Italian Opera Houses
and Festivals

Karyl Charna Lynn

The Scarecrow Press, Inc.
Lanham, Maryland • Toronto • Oxford
2005

SCARECROW PRESS, INC.

Published in the United States of America
by Scarecrow Press, Inc.
A wholly owned subsidiary of
The Rowman & Littlefield Publishing Group, Inc.
4501 Forbes Boulevard, Suite 200, Lanham, Maryland 20706
www.scarecrowpress.com

PO Box 317
Oxford
OX2 9RU, UK

Copyright © 2005 by Karyl Charna Lynn

British Library Cataloguing in Publication Information Available

Library of Congress Cataloging-in-Publication Data

Zietz, Karyl Lynn.
    Italian opera houses and festivals / Karyl Charna Lynn.
        p.   cm.
    Includes bibliographical references and index.
    ISBN 0–8108–5359–0 (pbk. : alk. paper)
        1. Opera—Italy.   2. Theaters—Italy.   3. Music festivals—Italy.   4. Italy—
Description and travel.   I. Title.
ML1733.Z92   2005
792.5'0945—dc22   2005013611

⊗ ™ The paper used in this publication meets the minimum requirements of
American National Standard for Information Sciences—Permanence of Paper for
Printed Library Materials, ANSI/NISO Z39.48–1992. Manufactured in the
United States of America.

In memory of my parents

8/31/13

to: PAPA P.J.

from: FOLKINS FAMILY

Contents

PART 3: SOUTHERN ITALY

PART 4: THE ISLANDS

~

Foreword

The reasons to visit Italy are many. Nature was generous with the verdant Italian peninsula surrounded by the clear blue waters of the Mediterranean, but the creativity of its inhabitants has endowed it with such an abundance of cultural resources that its attraction reaches even the most sophisticated traveler, especially those enchanted by bel canto and with opera as a passion.

Now, with *Italian Opera Houses and Festivals*, while spending your days in Italy, you can fill your evenings with the most rewarding musical experiences you can imagine. Or you can do just the opposite: spend most of your days visiting as many Italian opera houses as you can manage and indulge in only a few of the many other Italian attractions. Just think, sleep in late after a night at Milan's La Scala Theater, awake to a perfectly prepared cappuccino and croissant, and spend a relaxing day leisurely wending your way to your next city and opera house, with another great opera to enjoy. Then do it all over again and savor different surroundings, flavors, climates, and music.

When traveling to Italy to visit its prestigious theaters and opera houses, you will enjoy the pleasure of meeting a distinguished public largely composed of Italian music lovers. I don't know of a better way to get to know the locals! Your Italian might improve while discussing the merits of the singers with real connoisseurs or considering the famous maestro's tempo with your hotel's bartender. Italians love opera and they flock to opera houses all over the country. The Arena di Verona, where the summer opera season attracts the largest portion of its audience from abroad, still has no more than 50% foreign attendance. As an added bonus, you will discover that the regular opera season is definitely not high tourist season. This means less crowds and more comfortable accommodations.

Opera buffs embarking on a visit to Italy often ask, "Where do I begin?" and "Which is the most important opera house in Italy?" Actually, it would be difficult to say which is the most important. Truth be told, you needn't bother trying to find the most important theater. Opera houses in Italy are all important, especially to their faithful public. Just pick the theater that happens to be presenting your favorite opera or an opera you've always wanted to see and go from there. Let this book be your guide, trusting in the expert suggestions and up-to-date hints that Karyl Charna Lynn has crammed into it. Your exploration will be not only easy but fun and rewarding as well.

This guide, the product of Karyl's expertise, patience, love, and dedication to the Italian opera scene, is extremely useful to planning your visit to any of the numerous splendid opera theaters located in every region of Italy. It provides information on the opera houses' histories and will also help you book seats. No matter where your artistic interest may lie—in the Italian opera houses' regular season, in one of their special annual festivals, or in a quick look at their impressive interiors (often with adjoining museums)— *Italian Opera Houses and Festivals* will assist you with your travel choices before you leave home, accompany you while visiting Italy with its richness of information, and with its careful attention to detail, keep your special memories alive long after your return.

—Martin Stiglio, a director at the Italian
Cultural Institute

~

Preface

Opera houses in Italy are more than concrete, stone, glass, and wood with beautiful decorations. They are symbols of the world's greatest art form, which was born there. Italian opera houses are living, breathing entities, each with its own distinctive character. Every one is unique. In no other country will you find so many breathtakingly beautiful theaters. Some are hidden behind nondescript facades, especially in small villages and towns, while others are extensions of splendid exteriors. I have tried to give a taste of their different personalities by re-creating political, architectural, and performance histories with accounts and opinions from Italian newspapers, journals, and books of the time, most of which have never before been translated into English.

From the 17th century to the present, opera houses were built to give cities or towns importance and dignity. The grandeur of the theater indicated the prominence of the area. Theaters became the focal point of the city's cultural, political, and social life. They were a home away from home, places of elegance and peace, a refuge from the turmoil of everyday living. Many of the opera houses were paid for by the nobility who bought boxes in the theater. They were known as the *condomini* or *palchettisti* and treated their boxes like their second home, eating, drinking, and gossiping while the heroic feats and exploits of the mythological heroes and gods, kings, and emperors unfolded on the stage. When the castrati disappeared from the stage at the beginning of the 1800s, the theater became a place to express human passions, feelings, and emotions. It reflected the mood of the populace. As the century progressed, it became the hub of political activity. The name of the famous Italian composer Giuseppe Verdi was made into an acronym representing Italy's longing for freedom from the foreign powers who occupied the country until 1860: *Vittorio Emanuele, re d'Italia* (Victor Emanuel, king of Italy).

Opera in Italy enjoyed a culture all its own during the 1700s and 1800s. It was an experience different from that in any other country that apparently some foreigners did not understand, as evidenced by the impressions of a French and a German composer. Hector Berlioz described it in *Voyage musical en Allemagne et en Italie*: "The Italians were not at all interested in the poetic aspects of the music, but ready to consume a new opera like a plate of spaghetti." Otto Nicolai wrote to his father, "Moreover the opera is always composed in two acts, between which is presented a ballet, which has nothing to do with the opera and lasts two hours such that after the ballet, one has forgotten the first act of the opera. . . . Frequently one act of one opera is given with one act of another making a real mess."

Opera in Italy is still in a class by itself—an experience unequaled anywhere else, vastly different in some ways from the 18th and 19th centuries but similar in others. The emotion, flavor, and passion remain, not felt in any other country in the world. In some ways it is akin to a private conversation between the singers and audience, who react warmly and vociferously to glorious performances and violently to poor. Italians' behavior at the opera is similar to well-dressed spectators at a professional sporting event. They boo, cheer, and scream, but it is the opera singer, conductor, or director, not an athlete, who is the recipient. If the singer misses a high note or is flat, if the orchestra pacing is out of kilter, or if the heavy hand of the director is too visible, jeers and insults ring out, usually from the upper balconies but also from the orchestra section, even the boxes. The Teatro Regio in Parma is most famous for this behavior. The Regio is the house of experts, with a long history of unfinished performances, premature curtains, singers who were afraid to take curtain calls, and audiences so unruly that it was impossible to hear the opera, all because performances didn't live up to their exacting standards or warring (singer) factions were shouting out their differences. On the other hand, the audiences at the Teatro Ventidio Basso in Ascoli Piceno applaud everything, good or bad, even in the middle of an overture if the conductor pauses too long between passages. The Teatro Sociale in Mantua is an anachronism, still owned and run by the heirs of the *condomini*, who make it clear that outsiders are not welcome. The 17,000-seat, open-air arena in Verona has a tradition of lighting thousands of candles before the opera, creating a breathtaking sight, and Teatro alla Scala in Milan is so special that there is even an unwritten dress code for ladies: do not wear red because your attire will clash with the red seats, and nothing should distract from the beauty of the opera house. Turmoil at opera houses is front-page news. The lives of the opera singers are fodder for Italian gossip columnists, as the lives of movie stars are for everyone else.

All the 58 principal Italian opera houses and festivals in this book are grouped into several categories. The 12 largest are classified as *enti lirici* (public opera corporations). All their funding was once public, from the federal, state, and city governments. They received enough money to maintain a permanent orchestra, chorus, and technical staff with as many as 1,000 full-time employees. Near the end of the 20th century, these 12 theaters were required by law to form *fondazioni* (public-private corporations). This allowed them to solicit and receive private donations and sponsorship for up to 49% of their budgets in addition to public subsidies because the federal government was reducing financial support. Some houses have adjusted well to the change, mainly those with smaller permanent staffs such as the Teatro Carlo Felice in Genoa and the Teatro Reggio in Turin. Others are in fiscal turmoil, like the Teatro del Maggio Musicale Fiorentino in Florence, which is burdened with hundreds of full-time employees who were hired when money was plentiful; now there is little money to pay them but the theaters are unable to fire them because of the strong unions. Unions and opera house politics sometimes disrupt the opera seasons, and management is forced to spend an inordinate amount of time dealing with these problems instead of making artistic decisions. The 24 opera houses designated *teatri di tradizione* (theaters of tradition) because they have "stimulated local artistic and musical traditions" have not been as hard hit by the public subsidy cuts, since these theaters originally employed only a skeleton full-time staff, with almost everyone else hired on a per-opera or per-season basis. *Teatri di tradizione* either have formed *fondazioni* to receive private funding or they become totally supported and managed by the city administration. Of the remaining festivals and regional theaters, a few have formed *fondazioni*, but most are supported and run by the municipality. The reduction in public spending has resulted in an explosion of coproductions, which previously had been the exception. Opera houses that have formed foundations display a broadening of their repertory with more operas from the 1600s and 20th century and more creative, director-inspired, integrated productions.

Almost all the references used for this book and listed in the bibliography are in Italian. Because of space limitations only the most important are cited, but they are a good starting point for anyone wishing to delve deeper into the subject, for which a good reading knowledge of Italian is necessary, along with a familiarity with the specialized vocabulary of architectural and musical terms. For this book, I consulted hundreds of brochures, articles, papers, books, archival materials, and opera house programs (which, for example, for opening night at La Scala is a 250-page hardcover book) to gather and verify facts, figures, dates, events, operas, singers, and composers, which was difficult and frustrating at times because several "authoritative" sources would offer differing versions. A small glossary of Italian words used in the text appears near the end of the book, either because no English word or words convey the nuances in the Italian, or because I did not translate all the Italian names for the theaters. It also contains other Italian words I used in the text to maintain an Italianate flavor.

Many obscure operas by both famous and unfamiliar maestros have been recently revived, or might be in the future, as several Italian theaters and festivals rediscover the country's lost operatic patrimony. So that their names and works might be more recognizable, I have included world premieres of obscure operas at various opera houses and names of minor composers. In the text, I have used only the last names of composers due to the sheer volume of them, but I have followed the accepted format with all other names. The composer of an opera is mentioned either with lesser-known works if there is more than one opera by the same name or in a list of operas to avoid confusion. The opera titles are all in the original language, with those in Slavic languages being translated. The grammatical rules of the foreign language regarding capitalization are observed.

The book is organized by geographic region. Each chapter covers the opera houses and festivals in a particular city and journeys back in time by re-creating important events. Every chapter follows a similar format to allow comparison between opera houses and to facilitate searches. Each opens with the first theaters and performances in the city and follows the vicissitudes of the numerous constructions and destructions of the various buildings of both primary and secondary theaters (of which I have included more than a few hundred), including architectural descriptions and operatic performances at the secondary houses, and concludes with an architectural description of the principal theater. The operatic activities of the main theater (which often underwent several name changes) are covered in a separate section to avoid confusion with the performances at the less important theaters. Each chapter concludes with a practical information guide for visiting the opera house, including a recommended hotel almost all of which are within walking distance of the opera house. Brief descriptions of opera-related sites follow, including the birthplaces, dwellings, and museums of Italy's greatest composers. The chapters of some of the smaller theaters and festivals are not divided into separate sections, due to their brevity. I have visited almost every principal opera house, festival, and hotel included in this book—some only once and others numerous times. For those who can visit, I have tried to make this an indispensable companion for your trip; for those who are unable to make the journey, I hope the vicarious visit will be almost as exciting as a real one.

Acknowledgments

A book like this is not possible without the help, encouragement, and generosity of many people and the cooperation of many institutions, especially the opera houses themselves, archives, and libraries. I would like to express my deepest thanks to all my Italian colleagues and the Italian opera houses and festivals, especially the press and public relations offices, whose cooperation and generosity was essential to the book's success. The list would be too long to name them all, but you know who you are, and I give you a heartfelt thank you. I also owe a deep gratitude to my personal friends for their much appreciated assistance, advice, and support, especially during frustrating and stressful times when I thought I would never finish because the Italian had become confusing and unfathomable to me. Although the list would be too long to thank everyone individually, a few offered extraordinary assistance when I needed it the most: Emilio Viano deciphered complex and confusing Italian and Latin passages, Mel Leifer offered computer expertise, Robert Cole located needed materials, and Rod Johnson gave me photographic help. I'd like to thank Bruce Phillips, my acquisitions editor, and Scarecrow Press for believing in the importance of a book of this kind. Last and most importantly, I want to express my deepest appreciation to the entire staff of the Italian Cultural Institute in Washington, D.C., for their cooperation and support of this book.

ONE

Teatro Donizetti, Bergamo

The city of Bergamo is divided into two sections. One is known as Bergamo Alta (upper city), and the other as Bergamo Bassa (lower city). The first theaters in both parts were temporary structures called Teatri Provisionali (Provisional Theaters) that were set up for the performance season and dismantled afterward. In the 1700s in the upper city, the nobility frequented the Teatro della Cittadella, located on the second floor of the Palazzo del Capitano in the Cittadella, the headquarters of the military garrison. In the lower city, until Bortolo Riccardi built an opera house, the theaters took the form of large tents made of canvas and wood, erected on the fairgrounds for the season and then torn down.

Riccardi, who came from a wealthy Bergamo family that had made a fortune in the production and trade of silk, wanted to give the city a permanent theater located on the fairgrounds, but city regulations prohibited the erection of any fixed structure in that area. Riccardi would not be dissuaded. He laid a stone foundation, claiming the wet ground made that necessary, and began construction. After much controversy and delays, the theater called Teatro Nuovo, but also known as Teatro Nuovo al Prato di Fiera and Teatro di Fiera (New Theater on the Fairgrounds and Theater of the Fair), was born. Designed by Gian Francesco Lucchini, the Riccardi offered a small portico in front of the facade and an elliptical auditorium with three tiers of boxes topped by a gallery.

In 1796 French troops entered Bergamo, ending the military jurisdiction of the Republic of Venice over the city. Alessandro Ottolini, the last *capitano* sent by the Venetian republic, ordered the demolition of the Teatro della Cittadella on January 7, 1797, to prevent large crowds from gathering. Four days later, a fire of suspicious origin destroyed the Riccardi. Ottolini was accused of setting the blaze, but others accused the owners of the Cittadella of starting the fire in revenge for the demolition of their theater. Despite a trial that lasted for many years, the truth was never discovered. The municipality then commissioned Francesco Cerri to build a theater of wood on the second floor of the Palazzo della Ragione in the upper city. The Teatro Cerri, with 74 boxes divided among three box tiers and topped by a gallery, was inaugurated in 1798. It hosted both comic and serious opera until 1807, when it was demolished following a dispute between the theater and the municipality.

Meanwhile, Riccardi had immediately begun reconstructing his theater entirely in brick, and added a second balcony to the auditorium, which Vincenzo Bonomini decorated with chiaroscuro paintings. Lucchini was again the architect. The new Riccardo reopened June 30, 1800, with a play. An anonymous writer praised the theater in *Bergamo, o sia Notizie Patrie*: "Lucchini knew to select a curve that is harmonious, and perhaps you could not find an equal in any other theater in Italy." Stendhal, under his real name, Henry Beyle, was in Bergamo in Napoleon's army as second lieutenant of the cavalry. He described Bergamo's two theaters as "a very beautiful one in the village that is Bergamo on the plain [Bergamo Bassa, Teatro Riccardi], and the other, built of wood, is on the piazza of the city [Bergamo Alta, Teatro Cerri]."

Near the end of the 1700s, a small performance venue rose up in the lower city, the Teatrino della Fenice, so named because it was constructed where a hotel, Albergo della Fenice, had once stood. It hosted shows until the mid-1850s, when it was adapted for other uses. In 1803 an association of 54 of the richest and most respected families, tired of the fires and vicissitudes at the other theaters, erected their own opera house in the upper city, called the Teatro Sociale, but also known as Teatro della Società. Construction began in 1804 and lasted 4 years, with the inauguration taking place in December 1808. Leopoldo Pollach designed the building, which was decorated by Bonomini, Lattanzio Querena, and Francesco Pirovani. The auditorium offered three box tiers and a gallery. The Società hosted grand opera, including several works by Donizetti and Mayr, featuring well-known singers of the era. The *prima assoluta* of resident composer Petrali's *Giorgio di Berry* took place in 1854. A rivalry arose between the Sociale and Riccardi, but the Riccardo dominated and the Sociale went into decline. It is still extant. Two small theaters were erected in the upper city during the first two decades of the 1800s, Teatrino di Rosate, located on the piazza Rosate, and Teatrino di San Cassiano, situated where an ancient church once stood. They hosted musical and dramatic performances by amateur artists.

In 1835 a new stage curtain, painted by Carlo Rota, was hung in the Riccardi. The theater was very popular, attracting large crowds, who paid for their tickets in Austrian shillings, since the Austrians had thrown out the French. But by 1848, the population had had enough of the Austrians and carried out their own rebellion. That, combined with a cholera epidemic, closed the Riccardi for the 1848 and 1849 fair seasons. The structure was used as a military hospital. The following year, a fire destroyed part of the stage, which was quickly repaired. The Riccardi welcomed Vittorio Emanuele II in August 1859. Gas replaced oil lighting in 1868 and, at the same time, the theater was redecorated. In 1895 the building passed to a citizen association, its members becoming the owners and shareholders, an arrangement that lasted until 1936, when the theater was transferred to the municipality and managed by a civic commission.

To celebrate the centenary of Donizetti's birth, the theater was renamed in honor of the Bergamo maestro and a statue of the composer was created by Francesco Jerace. It overlooks a reflecting pond in the gardens on the east side of the theater. The facade was also reconstructed to its current appearance under the supervision of Pietro Via. Between 1958 and 1964, the interior was restructured, with Luciano Galmozzi, Peiro Pizzigoni, and Eugenio Mandelli in charge of the project. The Donizetti reopened October 10, 1964, with *Lucia di Lammermoor*. Two years later, the municipality took over direct management.

The Teatro Donizetti is distinguished by the unusual beige color of its facade. The names of five Donizetti operas, *Linda di Chamounix*, *Don Pasquale*, *Sebastiano*, *La favorita*, and *Lucia di Lammermoor*, are etched above the windows on the masonry building, one above each. Ionic pilasters frame the windows, which are crowned by lunettes. Engaged Corinthian columns, masks, and musical instruments embellish the building. The striking gray and rose, 1,154-seat auditorium holds 102 boxes in its three box tiers topped by two galleries. Putti in chiaroscuro and wreaths embellish the balustrades. Massive gilded Corinthian columns of green faux marble flank the proscenium boxes, and the coat of arms of Bergamo rests above the proscenium arch. Mythological scenes decorate the ceiling, the work of Francesco Domeneghini.

Operatic Events at the Teatro Donizetti

The earliest record of a performance at the Riccardi is in 1784, when Sarti's *Medonte, re d'Epiro* was staged in the half-finished building, when it had wood and cloth covering the roof. Two years later, *Didone abbandonata* was mounted, followed by Cimarosa's *I due supposti conti* and *Giannina e Bernard-one* in 1788. Bianchi's *Alessandro nelle Indie* was given the next year. Finally, the building was completed and baptized Teatro Riccardi, with *Didone abban-donata* inaugurating it on August 24, 1791. The theater held regular perform-ances during fair, spring, and summer seasons.

After the turn of the century, Mayr settled in Bergamo and played an important role in the musical life of the city. He was viewed as the teacher and spiritual father of Donizetti. His *L'equivoco* was offered in 1801, followed by *L'Elisa* and *Ginevra di Scozia*. When Bartolomeo Merelli became director in 1830, he invited Bellini to stage *La straniera*, followed by *Norma*. Donizetti operas started appearing in 1837. The Bergamo composer was honored 3 years later during a performance of his *L'esule di Roma*. Verdi paid a visit in 1844 to oversee his *Ernani*, and during a performance of *I Lombardi*, a patri-otic chord was struck with the "O Signore dal tetto natio" chorus. Verdi returned for the local premiere of *Rigoletto*. The Riccardi hosted some world premieres of minor composers, including Petrali's *Maria de'Griffi*, Pontoglio's *La schiava greca* and *La notte di Natale*, and Podestà's *I burgrave*.

Noted artists of the era were guests at the Riccardi—Giuditta Pasta, Giu-ditta Grisi, Giuseppina Strepponi, Domenico Reina, Erminia Frezzolini, Carlo Guasco, Napoleone Moriani, Angelica Ortolani, and Giovan Battista Rubini. When Giovannina Lucca took over the directorship of the Riccardi in 1879, she brought Meyerbeer's *Étoile du Nord* to Italy and offered Donizet-ti's unfinished work *Il Duca d'Alba*, with Matteo Salvi completing the miss-ing sections. Wagner's operas were introduced during the 1890s. With the dawn of the 20th century, Puccini, Mascagni, Leoncavallo, and Giordano became the favored composers, the operas being mounted along with movies, the new form of entertainment. World War I did not stop the performances, which included the *novità assoluta* of *Liacle*, by native son Edoardo Berlendis. Well-known artists continued to grace the stage—Beniamino Gigli, Toti dal Monte, Claudia Muzio, and on the podium, Riccardo Stracciari, Tullio Sera-fin, and Leopoldo Mugnone. A small number of performances continued dur-ing World War II, made possible by the orchestra and artists from La Scala, after their theater was destroyed.

When the municipality took over ownership of the theater, an ambitious program, known as the Teatro delle Novità (Theater of Novelties) was undertaken in which new, unpublished works were given a hearing. This was initiated in 1935 with a work by Gavazzeni, *Paolo e Virginia*. As musicologist Riccardo Allorto wrote in the program, "The 77 new works presented in Bergamo between 1937 and 1973, with interruptions between 1943 and 1950 and between 1962 and 1966, constitute a patrimony that belongs solidly to our musical civilization, to the Bergamo citizens who wanted and carried out the initiative, and to the musicians who rendered it possible." The 1948 season, which commemorated the centennial of Donizetti's death, unearthed some of the maestro's operas that had fallen into oblivion and was the catalyst for the festival Donizetti e il suo tempo (Donizetti and His Time), born in 1981. The festival brought to light some of his rarely performed works such as *Torquato Tasso*, *Fausta*, *Gianni di Parigi*, and *L'assedio di Calais*. It takes place every other year, with the nonfestival seasons usually excluding the maestro's operas. Another special Donizetti celebration was in 1997, the bicentennial of his birth. The season offered a couple of his unknown operas, *Don Sebastien* and *Il furioso all'isola di San Domingo*, along with favorites such as *L'elisir d'amore* and *Lucia di Lammermoor* and works from other composers, such as *I due Foscari*, *La Cenerentola*, and *Carmen*.

The Teatro Donizetti is part of the Teatri del Circuito Lombardo (Theaters of Lombardy Circuit) that either coproduce or share productions with the Teatro Ponchielli, Cremona, Teatro Grande, Brescia, Teatro Sociale, Como, and Teatro Fraschini, Pavia. Of course there is an emphasis on Donizetti's operas, especially the presentation of those rarely performed as a recent season showed, with *Parisina* and *La figlia del reggimento*, along with *Traviata* and *Andrea Chénier* on the schedule.

Practical Information

Teatro Donizetti, piazza Cavour 15, 24121 Bergamo; tel. 39 035 416 0613, fax 39 035 233 488; www.teatro.gaetano-donizetti.com.

The season takes place during October and November and offers four operas with two performances of each. Stay at the Excelsior Hotel San Marco, piazzale Republic 6; tel. 035 366 163, fax 035 223 201, a 5-minute walk from the opera house. Visit the sculpture of Donizetti with the Muse Melopea, next to the Teatro Donizetti, and Donizetti's birthplace, via Borgo Canale, where the maestro was born on September 29, 1797. The modest house, preserved from Donizetti's time, is located below street level. Visit the Istituto Musicale, via Arena 9, where the Donizetti Museum is located in a large hall. Opened in 1903, it contains Donizetti's manuscripts, documents, portraits, and mementoes. A smaller room contains the piano of the composer and other furniture, including an armchair and the bed in which he died. Donizetti's tomb is in the basilica of San Maria Maggiore, in the upper city. A cable car links the lower and upper city.

TWO

Teatro Grande, Brescia

The roots of the Accademia degli Erranti (Academy of the Erranti) go back to a theater society established in 1562 that in 1619 was transformed into an academy. The Erranti sponsored musical programs, among other types. The Republic of Venice, which ruled Brescia at the time, donated some buildings to the academy, which demolished them to construct a new building in 1637. Some three decades later, the impresario Antonio Barzino wanted a performing venue to fulfill his ambition to host operas for 3 years. Constructed under the arcade of the new structure in 1664, the theater was described as "little more than a tiny playhouse for oratorio, heated by warming pans and illuminated by oil lamps and candles." There were three boxes supported on wooden columns, one for the Venetian authorities, one for city authorities, and one for the board of directors of the academy. The members of the Erranti Academy brought armchairs from their homes to sit on. The orchestra section was on the same level as the stage, where the musicians and artists were seated.

What was described as the first true and proper theater was constructed in 1709 on the same site where the Teatro Grande is now located. Paid for by the *soci* (members) of the Academy of the Erranti, it was very small to keep down building costs. Within three decades, however, the town outgrew the theater, so the academy had to enlarge it. Known as the Teatro Nuovo, it was erected following the plans of Antonio Galli Bibiena and Andrea Seghizzi. Antonio Cugini realized the project, with Antonio Righini in charge of construction. The auditorium was U shaped and held four box tiers topped by a gallery. Every tier held 29 boxes and 4 proscenium boxes. The Erranti had reserved boxes for themselves on various tiers. The middle classes were welcomed in the orchestra level. There was a raised stage that was separated from the auditorium by a curtain. But the space was still heated by warming pans and illuminated by oil lamps and candles. Several modifications and interventions took place, including the addition of a facade with running columns, a small staircase, and the annexation of a foyer, before the structure was demolished.

Liberty was beating her drum and the Academy of the Erranti was dissolved, but the members remained. The Nuovo was renamed Teatro Nazionale by the governor of the Brescian republic, who in 1798 ordered that all the magnificent decorations and ornamentation of gold and silver be removed, creating a simplicity and uniformity consistent with the principles of democracy. This was short-lived, as only 8 years later there was talk of reconstructing the theater "to the peace and glory of Napoleon." Napoleon himself visited the opera house for a gala evening on July 28, 1796, and again on June 12, 1805. This latter visit lasted only a half hour. After 3 years of discussions, the plans of Luigi Canonica were chosen for the reconstruction of the theater. Native son Giuseppe Teosa executed the decorations.

The Teatro Nazionale was inaugurated on December 27, 1810, with Mayr's *Il sacrificio di Iphigenia*. Decorated in the temperate good taste of neoclassicism, there was a certain harmony in the auditorium, giving the impression of the gold background fusing with the gray and light-blue chiaroscuro of the parapets. The tapestry and drapery of all the boxes were a light-blue silk fringed with orange. The space abounded with allegorical pictures inspired by the victories of Napoleon. The painter Lorandi described them as the richest decorations comprising war emblems and symbols of the heroes of the times. But grandest of all was the large medal in the center of the dome where Napoleon himself stood, personified as Mars, crowned with olive leaves by Minerva and with a trembling Discord at his feet. The theater was illuminated by candles in the boxes and a ceiling chandelier for the orchestra level. In 1862 gas lighting replaced the candles and chandelier as part of a major reconstruction and redecoration. An elaborate, ornate neobaroque decor, the work of Girolamo Magnani, replaced the somber, tasteful neoclassical style. Only the royal box retained the original ornamentation comprising the allegory of Night painted by Domenico Vantini and Napoleon's insignia. *Un ballo in maschera* reopened the now-renamed Teatro Grande on August 1, 1863.

An imposing structure, the Grande presents a portico of Ionic columns and pillars with alternating bands of white and tan, crowned by a balustrade. Three banks of steps lead into the Hall of Statues where busts of Verdi and native son Girolamo Rovetta reside. The five-tiered, horseshoe-shaped 1,240-seat auditorium glitters with gold, cooled by a sea of red seats. Neobaroque-style decorations embellish the ivory-colored parapets with gilded putti, medallions, and monochrome inserts. Allegorical groups of figures representing Tragedy, Comedy, Music, and Dance ornament the ornately frescoed ceiling, the work of Luigi Campini. Also decorating the ceiling are monochrome inserts depicting various Roman and Greek gods, executed by Magnani.

Operatic Events at the Teatro Grande

During the first decades of the 1800s, operas such as Portogallo's *L'inganno poco dura*, Nasolini's *La morte di Mitridate*, Nicolini's *Traiano in Dacia*, Pacini's *La vestale*, Guglielmini's *La spelta dello sposo*, and Neri's *Saccenti alla Moda* were on the boards. In fact, 328 operatic novelties for Brescia were staged between 1800 and 1971, and in 1804 the world premiere of Orlandi's *Nino* was presented. In 1814 the first Rossini opera was performed, *Aureliano in Palmira*, followed by *Cenerentola*, *La donna del lago*, *La gazza ladra*, *Tandredi*, *Otello*, *Mosè in Egitto*, *Il turco in Italia*, *L'assedio di Corinto*, and *Edoardo e Cristina*. By 1840 around a dozen of the Pesaro maestro's works had been offered. The first Bellini opera heard was *Il pirata* in 1829. Over the next several seasons, *La straniera*, *La sonnambula*, *Norma*, *Beatrice di Tenda*, and *I Capuleti e i Montecchi* were on the boards. In 1831 Donizetti operas entered the repertory with *Olivo e Pasquale*. He was very popular, with more than a dozen of his operas gracing the stage, including *Belisario*, *Roberto Devereaux*, *Fausta*, *Lucia di Lammermoor*, and *Poliuto*. Also on the schedule were works by the Ricci brothers, Coccia, Vaccai, Persiani, and Mercadante with *Clotilde*, *Zadig e Astartea*, *Elena da Feltre*, *I Normandi a Parigi*, and *Il bravo* among others. In 1826 Meyerbeer's *Il crociato in Egitto* was mounted followed by his French works *Robert le diable* and *Les Huguenots*. Other French operas included Halévy's *La Juive* and Gounod's *Faust*. A few more *prime assolute* were staged, including Dominiceti's *La Fiera di Tolobos*, Pontoglio's *Tebaldo Brusato*, and Burgio di Villafiorita's *Jolanda*.

The first of many Verdi operas, *Nabucco* (*Nabucodonosor*), arrived at the Grande in 1843. Around a dozen of his works were hosted, including *I due Foscari*, *Ernani*, *Attila*, *Macbeth*, *I masnadieri*, *Il trovatore*, and *Giovanna d'Arco*. In the top five of the most performed operas in Brescia since 1893, three belong to Verdi: *Aida, Rigoletto,* and *La traviata.* As the 19th century drew to a close, French operas were much in evidence, including *Carmen, L'Africaine, Samson et Dalila,* Thomas's *Mignon,* and Massenet's *Le roi de Lahore.* The first Wagner opera, *Lohengrin* surfaced in 1891. Puccini operas and those of the verismo school were very popular. One of the highlights at the Grande was Toscanini conducting *Manon, I Puritani,* and *La traviata* during the 1894 fair season and returning 2 years later for *La bohème.*

Brescia, however, is best known as the place where on May 28, 1904, a revised *Madama Butterfly* (subsequently known as the Brescia version and the one most performed) found success after its disastrous world premiere 3 months earlier at Teatro alla Scala in Milan. On May 28, Cleofonte Campanini conducted, with Salomea Kruscenisky in the title role and Giovanni Zenatello as Pinkerton. The opera enjoyed 11 performances.

The Grande kept its doors open during World War I, although 1915 and 1916 were short seasons, with only two offerings each: *La fanciulla del West, Otello, L'elisir d'amore,* and *Don Pasquale.* Most of the operas between the wars were the well-known Italian works, but scattered among them were some lesser-known pieces such as Wolf-Ferrari's *Il segreto di Susanna* and *I quattro rusteghi,* Catalani's *Dejanice* and *Wally,* Zandonai's *Giulietta e Romeo* and *Francesca da Rimini,* Giordani's *La cena delle beffe,* and Mascagni's *Il piccolo Marat* and *Iris.* During World War II, the Grande not only kept open its doors but offered long and rich seasons of works, mainly from the *giovane scuola: Adriana Lecouvreur, La gioconda, La bohème, Manon Lescaut, Amico Fritz,* and *Fedora.* It was after the war, with many of Italy's major opera houses damaged, that the Grande reached its apex, offering memorable seasons and artists such as Maria Callas, Renata Tebaldi, Giulietta Simionato, Magda Olivero, Gianna Pederzini, Mario del Monaco, and Nicola Rossi Lemeni. Difficult times then befell the Teatro Grande. Although it has been unable to regain its glory from the years right after World War II, its lyrical seasons are assured by being part of the Teatri del Circuito Lombardo (Theaters of the Lombardy Circuit), as well as coproducing with the Teatro Verdi in Pisa, Teatro Comunale in Treviso, Teatro Sociale in Mantua, and the Teatro Sociale in Como.

The Grande is still partly privately owned by the *palchettisti* and partly publicly owned by the municipality. The funding is predominately public, with some private money. The repertory is fairly standard with an occasional novelty. Recent offerings include *La bohème, Le Comte Ory, Norma,* and a double bill of Togni's *Barrabas* and Margola's *Il mito di Caino.*

Practical Information

Teatro Grande, via Paganora 19/A, 25100 Brescia; tel. 39 030 297 9311, fax 39 030 297 9342; www.bresciainvetrina.it/bresciaarte/teatrograndebrescia .htm.

The season runs from October to December with four productions and two to three performances of each. Stay at the Hotel Master, viale 72; tel. 030 399 037, fax 030 370 1331. Situated in a quiet, peaceful location, the Master is a 15-minute walk from the theater.

THREE

Teatro Sociale, Como

In 1712 there existed in the Palazzo of Broletto a small wooden theater where the lower classes enjoyed the vulgar humor of commedia dell'arte. This annoyed the nobility of Como, who had to travel to Milan to enjoy *melodrammi*, although some of the aristocratic palaces had rooms where operas could be hosted. The nobility of Como wanted a theater more suitable to the dignity of the city and took the initiative to create one. In 1763 the Marquis Giorgio Porro Carcano and Count Marco Paolo Odescalchi met with authorities, and the following year another theater came into existence, inside dozens of small arcades topped by a large loggia. It was inaugurated for Carnival 1764/65. The operas of Paisiello, Galuppi, and Cimarosa were the ones most often performed, which "pleased the eyes more than the mind." It was closed in 1808, after the nobility decided they needed a larger, more modern theater with the turn of the century.

The site chosen was on the ruins of a medieval castle known as Torre Rotonda. The nobility formed the Società dei Palchettisti for the purpose of erecting the theater and hired architect Signor Cusi for the project. Francesco Bollini was the contractor in charge, assisted by Innocenzo Bossi. Construction began in February 1812. The Società had put in the contract that the theater was to be completed by August that same year, an impossible deadline to meet. The speed with which the building proceeded resulted in some construction disasters. Part of the ceiling of the entrance hall to the orchestra section collapsed, not once but twice. The first incident claimed three victims, and the second caused several injuries. The cause of the problem was traced to frigid winter temperatures during the construction of the ceiling that prevented a solid bond between the materials. It was determined that the portion of the ceiling still remaining should be demolished and

11

reconstructed in warmer April weather. The prefect agreed, "in regard for public security and past example," and ordered the entire ceiling demolished and reconstructed, prohibiting the opening of the theater. A couple of days before the opening, another architect, Cavalier Giuseppe Zanoja, was sent by the government to make an on-site inspection. He reported that there were irregularities in the side portico of the facade that faced the arena and that the architraves were not capable of supporting the weight of the floor, already indicated by cracks in them. He also reported that the construction was very poor and did not conform to the original design, which introduced additional dangers.

Finally, on August 28, 1813, Portogallo's *Adriano in Siria* inaugurated the Teatro Sociale, with the evening dedicated to the "ornatissima Società dei Palchettisti" (most honored Association of Box Holders) whose money made the opera house possible. The evening was described in *Il Teatro di Sociale di Como*: "For over an hour the public impatiently crowded the entrance, and then, almost in a fury, crowded the orchestra, boxes and the gallery. . . . Although the lighting was not very bright or luxurious, they admired the symmetry and the spaciousness of the auditorium, dimensions of the stage, and the architectural curves of the three levels of boxes and the gallery. . . . The governor's box was much praised with its beautiful caryatids which extended their arms to support the enclosure. The boxes, which tended to compete [with each other] in luxury, ornamentation, hangings, and tapestry, were also admired." Ironically, on the morning of the inauguration, the design of the opera house was severely criticized in a three-page letter in the weekly journal of Como, *Giornale del Lario*, written by Foscolo under the pseudonym Didimo Chierico.

In 1843 the Direzione Generale di Polizia (General Director's Office of the Police) published regulations governing the use of the theater: "The new method of lighting [boxes] with liquid hydrogen and other systems of heating was forbidden; in the case of mourning of a *palchista*, it was forbidden to close the box for more than three days; it was forbidden to smoke at any time or place in the theater."

By the early 1850s, the city had outgrown its theater. On May 23, 1854, an enlargement project was approved and work began with the engineer Rospini in charge. Thirty-eight boxes were added, for a total of 98, with 24 boxes on the first three tiers and 26 in the fourth tier. Gaetano Speluzzi supervised the interior decorations, with Croff executing the work. The ceiling was repainted by Pagliani and executed by Speluzzi with a theme involving the Arts and the Muses: Melpomene, Talia, and Euterpe with myrtle and a crown in their hands descend from Mount Olympus to crown the Arts. The Sociale was reopened December 28, 1855. The following year, a new rule was adopted that underlined that all the owner-members were "equal among themselves" and confirmed that the purpose of the Società was "to promote lawful and honest entertainment worthy of the culture and splendor of this city, with performance of comic and tragic works in music."

A frequent problem in Italian opera houses, including the Sociale, was keeping order during the performances. This prompted the management to post rules in December 1860: "It is forbidden to enter the theater in an evident state of inebriation or dress in an offensive or disrespectful manner; it is forbidden to bring dogs; it is forbidden to stand in the auditorium or hallways in a manner that would obstruct circulation. . . . Anyone breaking the rules will be expelled from the theater, arrested and subjected to the maximum punishment."

When Cusi conceived the Sociale, he had also included plans for an open-air arena to extend from one side of the opera house. With a U-shaped orchestra seating section, surrounded by amphitheater-type seats, flowers, and trees, the arena was eventually completed and used for outdoor summer performances of such diverse types of entertainment as plays, gymnastics, and equestrian shows. In 1930, because of an economic crisis, the Sociale could not host the opera season, so it unfolded in the arena. The arena was subsequently modified for the projection of cinema by transforming the seating sections into one large, rectangular, graded space. Movies began to be shown at the beginning of the 1900s and continued to the 1970s. Meanwhile in 1938, Carlo Ponci realized a new stage that was placed on the facade of the Sociale facing the arena. It was described as looking like "a box in armored cement that completely hid and disfigured Cusi's original facade." After performances stopped, the stage became storage space, and the old arena itself was used as a parking lot.

With the dawn of the 20th century, the opera house was once again too small to accommodate everyone who wanted to attend performances, so in 1908 two proposals were presented. The first offered the possibility of more seating in the Sociale by replacing the center boxes on the fourth tier with gallery seats and creating a second gallery. The second proposal suggested construction of another theater that could host all types of entertainment but reserved the Sociale for the traditional opera season. Although the first proposal was easier and far less expensive, the box holders believed that opening up their theater to "such a large public would destroy the fundamental origins of the theater." So another theater, a *politeama*, was constructed.

Designed by Federico Frigerio, it was inaugurated on September 14, 1910, with *La bohème*.

During the second half of the 1900s, the theater was in crisis, plagued by the indifference of its *palchisti* and the huge expense necessary for its restoration to guarantee the stability and security of the structure. In addition, the public was more interested in movies and television. The result was reduced profits and inferior performances of the standard repertory. The Sociale was regarded as a museum, a testimony of the past. It lacked good artistic direction. Finally, the building was closed at the end of the 1960s for restoration. But after it reopened, its operations did not last long. In May 1984, the local paper announced that "the Società Palchettisti had decided yesterday to close the theater for an undetermined time because of the instability of the structure." The climate was described as being like Hamlet, one decided not to decide. Among other things, there were discussions requesting the municipality to acquire the building, pointing out the anachronism in the box holders owning the theater in the 1980s. But the *palchettisti* did not want to give up control and finally agreed to the project proposed by Mario Bernasconi, and the theater was properly repaired. As the century drew to a close, the facade was renovated. With the dawn of the new millennium, over the course of several years the interior is being completely overhauled, thanks to an agreement between the Società Palchettisti, Associazione Lirica e Concertistica Italiani, the Lombardy region, the Como province, and the municipality.

A massive, six-Corinthian-column pronaos anchors the monumental neoclassical facade of the structure. Masks of Comedy and Tragedy flank a lyre that embellishes the tympanum on the dentil-delineated pediment. Shuttered windows line the three levels of the building. The 900-seat, elliptical auditorium of ivory, gold, and red holds five tiers. The allegorical fresco decorating the ceiling dome is populated with Muses and putti, crown wreaths and lyres, and horns evoking Apollo. The coat of arms of Como is displayed above the stage. The original stage curtain, painted by Sanquirico, shows the eruption of Vesuvius and Pliny the Elder dying from a cloud of gas and vapors.

Operatic Events at the Teatro Sociale

The repertory of the theater's early years saw works by Mosca and Portogallo, with one of Rossini's early works, *Demetrio e Polibio*, appearing during the inaugural season. The music of Rossini played an important role in the theater's repertory, including *La Cenerentola* and *Tancredi*. The opera season began in August with two or three productions repeated around 30 times. Ferdinando I and his consort were present at the reopening of the Sociale in 1838, with performances of Ricci's *Un'avventura di Scaramuccia* and *La sonnambula*. Ricci's *Chiara di Rosemberg* and Graffigna's *Un lampo di fedeltà* were staged in honor of the visit of the crown prince of Russia. The composer in those years who left the strongest mark was Bellini with *I Capuleti e i Montecchi* and *Beatrice di Tenda*. Other operas by the Ricci brothers and minor composers of the early 1800s graced the stage before Verdi's works entered the repertory. First came *Attila*, followed by *Rigoletto*, *Il trovatore*, *I due Foscari*, *Macbeth*, *La traviata*, *Nabucco*, and *I masnadieri*. Verdi's operas were the most performed at the Sociale. Other popular composers included Donizetti with *Don Pasquale*, *Lucrezia Borgia*, and *Lucia di Lammermoor*.

In the 1870s and 1880s, the operas of the French composers Gounod, Meyerbeer, and Bizet were on the schedule with *Faust*, *Les Huguenots*, *Robert le diable*, and *Carmen*. The seasons of the 1890s were marked by the works of the *giovane scuola*: Mascagni, Leoncavallo, Ponchielli, and Puccini. A writer of the era described the audience's response: "*L'amico Fritz*, which was new for Como, was given a good and pleasing execution, but the first evening, the public was confused about the music and maintained a cold and reserved demeanor for the first two acts. . . . *Carmen*, however, had a very unhappy execution, and lasted only a couple of evenings." The world premieres of Cipollini's *Il piccolo Haydn* and Ferroni's *Ettore Fieromosca* took place in 1893, but the Como *prima* of *La bohème* was an even more major event, as described by a chronicler of the day: "At the first performance, which took place January 25, 1896, there was a full house of extremely elegant people. The orchestra was filled; not an empty seat, not an empty box; the gallery was overflowing. All the daily newspapers and theaters of Milan had sent special critics. All the professors of the Milan Conservatory were present. The principal musical authorities including Verdi and Massenet had sent letters and telegrams of good wishes to the conductor."

With the dawn of a new century, the works of Giordano and Wagner were welcomed to the Sociale, along with those of Belioz and Massenet. Mascagni came twice to the opera house, for his *Iris* and then to conduct *Amica*. The 1913 season marked two centennial celebrations. A special evening was devoted to Verdi's music, commemorating the 100th anniversary of his birth, with the unveiling of a specially commissioned marble bust of Italy's greatest composer by the sculptor Fontana. Operas by Mascagni, Lualdi, Ferrari, Giordano, and Puccini played prominent roles in celebrating the 100th anniversary of the Sociale itself. World War I forced the closure of the opera house, after a performance of *Werther*. It reopened for the carnival season in 1919. The centennial of Bellini's death was commemorated during the 1935 season with productions of some of his operas, including *La sonnambula*. The Sociale remained open during World War II, hosting programs to commemorate the 40th anniversary of Verdi's death and the 50th anniversary of the world premiere of *L'amico Fritz*. Singers such as Mafalda Favero, Giulietta Simionato, and Mario del Monaco graced the stage. After Milan's famous opera house Teatro alla Scala was destroyed in August 1943, the 1943/44 season took place at the Sociale.

After the war, Giordano attended a performance celebrating the 50th anniversary of his *Fedora*. In 1951 Beniamino Gigli sang in *Manon Lescaut* and Tito Schipa in Cilea's *Arlesiana*. A few novelties for Como appeared in the following years, including Casella's *La giara*, Zandonai's *Francesca da Rimini*, and Mortari's *La scuola delle mogli*. The 100th anniversary of Puccini's birth was commemorated in 1959 with *Turandot*. When the theater reopened after a renovation, some unusual works were on the boards, such as Morini's *La vindice*, Soresina's *Tre sogni*, and Hazon's *Agenzia matrimoniale*. There were more novelties after the second restoration in the 1980s, including revivals of two 19th-century world premieres, Cipollini's *Piccolo Haydn*, Ferroni's *Ettore Fieramosca*, along with Monteverdi's *La favola d'Orfeo*, Rameau's *Platée*, and Bottacchiari's *Severo Torelli*. As the 20th century drew to a close, the seasons and productions were traditional with *La bohème*, *Andrea Chénier*, *Così fan tutte*, and Rossini's *La gazzetta* on the boards. Since January 1, 2002, the Associazione Lirica e Concertistica Italiani has managed the opera house with a noticeable broadening of the repertory and less-conservative productions. It is part of the Teatri del Circuito Lombardo (Theaters of Lombardy Circuit) with Teatro Ponchielli in Cremona, Teatro Donizetti in Bergamo, Teatro Grande in Brescia, and Teatro Fraschini in Pavia. Recent offerings have included *La traviata*, *L'elisir d'amore*, *Werther*, *El retablo del maese Pedro / El amor brujo*, *Lyubov'k tryom apel'sinam* (Love of Three Oranges), and *Il ritorno di Ulisse in patria*.

Practical Information

Teatro Sociale, via Bellini 3, 22100 Como; tel. 39 031 270 171, fax 39 031 271 472; www.teatrosocialecomo.it.

The season runs from October to March, offering seven operas with one and three performances of each. Stay at the Grand Hotel di Como, via per Cernobbio, 22100 Como; tel. 031 27 01 71, fax 031 271 472. Convenient to the theater but a long walk, the Grand Hotel is near the lake.

FOUR

Teatro Comunale Amilcare Ponchielli, Cremona

The Teatro Rangoni, also called Teatro Ariberti, opened in 1670 and was the first performance venue in Cremona. Built by the volition of Marquess Giulia Rangoni and her husband Giovanni Battista Ariberti, it was located where the Teatro Filodrammatici stands today. The first documented season took place in 1676, with the presentation of Cesti's *Il Tito* and Boretti's *Marcello in Siracusa*. *Enone gelosa* followed in 1698. The impresario Giacomo Cipriotti organized some of the opera seasons. The Ariberti remained active until 1717, when in a state of disrepair, it was donated by the family to a religious order.

In 1747 Giovanni Battista Nazari decided to give the city a real and proper theater "for the dignified and honest entertainment of the nobility and citizens of Cremona" in place of the temporary venues being used since the closure of the Ariberti. Named after and managed by its owner, the Teatro Nazari was inaugurated with an opera buffa on December 26, 1747. A local architect, Giovanni Battista Zaist, designed the theater, which was constructed of wood. It held four tiers of 25 boxes each, 2 of which were proscenium boxes, and 1 center box, which could be completely closed off, shielding its occupants and their activities from view of those in the auditorium. This permitted them to enjoy only the most interesting parts of the opera (without anyone else knowing). The auditorium was shaped like a U, widening slightly as it approached the stage. The late-baroque decorations in white, ivory, and gray were accented by gold lines. Giacomo Guerrini painted the curtain with an image of Hercules on Mount Beta dying in the flames of a funeral pyre, with soldiers and women surrounding him, expressing their admiration and sorrow at his death.

The Nobile Associazione (Noble Association, or Box-Holder Association) purchased the theater in 1785, renaming it Teatro della Società. The
Associazione dei dodici cavalieri (Association of the Twelve Cavaliers) managed it. To keep order in the opera house, strict regulations were issued as
the century drew to a close that prohibited games of chance in the boxes and
foyers and forbade the playing of encores, to "avoid tiring the singers and
have the performances run too late." In July 1805, a fire broke out during a
performance of a comedy. Although it caused limited damage, the result was
that the local authorities began deliberations about constructing a more solid
and secure opera house, in the then fashionable neoclassical style. But before
any definitive actions were taken, the Teatro della Società burned down. It
happened toward midnight on September 11, 1806, during a performance of
a *melodramma*, *Il fanatico in Berlina*. The *condomini* decided to rebuild immediately and selected Luigi Canonica to design the structure. Instead of keeping the name Teatro della Società or calling it Teatro dell'Associazione, the
Società elected to rename it Teatro della Concordia. The opera house was
inaugurated on October 26, 1808, with Paër's *Il principe di Taranto* and
Marinelli's *Il trionfo d'amore*, the latter having been specially commissioned
for the inaugural. On the frieze above the portico, "Sociorum Concordia Erexit" was inscribed.

The *Giornale di Milano* described the theater as having a portico with four
Ionic columns that dominated the facade, and between the columns were
three niches, each occupied by a bust of a famous dramatic Italian poet: Metastasio, Goldoni, and Alfieri. In the auditorium, the balustrades of the box
tiers were decorated with chiaroscuro ornamental designs on a gold background. On the parapet of the highest tier were lavish decorations of vines
and leaves; on the fourth, bacchanal with bacchantes, satyrs, and fauns; on
the third, ornate acanthus leaves and olives; and on the second, Iphigenia of
Euripides and Oedipus of Sophocles. The center box, reserved for the authorities, was adorned with the Eagle of Jove and the box itself luxuriously decorated with Jove, Themis, Mars, and their symbols. On the proscenium boxes
were medallions of Sophocles, Euripides, Aristophanes, and Menandro.
Corinthian columns with capitals decorated with olive leaves, imitating
those of the Temples of Giove Statore in Campo Vaccino, flanked the proscenium. The curtain, painted by Sanquirico and Legnani, showed the Patriotic Genius guiding the Performing Arts to the Temple of the Concordia to
be coronated and the motto "Concordia alit Artes." On the ceiling of the
auditorium, a curtain was painted with various symbols alluding to Phoebus
and the Muses that opened in the middle, showing the head of Apollo, radi-

ating in gold. On the frieze that circled the ceiling, there were medallions holding the heads of the principal Greek and Latin poets, painted in chiaroscuro that imitated stucco, on a background of gold.

On January 6, 1824, flames again consumed the structure with only the perimeter walls remaining. Rebuilt in record time by architects Luigi Voghera and Faustino Rodi following the plans of Canonica, the Concordia reopened September 9, 1824, with *La donna del lago*. The interior decorations, executed by Sanquirico in the neoclassical style, were described as being in gray tones, in a classic geometric style that was austere but "appropriate to the dignity of the place and its guests."

Another theater, known as the Teatro Ricci, was constructed in 1859, opening the following year. It was very popular with the Cremonese. Attracting a less elite clientele, it offered everything from horse shows and vaudeville to operetta and opera. The popularity of the Ricci had an adverse effect on the finances of the Concordia, which by 1874 were so dire that it could not mount its usual carnival opera season or the festive balls. The municipal administration was in crisis and without public support; there was not enough money for the theater to function. It was eventually reopened, but the financial situation remained precarious, aggravated by natural disasters, the political turbulence of the times, and the social unrest of the 1880s with its strikes and violent demonstrations. The name of the opera house was changed to Concordia-Ponchielli in honor of Cremona's native son Ponchielli in October 1892. But not all the *palchisti* were in agreement with this double name, which prompted the local newspaper, *La Provincia*, source of the original proposal, to suggest an alternative, Teatro Sociale Ponchielli, but it was never considered. It was not until 1907 that the opera house was officially renamed Teatro Ponchielli.

Meanwhile, the Teatro Ricci was destroyed by fire in December 1896. Reconstructed by architect Achille Sfondrini, it was named the new Politeama when it opened, since it offered a wide range of popular entertainment that attracted an increasingly larger audience, compared to the traditional programming at the Concordia-Ponchielli. To avoid further competition, an agreement was made between the two theaters, but the Concordia-Ponchielli did not respect it, scheduling *Fedora, Puritani,* and *Carmen* in 1900, during the Politeama's opera season. This caused a large drop in attendance at the Politeama, whose management then denounced the new president of the Box-Holder Association, Agostino Cavacabò. When Verdi died in January 1901, the Politeama managed to get even for this slight. The sister of Verdi's wife, Barberina Strepponi lived in Cremona, and while all the members of the association were in Milan for the funeral, the Politeama managed to get permission from Verdi's sister-in-law to name the theater Politeama Verdi in his honor. The *palchettisti* of the Ponchielli were not pleased.

During the 1900s, the Ponchielli was made less elite when the fourth box tier was converted into a gallery and a family circle was added, but it was not until 1930 that an orchestra pit was created in the auditorium. In 1935 the *condomini* proposed selling the theater to the municipality, because it was full of debt, most of which was uncollectible, including 200,000 lire from co-owners in arrears. Instead, it was decided to expel those in arrears and assess remaining co-owners 500 lire more per box. It was not until 1986 that the municipality purchased the opera house from the *palchettisti*, and added Comunale to its name.

The first performance at the Teatro Comunale Ponchielli took place the evening of October 4, 1986, using the most famous violins from the city's collection: the Stradivari "Il Cremonese" (1715) and the Guarneri "del Gesù" (1734). La Scala's philharmonic orchestra with Marlo Maria Giulini conducting played Brahms's *First Symphony* and Shubert's *Unfinished Symphony*. Since 1989 the theater has been completely renovated and restored, adding technically advanced stage equipment and bringing it up to current fire and safety codes.

A colonnade distinguished by four monumental Ionic columns dominates the facade with "Sociorum Concordia Erexit a MDCCCVII" etched on the frieze. The 1,249-seat, horseshoe-shaped auditorium radiates in ivory, gold, and red. The three box tiers, including a center royal box and proscenium boxes, are topped by two galleries. Gilded wood relief ornaments alternating with medallions of the classic poets in burnished silver-plated papier-mâché decorate the parapets. The parapets of the proscenium boxes are adorned with gilded masks. The dome ceiling is an unadorned sky-blue color.

Operatic Events at the Teatro Ponchielli

The opening of the Teatro Nazari saw many operas staged, including Chiarini's *Artaserse* and Galuppi's *Vologeso*. The programming was classified as cautious but having irregular intervals of experimental pieces such as Galuppi's *Semiramide riconosciuta* in the 1750s. The following decade offered opere buffe, with Piccinni's *La buona figliola*, Fischietti's *Il signor dottore*, Galuppi's *Il filosofo di campagna*, and Scarlatti's *La serva scaltra*. The 1770s ushered in Valentini's *La clemenza di Tito* and Guglielmi's *Il Ruggero*. There were also operas of Cimarosa and Cherubini on the boards, until fire reduced it to ashes in 1806.

When it reopened as the Teatro della Concordia, operas such as *Ginevra di Scozia*, *I zingari in Fiera*, *Elisabetta, regina d'Inghilterra*, and *Gli amanti comici*, as well as nonoperatic events, were on the boards. During the mid-1800s, the Concordia hosted the world premieres of two Ponchielli operas, *I promessi sposi* and *La Savoiarda*, along with Buzzi's *La sposa del crociato* and Campiani's *Bernabò Visconti*. Subsequently, Ponchielli took the post of the theater's musical director. The operas of the Ricci brothers, Meyerbeer, and Mercadante were in the repertory, but Rossini, Bellini, Donizetti, and finally Verdi indisputably dominated the seasons for several decades, such that for the 1890 carnival season all were Verdi's, offering *Aida*, *La forza del destino*, and *Un ballo in maschera* but with disastrous results. The box office from the second performance of *Ballo* collected only 196 lire. With a more diversified season in 1892, including *Carmen*, *Cavalleria rusticana*, *L'elisir d'amore*, *Pêcheurs de perles*, and a new edition of Ponchielli's opera *Il figliuol prodigy*, the season was a success. The theater hosted a couple of *prime assolute* during the 1880s—Coppola's *Cristoforo Colombo* and *Il Cid*—and from 1893 to the end of the century more than 20 different operas, including the world premiere of Branca's *La figlia di Jorio*, graced the stage.

Through good connections, the theater was able to entice Francesco Tamagno to give a benefit concert in April 1902 that was a success and garnered much praise. A change in the political administration allowed an adventurous (for the time) opera season to be programmed for 1903: *Tosca*, *Tannhäuser*, and *Un ballo in maschera*. It was the *Tosca* premiere for Cremona, and the opera was not well received. It fact, the public reaction was so hostile that the opera had to be pulled from the schedule and *Un ballo in maschera* performed in its place. But *Ballo* was also a fiasco, due in no small part to the mediocre tenor, Mario Roussell, although the soprano, Rosa Caligaris, had an excellent voice. So the impresario who arranged the season substituted another Verdi opera, *Il trovatore*, which happily pleased the public. With the new century, more contemporary fare, such as *La Wally*, *Amica*, *Loreley*, *Thaïs*, *Siberia*, Montemezzi's *Giovanni Gallurese*, and Pedrollo's *Terra promessa*, was on the boards, which caused discontent among traditionalists but pleased the rest.

World War I closed the theater from 1916 to 1920. After the war, the climate had changed. There were still some novelties: Catalani's *Dejanice*, Robbiani's *Anna Karenina*, and Mascagni's *Piccolo Marat*. With the winds of Fascism blowing, the inauguration of the 1925 season took place with *Tristan und Isolde*. The Fascists made the theater the focal point of political and cultural activities, opening it up to showing films, drama, and musical and literary exhibitions. In 1937 five operas were scheduled, *Lucia di Lammermoor*, *Rigoletto*, *Iris*, *Adriana Lecouvreur*, and a novelty by the Cremona composer Stradivari, *Nozze in Turenna*. The 1940 season opened with *La Wally*, followed by *Don Pasquale*, *Maristella*, and *La favorita*, but the theater was deserted, despite the good offerings. The ticket prices were raised in an attempt to improve the box-office take, but it made the loss even greater, prompting the Fascist leader to threaten to completely suspend the opera season. Although the seasons did continue, they were short and sporadic: summer of 1941, fall of 1942, and spring of 1944. Otherwise, the theater remained closed until after the war. The total expense had been more than 250,000 lire, whereas the box-office take was not more than 190,000 lire.

After the war, the initial responsibility of the theater passed to one of the old *condominio*, Giuseppe Zanotti, and more traditional repertory took hold, with Verdi, Puccini, Mascagni, Bizet, Ponchielli, Donizetti, Bellini, and Giordano on the program, although an occasional novelty graced the stage: De Martino's *La contessa Kernac*, Allegra's *Ave Maria*, Pasquale's *Mara*, Rossellini's *Uno sguardo dal ponte*, and Napoli's *Il rosario* and *Il malato immaginario*. The 1970s offered more popular fare with *Nabucco*, *Il trovatore*, and *L'italiana in Algeri*, as well as delving into the early periods with operas by Haydn and Paisiello. The 1980s witnessed, along with the traditional fare, an unknown work by Ponchielli, *I Lituani*, among its novelties.

The 1993/94 season commemorated the 350th anniversary of the death of the Cremonese composer Claudio Monteverdi with *L'incoronazione di Poppea*. A decade later, the Ponchielli began a Monteverdi project, in cooperation with the other Theaters of the Lombardy Circuit, to honor the famous Cremona composer, who was the first great figure in the history of opera, by mounting his first opera, *L'Orfeo*. Meanwhile, as the 20th century drew to a close, the seasons' offerings included one lesser-known work, for example, *I due Foscari* in 1999. By the beginning of the 21st century, the Monteverdi project opera had become the unusual, lesser-known work. Recent offerings included *Il ritorno di Ulisse in patria*, *Werther*, *La traviata*, *Andrea Chénier*, and *L'elisir d'amore*.

The Ponchielli is a member of the Theaters of Lombardy Circuit, which includes Teatro Donizetti in Bergamo, Teatro Grande in Brescia, Teatro Sociale in Como, and Teatro Fraschini in Pavia. These five theaters share their productions and offer similar, sometimes even identical, schedules. There are also coproductions with other Italian and European theaters and festivals.

Practical Information

Teatro Comunale Amilcare Ponchielli, corso V. Emanuele II, 52, 26100 Cremona; tel. 39 0372 022 001, fax 39 0372–022 099; www.teatroponchiel li.it.

The season takes place from October to December with five operas and two performances of each. Stay at the Continental, piazza della Libertà 25, 25100 Cremona; tel. 0372 434 141, fax 0372 454 873. A 10-minute walk from the theater, the Continental offers an excellent restaurant. Visit the Violinmakers Quarters: in the Palazzo del Comune, Hall of Violins, there is the Civic Collection of old instruments; in the Palazzo Fodri, there is the Cremonese Violinmaking Centre; in the Palazzo Affaitati, there is the Museo Stradivariano; in the Palazzo Raimondi, there are the International School of Violin-making and Organological Museum; Stradivari's home and his tombstone are in the public garden.

FIVE

~

Teatro Carlo Felice, Genoa

The first operatic performances in the city took place at the Teatro Falcone, one of the oldest public theaters in Italy. The Falcone was given to the city by the Adorno family in the 1600s. The theater held three tiers of boxes, 24 boxes to a tier, topped by a gallery. Pairs of Corinthian pilasters embellished the proscenium arch. Stradella's operas were popular fare in the late 1600s with *La forza dell'amor paterno*, *Le gare dell'amor eroico*, and *Trespolo tutore* on the boards, as well as works by Leo and Latilla. During the latter half of the 1700s, operas such as Cimarosa's *I due baroni di Roccazzurra*, Gazzaniga's *La moglie capriccios* and *Capriccio drammatico*, Zingarelli's *Il mercato di Montefregoso*, and Dalayrac's *Le due ragazzi savojardi* were performed. In 1796 Paisiello's *Il barbiere di Siviglia* was offered, and 21 years later Rossini's *Il barbiere di Siviglia* was given for the first time in Genoa. According to a reviewer of the time, the public was disappointed. Another commented after the second opera of the season, Mayr's *Gli originali*, "This good farce and principally the music was much more applauded and should repopulate the theater with spectators, [since] after the little success of the preceding opera [Rossini's *Barbiere*] the spectators have stayed away." *L'italiana in Algeri* was the final opera of the 1817 season. The last few years at the Falcone witnessed Donizetti's *I provinciali*, Mayr's *La rosa bianca e la rosa rossa* and *Elisa al monte*, Pacini's *Adelaide e Comingio*, Mercadante's *Elisa e Claudio*, and Rossini's *Zelmira*, *Mosè in Egitto*, and *Il barbiere di Siviglia*. The Falcone hosted opera seasons until 1825, when the last recorded opera, Mayr's *Ginevra di Scozia*, took place in the spring.

At the beginning of the 1700s, the Teatro Sant'Agostino was constructed and for 125 years was the primary operatic venue. Constructed of wood and seating 2,000, it hosted the carnival opera season, as well as any additional opera seasons presented in the autumn, spring, and summer. Genoa differed

24

from other major Italian cities such as Venice, Naples, Turin, and Rome regarding the desire or requirement to stage new works. Although there were novelties in Genoa, the impresarios demonstrated a certain caution in their selections, offering operas that had already met the approval of the public in other cities. Usually, notations accompanying opera performances in Genoa commented on where and how successful the work had been previously. Although the impresarios wanted to demonstrate that they were up to date, very few were inclined to be adventurous. Nonetheless, there were a few prime assolute such as *Alessandro nelle Indie* by Chiavacci, *Medonte* and *Lisandro* by Isola, and *Tito Manlio* and *Nicomede* by Giordano, known as Giordaniello. The composers who dominated the schedule were Cimarosa, Paisiello, Guglielmi, Piccinni, Sarti, and Anfossi, of whom only Cimarosa and Paisiello are recognized today. The operas staged, although popular in their time, are now forgotten, such as *I visionari*, *I zingari in Fiera*, *Olimpiade*, *La ballerina amante*, *Chi la dura la vince*, *Didone abbandonata*, *Il socrate immaginario*, *Il principe spazzacamino*, *Le trauma deluse*, *Cleopatra*, *Le astuzie femminili*, *Il convito*, and *La scuffiara*.

In June 1797, the French, after having been present for a while, effectively ended the aristocratic rule in Genoa. One of the most noticeable changes was on the cover of the theater programs that had been frequently dedicated "alle nobilissime dame e nobilissimi cavalieri" (to the most noble ladies and most noble gentlemen), but as early as the summer of 1793, a program was dedicated "al rispettabilissimo pubblico" (to the most respectable public), and that was repeated on numerous programs until Carnival 1798, when it was dedicated "ai cittadini liberi" (to the free citizens). At the same time, a Tree of Liberty was planted on the piazza in front of the Teatro Sant'Agostino. As the 18th century was drawing to its close, besides the Teatri Falcone and Sant'Agostino, Teatro San Francesco d'Albaro, Teatro della Crosa Larga, and Teatro delle Vigne also hosted opera.

The Teatro Sant'Agostino welcomed the 1800s with four operas, one of which was a prima assoluta, Nicolini's *Indatiro*, followed by his *Gli Sciti* and Mayr's *Adelaide* and *Lodoïska*. The next year, Nasolina's *Semiramide* graced the stage, followed in 1803 by Mayr's *Ginevra di Scozia*, about which a reviewer wrote, "The public crowded into the theater early to claim a good seat in the orchestra section, to see again with pleasure the celebrated Grassini. . . . She is more distinguished than the other Italian singers. . . . The sound of her voice is always correct, always harmonic, and her superiority is not a result of imitation, but the fruit of a long and deep study of the fundamentals of harmony. . . . We are not able to conceal that in this opera, the

poetry, music, and scenery did not appear to correspond with the expectations of the public. . . . Why? Because the public, whose tastes and perception
improve every year, remembers still the truly beautiful and tragic scene that
captivated them in the opera of *Semiramide*."

In 1804 at the opening performance of Pavesi's *Andromaca*, there was a
"curiosity" of a female Oreste. This was the first time a woman had sung the
role of a male, or what is known today as a "trouser role." That attracted an
extraordinary number of spectators who, from the first scene, never appreciated the opera. As a critic wrote, "One began to hear whistles and jeers,
together with scant applause, but the opera continued. Nonetheless, during
the second act the clamor of the public grew, demanding a certain aria that
prevented the prima donna from singing at the very instant when she was
about to sing. The scene became tumultuous and interesting. 'Andromaca'
did not sing anymore but requested a word with the public, giving a speech
in Italian with an English accent [to no avail]. Then the first male dancer
tried to change the mind of public, but the public, used to seeing him dance,
would not listen [to him talk]. The scene became strange and comical in a
rare and novel way. Then the curtain fell and the public had the liberty to
vent their feelings."

These composers, along with Zingarelli, Paër, Mosca, Coccia, Generali,
Farinelli, and Morlacchi, were much in evidence until Rossini overshadowed
them all. There were gradual changes in the operas and performances themselves that distinguished the dawn of the new century. The castrati had vanished as did the mythological heroes and heroines of the opera who were
now more romantic, historical figures. The chorus, which had almost disappeared from the *opera seria* of the 1700s, reappeared in an even more authoritative position, and the orchestra acquired new instrumentation, gradually
increasing in size.

The decade continued with successes: Mayr's *I misteri eleusini*, "the public
remained with reason, very satisfied"; Zingarelli's *Ines de Castro*, "at the performance there was very lively applause for each aria, duet, and the final
quartet. . . . Few works can boast such a flattering welcome"; and Fioravanti's
Amore a dispetto, "the first evening had obtained applause and success, but
the applause and success [were] very contested." There were also failures: Portogallo's *Il ritorno di Serse*, "The public had accorded little favor to this performance; they found the plot devoid of interest, the poetry detestable;
nothing new, nothing original . . . a mediocre work." During the second decade, Rossini arrived on the scene, eclipsing everyone. At the time, Mayr was
the king of opera in Genoa after the triumph of *La rosa bianca e la rosa rossa*,

but he was quickly dethroned. The Sant'Agostino staged one-third of Rossini's operas. But none of the numerous theaters in the city were large enough or important enough for a city like Genoa to accommodate the explosion of opera in the 19th century, which Rossini ushered in.

The first drawings for a new opera house date back to 1799, when architect Andrea Tagliafichi submitted plans that, after 26 years, were turned down. In December 1824, Eccellentissima Direzione dei Teatri (Most Excellent Management of the Theaters) was set up, presided over by the mayor of the city, to deal with the construction of a new opera house. On January 31, 1825, Carlo Barabino presented his plans for a new theater, which were approved in December of the same year. Initially, he proposed an elliptical auditorium, modeled after the Teatro Regio in Turin but ultimately decided upon the horseshoe shape of La Scala. The structure had five box tiers topped by a gallery. There would be two facades, the main one facing the piazza and a side one for carriages. In March 1826, Felice Noli was entrusted with the construction. The site chosen was where the church of San Domenico had once stood, but it had been demolished in 1821.

The construction of the opera house was a joint public-private venture, as was the management. In February 1825, the Most Excellent Management of the Theaters established, through the sale of boxes, the means to pay for the construction and a permanent endowment to run the opera house. The first-tier boxes cost 12,000 lire; second-tier, 14,000 lire; third-tier, 11,000 lire; fourth-tier, 8,000 lire; and fifth-tier, 5,000 lire. With the purchase contract came the stipulation that the "*palchettisti* and their heirs must always comply with all resolutions which the [now renamed] Most Excellent Royal Management adopts in the general interest of the co-owners." King Carlo Felice not only authorized that the theater be dedicated to him but purchased seven boxes, paying a total of 55,000 lire.

After 4 years of construction, the Teatro Carlo Felice was inaugurated on April 7, 1828, with Bellini's *Bianca e Fernando*. The local newspaper described the inaugural: "The theater is lit up as if it were daylight. Inside, nothing is more pleasing than a glance at the auditorium. One can easily imagine the magical effect produced by the newness of the frescos, by the gold reflecting the torch lights close to it. The presentation perfectly fit the beauty and the ornateness of the sumptuous hall. . . . As soon as the king and queen appeared in the royal box accompanied by the royal prince and princess of Carignano, a melodic and well-sung cantata (Donizetti's *apposita cantata*), alluding to their presence, began. Afterwards the first act of *Bianca e Fernando*. All the singers of opera competed to ensure the best outcome."

They were the well-known artists of the day, Adelaide Tosi, Giovanni David, and Antonio Tamburini. After the opera, the ballet *Gli adoratori del fuoco* was performed, as was the custom. When the opera house opened, the exterior was not completed, as noted in *Gazzetta di Genova* on April 12, 1828: "The beauty of the structure will have its glory complete when the arcades surrounding the theater, and the columns and all the marble of the magnificent pronaos are finished."

Barabino's theater, although following the neoclassical norms of the era, was atypical. He turned the building 90 degrees so it would overlook the old city and would have the main facade face the new piazza, which was the focal point of the new city. The main facade featured a stately portico with massive, fluted Doric columns of Carrara marble and the following inscription in Latin on the frieze: "Rege Carolo Felici duce nostro ordo genuensis satagente Hectore Yenneo Regio Gubernatore consuluit ne urbi tot insignibus monumentis instructae teatrum spectabilius deesset, MDCCCXXVII" (During the reign of Carlo Felice, our leader, the Civic Corps of Genoa, under the vigilant guidance of Ettore d'Yenne, the Royal Governor, decreed that the city, with many excellent buildings, should have a spectacular theater, 1827). A statue representing the spirit of Harmony, executed by Giuseppe Gaggini, crowned the portico. There was a separate carriage entrance on the side. Above the three entrance doors were bas-reliefs of Music by Davide Parodi, Comedy by Bartolomeo Carrea, and Tragedy by Ignazio Peschiera. A civic escutcheon was set on the tympanum. The richly decorated interior displayed numerous statues and works of stucco: *Nabucco* by Antonio Bozzano, *La gioconda* by Emilio de Lorenzi, *Poliuto* by Vittorio Lavezzari, *La vestale* by Lorenzo Mazza, *Marco Visconti* by Emanuele Giacobbe, *Norma* by Giuseppe Navone, *Guglielmo Tell* by E. Francesco Fasce, and *Saffo* by Luigi Orengo. The ornately embellished, 2,500-seat, horseshoe-shaped auditorium boasted five tiers with 33 boxes to a tier, and a gallery seating 141. There was a huge center royal box, topped by a gigantic crown that extended the entire width of the box. An elaborate fresco representing the Muses by Nicola Cianfarelli decorated the auditorium ceiling. A 72-flame chandelier hung in the center. Four Corinthian pillars defined the elliptical proscenium arch. Two Genoese artists, Giovanni Fontana and Francesco Baratta, painted the drop curtains, depicting *The Panathanaea Games* and *Selenus*. Over the years, restoration projects and restructuring work were executed on the building.

Genoa was a major port city that played an important role during World War II. This resulted in numerous bombing raids. The first took place between October and November 1942, damaging the Carlo Felice. It was the second strike on August 8, 1943, with incendiary bombs that delivered the fatal blow, reducing the once grand opera house to ruins. By 1948 the orchestra area had been readapted amid the rubble, and in August 1948 the opera house reopened as an open-air theater (since the roof had been destroyed) with *Aida*. The edifice was then so hastily patched together that by 1960 it had fallen into such a state of disrepair that it had to be abandoned, and 6 years later, razed. The Teatro Margherita, originally known as the Politeama Regina Margherita, became the primary opera house in the city.

The roots of the Margherita extended back to the Andrea Doria, constructed by Fasce and Costa on their property on the old via Giulia (now via XX Settembre) in 1853. Orsolino designed the structure. In 1884 Daniele Chiarella purchased the building, and in 1887 he completely transformed the inside, rendering it more comfortable and elegant. The Margherita was owned and managed by the brothers Achille and Giovanni Chiarella, sons of the deceased Daniele. The inauguration on December 25, 1885, with Halévy's *La valle di Andorra*, was described in the local journal: "Genoa has now been given a new theater destined to recall, in its properly elegant and abundantly charming atmosphere, a very distinguished and stylish public that one would seldom have had the occasion to come in contact with in the old theater, 'Doria' on whose ruins, one could say, was constructed this new Politeama Regina Margherita. . . . The theater presented an imposing appearance, and from every part, there was a chorus of admiration for the truly artistic ornamentation and fine gold, for the new arrangement of the boxes, for the similarity of the parapets all transformed into cast iron in a manner that resembled huge lace, for the magnificent lighting, for the rather rich and well-painted curtain and drop curtain, for the atrium itself, and finally for all the mirrors, decorated and gilded. . . . Now we come to the show. I do not believe that all were happy to have for the first opera given this season that of Halévy, an opera unquestionably beautiful, but of a genre not very accessible for the masses of the public that as you know, want to place their judgment from the first hearing although they then realize their mistake, but do not have the courage to indicate that openly. *La valle di Andorra* is an exquisite and most delicate musical work, but has need to be heard religiously. . . . It is not enough for one hearing." After opening, the theater became a venue for works such as *Carmen, Mignon, Mirella, Faust,* and *Fra diavolo.* Most seasons it hosted operetta and comic opera companies with works by Suppé, Planquette, Lecocq, and Offenbach. Occasionally, heavier fare such as *Trovatore, Norma,* and *La sonnambula* followed. The Margherita was subsequently converted into a movie house, but with the demise of the Carlo Felice, it was converted back into an opera house.

The struggle to rebuild the Carlo Felice had started right after the war, when the town council called for bids in October 1946, but then a different political party took power and the call was withdrawn. With a change again in political fortunes, the competition was reinstated in 1949, and on October 16, 1951, Antonio Chessa was declared the winner. His plans proposed a theater that blended the old with the new, the ancient with the modern and even included a 60-room hotel. His hotel concept was rejected (after 5 years had passed), and the council asked him to redraw his plans. He submitted revised drawings in 1958, but still nothing happened, and the following year he sued the municipality, demanding construction begin within 2 months. He lost. Next, Carlos Scarpa was entrusted with the commission, with Luigi Croce responsible for the structural side and Zavellani Rossi for the engineering-theatrical aspect. Scarpa kept the original facade but added a small 200-seat hall for chamber concerts. The municipality preferred a playhouse and requested Scarpa to modify his plans. The final drawings were done in 1977 and excavation began. The rebuilding of the opera house appeared imminent. Then during a trip to Japan, Scarpa died. This brought a tender-contract procedure to complete the opera house as quickly as possible. A group of enterprises led by the firm Mario Valle S.p.A. of Arenzano were chosen with three architects: Ignazio Gardella, Aldo Rossi, and Angelo Sibilla. The cornerstone was laid on April 7, 1987, and within 1,000 days the opera house was completed at the cost of 120 billion lire. *Il trovatore* opened the Carlo Felice on October 18, 1991, in time to host an inaugural season to commemorate the 500th anniversary of the discovery of America by Columbus, who was born in Genoa.

The original facade, with its imposing hexastyle portico, was preserved, but Barabino's elaborate horseshoe-shaped auditorium was not reconstructed. Instead, the auditorium re-created a Genoese piazza, to fuse the city with the artistic environment of the theater. The spacious auditorium is postmodern in style and offers an expansive 1,399-seat orchestra section, small side boxes with 76 seats, a 21-seat sliver of a balcony, and 504-seat gallery. The side walls, faced with blue-and-white-streaked gray marble and punctuated with green-shuttered windows and red and white balconies, re-creates the exteriors of buildings surrounding a piazza. Tiny spotlights sparkle from the ceiling, mimicking stars. *Viva Schönberg*, by Giovanni Ceccarelli, embellishes the fire curtain. The theater boasts some of the best state-of-the-art technical equipment in Europe, including four moving stages.

Operatic Events at the Carlo Felice

For the inaugural season in 1828, the Carlo Felice asked three composers, Bellini, Donizetti, and Morlacchi, to write works. Bellini offered a revised version of *Bianca e Fernando* for the opening opera, followed by Morlacchi's *Cristoforo Colombo* and Donizetti's *Alina, regina di Golconda*. The prima assoluta of *Alina* "found universal favor and the maestro was called to the stage numerous times. All the pieces of the score . . . were expertly composed." Also on the boards were Rossini's *Il barbiere di Siviglia*, *Otello*, and *L'assedio di Corinto*. A reviewer wrote of *L'assedio di Corinto* that "the much desired opera was staged last Saturday evening and had fully satisfied the public's expectation, and justified the praise of the Paris newspapers, where it had its first performance." The inauguration of the new opera house did not change the opera repertory offered by the impresarios, only increasing the number of new works, as opera houses of the level to which the Carlo Felice belonged traditionally opened with a new work. The most noticeable difference was that the productions appeared to be more grandiose because of the luxuriousness of the surroundings and the enlarged orchestra.

The repertory stayed with Rossini, Bellini, and Donizetti, who dominated, also offering Pacini, Morlacchi, and Mercadante. About *Semiramide* it was written, "The opera was awaited with impatience, not because it is new for us . . . but [for the reason] that the music of Rossini is preferred above the music of the other composers both antique and modern. . . . The opera master can only have a happy outcome. . . . There was unanimous applause, equally distributed for all the good singers, and [it] made clear the full satisfaction of the spectators." About *Cenerentola* the report was that "the opera was listened to by the public with prolonged enthusiasm, with which one listens always to the sweet melodies of Rossini." Other Rossini operas followed: *Zelmira*, *La gazza ladra*, *Tancredi*, *L'inganno felice*, *Il conte Ory*, *L'italiana in Algeri*, and *Mosè in Egitto*. One evening a Bellini opera, *I Capuleti e i Montecchi*, was substituted for Rossini's *Semiramide*, prompting one critic to compare the two composers. "That Bellini was substituted for Rossini, Bellini did not suffer in the comparison. If *Semiramide* succeeds at the highest level . . . and has all one could desire in an *opera seria*, *I Capuleti e i Montecchi* has so many excellent parts: it is a treasure of sweet and charming melodies so that in the heart one feels enraptured and moved by the most exquisite and deep emotions." Among other Bellini operas in the repertory were *La straniera* and *Il pirata*. Other composers and operas included Pavesi's *Ser Marcantonio*,

Meyerbeer's *Il crociato in Egitto*, Pacini's *Gli arabi nelle Gallie*, Mercadante's *Gabriella di Vergy*, *I Normandi a Parigi*, and *Ipermestra*, Nini's *La marescialla d'Ancre*, and Coccia's *Caterina di Guisa*.

As the decades progressed, the number of first performances of operas in Genoa decreased. In 1822, of 6 works, there was only 1 repeat. A decade later, of 12 operas, 5 were repeats, and in 1842, a year after Verdi first entered the Carlo Felice repertory, 8 were repeats. In 1832 an obscure opera, Granara's *Elisa dei Montaltieri*, was presented with one critic writing, "We have, perhaps, never had a more beautiful occasion to appreciate the success of a new opera. Its success was not only grand and complete, but striking, extraordinary and unique. More superlative words would not be sufficient to express the enthusiasm and torrent of applause." Tastes changed. Another example was in 1863, with Bona's *Vittoria*. Although the reviewer criticized the libretto, he praised the music: "The maestro had textured the score with much musical skill, with richness of instrumentation." No one has heard of these works since.

When Verdi arrived at the Carlo Felice in 1841 with *Oberto*, he would soon play a dominating role at the opera house. The maestro had an apartment in Genoa, and he described his strong connection to the city to Gino Monaldi: "You probably wonder why I've chosen Genoa instead of Milan as my usual residence. It is not that I love the sea or the desire to watch it from my window; you know I do not love the sea, and because of my aversion, I never went to America, and refused to go to Cairo for the production of *Aida*. I chose Genoa to keep myself a little distant from the musical world and all the people in that world who believe themselves to be my master." In 1867 he was made an honorary citizen of Genoa, for being a "European celebrity" and "for the glory of Italy." *Oberto* was well received at Carlo Felice, with one reviewer writing, "The success of this performance was complete, and one might even say major. It pleased to the highest degree, especially the finales of the acts, which demonstrated the distinctive manner and deep skill of the maestro." *Nabucco* was a resounding success, as was *I Lombardi*. "This opera is a worthy sister of *Nabucco*. . . . It is a triumph that our ancestors had never seen. The applause began at the first note and continued to the end." *Ernani*, *I due Foscari*, *Giovanna d'Arco*, *I masnadieri*, *Macbeth*, *Rigoletto*, and *Trovatore* followed, and by the mid-1850s, Verdi dominated the repertory. Although Verdi never composed an opera for the Carlo Felice, many were given there soon after their premieres.

On April 9, 1855, the Società Sanguineti opened a new theater. The society wanted to name the building after Verdi and staged *Rigoletto* as the inaugural work. But Verdi declined the honor, and it was called Teatro Paganini. He also declined an invitation the mayor of Genoa extended to him to write an opera in commemoration of the 400th anniversary of Colombus's discovery of America. Franchetti received the commission instead and on October 5, 1892, the world premiere of *Cristoforo Colombo* was staged in honor of Genoa's famous native son. The event was described as follows: "The auditorium was sold-out: The curtain rose. A short dialogue preceded the entrance of the procession and the orchestra struck up the triumphal march. The public was so moved by the grandiosity of the music that after having called to the stage with enthusiastic applause the maestro twice, requested a repeat. And the opera was begun from the first beat."

French opera was popular at the Carlo Felice, especially the works of Meyerbeer, Massenet, and Thomas. The theater also hosted the Italian premiere of Halévy's *La Juive*, but *Carmen* was performed at the Teatro Paganini. As the 19th century drew to a close, the Carlo Felice welcomed verismo and the new generation of Italian composers: Puccini, Mascagni, Leoncavallo, Giordano, and Cilea. Although Puccini's *Le villi* was staged in 1887, the maestro did not gain popularity in the port city until *Manon Lescaut* graced the stage some years later. Mascagni arrived in 1891 with *Cavalleria rusticana*. A critic wrote, "The final cry, 'Hanno ammazzato compare Turiddu,' struck as anything but dramatic; how it was pronounced did not obtain the desired effect. The music of Mascagni was clearly and genuinely Italian, clear and melodic, but with frequent returns to the conventional formula of 40 years ago." *Le maschere* was deemed a disaster. *I pagliacci* was first performed in 1893. "This much awaited opera had a favorable outcome. The opera was fresh, refined, and textured, rich with unpretentious and clear melodies, and dressed with unconstrained instrumentation. There was nothing vulgar, but without awaking grand enthusiasm, it was, nonetheless, pleasing enough." Like most Italian theaters, the Carlo Felice was slow to present operas of Mozart. *Don Giovanni* was first staged in 1867. "What a bizarre creation of Mozart, this *Don Giovanni* that for such a long time had been awaited and desired, and finally made its appearance on our grand stage. . . . When the curtain fell for the last time, first silence, then jeering and whistles."

Arturo Toscanini first conducted in 1891, staying for three seasons and initiating a so-called Wagner-Strauss cult. And although the Carlo Felice did not host the first Wagner opera in the city (Politeama Genovese staged *Lohengrin* in 1880), Strauss journeyed to Genoa to conduct the Italian premiere of *Arabella* in 1936. The following year, Stravinsky's *Solovey* (The Nightingale) was presented. The Fascist dictatorship banned works by

Schönberg and Berg. Only in 1970 was *Wozzeck* performed, followed 12 years later by *Lulu*. Many of the respected artists of the time performed at the Carlo Felice, including Beniamino Gigli, Aureliano Pertile, Enrico Caruso, Titta Ruffo, Toti dal Monte, and Gina Cigna, and conductors such as Marinuzzi, Capuana, Mancinelli, Toscanini, and Guarnieri were on the podium.

During World War I, a patriotic opera, *Mameli*, was premiered. In 1936 the impresario management of the opera house gave way to the appointment of the first *sovrintendente*, Corrado Marchi, and the formation of the *ente autonomo*. That same year, Mascagni's *Nerone* inaugurated the season, followed by *Le nozze di Figaro* and the world premiere of Malipiero's *Giulio Cesare*. *Fidelio* received its Genovese premiere the following year. Long seasons continued during the early years of World War II, with the last opera performance taking place on May 9, 1942, with *Cavalleria rusticana* and *I pagliacci*. A single concert was held on March 26, 1943, before the building was hit by bombs. The opera house reopened, amid the ruins of a roofless building, with *Aida* in 1948. Also on the schedule was *La gioconda* and *Turandot* with Maria Callas and Mario del Monaco and Tullio Serafin on the podium. Other well-known artists, such as Gina Cigna, Renata Tebaldi, and Ferruccio Tagliavini, sang at the theater, and works such as *Guglielmo Tell*, *Tosca*, *La forza del destino*, Bizet's *Diamileh*, Lualdi's *La granceola*, Menotti's *Amahl and the Night Visitors*, and *Die Meistersinger von Nürnberg* graced the stage. Despite the move to the Teatro Margherita, when the opera house had to be abandoned, the opera seasons did not suffer. Novelties continued with the Genoa premiere of Cherubini's *Médée*, Cavalli's *Giasone*, Prokofiev's *Ognennïy angel* (The Fiery Angel), Petrassi's *Cordovano*, Stravinsky's *Renard*, and Dallapiccola's *Volo di notte*. Although the inaugural 1991/92 season at the rebuilt Carlo Felice offered only two operas, *Il trovatore* and *La bohème*, by the following season, which opened with *Simon Boccanegra*, there were eight operas in the schedule, including Borodin's *Prince Igor* and Catalani's *Loreley*. The rest were popular Italian fare. The opera house gradually became less traditional and inaugurated the 1994/95 season with *Der fliegende Holländer* and the 1998 season with *Tristan und Isolde*.

Since its reopening, alongside a standard, predominately Italian repertory, the Carlo Felice has emphasized the rarely performed operas of Italy's most famous and less famous composers—Verdi's *Giovanna d'Arco*, *Jerusalem*, and *Oberto*; Donizetti's *Il Duca d'Alba* and *Adelia*; Rossini's *L'assedio di Corinto* and *Il conte Ory*; Mascagni's *L'amico Fritz*—and operas of foreign composers, especially Britten's *Rape of Lucretia*, *Death in Venice*, *Turn of the Screw*, and *Peter Grimes*; Hindemith's *Cardillac*; and Henze's *Venus und Adonis* and *Boule-*

vard Solitude. With the dawn of the 21st century and the transformation into a *fondazione*, as required by the legislative decree of April 23, 1998, the repertory is not as adventurous as previously, but the theater has continued staging rarely performed operas of Italy's famous composers, such as Rossini's *La donna del lago* and Verdi's *Il Corsaro*, in a predominately Italian repertory of beloved works, with a couple of foreign and 20th-century pieces. Some recent productions included *Billy Budd, Candide, Fidelio, Traviata, Simon Boccanegra, Norma, Così fan tutte, Cenerentola, La fille du regiment,* and *Fanciulla del West.* Genoa has become known for modern productions but ones that respect the tradition of the opera's origin. The Italian premiere of *Turandot* with the controversial new ending by Berio took place there.

Genoa was the European capital of culture in 2004, and the Carlo Felice was at the center of its cultural relaunching. This focus attracted some well-known conductors, such as Bruno Bartoletti, Daniel Oren, and Lorin Maazel, and directors, including Luca Ronconi, Robert Carsen, and Luis Pasqual. The opera season had a theme of voyage (appropriate for a major port city) with Rossini's *Il viaggio a Reims* (concrete voyage) and *Parsifal* (abstract voyage) staged. Other theme events will include three of Mozart's operas to celebrate the 250th anniversary of his birth and operas with a floral theme.

Practical Information

Teatro Carlo Felice, passo al Teatro, 16121 Genova; tel. 39 010 53811, fax 39 010 538 1233; www.carlofelice.it.

The season takes place from October to June and offers nine operas with five to nine performances of each. Stay at the City Hotel, via San Sebastiano 6, 16123 Genoa; tel. 010 5545, fax 010 586 301; www.bestwestern.com. Only a 3-minute walk from the opera house, the City Hotel offers splendid accommodations. Visit the Teatro Falcone in the Palazzo Reale, via Balbi 10; tel. 271 0211; Mueso di Risorgimento, via Lomellini 11; tel. 246 5843. The birthplace of Giuseppe Mazzini, it now houses documents and memorabilia relating to Mazzini and the Risorgimento.

Condominio Teatro Sociale, Mantua

In 1608 a Teatro Ducale was constructed by Antonio Maria Viani, restored in 1688 by Fabrizio Carini Motta, and had more work executed in 1732 by Ferdinando Galli Bibiena. By the beginning of the 1800s, there was a need for a new theater, and in 1817 a society of the most illustrious and wealthiest citizens was formed to give the city a new opera house. The members paid for the construction by purchasing their boxes. Luigi Canonica designed the building. The site selected required the demolition of several houses before construction could begin, which brought the total cost to 291,000 lire. Construction lasted from 1818 to 1822, when the Condominio Teatro Sociale was inaugurated the evening of December 26, 1822.

The box holders managed the theater when it opened, but unlike other opera houses in Italy, the box holders never surrendered their boxes to the city. Consequently, the Sociale is an anachronism, managed by the heirs of the original box holders, who administer it as if it were still the 1800s. Despite this elitist management and ownership, the *condomini* of the Sociale expected the municipality and province to sponsor their productions and join in the administration of the theater, which understandably these public entities refused to do. This led to the secretary of the Condominio Teatro Sociale, Ezio Ricci, to threaten in 1999 that the opera season might be the last. He was bitter because these public organizations refused to sponsor the one production created by the Sociale, *La forza del destino.* (It was canceled.) The Sociale, however, like all the theaters in Italy, receives a contribution from the state for every performance. The theater still hosts an opera season.

The neoclassical facade of the Sociale is dominated by a six-Ionic-column pronaos that supports a triangular relief pediment. The ground level of rusticated stone displays statues in niches of Melpomene and Talia by Antonio

Spazzi that flank the entrance. The deep red, ivory, and gold, 1,100-seat auditorium offers five tiers, three box levels, and two galleries. The parapets are embellished with gilded stucco masks of Comedy and Tragedy and cornucopia, designed by Tranquillo Orsi, who also decorated the ceiling with an allegorical motif. Girolamo Staffieri executed the stucco and Anselmo Berazzi the gilding. The proscenium boxes are framed by ornamental faux marble, gilded Corinthian columns. Above the proscenium arch is the coat of arms of Mantua surrounded by wreaths and a crown.

Operatic Events at the Sociale

Opera has been offered in Mantua since 1607, when La favola d'Orfeo was performed in the court of Mantua. The next year, Arianna was presented, the same year that saw Gagliano's Dafne. During the 19th century, the theater introduced several operas by minor composers, all of which have fallen into oblivion, Campiani's Alberto di Saviola, Elvira di Valenza, and Taldo; Graffigna's Veronica Cibo; Mela's Il convento di San Nicola and La testa di bronzo; and Mazzucato's Esmeralda. Although the theater was built for opera, it has also been used as a movie theater.

The current repertory continues to be primarily popular Italian fare such as Otello, Lucia di Lammermoor, Norma, La Cenerentola, Il turco in Italia, La sonnambula, and Turandot. The operas are coproductions with nearby Italian cities, so the productions are identical in all the theaters. Since the boxes are still privately owned, there are only a limited number of seats available for each performance, those in the orchestra and the top two galleries. Although the theater is usually "sold out," it is half empty. See the performances in a more welcoming environment, in one of the coproducing theaters.

Practical Information

Teatro Sociale, Piazza Cavallotti 1, 46100 Mantova; tel. 39 0376 323 860.

The season varies as does the number of productions. A bronze sculpture of Rigoletto (Duke of Mantua) is in the garden courtyard of the Casa di Rigoletto, Piazza Sordello 23.

SEVEN

Teatro alla Scala and Teatro Arcimboldi, Milan

Milan opened its first theater in 1598. Located in the interior of the court-
yard of the Palazzo Reale, it was called the Salone Margherita in honor of
Margherita of Austria, wife of King Phillip III of Spain, who reigned at the
time. A few operas were staged in the first half of the 1600s, including
Manelli's *Andromeda*. After the conversion of the Teatrino della Commedia
(Little Theater of Comedy) into an opera house in 1686, the number of
operatic offerings substantially increased. When fire reduced the Salone
Margherita to ashes on January 5, 1708, a very small theater was designed by
Gerolamo Quadrio and hastily constructed, opening on June 21, 1708. The
inadequacy of this new theater prompted the noble Milanese to obtain permission from the Austrian authorities (who had succeeded the Spanish ones)
to construct a proper theater at their own expense. Designed by Gian
Domenico Barbieri, it was called Teatro Regio Ducale, in honor of the Archduke Ferdinand, who governed Milan. The Milanese nobility, who were the
palchisti, paid for the construction. The opera house was inaugurated on
December 26, 1717, with Gasparini's *Costantino*.

An English musicologist visited the Regio Ducale in 1770. He observed
that the opera house was primarily a place to socialize rather than to appreciate opera, and that the audience, which ate and played cards during the performance, was noisy. Opera seria was offered only during carnival; otherwise,
farces or comic operas were performed. He saw Gasman's farce *L'amore artigi-
ano*, which began at eight and ended at midnight. He felt the music was
charming and the seven characters of the opera were well delineated. But the
noise during the performance was incredible, not stopping even during arias

or duets. However, at the end of an aria or duet, applause exploded in the auditorium, continuing until the singers stopped doing encores. The audience had learned that this was the way to hear their favorite arias repeated. There were performances every day except Friday, and the seasons lasted from November to August. The opera was financed by 30 gentlemen, each a member of the nobility. They paid 70 zecchini, and each had a box reserved for himself. The remaining boxes were rented for 50 zecchini on the first level, 40 on the second, 30 on the third, and so on. The cheapest seats were in the orchestra and the gallery, which was called the *piccionaia*. Between acts, the spectators in the orchestra climbed to stroll in the galleries. The opera house was large and luxurious, with five tiers of boxes, 36 boxes to a tier. Each box accommodated six people. On the fourth tier, rooms were opened during the performance for faro players. During its 59 years of existence, the Regio Ducale hosted the first performances of operas by Porpora, Albinoni, Paisiello, Hasse, Piccinni, Scarlatti, and Galuppi. Gluck's *Artaserse* was performed in 1741, and later in the century, Mozart's *Mitridate, re di Ponto, Ascanio in Alba,* and *Lucio Silla* were offered. The celebrated castrati Gasparo Pacchiarotti, Giuseppe Farinelli, Giovanni Manzuoli, and Luigi Marchesi, along with Lucrezia Anguiari and Caterina Gabrielli, performed there. It was after a performance of Traetta's *La Merope* during the night of February 26, 1776, when perhaps not all the candles that had illuminated the performance were extinguished, that a fire claimed the wooden structure.

After exhaustive negotiations between the government of Vienna, the Archduke Ferdinand, the empress of Austria and duchess of Milan Maria Theresa, and the *palchettisti* of the destroyed Teatro Regio Ducale, a project to construct two new theaters with integrated programming was approved: Teatro alla Scala, referred to as the *teatro grande*, was reserved for opera seria in the more important season of carnival, and the Teatro La Canobbiano, referred to as the *teatro piccolo*, was relegated to hosting *opera comica*, or a nontragic repertory. The site chosen for La Scala was where the crumbling 14th-century church Santa Maria alla Scala stood. The demolition of the building began in August 1776. La Scala was constructed of masonry to reduce the fire risk and consequently took a long time to build, so a Teatro Interinale (temporary theater) of wood with a copper roof and 120 boxes was erected for the interim. Designed by the architect of La Scala, Giuseppe Piermarini, it opened September 13, 1776, and hosted performances until the new opera house was ready.

As construction neared completion, Maria Theresa prophetically proclaimed, "Already the new theater which rises is destined to eclipse the celebrity of the most famous in Italy." Originally known as Nuovo Regio Ducale Teatro, it was subsequently renamed Teatro alla Scala after the demolished church. Salieri's *Europa riconosciuta* with the famed castrato Gasparo Pacchiarotti inaugurated La Scala on August 3, 1778. Archduke Ferdinand and Archduchess Maria Ricciarda Beatrice d'Este, princess of Modena, attended the inaugural. Their names on the title page were larger than the opera's title, and neither the composer's name nor the singers were mentioned. As a chronicler of the time wrote about the structure, "If I criticize the facade, that the protruding loggia had major imperfections, I will only praise the interior of this magnificent building. It is overall immensely elegant." Another wrote, "I do not like the facade. In the design you see the facade as a single surface, but in the execution there are three sections. The portico of ashlar, which serves as an entrance to protect those arriving by carriage from the rain, extends too far and hides part of the facade. Only if you move away does the 'malformation' diminish."

The facade was erected where the side of the church had been located, so it faced a street and not a piazza, justifying the protruding central portico. Only in 1858 was the present piazza created. The austere style of the facade contrasted with the richness of the interior, which held five tiers of boxes, 36 on each of the first three tiers to leave room for the royal center box and 39 on the fourth and fifth tiers, in addition to the gallery. There were no fixed seats in the orchestra level, so around 600 people were crammed in. The original illumination was by candle, which in 1787 was replaced with oil lamps: 996 were hung from the ceiling in the auditorium and 84 placed behind the stage. The original curtain depicted *Muses in Parnaso*, and was painted by Domenico Riccardo. Construction costs reached 400 million lire, paid by the *palchettisti* of the destroyed Teatro Regio Ducale, who took ownership of the boxes in the new opera house and the land on which it was built. The boxes became their private salons, where they spent the evening eating, drinking, socializing, playing cards, and gossiping, interrupting their activities only to watch a particular aria or climactic scene or to applaud their favorite singer. Each box was decorated differently, according to the owner's taste. Silk, tapestry, or scenes from favorite operas covered the walls, and frescoes, mirrors, or carved wood adorned the ceilings. The boxes could be closed off, allowing "intimacies" in the box, which gave rise to gossip of every type. On the front of the box, the family's coat of arms was displayed. The foyers of the boxes were designated for playing *gioco d'azzardo*, a game of chance that was a good source of income for the theater management. Hard wooden benches were placed in the orchestra section for the military and the servants

of the rich, whose behavior was unruly. Most often they were drunk and boisterous, yelling and shouting during the performances, frequently drowning
out the performers. Their applause took the form of beating their sticks
against the benches. The lower classes occupied the galleries, from where, in
place of applause, they showered the stage with paper. To bring some civility
to the performances, dozens of bylaws were passed that forbade, for example,
displaying disapproval of a performance either during or after, applauding in
a manner that did not represent the true worth of the performance, playing
encores, or calling singers back onto the stage more than once.

The year after La Scala opened, Salieri's *La Fiera di Venezia*, a *commedia
per musica* inaugurated the Teatro della Cannobiana in August 1779. Piermarini also designed this opera house, located in Contrada Larga. It introduced several operas to the world, the most famous being *L'elisir d'amore* in
May 1832. Most, however, were by now-forgotten minor composers of the
1800s: Cordella's *Gli avventurieri*; Vaccai's *Giulietta e Romeo*; Mazzucato's *Don
Chisciotte*; Bazzoni's *I tre mariti* and *Salvator Rosa*; Coppola's *La bella Celeste
degli Spadari*; Benvenuti's *Adriana Lecouvreur* and *La stella di Toledo*; Cagnoni's *La valle di Andorra* and *Claudia*; Foroni's *I gladiatori*; Muzio's *Le due
regine*; Pedrotti's *Guerra in quattro*; and Torriani's *Anna Campbell*. Probably
the only opera of note is Vaccai's *Giulietta e Romeo*. Some considered Vaccai
on the same level as Donizetti and Bellini. In fact, Maria Malibran, who did
not like the fourth act of *I Capuleti e i Montecchi*, substituted for it the third
act of Vaccai's *Giulietta e Romeo* when she performed the opera, and Teatro
Pergolesi in Jesi revived the work in the late 1990s.

When the French occupied Milan in May 1796, they removed from the
boxes the coats of arms of the nobility, calling them "relics from an age of
barbarity and slavery," and carved five regular boxes out of the center box.
But their stay was brief, and in 1799 the Austrians returned and so did the
coats of arms and center box. During their rule, the Austrians offered good
shows and cheap tickets, to prevent the defiant Milanese from engaging in
patriotic or terrorist activities.

In 1801 the Società Teatrale della Casa Carcano decided to build a theater on Porto Romana. The location chosen was the site of the ex-convent
of San Lazzaro, bought by Giuseppe Carcano. Luigi Canonica was the architect who modeled the building on the theaters of La Scala and Cannobiana.
Decorated in the neoclassical style in stucco and gold, with a large center
medallion, the theater offered between 1,200 and 1,500 places in four box
tiers. Federici's *Zaira* inaugurated the Carcano on September 3, 1803, with
the nobility and rich bourgeoisie in attendance. Although overshadowed by

La Scala, during its first few decades the Carcano played an important role as an opera house hosting the world premieres of *Anna Bolena* and *La sonnambula*. Although it continued to present world premieres, they were by minor composers and of obscure operas: Orlandi's *Le nozze chimeriche*; Manfroce's *Manfredi*; Gerli's *Il pitocco*; Frondoni's *Un terno al lotto*; Fontana's *I baccanti*; Meiner's *Elodia di San Mauro*; Gambini's *Eufemio di Messina*; Mazza's *La sacerdotessa d'Iside*; Graffigna's *Gli studenti*; Canepa's *David Rizio*; Abbà-Cornaglia's *Isabella Spinola*; Maggi's *Gabriella di Belle Isle*; Gallagnani's *Atala*; and Ferrari's *Il cantico dei cantici*. Legendary singers such as Giuditta Pasta and Maria Malibran graced the stage, but after 1850, drama, band concerts, and circuses shared the stage with opera, which continued to be performed.

La Scala underwent its first renovation in 1807 under the watchful eyes of Giovanni Perego, Gaetano Vaccari, and Angelo Monticello. In 1814 the stage was enlarged, with Pietro Canonica responsible for the project. A magnificent chandelier with safety bulbs known as argants and designed by Alessandro Sanquirico was hung in 1823. Gas lighting was introduced in 1860 and electricity in 1883. Then in 1897, the city withdrew its subsidy and La Scala had to close. A sign was nailed to the door, "La Scala, closed on the occasion of the death of all feeling for art, of civic pride, and of good sense." Guido Visconti intervened, establishing the Società Anonima, composed of a group of *palchettisti*, who reopened the opera house, hiring Giulio Gatti Casazza as general director and Arturo Toscanini as artistic director.

On May 15, 1850, the Teatro della Comedia opened, offering 1,050 seats distributed in four tiers of boxes and decorated in red, white, and gold. Renamed Teatro Manzoni, it also introduced operas: Litta's *Raggio d'amore*; Zuelli's *La fata del nord*; Usiglio's *Le nozze in prigione*; and Bottagisio's *Elida* and *Ondina*. The building has since been restructured and modernized and is a home for drama.

In 1872 the Teatro Dal Verme opened with *Les Huguenots*. It joined the other Milan opera houses in presenting world premieres. Most were by minor composers, such as Sangiorgi's *Giuseppe Balsamo*; Podestà's *Un matrimonio sotto la repubblica*; Bossi's *Il veggente*; Bandini's *Fausta*; Pizzi's *Editha*; Dominiceti's *Morovico* and *L'ereditiera*; Mistretta's *Marcellina*; Ferrari's *Notte d'aprile*; Marenco's *I Moncada*; and Sessa's *Re Manfredi*. But not all were minor. Puccini's first opera, *Le villi*, was born here, as was Zandonai's *Conchita*. The only prima assoluta that became famous was Leoncavallo's *I pagliacci*. In the early part of the 20th century, the Dal Verme was transformed into a cinema, and in the 1950s began hosting musical reviews and political conventions. In 1964 architects Ernesto Rogers and Marco Zanuso proposed a project to make it the new seat of the Piccolo Teatro, but financial problems prevented it from coming to fruition. In 1981 the city purchased the theater and transformed the auditorium into a 1,420-seat concert hall. It reopened April 5, 2001, with a week of concerts and shows. The Dal Verme is managed by the Fondazione I Pomeriggi Musicali.

Operatic activities at the Teatro Cannobiana continued when Edoardo Sonzogno purchased the building in 1894 and Achille Sfondrini reconstructed it. Renamed Teatro Lirico, the theater reopened with Samara's *La martire*. As the 19th century drew to a close, it hosted world premieres of famous verismo composers—Cilea's *Adriana Lecouvreur* and *L'Arlesiana* with Enrico Caruso creating the role of Federico; Giordano's *Fedora*; and Leoncavallo's *Zazà*—and minor composers such as Coronaro's *Claudia*; Nardis's *Stella*; Ferroni's *Il carbonaro*; Galli's *David*; Cipollini's *Ninon de Lenclos*; and Orefice's *Chopin*. The Teatro Lirico staged contemporary opera during the latter part of the 20th century, including Der Aufstieg und Fall der Stadt Mahagonny, Nono's *Al gran sole carico d'amore*, and Vacchi's *La Station thermal*. Since 1998 the Orchestra Sinfonica Giuseppe Verdi has run the theater, which hosts avant-garde dance and classical music.

The Teatro Carcano closed in 1904 but opened a decade later, restored by Nazzareno Moretti. It was restructured in 1946, with large orchestra and balcony sections replacing the box tiers, reopening in October 1948 with the show "Le 4 arti" (The 4 arts), which paid homage to music, dance, prose, and operetta. Beginning in the 1950s experimental drama appeared, and by 1965 it was a home exclusively for drama. The gently curved, monumental building is today partially concealed by a structure in front of it.

At La Scala, the fifth tier of boxes was transformed into a gallery in 1907 and the orchestra pit was created. In 1918 Uberto Visconti was forced to resign as head of the box-holder association, Società Anonima, because of the economic crisis gripping the country, caused by the war. His resignation closed the opera house. Three years later, the administration of La Scala was transformed into an *ente autonomo* and the *palchettisti* handed over their boxes to the municipality. Between subsidies from the city and state and subscription sales, La Scala had guaranteed financing. During a bombing raid the night of August 15, 1943, the opera house was hit, collapsing the roof and part of the galleries, boxes, and stage. The *Corriere della Sera* reported the event: "The major loss that Milan has suffered, has been the destruction of our great opera house. . . . The grand auditorium, to which memories of so many artistic and historic events are tied, is only an immense abyss, and the orchestra level is buried under a heap of rubble." The dangerous sections of the bombed structure were removed and a temporary roof installed. Luigi Secchi received the commission to reconstruct the building following Piermarini's original plans. The motto was "*Com'era, dov'era*" (How it was, where it was). The reconstruction was paid for with gate money from soccer games combined with a 2% amusement tax in the Lombardy region (where Milan is located). Toscanini conducted music by Verdi, Rossini, Boïto, and Puccini, with Renata Tebaldi as soloist, at the gala reopening concert on May 11, 1946. *Nabucco* inaugurated the regular opera season on December 26, 1946.

At the beginning of the 1950s, there was a need for a smaller venue better suited for 16th- and 17th-century chamber works and certain contemporary pieces, resulting in the birth of La Piccola Scala (the Little Scala). Designed by Piero Portaluppi and Marcello Zavelani Rossi, La Piccola Scala opened December 26, 1955, with *Il matrimonio segreto* with Giorgio Strehler directing. The 500-seat auditorium held an orchestra section, boxes, and small balcony. During the next couple of decades, it hosted several world premieres, including Ghedini's *L'ipocrita felice*, Malipiero's *La donna è mobile*, Mortari's *La scuola delle mogli*, Rota's *La notte di un nevrastenico*, Manzoni's *Atomtod*, and Negri's *Dairio dell'assassinata*. The venue for early chamber works and modern pieces shifted at the end of the 20th century to the Nuovo Piccolo Teatro, which witnessed on October 16, 1998, the *prima rappresentazione assoluta* of Clementi's *Carillon*, commissioned by La Scala. During the renovation of La Scala at the start of the 21st century, La Piccola Scala was transformed into a storage area for Teatro alla Scala.

At the end of the 1990s, state financing for opera houses was drastically reduced, and a new law required La Scala as an *ente autonomo* to form a *fondazione di diritto privato* to raise money from private sources to supplement the public funding. Known as Milan for La Scala, the *fondazione* promotes, assists, and supports the activities at La Scala. With 1,000 full-time employees, the theater has enormous financial obbligations. Nevertheless, since its transformation from a municipal department, the opera house has had greater freedom in all aspects of its operations, with independent management and private sponsors, although the city, province, region, and state still provide a majority of its budget.

At the end of the 1990s, the facade of La Scala underwent a thorough cleaning, revealing a creamy beige patina, which was much different from the yellow mustard hue that everyone knew. That only highlighted the need for renovation of the interior. There were other requirements as well: modernization of the stage machinery, expansion of backstage and storage area, bringing the building up to fire and safety codes, and increasing the amount

of office and rehearsal space. Work began in January 2002 under the direction of chief architect Mario Botta. The cost was $54 million. A new cube
tower, designed by Franco Malgrande, sprouts skyward from behind the 18th-
century neoclassical facade of Piermarini to house the new stage machinery.
A second, elliptical tower rises next to the first, to house the administrative
offices and artists' rooms. The usual controversies ensued, with preservation-
ists bringing a court challenge to block demolition of backstage and side
spaces and the destruction of La Piccola Scala. They lost on all three. For
fire and safety reasons, standing-room privileges and many seats were
removed from the top gallery, causing the *loggionisti* to sue. They also lost. In
compensation, however, at every performance 140 seats in the top gallery are
held for same-day purchase (as if they were standing room). Botta responded
to the criticism by stating that "the history of La Scala is one of continuing
transformation and the use of outdated stage machinery, lack of storage
space, and limited stage area [that] restricted the number of performances to
90." Eventually that number will be 160. Unfortunately, the renovation
could do nothing to improve the terrible sight lines from all but the orchestra
and center boxes. However, the acoustics were rendered excellent, according
to Riccardo Muti.

During the project, activities were transferred to the Teatro Arcimboldi,
designed by Vittorio Greggotti and built by the Pirelli tire company in an
abandoned Pirelli factory in an area of northern Milan known as Bicocca.
Erected in 27 months at a cost of $44,000, the theater was paid for jointly by
the city and Pirelli. The Arcimboldi is a modern structure with clean lines
of granite and plaster. The fan-shaped, 2,375-seat auditorium holds two tiers
and an elevated seating area behind the orchestra, shaped like a moon cres-
cent. Unlike La Scala, the Arcimboldi offers excellent sight lines from every
seat. On January 19, 2002, *La traviata* inaugurated the Arcimboldi, but only
12 days later it was closed, the result of a 440-pound lighting and acoustic
panel falling in the auditorium during a ballet performance. Fortunately, the
hall had been evacuated and no one was hurt. The remaining 99 identical
glass panels were then removed. The Arcimboldi reopened February 17,
2002, with *Samson et Dalila*.

On December 7, 2002, for the first time in 224 years, the opening of La
Scala's season took place away from La Scala, at the Teatro Arcimboldi.
Besides the usual collection of protesters against the wearing of fur and the
destruction of the environment, there were doctors protesting lack of a contract, residents of the area protesting a new tram that had already been built,
and most prominent, the just-laid-off workers from the Alfa Romeo car fac-

tory with a letter from them read before the opera, which prompted one minister to comment, "You see, in the USA when workers are fired, they leave. In Italy, they go on strike and the bourgeoisie applaud!"

The protesting workers of Alfa Romeo returned 2 years later, when La Scala reopened its historic home on December 7, 2004. They held up signs that read, "Take the money and run." Animal-rights activists demonstrated against the fur coats on the guests, and the Disobbedienti di Azione Milano (The Disobedient of Action Milan) blasted music of Mozart to protest the money spent on culture and call attention to the high unemployment and other social problems. Five hundred police guarded the arrival of the rich and famous who attended the inaugural gala of Salieri's *Europa riconosciuta*, a work that had not been performed for 226 years, since it inaugurated La Scala in 1778. There was much speculation (and grumbling) on why Muti chose a long-forgotten opera, instead of commissioning a new work or opening with one of Verdi's beloved pieces, to which Muti replied, "We must reestablish Salieri as the great musician he was after all the infamy that has been thrown at him in the Mozart story." But it appeared the real reason was that the opera and its 25 rapid scene changes showed off the new stage machinery and did not draw attention to itself. It let the opera house be the prima donna for the evening. One headline in an Italian newspaper read, "Milan at the center of the world," and maybe for the evening it was. The opera house was not yet finished when it opened for the gala inaugural. In fact, most of the opera season continued at the Arcimboldi. At least another year of work is required before the opera house is fully operational, and the costs could become astronomical and maybe unsustainable.

La Scala's austere, neoclassical facade is divided into three sections. A three-arch ashlar portico at the street level offers a spacious terrace above. Pairs of Corinthian pilasters and engaged columns flank Palladium-style windows in the middle level. On the top, a balustrade wraps around the roof, and a center pediment crowns the structure, with the tympanum decorated with a relief of Apollo and his chariot being pulled by four horses. Larger-than-life statues of Verdi, Donizetti, Bellini, and Rossini, and busts of Giordano, Puccini, and Mascagni are in the foyers. Four tiers of boxes topped by two galleries soar in red, ivory, and gold splendor around the horseshoe-shaped auditorium. Gilded cherubs, griffins, lyres, medallions, anthemia, and acanthus embellish the ivory parapets. Gilded caryatids flank the former royal box and pairs of massive, fluted Corinthian columns border the four levels of proscenium boxes. The ivory coffered ceiling is trompe l'oeil. The plush red velvet seats have led to an unwritten rule (among the cognoscenti) that ladies should not wear red, because it would clash with the color of the seats and nothing should detract from the beauty of La Scala.

Operatic Events at Teatro alla Scala

Gluck was first offered the commission to write the inaugural opera for La Scala, but he refused. Then Salieri was asked, and he composed *Europa riconosciuta* for the occasion. A reviewer in 1778 wrote in *La Gazzetta di Milano*, "I am not able to sufficiently praise the excellent music of maestro Salieri. The rivalry of the most celebrated singers, united here, with each offering a different [singing] style which distinguished each one, was admired. . . . Never until now had the audience been so attentive, and not distracted by their usual secondary pursuits [of eating, gossiping, and card playing]. The large chorus ably executed the music; the scenery was beautiful, with each event of the story well-arranged: the procession, the triumph, the sacrifice, the combat, the struggle, the imprisonment, the throne. The ballet was executed by a large corps of good ballerinas. . . . The opera encountered such approval that by request of the court and the public the celebrated composer and director appeared on the stage to receive well deserved applause which resounded throughout the auditorium. . . . The three illustrious Cavalier Associates who assumed the [financial] burden of the theatrical entertainment, in their generosity, did not spare any expense." There was also criticism, aimed primarily at Mattia Verazi, the librettist and director. He had been active in the court in Germany for many years; the Milanese considered him a foreigner and therefore mistrusted him. They also felt his compensation of 1,000 zecchini was excessive in view of the work he had done.

During the early years, opera buffa from the Neapolitan school reigned. Paisiello and Cimarosa were the most prominent composers in the repertory with *La frascatana*, *L'italiana in Londra*, *Il barbiere di Siviglia*, *Nina pazza per amore*, and *Il matrimonio segreto*. Works by Zingarelli and Sarti were also popular, with *I due litiganti* receiving its world premiere on September 14, 1782. This initialed the tradition of introducing new works, which led to the world premieres of 350 operas during the first 150 years. In 1788 the impresarios Gaetano Maldonati and Francesco Benedetti Ricci took over the management of the opera house and published the theater's first regular season program. In 1793 works by Paër entered the repertory followed by those of Mayr, forming a bridge between the opera buffa of the past and the romantic operas of the great 19th-century composers that followed.

Those composers, along with the artists who interpreted the roles and the conductors who led the performances, made La Scala, during the next century, the most important opera house in the world. It began with the arrival of Rossini. In September 1812, he introduced the first of five operas that La Scala premiered, *La pietra del paragone*. During the next 7 years, *Aureliano in Palmira*, *Il turco in Italia*, *La gazza ladra*, and *Bianca e Falliero* would see the light. *La pietra del paragone* was an immediate success, with *La Gazzetta Piemontese* writing, "The beautiful musical phrases of this Italian genius . . . steal with such ease into the ears of those who heard [the opera and] . . . a few months later will be on the mouth of everyone." Rossini composed *Aureliano in Palmira* as an opera seria to show he could write in the genre, but the opera was not favorably received. Rossini's operas dominated the repertory until 1825, including *Il barbiere di Siviglia*, *La donna del lago*, *Otello*, *Tancredi*, *Il turco in Italia*, *La Cenerentola*, *Mosè*, and *Semiramide*. Of the 52 performances between 1823 and 1825, 32 were by the Pesaro maestro.

Next, Donizetti arrived at La Scala in October 1822, with the prima of *Chiara e Serafina*. It was coolly received. There were five more world premieres of Donizetti works: *Ugo, conte di Parigi*, *Lucrezia Borgia*, *Gemma di Vergy*, *Gianni di Parigi*, and *Maria Padilla*. Donizetti soon dominated the stage. Between 1830 and 1840, there were 430 performances of 16 different Donizetti operas, including *Lucrezia Borgia*, *Torquato Tasso*, *La favorita*, *Poliuto*, *Linda di Chamounix*, *Don Pasquale*, *Anna Bolena*, and *La figlia del reggimento*. In 1826 Domenico Barbaia took over as impresario, commissioning Bellini to write three operas. The first, *Il pirata*, performed on October 27, 1827, was successful. *La straniera* followed 2 years later, with *Norma* appearing in 1831. The premiere of *Norma* was a disaster. As the story goes, Marchesa Bianchi was in love with Bellini, but Bellini did not return her love, and true to the expression "Hell has no fury as a woman scorned," she paid spectators to disrupt the opening performance by whistling, hissing, and booing. Fortunately for Bellini, she did not have the funds to pay for the disturbances to continue. When Stendhal visited, he wrote, "I exit from La Scala and in truth my admiration does not fall. For me, La Scala is the first theater of the world because it is this theater that gives the most pleasure from the music. . . . There is no chandelier in the auditorium: it is illuminated only by the light reflected from the stage. It is impossible even to imagine something more grand, more magnificent, and most unusual of all, is the architecture."

The most important singers of the bel canto era performed at the opera house, including the tenors Luigi Pacini and Giovanni Battista Rubini, bass Luigi Lablache, the castrati Gasparo Pacchiarotti and Giovanni Battista Velluti, sopranos Isabella Colbran, Giuditta Pasta, Giuditta Grisi, and Teresa

Belloc, and mezzo soprano Maria Malibran. When Verdi's operas followed, they attracted the greatest singers of the day, including Adelina Patti, Teresa Stolz, Francesco Tamagno, and Victor Maurel.

Barbaia left La Scala in 1832, and 4 years later Bartolomeo Merelli took the helm, remaining until 1850. It was Merelli who elevated La Scala to its untouchable position in the world of opera by indelibly uniting the opera house with Verdi. Verdi's first opera, *Oberto*, was staged in November 1839 and was fairly well received. Merelli then contracted Verdi to write three more operas, which led to more than a half-century association between the maestro and La Scala, despite a few decades of "differences." The first contracted work was a comic opera. While Verdi was composing it, family tragedies befell him. First, his two children died, then his wife, Margherita. He could not write a comic opera and requested a release from his contract. Merelli refused and *Un giorno di regno* was introduced on September 5, 1840. It was an unmitigated disaster. Verdi sank into a deep depression, refusing to compose anymore. Merelli returned the contract, but he did not give up. The story goes that one cold winter evening he met Verdi and placed a libretto by Temistocle Solera into the composer's hands. Upon arriving home, Verdi threw the libretto on the table and it opened to "Va, pensiero sull'ali dorate" (Fly, thought, on wings of gold), and so inspiring was it to the farmer from Bussetto that he wrote *Nabucodonosor* (*Nabucco*). Its prima assoluta took place on March 9, 1842, with Giorgio Ronconi in the title role and Giuseppina Strepponi (who would become Verdi's second wife) as Abigaille. It was an unqualified triumph. Verdi became an idol overnight, and his name was transformed to the acronym for *Vittorio Emanuele, re d'Italia* (Victor Emanuel, king of Italy), who would be the first to rule a united, independent Italy. One reason for its great success was the topic of an oppressed population longing for freedom. Every Milanese identified with the Hebrews' persecution at the hands of the Babylonians, establishing "Va, pensiero" as the Italians' call to unite against their Austrian rulers. *Il Lombardi* followed in February 1843 and *Giovanna d'Arco* 2 years later.

Although Verdi's operas remained a staple of La Scala's repertory, after *Giovanna d'Arco* the Busseto maestro left La Scala, returning only in 1869 with a new version of *La forza del destino*. The European premiere of *Aida* followed a year after its world premiere in Cairo, and in 1874 when Alessandro Manzoni died, Verdi wrote the *Messa da Requiem*, which was performed at the theater. Next came the revised version of *Simon Boccanegra* in 1881. He then offered La Scala the prime assolute of his final two masterpieces, *Otello* in February 1887 and *Falstaff* 6 years later. With the triumph of *Fal-*

staff, Verdi's second era at La Scala drew to a close. As Italy's greatest composer lay dying in the Grand Hotel nearby, straw was placed on the street outside his window to muffle the sound of horses' hooves so he would not be disturbed. Verdi died of a stroke on January 27, 1901, and La Scala shut its doors. A few days later, a concert of Verdi's music was performed, with Enrico Caruso singing and Toscanini conducting. When the maestro was buried, those at the grave site spontaneously sang "Va, pensiero sull'ali dorate."

The world premiere of *Mefistofele* took place on March 5, 1868, and it provoked violent protests between Boïto's admirers and his enemies. When the disturbances continued during the second performance, Milan's chief of police ordered the opera withdrawn from the repertory. The *prima esecuzione assoluta* of *Gioconda* followed in 1876. The works of Puccini first entered the repertory in 1885 with *Le villi*, but the world premiere of *Edgar*, 4 years later, was not warmly received. *Manon Lescaut* received its La Scala *prima* in 1894, and *La bohème* opened the 1900 season.

Meanwhile, in 1873, La Scala welcomed a new impresario who introduced Wagner operas, beginning with *Lohengrin*. Toscanini opened his first season in 1898 with *Die Meistersinger von Nürnberg*, followed by *Siegfried*, and so on, such that by 1903, *Der Ring des Nibelungen* had been presented. More German works followed, with *Salome* in 1906, *Elektra* 3 years later, and *Der Rosenkavalier* in 1912. The opera house had become more receptive to new musical movements and foreign operas. *Pelléas et Mélisande*, *Boris Godunov*, and works by Respighi, Stravinsky, Busoni, Zandonai, and Pizzetti graced the stage. Some of the great voices of the era included Victor Maurel, Enrico Caruso, Giovanni Zenatello, Giuseppe de Luca, Fernando de Lucia, Gemme Bellincioni, Rosina Storchio, Félia Litwinne, Claudia Muzio, and Tito Schipa.

By the end of the 19th century, the role of conductor took on greater importance at La Scala than in most opera houses, and since that time, many exceptional maestros have stood on the podium. Probably the greatest conductor of all time was Arturo Toscanini, who dominated the house's musical life during his different tenures. Toscanini's first tenure began in 1898, and he turned the opera house into a battlefield with the audience. Ladies with large hats were not allowed into the auditorium, and the no-encore rule was strictly enforced. His first tenure ended abruptly in 1903 during a performance of *Un ballo in maschera*. Angered by the incessant demands for encores that were disrupting the performance, he threw down his baton and stormed out of the theater. The performance was not finished and he did not set foot in La Scala again that season. He returned for the world premiere of *Madama*

Butterfly on February 17, 1904, which was a disaster. The story goes that the noise was so deafening that Puccini appeared on stage to restore order. There were many reasons for the failure. There was conjecture that Puccini's enemies, which included a faction that supported Mascagni and his publisher Sonzogno, had a claque organizing disruptions. But they were not responsible for all the unrest. The story of an American sailor jilting a geisha girl sung to strange new melodies and harmonies, with an extremely long, slow-moving second act, simply bored the Milanese, and the singer in the title role, Rosina Storchio, who was very close to Toscanini, was obviously pregnant (which the audience knew was by the conductor), neither of which they were ready to forgive. *Madama Butterfly* was pulled from the schedule and not staged again until 1925. Meanwhile, Toscanini followed Gatti Casazza to the Metropolitan Opera in New York in 1908, and Tullio Serafin succeeded him at La Scala. Other noteworthy conductors include Victor De Sabata, Antonio Guarnieri, and Gino Marinuzzi.

Puccini fared better with his *Manon Lescaut* and *La fanciulla del West*, but the maestro did not live to see another world premiere at La Scala. He died before finishing *Turandot*, introduced in 1926. Completed by Franco Alfano, *Turandot* was conducted by Toscanini, and when the maestro arrived at the point where Puccini stopped composing, he turned to the audience and said, "Here the opera is finished, because at this point, the maestro died," and left the podium. *Cavalleria rusticana* arrived in 1891, followed by other Mascagni titles, *Iris* and *Le maschere*, and operas of Leoncavallo, Giordano, and Cilea. The centennial of Verdi's birth was marked with *Falstaff* and *Messa di Requiem*.

La Scala reopened after World War I on December 26, 1921, with Toscanini conducting *Falstaff*. During the maestro's final tenure, he turned the place into a shrine of opera. But his legendary clashes with Benito Mussolini forced him in 1929 to leave not only La Scala but Italy. De Sabata took over, remaining until 1953. When Toscanini died on January 6, 1957, in New York, his body was flown back to Milan, according to his wishes, and his coffin was placed in the atrium of La Scala, where throngs of people paid their last respects. As the funeral cortege left the opera house, De Sabata conducted Beethoven's *Funeral March* in the deserted auditorium. The music was transmitted to the piazza, where thousands had gathered.

One of La Scala's low points was introducing Mascagni's *Nerone*, an opera that glorified Mussolini and Fascism in 1935. The era between the wars brought Beniamino Gigli, Fyodor Chaliapin, Toti dal Monte, Titta Ruffo, Gino Bechi, Magda Olivero, Gilda dalla Rizza, Giacomo Lauri-Volpi, and

Aureliano Pertile to the opera house. After its bombing in 1943, performances took place at the Teatro Sociale in Como, the Teatro Donizetti in Bergamo, and at the Teatro Lirico, where on an afternoon in April 1945, *Don
Giovanni* was given. Performances of *La bohème* followed in May.

Maria Callas's La Scala triumph occurred in *I vespri siciliani* on opening
night of the 1951/52 season. Her success was repeated in the following
months with *Norma* and *Die Entführung aus dem Serail* and again on December 7, 1952, in *Macbeth*. It was written that Maria Callas had an "innate
ability to master the gestures, the words, the phrases, the space while search-
ing to express the internal motive of the character identified with the score."
Callas joined with Franco Corelli in Spontini's *La vestale*, the opera in which
Luchino Visconti made his directorial debut. The Callas phenomena lasted
a decade, ending in 1961/62 with *Medea*. The much written about and
talked about rivalry with Renata Tebaldi had no reason to exist. Their voices,
temperaments, and roles were each unique. Tebaldi made her mark with
Margherita, Desdemona, Mimi, and Cio-Cio-San, among others. But she was
from the grand Italian school of singing, whose time was coming to an end.
Beverly Sills, Monserrat Caballé, Fiorenza Cossotto, and Mirella Freni were
the new prima donnas. On the male side, Mario del Monaco, Giuseppe Di
Stefano, Corelli, Tito Gobbi, and Ruggero Raimondi were the stars, to men-
tion but a few.

After the war, contemporary repertory began creeping into the schedule,
although it was not initially welcomed. The reception to *The Consul* was
downright hostile, and during *Wozzeck* the audience was so unruly that maestro Dmitrij Mitropoulos had to personally intervene to bring quiet to the
house so the opera could be completed. Operas of Hindemith, Dallapiccola,
Schönberg, and Shostakovich entered the repertory during the mid-1960s,
and in 1979 the European premiere of Krzysztof's *Paradise Lost* took place.
The 1980s introduced Stockhausen's *Donnerstag aus Licht*, *Samstag aus Licht*,
and *Montag aus Licht* and Manzoni's *Doktor Faustus*, among others, with
Berio's *Outis* appearing for the first time in the mid-1990s. Some of the well-
known artists included Luciano Pavarotti, Jane Eaglen, June Anderson,
Renato Bruson, Carol Vaness, Mariella Devia, and Plácido Domingo and
conductors Claudio Abbado, Riccardo Chailly, and Muti, who became La
Scala's music director in 1986.

La Scala has been plagued at various times in its career with political
infighting, inadequate budgets, traditional (unexciting) repertory, and union
problems. One crisis occurred in 1974/75 when there was no money and the
unions made large demands. A difficult fight followed, resulting in the *sovrin-*

tendente, Paolo Grassi, requesting a reform of the *enti lirici* (opera corpora-tions) and a special law to define the role of theater. Another crisis occurred at the beginning of 2005, after the *sovrintendente*, Carlo Fontana, was fired and the unions demanded Muti's resignation. During the last decade of the 20th century, contributions from the state had been drastically cut and the amount of earned money had to be increased, leading to Fontana wanting a more "popular" repertory, which Muti opposed, and resulting in the firing. La Scala increased its earnings by raising ticket prices and costs of scenery rentals, as well as finding private sponsors. La Scala's budget at the beginning of the 1990s was $100 million, of which 64% came from public subsidy— down from at least 85% and diminishing even more as the decade progressed. At the same time, the budget has increased, resulting in a large deficit. The commercialization of Milan's great opera house has come at a price, evident at times in the productions and atmosphere. But La Scala has learned the art of 21st-century fund-raising very well. Opening night orchestra seats now cost $2,000 each. On the positive side, since the formation of the *fondazione*, the productions have become more creative, adventurous, and innovative and the schedule broader with more foreign and contemporary, or "difficult," works on the boards, as is evidenced by the 1999/2000 season: *Fidelio*, *Adriana Lecouvreur*, *Wozzeck*, *Tosca*, *Ariadne auf Naxos*, *Dialogues des Carmélites*, *Peter Grimes*, *West Side Story*, *Bohème*, *Voyna i mir* (War and Peace), Nono's *Prometeo*, and the world premiere of Corghi's *Tat'jana*.

With the dawn of the millennium came the commemoration of the centennial of Verdi's death and performance of six of the maestro's operas: *La traviata*, *Rigoletto*, *Un giorno di regno*, *Un ballo in maschera*, *Il trovatore*, and *Otello*. The last opera opened the 2001/02 season on December 7, 2001, at La Scala's traditional home. The season continued with *La traviata* at La Scala's temporary home, the Teatro Arcimboldi. The 2002 and 2003 seasons were inaugurated at the Teatro Arcimboldi with *Iphigenia in Aulide* and *Moïse et Pharaon*, respectively. When the company returned in 2004, the same work that inaugurated the house in 1778, *Europa riconosciuta* was performed. The Milan and Rome papers wrote that the applause lasted 15 minutes. Newspapers from other Italian cities said it was only 12 minutes, but in any case, the opera was an unqualified success. With the reopening of La Scala on December 7, 2004, the opera season now unfolds in two venues, allowing a type of repertory system but in two different spaces. For the 2004/05 season, the operas at La Scala itself were limited to either "difficult" and contemporary works, such as *Pelléas et Mélisande*, the prima assoluta of Corghi's *Il dissolute assoluto* with Hindemith's *Sancta Susanna* (although a strike caused the cancellation of the scheduled double bill of *Il dissolute assoluto* and *Sancta Susanna*), and Tchaikovsky's *Cherevichki* (Slippers), and popular Italian fare, such as *Bohème* and *Cenerentola*. The core of the season's schedule was (still) at the Arcimboldi: *Tannhäuser*, *Otello*, *Elektra*, *Rinaldo*, *Pikovaja dama* (Queen of Spades), and *Carmen*, where it will remain until the reconstruction and renovation work is completed at La Scala.

Practical Information

Teatro alla Scala, via Filodrammatici 2, 20121 Milan; Teatro Arcimboldi, viale dell'Innovazione, Milan; tel. 39 02 7200 3744, fax 39 02 887 9331; www.teatroallascala.org.

The season runs from December to November, with a break in August. There are 12 operas, 6 at La Scala and 6 at the Arcimboldi (which might change with the completion of La Scala), with the number of performances ranging from 7 to 13. Stay at the Grand Hotel et de Milan, via Manzoni 29, 20121 Milano; tel. 02 723141, fax 02 86460861; www.grandhoteletdemilan .it. The Grand Hotel was Verdi's Milan home for 27 years, and the apartment where the composer lived has been preserved. It is a 5-minute walk to La Scala. Each room is individually and luxuriously decorated with musical or operatic themes. Visit Verdi's apartment in the Grand Hotel et de Milan and the Casa di Riposo per musicisti (Rest Home for Musicians), piazza Buonarroti, which was built according to Verdi's wishes and with his money. Verdi's tomb is located on the grounds of the Rest Home, inside a crypt, where he is buried next to his wife, Giuseppina Strepponi. Teatro Carcano: corso di Porta Romana 63; tel. 5518 1377; www.teatro.carcano.com. Teatro Lirico (originally Teatro Cannobiana): via Larga 14; tel. 809 665. Teatro Dal Verme: via San Giovanni sul Muro 2; tel. 87905; www.dalverme.org. Teatro Manzoni: via Manzoni 42; tel. 7636 901; www.teatromanzoni.it. Teatro Grassi (Piccolo Teatro): via Rovello 2; tel. 7233 3222; www.piccoloteatro.org.

EIGHT

Teatro Coccia, Novara

In 1695 the first documented *dramma per musica, Antemio in Roma,* was staged in the Teatro Nuovo. It was not until 1757 that another *melodramma, Il filosofo di campagna,* was performed in the house of the aristocratic family Petazzi. Operas then followed in quick succession between 1757 and 1775, including *La cascina, Le serve rivali, L'amore arrigiano,* and *La moda.* The predilection for the public was to follow the operas of the Venetian school, and then those of the Neapolitan school. *Opera comica* was most popular, with the music of Cimarosa, Paisiello, Anfossi, Sarti, Salieri, Bianchi, and Piccinni favored. It was written that these composers altered the panorama of music in Novara.

Since Novara did not have a permanent theater, operas were performed in courtyards and rooms of the palaces of noble families, especially the Casa Petazzi, which was equipped with a theater complete with boxes and a gallery. This only emphasized the need for a permanent performing venue, which finally was assured. The funds for the new theater came in part from Count Luigi Maria Torinelli, and from the recently formed *Società dei Palchettisti* (Society of Box Holders), who purchased the boxes in the theater, becoming the *condomini.* Construction began in 1777 on the new opera house, called the Teatro Civico but also known as Teatro Nuovo. Located on one side of the piazza Rivarola, it was completed in 2 years and inaugurated in 1779 with Sarti's *Medonte, re d'Epiro.* The architect was Cosimo Morelli, with the Galliari brothers responsible for the interior decor and the stage curtain, on which Ercole, the founder of the city, was represented. Built only for aristocracy, the theater was rather small, with the auditorium shaped like a U and holding three levels of boxes divided by rows of small pillars. It was decorated with painted garlands in wood that continued on the parapets of the boxes. The boxes themselves were decorated with blue silk and held carved seats covered in rich brocade. The proscenium arch, ornamented with gilded wooded carvings, was supported by two pairs of fluted columns. The facade was not monumental, as the custom of the time was that it should resemble the outside of a nobleman's house.

The Civico was restructured in 1830 by Luigi Canonica and Antonio Agnelli, when the auditorium was given its first orchestra pit and took on a brighter appearance. Carved swans decorated the small columns on every box tier, and the parapets were decorated with floral festoons and heads of animals. The white and gold hue of the room contrasted with the red drapery hung from the boxes, whose ceilings were painted with allegorical figures. In the center, a chandelier of Bohemian crystal hung. Bellini's *La straniera* reopened the theater in 1832. The next year, the cream of Novara society formed *La Società del Casino* (Association of the Casino) to manage the theater, which was open every day from 9 a.m. to 11 p.m. for conversation, balls, games, politics, and opera performances. To control the behavior of the visitors, rules were set in 1850 requiring proper attire, prohibiting smoking, and not allowing the audience to demonstrate approval or disapproval by whistling, yelling, or shouting.

Between 1853 and 1855, a second theater, Teatro Sociale, opened. Designed by Paolo Rivolta, it hosted minor companies and young, up-and-coming talent. Within a few years, however, a fierce competition developed between the Sociale and the Teatro Civico (Nuovo), subsequently renamed Teatro Antico. In 1873 the maestro of the cappella in Novara, Carlo Coccia, died and the Antico was again rebaptized, becoming Teatro Coccia in his memory. As the 1800s were drawing to a close, it became apparent that the Teatro Coccia, which dated from the 1700s, was inadequate for the needs of the city, which required a performance venue with a greater capacity and suitable for a variety of shows.

The municipal council acquired both theaters in 1880 for the purpose of replacing them with a new construction. To facilitate this undertaking, the Società dei Palchettisti of the Teatro Coccia dissolved itself. The following year, Andrea Scala presented a project for a new theater. According to his proposal, the theater would be constructed on the side of the castle in the piazza Rivarola and the two existing theaters would be converted for other usages. The project was too expensive for the municipal council's taste, and it requested modifications. Scala delegated the project to Giuseppe Oliverio, who after some years and modifications and only involving the Teatro Coccia, was given the approval for the work. In 1885 the Società dei Palchettisti was reestablished under the direction of the mayor of Novara, Marquis Luigi Tornielli, and in February the following year, the theater's owners removed everything of value from their boxes, including furniture and lighting fixtures. The next month, construction began. In 1887, however, after having made numerous requests for modification during the course of work, the *palchettisti* brought a civil suit against the architect for breach of contract. The work ended the next year, although the theater was not completed. The rear part of the stage was missing, so the space was enclosed by a wall and transformed into a garden, with plans to complete it in more economically favorable times.

The "new" Teatro Coccia was inaugurated the evening of December 22, 1888, with *Les Huguenots*. There was not much enthusiasm for the work, probably because of the complexity of the music. As the critic for the *Corriere di Novara* wrote December 22, 1888, "If one did not have the ears of a professional, a profound culture of the art, or was not a lover of the theater, there was a danger of boredom and the need to pay attention and to study [the opera] before enjoying it completely." Construction resumed in 1914 and continued until 1928. "The construction faithfully respected the formal concept of the initial project from 1883, accurately imitating the decorations of the 19th-century building to maintain a uniformity within the structure," as Carbone wrote in *Perizia tecnica*. Giuseppe Passerini directed the work. Other modifications and modernizations were performed, and beginning in 1914 movies were shown, requiring the construction of a projection room, much to the dismay of opera lovers. The interior of the Coccia was restored in 1986 and the facade during 2004/05.

Meanwhile, the Teatro Sociale had been renamed Teatro Municipale and was renovated a few years later. A third theater, the Teatro Faraggiana, was inaugurated on April 2, 1905, with *La sonnambula*. Also designed by Oliverio, the building was erected by Senator Faraggiana, who did not like the other box holders at the Coccia and built his own theater!

The Coccia is a neoclassical-style building of pale yellow hue subdivided into three distinct parts. One section preserved the preexisting 18th-century structure incorporated into the new construction. The second section was built between 1886 and 1888, parts of which have subsequently been remodeled. The third section was erected in the temporary garden during the 1920s. The exterior has two principal facades, one facing via Fratelli Rosselli, and one facing Piazza Martiri della Libertà, with doors on three sides. Doric columns define a front peristyle topped by a glass-enclosed balcony. Ionic pilasters flank rectangular windows that punctuate the facade. Busts of Tornielli and Coccia are located at the entrance to the horseshoe-shaped, 925-seat auditorium, which took on the "modern" colors of gray and rose during the 1986 restoration. Decorated in the Renaissance style, the space offers three tiers of boxes topped by a gallery. The parapets are decorated in ivory and gold, with cast-iron columns between each box.

Operatic Events at the Teatro Coccia

After the Teatro Civico opened, it witnessed several important events: The marriage of Prince Vittorio Emanuele of Savoy to Princess Maria Teresa of Austria saw *Enea e Lavinia* staged in their honor. Napoleon's birthday was celebrated in 1808 with *Cantico*. The visit by King Carlo Felice in 1822 was commemorated with *Il barbiere di Siviglia*. During this time, several Rossini operas graced the stage, followed by those of Bellini and Donizetti. Beginning in 1837, Donizetti was the preferred composer, but not all of his operas were successful. There was a particularly bad execution of *Gemma di Vergy* in 1839, the fault of the artists. The presentation of Mercadante's *Il giuramento* was considered an important event, since at that time he was the choirmaster in Novara. Other favorite composers included Coccia, Pacini, and Morlacchi. An impresario ran the theater, economizing wherever he could, mainly with the orchestra, chorus, and dancers; he hid out-of-tune choristers amid good ones, mixed bad and good violinists, and concealed ugly ballerinas behind the beautiful ones. If he still did not succeed financially, he fined the artists. Amusing incidents include an intemperate Signora Parodi being fined 5 lire on January 4, 1892, for not having taken off a black corset during the performance as ordered by the administration; again, on January 24 for undignified behavior on stage; and yet again, on January 27 for having fought in the theater with Signora Traversi. The use of the claque began around this time, which promoters, impresarios, and directors found useful to guarantee the success of the shows. Besides opera, the theater hosted plays, variety shows, and even Roman circuses.

During the second half of the 1800s, the most performed composers were Verdi, Ricci, Donizetti, Bellini, and Rossini, with occasional operas from Pacini, Peri, and Petrella and the French composers Auber, Gounod, and Meyerbeer. In fact, it was a Meyerbeer opera, *Les Huguenots*, that had opened the "new Coccia." *Aida* followed, and it was even less successful. The staging was so dark that everyone was calling "*luce, luce, luce*" (light, light, light). The season closed with *La forza del destino*, also with an unhappy result, such that the critic in the *Corriere di Novara* praised the Novara public for not protesting in the piazza but going directly to the impresario to voice their displeasure. The repertory continued in the Italian vein with mainly Verdi operas, including *Ernani*, *Traviata*, *Otello*, *Trovatore*, *Ballo in maschera*, and *Rigoletto*, along with *Edmea*, *Mefistofele*, *Le precauzioni*, and a smattering of French works, *La Juive*, *Mignon*, *Carmen*, and *L'Africaine*. The first Wagner opera, *Lohengrin*, was staged during the 1892/93 season. As the 20th century was ushered in, the works of Mascagni, Leoncavallo, Cilea, Ponchielli, Giordano, Verdi, and Puccini were in favor, along with operas of some minor composers, such as Varese's *Nerina*, Zanetti's *Madre*, and Alfano's *Risurrezione*. During World War I, life remained normal in Novara and the Coccia kept its doors open with the mainstream Italian repertory, but a different type of crisis struck: the growing popularity of cinema to the detriment of theatrical performances.

By spring of 1914, opera was sharing the stage with cinema. The *Corriere di Novara* expressed its indignation in its September 13, 1914, edition: "Poor Coccia, destined for the more pure expression of the arts, has now been reduced to the level of the other theaters." Between the two world wars, Leoncavallo, Mascagni, Giordano, and Puccini continued to be the composers of choice. Although Verdi operas were also staged, they were regarded as "old." There were novelties as well, such as Trentinaglia's *Rosmunda*, Smareglia's *Pittori Fiamminghi*, Zuffellato's *Un astuzia di Colombina*, Colonna's *Beatrice Cenci*, and Cagnoni's *Papà Martin*. During World War II, the theater stayed open, staging more novelties such as Colonna's *Sagre Ampezzane*, Lualdi's *Le furie di arlecchino*, and Garau's *La guardia innamorata*. After the war, popular Italian operas prevailed along with more unusual fare such as Mannino's *Vivì*, Cinque's *Pierrot innamorato*, Allegra's *Medico suo malgrado*, Massaron's *La prima notte*, and the rarely staged *La battaglia di Legnano* of Verdi. As the 20th century drew to a close, unusual or contemporary operas disappeared from the repertory and the productions became traditional.

The Coccia is administered by the municipality, and classified as a *Teatro di tradizione*. The thinking had been that, since Novara was only 30 miles from Milan, one went to Milan to see nontraditional offerings. The budget was not large, which limited the number of both productions and performances. The situation changed beginning with the 2002/03 season and the hiring of the first artistic director at the Coccia. The 2002/03 season offered four operas, including a rarely performed one-act farce by Donizetti, *Il campanello dello speziale*, along with popular Italian fare. In addition, eight operettas and musicals were staged. The next season saw staged the first Coccia opera ever performed at the theater named after him, *Clotilde*. The hope is that the opera house will establish a *fondazione* for its funding and increase the number of lesser-known operas and daring productions offered—but only after the horizons of the conservative Novara audience are broadened, to avoid an empty theater. Recent repertory included *Faust*, *Rigoletto*, *L'italiana in Algeri*, and *Pagliacci* / *Cavalleria rusticana* and three operettas by visiting companies, Straus's *Sogno di un Valzer*, Kálmán's *La Principessa della Czardas*, and Lehár's *Die lustige Witwe*.

Practical Information

Teatro Coccia, via Fratelli Rosselli 4, 28100 Novara; tel. 39 0321 620 400, fax 39 0321 640 962; www.teatrococcia.it.

The season runs from November to April and offers four operas and two operettas, with two to three performances of each. Stay at the Albergo Italia, via Solaroli 12, 28100 Novara.

NINE

~

Teatro Comunale
"Giuseppe Verdi," Padua

A large room in the Palazzo del Capitanio was the city's first theater. Constructed in 1642, it hosted the city's first opera, Gabrieli's *Maurizio*, in May 1691. But by that time, the building had substantially decayed. Subsequently abandoned, it burned to the ground in April 1777. Next, the Teatro degli Obizzi opened. Constructed in 1652 by Poi Enea Obizzi, the theater hosted only comic performances until 1693, when opera shared the stage. The Obizzi was renamed Teatro Novissimo and then Teatro dei Concordi after the Società purchased it. The building continued to operate as a performance venue until 1884, when in a precarious state, the Società sold the building. It was subsequently transformed into a movie theater.

By the mid-1700s, some of the noble families disagreed with the management of the Obizzi, as well as feeling that the Obizzi could no longer adequately accommodate the new production requirements, so they formed the *Nobile Società del Teatro Nuovo* for the purpose of constructing a new theater. A site in the San Nicolò district was chosen and work began in 1749. It took 2½ years to complete. Antonio Cugini designed the building, and Giovanni Gloria was in charge of the construction. The Teatro Nuovo was inaugurated on June 11, 1751, with Galuppi's *Artaserse*, a work especially commissioned for the occasion. The journals of the era wrote that it was a luxurious event and the theater left a favorable impression. A "foreigner," De La Lande, wrote in French, "We would say that the music is very well cultivated in Padua . . . and the auditorium of the theater is rather pretty." The new opera house offered a horseshoe-shaped auditorium with four box tiers of 29 boxes each. The fifth tier was a gallery for the servants. The orchestra section held

250 stools and a standing area separated by a balustrade. Above the entrance hall there was a saloon for games and balls. In 1764 the Duke of York visited the theater, followed some years later during the fair season by the grand duke of Tuscany, Pietro Leopoldo. The first intervention took place in 1775 to correct mistakes of the initial construction and alleviate inconveniences for the public. A decade later, Bernardino Maccaruzzi corrected the acoustical distortions in the hall, among other work performed. In January 1846, Giuseppe Jappelli reworked the facade and auditorium, increasing the number of boxes to 31 on all the tiers except the first, which had 30. The theater reopened June 12, 1847, with Pacini's *Lorenzino de'Medici*. A new curtain was painted by Vincenzo Gazzotto in 1856 showing *The Entrance of the Carroccio into Padua*. The Nuovo was again reconstructed between 1882 and 1884 under the supervision of Achille Sfondrini, obtaining the appearance it has today. The auditorium received new stucco and gilding. Giacomo Casa decorated the vault with an allegorical fresco of music with scenes from six Verdi operas: *Nabucco*, *Aida*, *I due Foscari*, *Ernani*, *I Lombardi*, and *Macbeth*. The theater was renamed Teatro Verdi when it reopened June 8, 1884, with *Aida*.

Verdi was invited by the theater's president to the inaugural gala at the theater that now carried his name. But he declined, writing in a letter, "What I had the honor to tell you before, and what I repeated to the honorable architect Sfondrini is that I am not able to come to Padua for the opening of the new theater. I am very sorry to have to repeat it for the last time. Everything is working against it: my age, my health, and most of all my tastes. And permit me, Mr. President, to ask, What will I come to do? To make myself be seen? To receive applause? That I cannot do. I should, it is true, come to thank you for the honor that you wanted to do for me, but I hope that you will accept, also in writing, these thanks that I make to you with the deepest feelings and sincerest gratitude. . . . Busseto at Sant'Agata, June 6, 1884, Yours, Giuseppe Verdi."

The opera house was severely damaged by Austrian bombs on December 29, 1917. When the building was repaired, the frescos on the cupola were repainted with allegorical themes. Giuliano Tommasi was in charge of the work. Vittorio Emanuele III attended the reopening of the opera house with *Mefistofele* on December 21, 1920. After the war, the municipality acquired the theater. It was restructured again in 1958 and 1996.

The Teatro Verdi presents a gently curved facade of yellow ochre. Surrounded by a portico on the lower level, and punctuated with lavishly framed windows on the upper, the facade is adorned with musically inspired reliefs and ornamentation and crowned by statues. The 890-seat, horseshoe-shaped auditorium holds three tiers of boxes and a gallery. White stucco masks, putti, and embellishments decorate the chocolate-colored parapets. The seats, which had been red, are now gray, and the curtain, which had been blue, is now red. The coat of arms of Padua decorates the proscenium arch.

Operatic Events at the Teatro Verdi

After the inaugural *Artaserse*, Galuppi wrote several more operas for the Nuovo, including *Demofonte, Solimano*, and *Arianna e Teseo*. In 1752 Scarlatti was commissioned to write a new opera and *Demetrio* was presented. In 1773 the Nuovo began hosting drama as well. The theater offered two seasons, carnival with comic opera, and Santo with opera seria. With both the Teatro Nuovo and Teatro degli Obizzi hosting opera, a silent agreement to divide the opera seasons was made between the two theaters. But during Carnival 1790/91, a fierce competition broke out between the two venues. The Marquis Tomaso degli Obizzi, having just restored his theater, decided to open it during carnival, when the Nuovo was open. The Nuovo then opened during the spring when the Obizzi was open. After a couple of seasons of this "bruising competition," the Nuovo was declared "victorious," and an official accord was signed on August 27, 1792, between the two theaters that divided the seasons. The Nuovo had the seasons of Santo and San Giustina; the Obizzi, carnival and spring.

Between 1793 and 1800, several new works by Sarti, Alessandri, Fabrizi, Paër, and Montellari graced the stage. Then Carlo Eugenio Napoleon visited in 1806, followed by the Duke of Modena in 1814 and Ferdinando I in 1838. During the first part of the 1800s opera buffa dominated the repertory, although the genre was already in decline. "New blood" appeared with the works of Rossini, first seen in 1811, and 3 years later, two-thirds of the operas on the schedule were by the Pesaro maestro. Other names new to Padua entered the repertory: Pacini, Donizetti, Bellini, Mercadante, and Mayr. In 1843 *Nabucco* graced the stage and was accorded a reception equal to that received at La Scala. The next year it was *Ernani*, and during Carnival 1841/42 Malipiero's *Giovanno, prima regina di Napoli* received its prima assoluta. The 1850s saw *I due Foscari, Poliuto, Luisa Miller, Rigoletto*, and *Trovatore*. In 1818 Giuditta Pasta sang in Padua for the first time, followed by other celebrated singers of the era, including Teresa Stoltz, Francesco Pandolfini, and Marietta Brambilla.

After the theater reopened as the Teatro Verdi, contemporary works of the time, including *Lohengrin, Otello*, and *Cavalleria rusticana*, were offered.

The popular Italian repertory dominated, with the occasional novelty such as *Donne curiose* or foreign piece such as *Parsifal*. The 20th century witnessed Edward Johnson, under the name of Edoardo di Giovanni, make his operatic debut as Andrea Chénier in 1912. Nello Santi made his debut conducting *Rigoletto* there in 1951. Between 1973 and 1986, the opera seasons were managed by the municipality, and the repertory kept a mixture of mainstream Italian operas with lesser-known ones, including *I due Foscari*, *Il piccolo Marat*, and *I quattro rusteghi*. Then the seasons were organized in collaboration with the Teatro La Fenice in nearby Venice. *L'inganno felice*, *Rigoletto*, and *Tosca* were some of the offerings just before the arrival of the 21st century. With the subsequent scheduling of predominately dramatic fare, theater management passed to the Corporation of Italian Theaters, and the municipality again took over the opera seasons. This resulted in the Orchestra of Padova and of Veneto making its first foray into the opera arena in November 2002 by playing at a new production of *Così fan tutte*, chosen to commemorate the reopening of the Teatro Da Ponte in Vittorio Veneto. Although the orchestra had been in existence since 1966, it gave only classical music concerts, around 150 a year. The Verdi, originally constructed in 1751 as an opera house and opening its doors to short seasons of prose in 1773, has come full circle, now being a fortress for drama with only a short opera season.

Practical Information

Teatro Comunale "Giuseppe Verdi," via dei Livello 32, Padua; tel. 39 049 876 0339; www.teatroverdipd.it.

The opera season, which runs in either September or October, offers one opera with two performances. Stay at the Majestic Hotel Toscanelli, via dell'Arco 2; tel. 049 663 244.

TEN

~

Teatro Fraschini, Pavia

The first theater opened in 1671 and was replaced by the Teatro Omodeo in 1728. Discussions concerning the construction of a new, more elegant theater began in 1771. A group of noblemen, known as *I quattro Cavalieri Associati* (Association of the Four Cavaliers) formed to pay for the construction and claim their boxes in the new building, designed by Antonio Galli Bibiena. Two years later, the Nuovo Teatro dei Quattro Cavalieri was inaugurated with Mjsliweczek's *Demetrio*. The large central box was assigned to the prince and the first three tiers were reserved for the nobility and aristocracy. In 1845 one of the many restorations took place, with the theater subsequently renamed Teatro Fraschini, in honor of the celebrated Verdian tenor from Pavia, Gaetano Fraschini. The most recent restoration began in 1984 and took a decade to complete, with the Fraschini reopening in December 1994.

The neoclassical facade is divided into three levels. Tuscan-order columns form a three-arch portico entrance on the street level. Rows of windows surmounted by a pediment and separated by pilasters define the upper two levels. The 800-seat auditorium was restored in 1994 to its original subtle green color, popular in Italian theaters of the 1700s. There are four tiers topped by a gallery. Carved individual balustrades, a hallmark of Bibiena, set apart each box, and boxes are defined by a series of arches with beige marble columns, the order of which differs on each tier. The first is Tuscan; the second is Ionic; and the third is Corinthian. A green blue hue fills the spandrels, highlighted by a gilded keystone and arch ring. Massive gilded Corinthian columns of beige marble flank the proscenium boxes, which are angled toward the auditorium. Allegorical motifs carrying a musical theme decorate the ceiling, painted to look like a dome. The coat of arms is displayed on the valence above the stage curtain.

Operatic Events at the Teatro Fraschini

After the theater reopened in 1994, it hosted opera seasons of surprising length given the small, provincial nature of the town and opera house. Popular operas and lesser-known ones, both contemporary and those from the 18th and 19th centuries, were on the schedule, including Paisiello's *Il barbiere di Siviglia*, Malipiero's *Tre commedie goldoniane*, Henze's *Pollicino*, Piccinni's *Cecchina*, Rossini's *Cenerentola*, and Puccini's *Tosca, Gianni Schicchi*, and *Madama Butterfly*. There are coproductions with the Teatro Sociale in Como, Teatro Grande in Brescia, Teatro Donizetti in Bergamo, Teatro Sociale in Mantua, and Teatro Ponchielli in Cremona. Often these opera houses offer identical opera schedules. Recent repertory included *Traviata, Werther, L'elisir d'amore, Andrea Chénier*, and *Ritorno in Ulisse in patria*.

Practical Information

Teatro Fraschini, corso Strada Nuova, 136, 27100 Pavia; tel. 39 0382 371 214, fax 39 0382 371271; www.teatrofraschini.it.

The season, which takes place from October to January, offers five operas with two performances. Stay at the Albergo Ariston Pavia, via Scopoli 10/D, 27100 Pavia; tel. 0382 34334, fax 0382 25667. The hotel is a 12-minute walk from the theater.

ELEVEN

Teatro Sociale, Rovigo

In 1816 the owner of the Teatro Roncali, Antonio Roncali, proposed erecting a new theater and obtained the necessary authorization from the Austrian government. The idea of a new performing venue was welcomed by the residents, due to their special interest in opera. The Società del Teatro, a private association of opera lovers, was established to pay the construction costs of 120,000 Austrian lire. Additional funding came from the municipality and Cassa di Risparmio (Savings Bank). Work began in 1818. The Teatro della Società, as the Teatro Sociale was originally titled, opened its doors on March 3, 1819, more than a month before the official inauguration, for a visit from Emperor Franz Joseph. A cantata was played in his honor. The official inauguration took place on April 16, 1819, with Generali's *Adelaide di Borgogna*, a work written especially for the occasion. Sante Baseggio was the architect with Nicolò Pellandi responsible for the interior decorations. There were five box tiers when the theater first opened, but one tier was eliminated during the 1858 restoration, which took place under the direction of Giovanni Viaello. The restoration was so expensive, 122,000 Austrian lire, that it was more costly than the building's original price tag. The parapets of the auditorium were redecorated with the following designs: first tier, a series of multicolored fauns in gilded relief and clusters of flowers; second tier, a series of portraits of the most famous Italian composers; third tier, a series of putti with symbols alluding to Comedy and Tragedy; fourth tier, a variety of flowers and a soft valence draped over each box; and on the large center box, two putti write the names of some of the most illustrious Italians in a Book of Eternity.

The theater went up in flames in January 1902, but the Società Teatrale quickly reconstructed the edifice. Before the reopening performance, a stone slab was unveiled, built into the peristyle of the theater, inscripted, "During the night of January 22, 1902, a fire destroyed the Teatro di Società, built according to the design of Sante Baseggio in the year 1818. With like-minded purposes, the Società Teatrale, the municipality and the savings bank, with architect Daniele Donghi of Milan, restored with 'new form' that antique monument given to the culture and education of the arts of the people, 1904." Mascagni conducted his *Iris* for the inaugural opera on October 21, 1904.

The Società Teatrale managed the theater from its inauguration until 1908, when the building was sold at auction to Antonio de Paoli, who preferred commercial enterprises. In addition to the opera seasons, movies were projected. The Società Teatrale regained their theater in 1925, and since 1964 the municipality has managed it. Three years later, it was recognized as a *Teatro di tradizione*. A much needed restoration and modernization took place in the early 1970s, and the 2004/05 season marked the 100th anniversary after the devastating fire of the rebuilt Sociale.

The facade is divided into two distinct sections. On the lower part, two arched doorways surrounded by rusticated stone flank a center colonnade, and two pairs of Tuscan-order columns support an architrave etched with "Societas MDCCCXIX," crowned by a balustrade. Five rectangular windows, topped by reliefs of musical instruments, symbols, and masks, define the upper part. The 750-seat, beige and red auditorium, decorated in the Liberty style, offers four tiers: two box tiers topped by two balconies. Cherubs, chiaroscuro musical symbols and motifs, masks of Comedy and Tragedy, and colored portraits of composers—Franchetti, Ponchielli, Mascagni, Rossini, Boïto, Bellini, Donizetti, Catalani, Pergolesi, Cimarosa, Leoncavallo, Puccini, Verdi, Spontini, and Mercadante—adorn the parapets. The coat of arms of Rovigo is displayed on the valence of the proscenium arch. Nine Muses chased and crowned by various putti decorate the ceiling, the work of Giovanni Vianello.

Operatic Events at the Teatro Sociale

When the Sociale first opened, the main interest of the patrons was to listen to the celebrated singers of the era: Luigia Boccabadati, Vincenzo Negrini, Sebastinano Ronconi, and Domenico Cosselli. After the 1858 restoration, the inaugural season offered *La favorita*, *Il trovatore*, and *Giovanna di Guzman*. When the theater reopened after the 1902 fire, many international artists performed there, usually before they achieved fame. Two of the most celebrated made their operatic debuts at the Sociale: Beniamino Gigli as Enzo in *Gioconda* in 1914 and Renata Tebaldi as Elena in *Mefistofele* in 1944. Gigli returned for *Lucia di Lammermoor* and *Il trovatore* and Tebaldi for *Andrea Chénier*. The theater also hosted Maria Callas as Aida, Mario del Monaco as Andrea Chénier, Toti dal Monte, and Cesare Siepi, among others. The repertory consisted of mainly popular Italian fare, sprinkled with French operas, such as *Werther*. Since the 1950s, some of the better known singers performing at the theater early in their careers have included Franco Corelli, Magda Olivero, Giulietta Simionato, Alfredo Kraus, Nicola Rossi Lemeni, Ruggero Raimondi, Mariella Devia, Katia Ricciarelli, and in 1962 Luciano Pavarotti as the Duke of Mantua.

Beginning in 1965, a few contemporary works were staged, including *Assassinio nella cattedrale*, *La guerra*, *Uno sguardo dal ponte*, and Bartók's *A Kékszakállú herceg vára* (Bluebeard's Castle). Two decades later, Rossini's *Sigismondo* was unearthed for the first performance in modern times. In the 1980s, coproductions began with the Teatro Comunale of Treviso, and the two theaters formed the Orchestra Filarmonia Veneta, which plays for both opera and concerts. The last few seasons of the 20th century saw *Fedora*, *Il matrimonio segreto*, *L'elisir d'amore*, *Tosca*, *Norma*, *Il barbiere di Siviglia*, and *Simon Boccanegra* in the schedule. In November 2004, the Sociale hosted the *prima esecuzione assoluta* of Coli's *The Tell-tale Heart*, a monologue for baritone with text of Edgar Allen Poe, paired with another contemporary piece, Scogna's *Anton*, conducted by the composer. February 2005 marked 90 years since Gigli had made his debut in *La gioconda*. The opera was staged in honor of the occasion, along with a gala benefit concert. Recent repertory includes *Ballo in maschera*, *Ideomeneo*, and *Madama Butterfly*.

Practical Information

Teatro Sociale, piazza Garibaldi 14, Rovigo; tel. 39 0425 27853, fax 39 0425 29212; www.comune.rovigo.it.

The season runs from September to February, offering five operas with two to five performances of each. One performance is reserved for students. Stay at the Hotel Cristallo, viale Porta Adige 1, 45100 Rovigo; tel. 0425 30701, fax 0425 31083. The Cristallo, which supports the opera and hosts the artists and the cast parties, is a 12-minute walk from the opera house.

TWELVE

Teatro Comunale Chiabrera and Teatro dell'Opera Giocosa, Savona

In the era before the construction of public theaters, performances took place in the courts of the princes and the palaces of the aristocracy. Traveling companies performed *commedie musicali* in the now demolished Palazzo delle Cause. During the 1647 carnival, as Lamberti noted in his *Memorie*, "a comedy company came to Savona and staged many 'musical comedies' in the Palazzo of the marquis of Garessio [Rovere]." Then more than 125 years passed with no news about musical performances. Toward the end of the 1700s, the Teatro Sacco, also known as Teatro della Città di Savona, came into being in the Palazzo Sacco, paid for with funds that the Savonese patrician Girolamo Sacco left to the city in 1555 to be used "when the city decided to build a theater." The Sacco held a maximum of 300 and had a narrow stage, two tiers of boxes, and a small orchestra section. It witnessed all the artistic and political events from the Napoleonic period to 1853. There was strict censorship by the political commissioner, who prohibited any inflammatory production. Police agents, reinforced by troops, guarded both the inside and outside of the new theater. The curtain rose at 7 p.m. in the winter, 8:30 p.m. in the spring, and 9 p.m. in the summer. There were strict rules governing the theater, and whoever broke them was immediately arrested: The audience had to remain silent with heads uncovered during the performance and could not bring in dogs. One encore was allowed but two were absolutely prohibited. Proper attire was required.

At the beginning of the 1800s, two travelers, Davide Bertoletti and Giacomo Navone, who had separately visited the Teatro Sacco, wrote unfavorably about it. In Bertoletti's view, "When a beautiful theater will be substituted for this cave . . . Savona will be a pretty city," and Navone wrote, "We went last evening to the Teatro of Savona, a building of little value." On January 17, 1829, there was a scandal in the theater, as a report sent by Savona mayor Gio Batta Pico to the head office of the province revealed. A servant in livery sat in the orchestra section and refused to move, although there were rules prohibiting anyone in livery from entering that area. By December 1833, the rules were changed, permitting servants to sit there but only if they did not have any indication or sign that they were servants (not in livery, not carrying a lantern) and if they had bought a ticket. In 1841 there was much talk about the necessity of enlarging the tiny opera house. Pietro Zerbini offered to pay 40,000 lire for the work in exchange for a special concession regarding the management of the theater, but nothing was done. In the early 1800s, the most popular composers performed in the Sacco were Donizetti, with L'elisir d'amore, Il furioso all'isola di San Domingo, Olivo e Pasquale, Il Belisario, Parisina, Lucia di Lammermoor, Anna Bolena, Torquato Tasso, Lucrezia Borgia, Bertly, Roberto Devereux, and Linda di Chamounix. Rossini was the next most popular, with Semiramide, Cenerentola, Il turco in Italia, Matilde di Schabrand, Tancredi, Il barbiere di Siviglia, and La gazza ladra, followed by Bellini, with I Capuleti ed i Montecchi, Norma, Beatrice di Tenda, La straniera, Sonnambula, and I Puritani. Operas by the Ricci brothers, Mercadante, and Pacini were also well liked. During the final decade before the new opera house opened, early Verdi works Ernani, Nabucco (Nabucodonosor), I due Foscari, and Attila were offered.

In 1842 the municipality discussed the idea of a permanent theater, located in the area of the piazza of the Mercato, since the Sacco was insufficient for the growing population and the ambition of the citizens to have a larger, more elegant theater. The following year, Giuseppe Galleano presented a project, modeled in large part on the Teatro Carlo Felice in Genoa, with a capacity of 1,200 and a cost of 138,000 Piedmont lire. The theater would have been dedicated to Carlo Alberto, who was then sovereign. For various reasons, Galleano's plans were not approved. In 1847 Gioachino Dellisola submitted a project, but the cost was judged excessive. Two years later, in November 1849, the city council unanimously decided to construct a theater, to be called Chiabrera after the Savonese poet Gabriello Chiabrera, with three box tiers, 20 boxes on the first level and 21 on the other two, in addition to a gallery, with the cost not exceeding 110,000 Piedmont lire. Funds were raised by the sale of boxes, but unlike other Italian cities, the municipality would reimburse the palchettisti the purchase price in 20 to 30 years. During that time, the palchettisti had exclusive use of their boxes. The municipality was obligated to open the theater for two seasons per year, with no fewer than 30 performances of opera or drama.

After royal approval was received in February 1850 from Vittorio Emanuele II for the construction, an architectural contest was held that attracted 19 entrants. Luigi Falconieri won the contest and designed the building. The theater took 3 years to erect and, when it was finished, was considered the third most important in the Kingdom of Sardinia, after the Teatro Regio in Turin and the Teatro Carlo Felice in Genoa. Two-thirds of the cost was paid by subscription of the *palchettisti* and one-third by the municipality. On October 1, 1853, the Teatro Comunale Chiabrera was inaugurated with *Attila*. The theater should have been inaugurated with *Ginevra di Scozia*, by native son Noberasco, but some members of the city council objected, and the performance of Noberasco's opera was postponed until Carnival 1856/57. By 1883 the city had repaid the *palchettisti* and was the sole proprietor of the building.

In 1888 the Teatro Sacco was radically restored, and the elaborate and elegant decorations from the 1700s were eliminated. It was retitled Teatro Colombo. After a fire in March 1893 caused 20,000 lires' worth of damage, the newspaper *Cittadino* wrote, "The entire stage was destroyed by flames and a large number of the proscenium boxes as well. The firefighters cut part of the roof in order to put out the flames that smouldered in the rafters of the ceiling. The rest of the theater is in bad condition." The patchwork restoration that followed degraded the auditorium even further from that of the 1888 restoration.

Meanwhile, the financial subsidy from the municipality for the Chiabrera slowly diminished, stopping entirely in 1910. Two citizen's associations, the Amici dell'Arte (Friends of Art) and Amici della Musica (Friends of Music) programmed the seasons, offering productions of respectable quality. In 1954 the theater was closed for a restoration that lasted until 1963. Four years later, the city took over the management, with additional restructuring in 1984. Then on the morning of October 11, 1999, the ceiling of the auditorium suddenly collapsed. A platform was constructed to protect the audience from any additional falling debris so the 1999/2000 season could continue. At the end of the season, the opera house was closed and the restoration of the ceiling frescoes and the rest of the structure began. In October 2005, the opera house reopened.

The Chiabrera is a large neoclassical structure. The facade offers a colonnade of four large Doric columns on the lower level. The upper level has a row of Ionic columns with pairs of Ionic pilasters at each end and statues of

Metastasio and Rossini in niches on either side. In the tympanum is a relief of Gabriello Chiabrera presenting "Amedeide" to Carlo Emanuele I of Savoy on his throne. On the fascia, "Gabriello Chiabrera . La Patria . MDCC-CLIII" is inscribed. Statues of Goldoni and Alfieri flank the entrance. Antonio Brilla executed the sculpture work of the facade, based on sketches by Santo Varni. The 700-seat, red, ivory, and gold auditorium is horseshoe shape. There are four tiers, the first and third of which were transformed from boxes into open balconies during the restoration of the 1950s and 1960s. The second tier is the only box tier. A gallery is on top. Gilded stucco adorns the ivory-colored parapets. The eight figures on the dome ceiling represent Tragedy, Comedy, Poetry, Music Dance, Painting, Architecture, and Sculpture. The original historical-mythological curtain by Gaetano Borgo Caratti, which represented the deification of the poet Chiabrera, was destroyed in the 1883 fire.

Operatic Events at the
Teatro Comunale Chiabrera

After the opening of the Chiabrera with *Attila*, the inaugural season continued with *Macbeth* and *Poliuto*. The theater was managed by an impresario and subsidized by the municipality. The grand masters of the 1800s were the most performed, with Verdi the most popular, including his works *Trovatore*, *Luisa Miller*, *Traviata*, *Rigoletto*, *Ballo in maschera*, *Aida*, and *Otello*. Donizetti continued to find favor with *La favorita*, *Don Sebastiano*, and *Maria di Rohan*. Several minor composers whose works were liked included Petrella, Pedrotti, De Giosa, Perrari, Peri, Apolloni, Mercadante, and Marchetti. As the 19th century drew to a close and the 20th century arrived, the operas of the verismo school by Puccini, Mascagni, Leoncavallo, Cilea, Ponchielli, Catalani, and Wolf-Ferrari among others dominated the repertory. Foreign composers' works were not neglected, and especially popular were French operas by Meyerbeer, Bizet, Massenet, Gomez, Halévy, Gounod, Flotow, Thomas, and Auber among others. Apparently, Wagner's work appeared only once, in 1891/92, with a performance of *Lohengrin*, which received an icy reception. The first Mozart opera, *Don Giovanni*, was not even offered until 1967.

The Teatro dell'Opera Giocosa now produces the opera season. Founded in Genoa in 1956 as part of the Centro Culturale Sperimentale Lirico Sinfonico, the Opera Giocosa moved to Savona in 1987. Unlike the setup in most Italian opera houses, the opera company (Teatro dell'Opera Giocosa) and the opera house (Teatro Comunale Chiabrera) are two separate entities. The Opera Giocosa was recently classified as a *Teatro di tradizione*. Their mission is to launch the professional careers of young artists in the opera world by creating the conditions for the "development of permanent, artistic structures and for promoting new productions which have a historic-cultural interest." This means for the Opera Giocosa that their raison d'être is to produce neglected operas of the 1700s and 1800s by important Italian composers and the obscure works of the forgotten composers. Included in their repertory have been Rossini's *Aureliano in Palmira* and *Sigismondo*, Donizetti's *Torquato Tasso* and *L'esule di Roma*, Pacini's *Medea*, Apolloni's *L'ebreo*, Coccia's *Caterina di Guisa*, Salieri's *Arlecchinata*, Traetta's *Le serve rivali*, Paisiello's *La pazza per amore*, and Pergolesi's *La contadina astuta*, among others. Operetta is offered in a separate season. The casts are a mixture of established and up-and-coming artists. At the end of the 20th century, the company brought to light Porpora's *Arianna in Nasso*, along with *La Cenerentola* and *La bohème*. During the reconstruction of the Chiabrera, the company presented popular operas, including *Traviata* and *Il barbiere di Siviglia*.

Practical Information

Teatro Comunale Chiabrera, piazza Diaz 2, 17100 Savona; tel. 39 019 836 6995, fax 39 019 820 409; www.comune.savona.it. Teatro dell'Opera Giocosa; tel. 39 019 821 4904, fax 39 019 833 9881; www.operagiocosa.it.

The season takes place during either the fall or summer, offering two operas with four performances of each. Stay at the Hotel Riviera Suisse, via Paleocapa 24, 17100 Savona; tel. 019 850 853, fax 019 853 435. A 10-minute walk from the opera house, the Riviera Suisse is a supporter of the opera.

THIRTEEN

Teatro Comunale, Treviso

During the 17th century, opera was first heard at the Teatro di Santa Margarita, until it burned to the ground. On the initiative of Count Fiorino d'Onigo, who in 1691 obtained permission from the Republic of Venice under whose jurisdiction Treviso fell, a theater for opera and comedy was built in the form of a *Teatro all'italiana* with many box tiers. The site chosen was owned by Onigo, and it held decaying houses with shops and warehouses, which were quickly demolished. A year later, in October 1692, the new theater opened with *La Rosiclea*, a musical work by Giovanni Frezza probably written especially for the inauguration. The origins of the Comunale are traced to the Teatro d'Onigo, named for Count d'Onigo. D'Onigo died shortly after the opera house was completed, and the theater passed to his son Gerolamo. The D'Onigo distinguished itself over the years with a high level of programming, especially during the autumn *fiera* of San Luca, which was much appreciated by the Venetian nobility. Performances were suspended after 1714 and the opera house abandoned.

Almost 50 years passed before it reopened. Guglielmo d'Onigo, who had inherited the theater, obtained permission in March 1763 from the Consiglio dei X to enlarge and renovate the building. The work, which lasted 2 years, was entrusted to Antonio Galli Bibiena, who built a structure with five levels of boxes, holding 1,175 seats. The facade and atrium were realized by Giovanni Miazzi. The theater was inaugurated on April 18, 1765, with the prima assoluta of Guglielmi's *Demofonte*. The D'Onigo was described in 1765 in the *Memorie Trevigiane del Federici*: "The stairs are convenient and huge from the top to the bottom, the corridors spacious with rooms for conversation and halls for gaming . . . and on the curtain, Parnassus was represented." The decor was in the imperial style of the original La Fenice of Giannantonio Selva and the pediment displayed an inscription in Latin commemorating Guglielmo, Miazzi, and the theater's restoration: "Guglielmus Hier Fil. Comes de Vonigo cultu splendidiore Theatrum restituit ampliavitque. A.A.V. MDCCLXV Io. Miazzi Archit" (Guglielmo, Count of Vonigo, restored and enlarged the theater for more splendid performances, 1765, Miazzi, architect.)

On May 28, 1836, the not-easy-to-please critic Tommaso Locatelli wrote in the *Gazzetta di Venezia*, "The theater in Treviso is the most lovely and charming example of its kind that anyone could ever imagine. The theater's grace is born of the simplicity of its design, a perfect blending of colors, the good taste and sparing use of ornaments which ring the ceiling. The entire complex boasts such freshness and elegance that it would be difficult to find words to describe it." A fire later that year damaged the theater's wooden framework, abruptly ending its activities until the Società dei Palchettisti was formed in 1844. As Signor Semenzi wrote in his monograph after the 1846 restoration, "It is marvelously proportionate, the curve well integrated, with four tiers, each with 23 boxes besides the gallery. . . . Thanks to the efforts of that excellent craftsman Negri, it [the theater] was rightly decorated with gilded stucco of a great variety, suitable for any theater it might adorn." The opera house was rebaptized Teatro Sociale, but was also referred to as Teatro di Società.

Another fire, this one caused by an escaping rocket, reduced the theater to ashes on October 2, 1868. The theater's custodian, a man named Triaca, had a side business of making fireworks and, not having a suitable place, used the stage of the theater. One night, a rocket exploded and quickly ignited the other fireworks stored in the theater. Within a short time, a blazing inferno engulfed the building. All that remained were the outside walls. The theater, which was reconstructed in just 1 year, is the one we see today. The project was entrusted to Andrea Scala, who designed the building. Signori Stella and Andreotti were responsible for the elaborate decorations, and the ones in stucco were the work of Fausto Asteo. The Sociale reopened in October 1869 with *Faust*, as part of the *stagione di San Martino*. In the archives, an anonymous letter was found and traced to Luigi Bailo, written to his friend Antonio Caccianiga describing his feelings and impressions regarding the destruction of the opera house. "When a place which is the repository of our memories is destroyed, we are bitter about the loss that strips from our recall the true source of the purest of our pleasures and perhaps the most endearing of those pleasures: those associated with memory. And when an unfortunate event destroyed the theater last year, many of us felt deep sorrow, so much so that we feared the financial problems facing the city might delay or even prevent the rebirth of this small La Fenice . . . . The works presented were in good taste and blessed by performances of the best voices in the land."

Upon the death of Count d'Onigo, the direct rule of the theater passed to his daughter, Countess Teodolinda Jacquillard d'Onigo, and then to her mother, Caterina Jacquillard d'Onigo. The Società requested that Caterina Jacquillard sell them the building (excluding the Onigo box), which they had been renting. They paid her 39,505 lire, which corresponded to 20 times the annual rent indicated in the deed that had been drawn up September 1844. In July 1919, the charitable institutions of D'Onigo gave as a gift to the municipality box 12 in the second tier, the "box of d'Onigo," which made the city a co-owner of the theater. Differences of opinion arose between the municipality and the Società dei Palchettisti that resulted in the city acquiring the building from the box holders on October 26, 1931, for 192,000 lire. The opera house was then renamed Teatro Comunale.

During World War II, with most of Treviso bombed out, the city sold the theater to Venerio Monti, his wife, and his sons for 3.9 million lire on June 26, 1944. Almost 6 years later, in December 1950, the courts of Treviso declared the sale null and void. With appropriate compensation paid to the owners, the city took back the theater. Restructured in the early 1960s, the edifice was listed in 1968 as one of the 24 Italian theaters considered by law to be a national landmark. The building was closed in 1998 because it did not meet building and fire safety standards. After a 5-year renovation and updating, it was reopened November 15, 2003, with a concert by the London Royal Philharmonic Orchestra.

The neoclassical facade is divided into two sections. The lower part is of rusticated stone with arch entrances. Windows crowned by frontons punctuate the upper part, with the facade decorated by reliefs of musical motifs and Ionic pilasters. A balustrade runs across the top of the theater. The 700-seat, horseshoe-shaped auditorium radiates with ivory, red, and gold. There are four box tiers topped by a gallery. A rococo-type design with colorful floral motifs, studded with gilt Murano pearls, embellishes the front part of the boxes and the proscenium arch. Delicate female figurines sprout from the box dividers and putti frolic on the allegorical-theme ceiling.

Operatic Events at the Teatro Comunale

When the D'Onigo opened after reconstruction in 1763, it hosted a variety of activities, from opera buffa, opera seria, and concerts to benefit evenings and carnival balls. There were elaborate celebrations for illustrious visitors, among whom were Nicolò Paganini, the emperors Ferdinand and Francis I, and Viceroy Archduke Ranieri. A luxurious feast took place for the marriage of Napoleon.

When the theater reopened after the second fire in 1869, *La traviata* was on the boards as part of the inaugural season. A golden era at the Sociale followed: Emma Calvè made her debut in the fall of 1890 in *Hamlet*, singing 12 performances in the role of Ophelia. Arturo Toscanini arrived in 1894 to conduct *Falstaff* and *Cristoforo Colombo*, returning the next year for *Tannhäuser* and *Loreley*. At the turn of the century, Enrico Caruso offered a memorable Cavaradossi; other well-known artists included Giacomo Lauri-Volpi in *Andrea Chénier* and Toti dal Monte in *Lodoletta*, *Il barbiere di Siviglia*, *La traviata*, and *Madama Butterfly*.

In 1940 the management of the theater was entrusted to the Società Autonoma Gestione Teatri, which had its headquarters in Treviso. The agreement lasted until 1952. After a few years, the city decided the contract was against their interests and, through legal means, had it declared null and void. After the municipality reacquired the building in 1950, the *Società Amici della Musica* managed the seasons for the next 7 years. Meanwhile, the musical life of the theater continued, alternating the traditional autumn and spring opera seasons and hosting such famed singers as Licia Albanese, Tito Gobbi, Aureliano Pertile, Mario del Monaco, Magda Olivero, Nicola Rossi Lemeni, Giuseppe di Stefano, and Ferruccio Tagliavini. A management firm guided the theater until September 1969. Two years later, the Ente Teatro Comunale of Treviso was establish to organize opera performances, as well as concerts, ballet, drama, and other cultural events. It was a private corporation started by a public initiative. The Comunale was named a *Teatro di tradizione* in 1968 and beginning in 1979 has collaborated with the Teatro Sociale in Rovigo. In 1969 the Toti Dal Monte International Competition was established, which became a springboard for young singers who went on to international careers, including Ghena Dimitrova, Mariella Devia, and Ferruccio Furlanetto. Established singers continued to perform there, Katia Ricciarelli, Renato Bruson, and Piero Cappuccilli, among others. With the arrival of the new millennium, the roster of singers is not as illustrious as previously. With the reopening of the Teatro Da Ponte in Vittorio Veneto, the Comunale has united with the Da Ponte and hosts the operatic portion of the subscriptions. Since the Comunale reopened in 2003, the Fondazione Cassa Marca has underwritten the expenses to manage the theater for the next 30 years, which the city has gratuitously lent to the *fondazione*.

Before the dawn of the millennium, the repertory had been predominately Italian, with an occasional non-Italian work: *Macbeth*, *Die Zauberflöte*, *Tosca*, *Fedora*, and *Il matrimonio segreto*. The final season before closing for restoration saw *Faust*, *Don Giovanni*, *L'elisir d'amore*, *Cavalleria rusticana*, and *Pagliacci* on the boards. Since 2003 the seasons have been all popular Italian fare such as *Le nozze di Figaro* and *Il barbiere di Siviglia*.

Practical Information

Teatro Comunale, corso del Popolo 31, 31100 Treviso; tel. 39 422 540 480, fax 39 0422 513 311; www.fondazionecassamarca.it.

The season takes place during November and December with three performances each of two operas. Stay at the Al Fogher, viale della Repubblica 10, 31100 Treviso; tel. 0422 432 950, fax 042 243 0391. There is a direct bus connection to the opera house.

~

Teatro Lirico Giuseppe Verdi, Trieste

The first performance venue in Trieste dates back to 1705, when the Sala del Consiglio in the Palazzo Municipale hosted performances on a moveable stage. After a long period during which the *sala* was used for both pubic functions and recreational purposes, it was permanently adapted in 1751 as a theater and named Teatro di San Pietro after the saint of a nearby church, following the Venetian custom of the era. Located near the ruins of the Teatro Romano, the new structure offered 800 seats among three box tiers and a gallery. The repertory resembled that of the Venetian theaters of San Moisé and San Samuele, with the operas of Pergolesi, Galuppi, Paisiello, Anfossi, and Piccinni gracing the stage. When the Austrians arrived in 1760, they added Cesareo Regio to the theater's name, so it was known as Cesareo Regio Teatro di San Pietro. With only 800 seats, it soon became inadequate to accommodate all the public that wished to attend performances. The technical facilities also proved to be inadequate. The captain of the police and director of the theater, however, were against every suggestion to abandon the building or renovate it, stating that neither the Austrian government nor the municipality wanted to undertake the financial burden, and for a long time there did not appear to be any possibility of a privately financed project.

Beginning in 1776, however, the rising merchant class began submitting designs, proclaiming their willingness to finance a more suitable structure, but conflicts arose between renovating the San Pietro or erecting a new building. The first two proposals were from Antonio Mezzodì and Carlo Giuseppe Maurizio for a new theater, but they were refused for various reasons. Giuseppe Bobolin then presented a project to enlarge the Teatro San Pietro, but that too was denied. As the 18th century drew to a close, the San Pietro was in a state of decay, permanently closing its shutters in 1800.

Fortunately, 2 years earlier, on February 13, 1798, the Austrian Chancery in Vienna had selected the proposal of Giovanni Matteo Tommasini, diplomatic representative of the grand duke of Tuscany in Trieste, who had presented in 1795 a request to build a theater at his own expense in an unoccupied area along the sea and the piazza Grande. The site was located in the economic and commercial center of the city. In June 1798 a contract was drawn up for which Tommasini, in exchange for constructing the theater, would be paid from the municipal budget 6,400 fiorini annually; would possess in perpetuity box 7 *a pepiano*; and as compensation for possible cost overruns, would have the right to all the boxes of the fifth tier. He then, with the consent of the civic authorities, transferred the contract to Count Antonio Cassis-Farone, who became the first owner of the theater, claiming box 20 on the first tier. Giannantonio Selva, best known as the architect of Teatro La Fenice in Venice, was hired to design the structure. This choice angered two local architects, Ulderico Moro and Giacomo Marchini, who protested the awarding of the project to a Venetian. The director of the Civiche Fabbriche, Carlo Steinlein, joined in the protest by criticizing Selva's designs. He questioned the security of the steps and the ceiling and complained that the auditorium was too ovoid, impeding the view of the stage from the boxes. Vienna had also sent designs for the new opera house, which differed from those of the architect, especially those for the facade. Vienna considered Selva's facade too plain and simple; the Austrians desired more decorative elements. Selva submitted a second set of drawings, but these were also deemed unacceptable. He refused to alter his plans, defending point by point the criticisms, and insisted vehemently that altering the ornamentation would eliminate the effect he was trying to achieve. Another architect, Matteo Pertsch, was appointed to resolve the problem. Pertsch redesigned the facade by blending elements of Selva with those from Giuseppe Piermarini, architect of La Scala and Pertsch's teacher.

The theater took 3 years to complete and was inaugurated on April 21, 1801, with Mayr's *Ginevra di Scozia*, the opera chosen from among the many entries submitted to be the inaugural opera. Opening night was described by Giuseppe Stefani as attended by a "monopoly of merchants, who took advantage of the privilege of a class which had recently exited from the warehouses, and was enticed to climb into another world, that of culture and art. It was an exceptional evening, given the measure of their immense wealth, ambition, and vanity." Originally known as the Teatro Nuovo, to distinguish it from the old Teatro San Pietro, the theater held six tiers, five of which were box tiers, and the sixth had 11 boxes in the center with the sides holding galleries for the lower classes. Reed and lyre adorned the parapets. The boxes were decorated by their owners and were assigned according to the location of the owner's box in the Teatro San Pietro, the owner's wealth, and the owner's generosity in contributing to the city and state. Unmarried individuals were assigned a seat in the orchestra section. The new wealthy mercantile classes owned most of the boxes, with only a few owned by the aristocracy.

It soon became evident that the Nuovo was built primarily for the box holders, with little consideration for the artists, whose rooms were few and poorly located; the stage was small and difficult to heat; and the technical capabilities were very limited. The theater, however, was ideal for dances, masked balls, and playing games of chance. It hosted all the important occasions in the city. When the French occupied the city from November 1805 to March 1806, the public stopped frequenting the theater. The occupiers were forced to encourage the inhabitants to go to the opera house. Then rules were issued that prohibited encores, whistling, too boisterous applause, whacking sticks, stomping feet, bringing in dogs, and congregating in the atrium before, during, or after the show. When the Austrians returned, the theater came to life again. But the French were back in 1809, and the same crisis of an empty house befell the management such that to fill the theater for Napoleon's birthday the manager kept it illuminated during the day and offered free entrance to everyone that evening. The Austrians returned in 1813, but only after an exchange of artillery that hit the facade of the opera house, the evidence of which is still visible today.

There were other theaters in the city, so in 1820 the Nuovo was renamed the Teatro Grande, to distinguish it from those less illustrious. In April 1835, Moisè Hierschel acquired the Teatro Grande from the heirs of the original owners, Tommasini and Cassis Faraone. Then a horrific incident took place. It seems an insane person, Simone Hovall, entered the Hierschel box during a performance and killed Hierschel's mother-in-law and daughter-in-law with a knife. In 1861 Count Leone Hierschel, an heir of Moisè Hierschel, sold the theater for 250,000 fiorini to the municipality, with the exclusion of box 7 and box 20, which remained with the heirs of Tommasini and Cassis Faraone. To mark its passing from private to public ownership, the Grande was rebaptized Teatro Comunale. Electricity replaced the gas lighting in 1889, which had replaced the candles and oil in 1846. When the opera house originally opened, it could accommodate 1,400 spectators, increasing to around 2,000 from mostly additional standing room space, before it was closed in December 1881 because it was deemed unsafe. Authority was granted for restoration. Upon reopening, its capacity had been reduced to 1,000.

In 1827 the Anfiteatro Mauroner opened, surviving 49 years before fire consumed it in 1876. It hosted the world premiere of native son Sinico's *Marinella* in 1854. The Teatro Politeama Rossetti was inaugurated on April 27, 1878, with *Un ballo in maschera*. Named after the famous citizen, politician, and scholar of the early 19th century, the Rossetti offered a 3,200-seat auditorium and a 54-foot stage. The opera season was limited to avoid competition with Comunale. It presented a couple of *prime mondiali*, Giovannini's *Adele di Volfinga* in 1880 and 6 years later Sinico's *Spartaco*. The Politeama was converted into a cinema in 1913 before World War I forced its closure. Reopening in 1918, it underwent major restructuring a decade later, but continued to be used mainly as a movie theater. It remained open during World War II, and between 1945 and 1947, the American and British armed forces requisitioned the theater and Louis Armstrong and Josephine Baker played there. It was, however, again in need of restoration work and closed in 1956. Thirteen years passed before the construction was completed, the theater reopening in 1969 as a multipurpose performance venue, hosting on occasion the International Festival of Operetta.

On January 27, 1901, just hours after Verdi's death was announced, the Comunale was officially renamed the Teatro Verdi, the first theater in Italy to claim the honor. The opera house underwent a major reconstruction in 1992 at the cost of 36 billion lire. The work, supervised by Dino Tamburini and executed by the Consorzio di Imprese Edili Triestine, closed the building for 5 years. On May 16, 1997, the Teatro Verdi reopened with a *Viva Verdi* concert that featured excerpts from several of the maestro's operas and concluded with the Grand March from the second act of *Aida*. At the end of the 1990s, the Teatro Verdi, as an *ente autonomo* and required by law, formed a *fondazione*, allowing it to accept private funding, securing its financial future.

During the restoration, an alternative performance venue was created in a former bus station and named the Sala Tripcovich, after the shipping company that paid for the conversion. The work was done in record time. The contract was signed in May 1992 and on December 15 of the same year, the inauguration took place. The exterior stucco was painted a faux marble peach color, decorated with a deep-red stage curtain. Inside, the 934-seat auditorium showed contrasting colors of red and black, embellished with pilasters with gilded capitals. After the Verdi reopened, the Tripcovich continued hosting performances, its cozy space ideal for chamber opera, operettas, and works better suited for smaller venues.

The Teatro Verdi displays a yellow ochre facade resembling that of La Scala and an auditorium resembling La Fenice. The neoclassical front offers a three-arch, rusticated stone pronaos, which supports a large terrazzo above. Statues representing Mars and Pluto with Cerberus occupy niches at either end of the building. Ionic pilasters line the upper level, punctuated by two rows of windows with fronton. A marble statuary group, an Apollo flanked by seated figures of Lyric Art and Tragic Art, crowns the structure. The 1,400-seat, horseshoe-shaped, ivory, red, and gold auditorium holds three box tiers topped by a gallery. The latest renovation restored the auditorium's original shape and decor, with figurines adorning the box dividers of the lower tiers and gilded musical symbols, masks, and floral patterns embellishing the parapets. During the reconstruction, the stage machinery and technical capabilities of the theater were modernized, equipping it to handle technically complicated productions of the 21st century.

Operatic Events at the Teatro Verdi

The opening opera, *Ginevra di Scozia*, featured solid bel canto artists of the day. It was reported that the 25-year-old soprano, Teresa Bertinotti, had good sound quality, the 51-year-old tenor, Giacomo David, was still in fine voice and a favorite of the composer, and the castrato Luigi Marchesi, called Marchesini, was considered the champion of arrogance—he refused to sing for Napoleon. Salieri was also invited to compose an inaugural opera, and although Mayr's opera *Ginevra* received the honor to open the theater, Salieri's *Annibale in Capua* was considered worthy of staging and was performed in May 1801. Salieri felt Trieste's new opera house was important enough to travel to the city to supervise the production. Despite the composer's presence, and 17 performances, it never enjoyed the success of *Ginevra*. There was speculation that it, being a serious opera and written in the Gluck mode, was not familiar enough to the Trieste audience to be fully accepted. During the first seasons opera buffa dominated the boards, with works by Paisiello and Cimarosa favored.

Opera seria and works such as Nicolini's *Adriano in Tracia*, Pavesi's *Fingallo e Comala*, Nasolini's *Merope*, Zingaretti's *Giulietta e Romeo*, and Farinelli's *Il Cid* were emphasized. Other composers in the repertory included Sarti, Trento, Generali, and Paër. The well-known castrato Giovanni Battista Velluti came to Trieste in 1809, enrapturing the public with his voice. The world premiere of Pacini's *La sacerdotessa d'Irminsul* took place in 1817, followed by Pucitta's *Il maestro di cappella*. The programming then followed the path of most other Italian theaters, with Rossini first reigning with *Tancredi*, *L'italiana in Algeri*, *Il barbiere di Siviglia*, *Il turco in Italia*, *L'inganno felice*, *L'Aureliano in Palmira*. Then Bellini's *Il pirata*, *I Capuleti e i Montecchi*, and *La straniera* and Donizetti's *Anna Bolena*, *L'elisir d'amore*, *Le convenienze e le inconvenience teatrali* played major roles in the repertory, followed by Nicolai and Mercadante. Mercadante formed a bridge between Rossini's reign at the opera house and the arrival of Verdi. Well-known artists of the day such as Eugenin Tadolini, Serafino Panzizi, Napoleone Moriani, and Erminia Frezzolini performed. Frezzolini, called the heir to Maria Malibran, dazzled both onstage and off: onstage in *Beatrice di Tenda* and all 20 performances of *Ernani*, and offstage she broke the heart of composer Nicolai. Engaged to the baritone Felice Varesi, she left him for Nicolai but then deserted the composer to marry the tenor Antonio Poggi. It was said that Nicolai was so bitterly disillusioned by the ill-fated love affair that he sank into a creative starvation and, when he emerged, not even the triumph of his major work, *Die lustige Weiber von Windsor*, saved him. He died 2 months after its Berlin premiere at age 39.

During the 1820s and 1830s, the Grande hosted the prime assolute of several minor composers: D'Antoni's *Amina*; Generali's *Chiara di Rosenbergh*, *Il divorzio persiano*, and *La vestale*; Pacini's *Crociati a Tolemaide*; Panizzi's *Son'eglion maritati* and *Gianni di Calais*; Tadolini's *Almanzor*; Ricci's *La prigione di Edimburgo*, very popular in its day; and Riesck's *La fidanzata di Lammermoor*. Levi's *Genevra degli Almieri* was introduced in 1840.

By 1846 Verdi operas had eclipsed them all, with *Nabucco*, *I due Foscari*, *Attila*, and *Ernani* on the schedule. The Grande was also the scene of two prime mondiali of Verdi's. *Il corsaro* took place in October 1848. Gaetano Fraschini created the title role and Carolina Rapazzini created Corrado's mistress, Medora. Verdi, suffering from a cold, did not attend the world premiere. He wrote his sculptor friend Vincenzo Luccardi from Paris, "I had intended to take it [*Il corsaro*] to Italy myself, but I decided instead to send it because I did not feel well enough to take the long and tiring journey at this time of year." The first performance was not successful, with only two of the numbers receiving applause. After a few more performances in other Italian cities, it disappeared from the stage. The second opera, *Stiffelio*, fared better. Verdi went to Trieste to supervise the production. *Stiffelio*, the story of the adulterous wife of a minister, not surprisingly, ran into censorship problems. Verdi responded with, "Leave the libretto as it is or I will withdraw the opera!" After numerous cuts and a total mutilation of the third act, it was staged on November 16, 1850, with considerable success. Fraschini was again in the title role, and Marietta Gazzaniga was his adulterous wife Lina. World premieres of several minor composers also took place during the 1850s, Cortesi's *Il trovatore*, Badia's *Flavio Rachis*, Buzzi's *Ermengarda*, Graffigna's *Maria di Brabante*, Traversari's *Don Cesare di Bazan*, Rota's *I Romani in Pompeiano*, and Sinico's *I moschettieri*.

French works were also popular, and the Grande hosted the Italian premieres of *La muette de Portici* and *Mignon*, along with Rossini's French works, *Le Comte Ory* and *Guillaume Tell*. In 1866 the Trieste *prima* of Halévy's *La Juive* took place. Other French operas included *Faust*, *L'Africaine*, and *Dinorah*. Italian works such as Apolloni's *L'ebreo* and Pedrotti's *Tutti in maschera* were also featured.

There were not only successes at the Comunale, as the Grande was renamed in 1861, but also failures. During Petrella's *Contessa d'Amalfi*, the public whistled and hissed at the protagonist, Violetta Saurel, who responded with an ironic curtsy. The next day, public apologies were given in pamphlets distributed at the entrance to the theater. In 1873 *La favorita* was also a fiasco, the result of the inadequacies of the baritone, Lorenzo Lalloni. The first night he was tolerated, but at the second performance the opera was drowned out by boos. Then, according to Signor Bottura, a writer of the day, "After the second act, Lalloni, enraged by the boos, tore into anyone who had the misfortune to encounter him backstage, punching and kicking like a crazy man. He then fled the theater. The call boy must have noted what had happened and suppressed the third act. The protests by the spectators then exploded more furious than ever. Anyway, it was impossible to continue the performance." The opera house hosted more prime assolute between the 1860s and the end of the century, Rota's *Aurora di Nevers*, Zescevich's *Orio Soranzo* and *Le false apparenze*, Marchetti's *Romeo e Giulietta*, Apolloni's *Gustavo Wasa*, and Smareglia's *Nozze istriane*.

The end of the century brought from the French repertory *Samson et Dalila*, *Werther*, and *Carmen*, among others; the Italian verismo *Cavalleria rusticana*, *I pagliacci*, *Andrea Chénier*, and *Adriana Lecouvreur*; and the operas of Puccini. The Trieste public did not embrace these operas from the *giovane scuola* as enthusiastically as the rest of Italy, where one was killed with a knife and not a sword and passions, situations, and gestures were more akin to realism than the grand operas, but they were accepted and performed. The conductor who left the most indelible mark on the theater was Gianandrea Gavazzeni, who after conducting *La fanciulla del West*, wrote to his sister on how Puccini had finally conquered Trieste, "I had a wonderful success, but we had to conquer the resistance of the public. It was like an assault by a bayonet, but by the second act, they were on their feet." Wagner's *Götterdäm-merung* and *Tristan und Isolde* also arrived at the theater, with Wagner works continuing into the 20th century with *Parsifal*, *Die Meistersinger von Nürn-berg*, and *Götterdämmerung* especially well liked. The rest of the Ring Cycle was also staged, with much success. A young Tullio Serafin conducted many of the works, and within a short time, Verdi and Wagner operas became the pillars of the seasons, along with other works from the 1800s and 1900s, espe-cially Puccini operas. Singers such as Aureliano Pertile, Gemma Bellincioni, Toti dal Monte, Lina Pagliughi, and Maria Callas performed at the theater and Richard Strauss, Victor de Sabata, and Gino Marinuzzi conducted.

After World War II, the repertory continued with German operas, adding Russian ones as well, and during the 1980s and 1990s, more Russian and East-ern European operas entered the repertory, including *Pikovaya dama* (Queen of Spades), *Khovanshchina*, *Jenůfa*, and *Rusalka*. There were Trieste novelties such as De Banfield's *Lord Byron's Love Letter* and Shostakovich's *Ledi Mak-bet Mtsenskovo uyezda* (*Lady Macbeth of the Mtsensk District*). The Teatro Verdi offers a broad and balanced repertory, including French, German, and American opera, from baroque to contemporary, from favorites to obscure works. A recent season presented *Ariadne auf Naxos*, *Cavalieri di Ekebù*, *Un ballo in maschera*, *Macbeth*, *Lohengrin*, *Faust*, *The Rake's Progress*, and *Madama Butterfly*. At the Sala Tripcovich, *L'isola disabitata* and *Rita* were offered recently.

Every summer an International Festival of Operetta takes place in the Teatro Verdi and at various other venues in Trieste, the purpose of which is to rediscover and relaunch this genre of music. The seeds for the festival were planted at the end of the 1800s, when major Viennese operetta companies visited the city, and continued into the early 1900s, the companies offering works such as *Eva*, *Moglie ideale*, and *Federica*. This is not surprising given that Trieste was part of Austria for a long time, not joining Italy until 1918. The festival celebrated its 35th anniversary in 2004, offering Lehár's *Paganini*, *My Fair Lady*, *Elisabeth*, and *Al Cavallino bianco*. The festival marked the reopening of the Teatro Verdi after its restoration with performances of *Die lustige Witwe*, *Czárdásfürstin*, and *Das Land der Glocken*.

Practical Information

Teatro Lirico Giuseppe Verdi, piazza Verdi 1, 34121 Trieste; tel. 39 040 6722 298, fax 39 040 6722 249; www.teatroverdi-trieste.com.

The season, which runs from October to June, offers eight operas with seven to eight performances of each. The Sala Tripcovich offers two operas with four performances of each, usually in December and March. The Operetta Festival takes place during July and August and presents three to four works. Stay at the Grand Hotel Duchi d'Aosta, piazza Unità d'Italia 2, 34121 Trieste; tel. 040 760 0011, fax 040 366 092. The opera house is just across the piazza, a 3-minute walk. Visit the Civico Museo Teatrale, via Imbriani 5, and the Liceo Musicale "Giuseppe Tartini" in the Palazzo Rittmeyer, via Ghega.

FIFTEEN

Teatro Regio, Turin

From the beginning of the 1600s, performances and festivals were given in the salons and halls of the palaces and castles scattered around the dukedom. The first theatrical creation with music, Guarini's *Il pastor fido*, a pastoral fable, took place in 1585 to celebrate the marriage of Carlo Emanuele I to Caterina, daughter of Filippo II of Spain. That genre of music found much favor in the Piedmont court. The first melodrama offered is believed to have been d'India's *Zalizura* in 1612. But as Marie-Thérèse Bouquet wrote in *Il Teatro di Corte dalle origini al 1788*, "It is in fact necessary to wait until 1662 and the success of Ziani's *Fortune di Rodope e Damira* to find again a *dramma per musica* in Turin." Cesti's *Orontea, regina d'Egitto* and *Dori* followed in quick succession. As the 1600s progressed, the other popular entertainments of the era, comedy-ballets, comedy with "machines," horse festivals, and royal balls, slowly gave way to *dramma per musica* such that between 1662 and 1688, at least 10 were performed, including Cavalli's *Artemisia e Xerse, Atlante,* and *Eliogabalo.*

With the growing popularity of opera and the increase in performances, it was decided in 1680 to create a permanent theater in the Salone delle Feste (Hall of Festivals) in the Palazzo Vecchio. Known as the Teatro delle Feste, the first royal theater was inaugurated the following year with Ivanovich's *Lisimaco*. With an auditorium shaped like a beehive, the Feste hosted seasons of opera until 1703 when, after performances of Martinenghi's *Arsiade* and Pollaroli's *Tito Manlio*, it closed because of hostilities. Subsequently reopened and refurbished in 1722, it continued with seasons of opera until 1740, when the Teatro Regio opened. Works such as Giay's *Eumene*, Hasse's *Olimpiade*, Brivio's *Demofoonte*, Arena's *La clemenza di Tito*, and Leo's *Achille in Sciro* were on the schedule. Private impresarios were contracted to organize the seasons. In the beginning, the court had four permanent singers on its payroll: the sisters Cecilia and Margherita Bonessia, Countess Catterina Canossa, and Isabella Lessona. There were other important singers applauded at the court, especially the castrati Giuseppe Bianchi, Marco Godia (known as Marchietti), and Giovanni Secondo Oseglia, to whom the court paid large sums of money for their services, with Oseglia receiving almost as much as the maestro of the cappella. Additional singers were hired for carnival. On October 9, 1745, the theater was devoured by fire, which destroyed the entire Palazzo Vecchio. As one of the princesses described it, "When the theater burned, it was a terrible fire. Everyone lost a lot. Everything that did not burn, fell in ruins."

In 1703 Prince Emanuele Filiberto of Savoy Carignano bought for 18,200 lire in silver the Trincotto Rosso, a type of rectangular gymnasium adapted for playing tennis, with tiers of seats for spectators. Filiberto transformed it into a horse farm and riding school and used it to store hay. In July 1708, Vittorio Amedeo, Filiberto's son, modified the space to host theatrical performances by constructing 56 boxes. It opened during carnival in 1711 as a private theater called Teatro Carignano. Beginning in 1714 and until 1722, it hosted regular seasons of opera, including works by two native sons: Fiorè's *Sesostri re d'Egitto*, *L'Arideno*, *La Merope*, and *Il trionfo di Lucilla* and Giay's *Il trionfo d'amore*. Gasparini's *Democrito*, Boniventi's *Venceslao*, and Orlandini's *Il carceriere di se stesso* also graced the stage. When the Teatro delle Feste was reopened in 1722, the Carignano hosted opera buffa, which was not performed at the royal opera house, and drama.

The decision to construct a true and proper opera house came in 1713 with the transformation of the dukedom into a kingdom and the creation of the Nobile Società of the Cavalieri. In 1714 King Vittorio Amedeo II invited the architect Filippo Juvarra to design a new opera house befitting the prestige of the court, but it was not until his son Carlo Emanuele III became king in 1730 that the project came to fruition. Benedetto Alfieri took over the project after Juvarra's death in 1736. The cornerstone was laid in April 1738 and construction was completed in 2 years. Originally called Nuovo Teatro Regio (New Royal Theater), it was inaugurated under the auspices of Emanuele III on December 26, 1740, with Feo's *Arsace*. The Regio held 1,500 spectators in 139 boxes distributed among the five tiers and a gallery. The inaugural opening was described by Luciano Tamburini in *L'architettura dalle origini al 1936*: "The seats were red-gold, accentuating the general elegance of the lavish eveningwear of the aristocracy. . . . The audience seated in the orchestra were not the usual public, but distinctive for the dignity of their attire and behavior. . . . The auditorium was illuminated solely by candles, heated by stoves and fireplaces. . . . From the outlines of the boxes to the balustrade of the gallery, the pictures painted on the ceiling and the allegorical decor of the proscenium arch, all offered an indelible image to the public the evening of December 26, 1740." The French astronomer Francesco Gerolamo Lalande described the Regio in his *Viaggio in Italia* as "the best constructed and the most richly decorated [opera house] that existed in the modern style . . . and has served as a model for the theater in Naples and for many others that have been constructed afterwards." The cost of the theater reached 822,606 lire, an enormous sum of money for that era.

The Teatro Carignano collapsed in May 1752, and the following month Prince Luigi of Carignano received permission from King Carlo Emanuele II to reconstruct it. Prince Liugi commissioned Alfieri to design the building, with Giovanni Battista Borra responsible for the exterior and Carlo Emanuele Rocca in charge of the construction. The first stone was laid on July 13, 1752. Diverse artists decorated the interior: Pietro Antonio Porro painted the parapets of the 84 boxes with garlands, flowers, and medallions; Gaetano Perego did the cornices of the ceiling; and Mattia Franceschini embellished the center with flowers and garlands. Bernardino Galliari executed the *Birth of Venus* on the curtain. On February 16, 1786, a sudden fire devastated the structure, leaving only the exterior walls. It was immediately reconstructed, reopening on September 2, 1786, with Guglielmi's *L'impostore Punito*. Designed by Giovanni Battista and Francesco Ferriggio, the theater held an orchestra section with 22 benches, four box tiers topped by a *piccionaia* (gallery). There were caryatids of papier-mâché representing faces of men and women on which rested Ionic capitals. In 1810 it hosted the prima assoluta of Giuseppe Mosca's *Monsieur de Montanciel*, followed 11 years later by his brother Luigi's *La voca misteriosa*.

The Regio was ordered closed by the sovereign on October 17, 1792, and 2 years later it became a warehouse, with grain piled high in the orchestra section and rice between the gilded putti and decorations. The Regio, however, reopened its shutters on December 26, 1797, to allow the Società to recover whatever they could. General Joubert invaded on December 5, 1798, and 4 days later Carlo Emanuele IV went into exile. With the French occupying the city, the Regio was renamed Teatro Nazionale, and the municipality invited the citizen architect Giuseppe Battista Piacenza to remove the royal coats of arms. In 1801 it became the Grand Théâtre des Arts, and with Napoleon ascending the throne, it was rebaptized the Teatro Imperiale. With the defeat of Napoleon in 1814, the coat of arms of the House of Savoy was restored to the royal box, and it became once again the Teatro Regio. Four years later, the harmonious neoclassical decorations gave way to a baroque decor, the work of Ernesto Melano and Pelagio Pelagi. In 1861 Angelo Moja redecorated the auditorium again, still in a baroque style but "far from the exquisite lightness of rococo." The first tier was simulated yellow marble with a dark lower fillet and gilded cornice; the second displayed portraits of famous maestros in chiaroscuro, putti in gilded frames, painted flowers, and red pearls with ornamentation of gilded wood relief; the third alternated framed painted flowers with wooden gilded heads; the fourth was painted with garlands of flowers in gilded frames that alternated with golden wooden lion heads; and the fifth was decorated with gilded, wooden medallions with a painted head of a lady, wreaths of painted flowers, and pearls in golden, wooden frames. All the boxes were divided by gilded, carved wooden caryatids. The opera house suffered periods of grave financial crisis, especially between 1850 and 1860, notwithstanding public contributions to its operations. The crisis reached a point that the government of the crown forced the municipality to contribute to its maintenance, which was initially 40,000 lire and incrementally increased until the city acquired the opera house free of charge on July 6, 1870. The seasons were organized by contract with private impresarios.

The Teatro Carignano, by direction of King Carlo Alberto, underwent restoration, with Ferdinando Bonsignore overseeing the work, and reopened April 23, 1824. That same year it hosted the world premiere of Vaccai's *La pastorella feudataria*. Many additional prime mondiali by minor composers followed: Bordese's *Zoraide* and *I gemelli di Preston*; Cagnoni's *Il vecchio della montagna*; Strepponi's *Amore e mistero*; Casalini's *La sposa di Murcia*; Litta's *Maria Giovanna*; Lucilla's *Il conte Rosso*; Speranza's *L'aretino* and *I due Figaro*; Mabellini's *Rolla* and *Ginevra di Firenze*; Mandanici's *Il segreto*; Marchetti's *Le demente*; Nini's *Il corsaro*; Pacini's *La schiava di Bagdad*; Roberti's *Piero de Medici*; Villanis's *La figlia del proscritto*; and Rossi's *Gli artisti alla fiera*. It also offered the Italian premiere of Donizetti's *Linda di Chamounix* in August 1842. The building was restructured in 1877, but 6 years later it was put up for public auction. The Società di Capitalisti acquired it and had it restructured again, under the direction of Pietro Carrera, including the transformation of the fourth tier of boxes into a gallery and the installation of heat and ventilation. In 1889 the theater introduced Orefice's *Mariska*. The building again changed hands in 1912 when Giovanni Archille Chiorelli bought it from the Società, keeping it for 20 years before ceding it to the municipality on September 24, 1932. Enrico Bonicelli was hired to do additional structural modifications. After fire destroyed the Teatro Regio in 1936, the Carignano was adapted to host opera seasons. The auditorium was reconstructed in cement to minimize the hazard of fire and make it more stable, leaving only the decorations in wood. The theater offers a four-tier, baroque-style hall decorated with gilded stucco and red velvet. With the reopening of the Regio in 1973, the Carignano became a home for drama.

The Vittorio Emanuele II Royal Hippodrome was constructed in 1856 by Bogetto and Leopoldo Galli, based on the designs of Gaetano Bertolotti. Originally built as a public racecourse and circus that could hold 4,500 spectators, it was soon adapted for opera and dance performances and called Teatro Vittorio Emanuele. In that role, it hosted several world premieres, beginning in 1859 with Turin composer Roberti's *Petrarca alla corte d'Amore*, Usiglio's *La locandiera*, Bandini's *Janko* and *La fidanzata di Corinto*, Cordara's *La tentazione di Gesù*, and Coronaro's *Un curioso accidente*. The best known *prima esecuzione assoluta* at the theater was Alfano's *Risurrezione* in 1904.

With the dawn of the 20th century, the Teatro Regio was showing its age. Some who wanted to build a new theater instead of reconstructing it were saying, "The Regio appears by now a beautiful, elegant cadaver, but still, always, a cadaver" and "[the Regio is like] an old person who wants to put on make-up, but with make-up would still remain an old person." But the side for reconstruction won. Two projects were considered. One was from Antonio Vandone and the other from the engineer Cocito. Vandone's proposal modified the auditorium as little as possible. He kept five boxes on each side of the fourth and fifth box tiers, transforming only the center section of those tiers and the gallery into one large balcony divided into three sections with 540 seats and 200 standing places at a cost of 290,000 lire. Cocito's proposal preserved only the general line of the auditorium but substituted the fourth and fifth tiers and gallery with one vast open amphitheater with three distinct levels that extended to the ceiling with 915 seats and 200 standing places for a cost of 540,000 lire. Cocito's plan was selected because of its increased seating capacity, and the Regio underwent its final intervention in 1905. The seating capacity reached 2,415, making the theater more "democratic." The management of the theater, which had been private, passed to the Società Anonima del Teatro Regio. World War I closed the opera house in 1916, and the following year the military authorities used it as a depository for "furnishings." When the theater reopened in 1919, the Società Anonima again ran the opera house until, during the night between February 8 and 9, 1936, a short circuit under the stage ignited a blazing inferno that destroyed

196 years of history in a few hours. Only the baroque facade of Alfieri was spared. The struggle to rebuild the opera house lasted 37 years.

During the reconstruction, the opera seasons were held at various theaters around the city. Between 1936 and 1942, the activities moved successively from Teatro Caginano to Teatro della Moda to Teatro Vittorio Emanuele. After the war, the seasons moved from Teatro Lirico (formerly Vittorio Emanuele), back to the Carignano, and to Teatro Alfieri. The Alfieri had been active in the 1800s as an opera house, presenting several world premieres of now forgotten composers and operas, including Mabellini's *Matilde a Toledo*; Cottrau's *Griselda*; Ricci-Stolz's *Per un capello* and *La coda del diavolo*; Bacchini's *La damigelle di St. Cyr* and *In congedo*; and Ferrari's *Il candeliere*. By the spring of 1949, the Regio's seasons were hosted by the Teatro Nuovo.

The reconstruction began with a national competition in February 1937, which architects Aldo Morbelli and Robaldo Morozzo won. But the outbreak of World War II, numerous changes to the plans, and an economic recession delayed the laying of the first stone until September 25, 1963, and then construction was abandoned. The project was then assigned to architect Carlo Mollino and engineer Marcello Zavelani Rossi and construction resumed in September 1967. The Regio took on an innovative and contemporary design with a curved brick-and-glass structure hidden behind Alfieri's original facade. *I vespri siciliani*, with Maria Callas and Giuseppe di Stefano, inaugurated the Teatro Regio on April 10, 1973.

The opera house was integrated with the neighboring structures by using brick, rusticated stone, and an expansive glass facade. The roof, the work of Felice Bertone, fuses a variety of geometric shapes and forms, which are interspersed by 15 skylights. A "metal curtain" called *Musical Odessey*, by Umberto Mastroianni, fronts the opera house and acts as a gate. Large foyers distribute the audience to aerial bridges and gangways that lead into the auditorium. The 1,750-seat, ellipsoidal hall holds a large, steeply raked orchestra level, with 37 boxes tracing the perimeter of the space, suspended outside the ellipsoidal sphere. The ceiling, a gridiron constructed of metallic staves, is decorated with geometric patterns that form a chromatic vibration with colors diminishing from deep blue to white, the work of the designer Castellano. Almost 2,000 needle-shaped columns of Perspex, suspended from the ceiling and looking like perfectly shaped thin icicles, illuminate the space. The initial acoustics were poor, so an acoustic shell has been added in the modern, unadorned proscenium arch.

Operatic Events at the Teatro Regio

The Nuovo Teatro Regio was inaugurated in 1740 and offered only one opera season, which lasted from December 27 to the last day of carnival. The season usually scheduled two operas, but tradition required that both works be new, one written expressly for the Regio. Some of the operas performed during those first years included Arena's *Artaserse*, Latilla's *Zenobia*, Jommelli's *Semiramide riconosciuta* and *Tito Manlio*, Gluck's *Poro*, Sordella's *La conquista del vello d'oro*, Lampugnani's *Andromaca*, Scarlatti's *Partenope*, and Terradellas's *Didone*. The rest of the year the theater remained shut. Only opera seria was presented, with ballet performed between the acts of opera, as was the custom at the time. The Società dei Cavalieri, created in 1727 with 40 members, managed the theater, commissioning operas from a large number of composers, including Traetta, Cocchi, Piccinni, Galuppi, Zingarelli, Balbi Abos, Manna, Bertoni, Pasqua, Monza, Colla, Paisiello, Sarti, Martín y Soler, Bianchi, Ottani, Cherubini, Cimarosa, Pugnani, and Gasparini. Counted among the works introduced during the early years were *Enea nel Lazio, Bajazet, Andromeda, Trigrane, Sofonisba, Annibale in Torino, Siroe, Iphigenia in Aulide, Volodimiro, Achille in Sciro, Issea, L'aurora, Demofoonte,* and *Mitridate, re di Ponto*. This custom resulted in all 112 operas staged between 1740 and 1800 appearing only once on the schedule. In fact, it was not until 1815 that an opera was repeated, Paër's *Griselda*, which was first produced in 1801. During the first half of the 1800s, only eight additional operas were staged a second time out of 119 mounted. They were Farinelli's *I riti d'Efeso*; Rossini's *La pietra del paragone, Tancredi,* and *Mosè in Egitto*; Mercadante's *Didone abbandonata; Norma; Lucia di Lammermoor;* and *Lucrezia Borgia*.

On December 21, 1798, when the French occupied the city, the management of the theater was transferred from the Società dei Cavalieri to two citizens, Giovanni Alberto Rossignoli and Luigi Somano, who managed to produce two *opere serie* during Carnival 1798/99, Alessandri's *Argea* and Zingarelli's *I veri amici repubblicani*, both prime assolute. Rossignoli and Somano ceded the management the next year to an association directed by Teobaldo Roatis. He encountered many problems. The season was suppressed, and he passed the management on to Giacomo Pregliasco. So it went until the Società dei Cavalieri returned in 1824, staying until 1833, when it went bankrupt. From the turn of the century to the end of the reign of the Società dei Cavalieri in 1833, presentation of 31 new operas de rigueur was recorded, including Mercadante's *Ezio, Didone abbandonata, Nitocri,* and *I*

Normandi a Parigi; Mayr's *Demetrio*; Pavesi's *Elisabetta, regina d'Inghilterra* and *Nitteti*; Federici's *Sofonisba*; Farinelli's *Lauso e Lidia*; Generali's *Bajazet*; Mosca's *Sesostri* and *Ginevra di Scozia*; Fioravanti's *La trasformazione immaginaria*; Nicolini's *L'eroe di Lancastro*; Orlandi's *Corrado* and *Rodrigo di Valenza*; Lavigna's *Hoango*; Paganini's *Cesare in Egitto*; Soliva's *Berenice d'Armenia*; Ricci's *Annibale in Torino*; Coccia's *Medea e Giasone*; and Vaccai's *Bianca di Messina*.

With the end of the reign of the Società dei Cavalieri in 1833, the way the Regio was managed changed, with a repertory system put in place instead of always staging novelties. The impresarios who organized the seasons presented the great names of the 1800s, Rossini, Bellini, Donizetti, Meyerbeer, and later Verdi. Between 1834 and 1879 only 20 prime assolute were offered: Coppola's *Gli Illinesi*, Vaccai's *Marco Visconti*, Nicolai's *Templario*, Mercadante's *Francesca Donato* and *Il reggente*; Coccia's *Il lago delle fate*, Pacini's *La regina di Cipro* and *Ester d'Engaddi*, Bona's *Il gladiatore*, Sanelli's *Camoëns*, Villanis's *La vergine di Kent*, Cianchi's *Leone Isauro*, Bazzoni's *Il rinnegato fiorentino*, Petrella's *La contessa d'Amalfi*, Gandolfi's *Il paggio*, Pedrotti's *Il favorito*, Montuoro's *Re Manfredi*, Rossi's *La contessa di Mons* and *Cleopatra*, and Cagnoni's *Francesca da Rimini*. Verdi's works were the most selected by the impresario, with 22 titles claiming 101 performances; followed by Donizetti, 16 titles and 56 performances; Rossini, 14 titles and 40 performances; and Bellini, 7 titles and 35 performances.

Nevertheless, the story of the Regio is more closely intertwined with Mercadante, Massenet, Puccini, Strauss, Wagner, and Zandonai than Verdi, Donizetti, Rossini, or Bellini. The Regio hosted 12 operas of Mercadante, 6 of which were world premieres. But it was the prime assolute of 2 of Puccini's masterworks that united the opera house with the maestro from Lucca: *Manon Lescaut* in February 1893 and *La bohème* 3 years later. The first Puccini opera staged at the Regio was *Le villi* during the 1884/85 season, followed a few years later by *Edgar*. Interest in the Tuscan composer grew after the success of *Manon*. Puccini was not as lucky with *Bohème*. The world premiere, which took place February 1, 1896, was a gala occasion with several members of the royal family in attendance. Mascagni and Franchetti came to the Regio, as did critics from all over Italy. Arturo Toscanini, music director of the opera house from 1895 to 1898 and 1905 to 1906, conducted. The critics were scathing in their reviews. The most famous, written by Carlo Bersezio after the premiere, appeared in *La Stampa* on February 2, 1896: "*La bohème*, I believe, will not leave a grand impression in the spirit of its listeners, so it will not leave a great mark in the history of our lyrical theater, and it will be well if the author would consider it (if one permits me the expression) as a passing error."

The first official programming of a comic opera during the season at the Regio did not occur until 1855, with *Il barbiere di Siviglia*. Until then, for more than a century, only 13 opere buffe were presented, all for special occasions, which were not part of the regular season. In September 1773, Salieri's *La Fiera di Venezia* celebrated the marriage of Princess Maria Teresa of Savoy. Ten years later, a second *dramma giocoso*, Soler's *L'accorta cameriera*, was performed in honor of the archduke of Austria Ferdinando and Beatrice d'Este. When the fall seasons of the Regio were hosted by the Teatro Carignano in 1801 and 1802, they included *drammi giocosi*, such as Mayr's *L'equivoco*, Fioravanti's *Il turbo malaccorto* and *La trasformazione immaginaria*, Farinelli's *L'amante per forza* and *Teresa e Claudio*, Trento's *Teresa vedova*, and Orlandi's *Il Podestà di chioggia*. There was little enthusiasm for the comic opera genre at the Regio, and the most popular ones of the era, such as *L'italiana in Algeri* and *La fille du regiment*, were never performed. *La Cenerentola* appeared only in the 1855/56 season, 38 years after its world premiere, whereas it had already been staged at the Carignano 9 months after its world premiere. Rossini's *drammi per musica*, however, were frequently on the program. Donizetti's comic operas suffered the same plight. Cimarosa was performed between 1784 and 1806 and then his works disappeared for 125 years, until a Cimarosa renaissance took place in the 1930s.

During the final decades of the 1800s, the Regio enjoyed the operas of Massenet, including *Le roi de Lahore*, *Cendrillon*, and *Manon*, and presented the world premieres of Zandonai's *Francesca da Rimini* and Catalani's *Elda* and *Loreley*. Between 1890 and 1936, 51 operas from the *giovane scuola* were mounted, including 27 of Puccini's. Wagner was presented 40 times, and the Regio became known as a "temple to Wagnerian and Straussian art," as these German composers were not often performed in Italy. (Bologna was the other Wagner stronghold in Italy.) The first Wagner opera to appear was *Lohengrin* during the 1876/77 season. It was staged 6 more times for a total of 82 performances. The first complete Ring Cycle was presented in the spring of 1883, and in the beginning of the 1890s, *Die Walküre*, *Götterdämmerung*, and *Tristan und Isolde* became regular parts of the repertory. The Italian premiere of *Salome* took place in 1906 with the composer on the podium. His *Der Rosenkavalier* followed in 1923 and *Elektra* in 1930.

From the opening of the Teatro Regio on December 26, 1740, until its last performance on February 1, 1936, before the devastating fire, 416 different operas had graced the stage, of which 322 were produced only once. The

1940s and 1950s saw *Manon, Werther, Aida* (featuring Maria Callas), *Lohengrin, Siegfried, Tristan und Isolde, Pelléas et Mélisande, Boris Godunov, Der Freischütz, Les pêcheurs de perles,* and *Prince Igor,* among others, grace the various performance venues in the city. During the 1960s and until the Regio reopened in 1973, an equally broad repertory was offered, with *Matrimonio segreto;* Rota's *Il cappello di paglia di Firenze, I Puritani,* and *La sonnambula; Die Entführung aus dem Serail; The Rake's Progress; Peter Grimes; Der Rosenkavalier; Der Aufstieg und Fall der Stadt Mahagonny;* and *La forza del destino.*

After *I vespri siciliani* inaugurated the Teatro Regio in 1973, the first prima assoluta, Fuga's *L'imperatore Jones,* took place 3 years later. Bussotti's *Phaidra/ Heliogabalus* was introduced in 1981 and Corghi's *Gargantua* in 1984. The mid-1980s brought an innovative and naturalistic style to the contemporary and foreign works, especially *Ulisse* and *Der Ring des Nibelungen.* The last decade of the 20th century saw operas both Italian and foreign from the 1700s through the 1900s, from Mozart's *Mitridate, re di Ponto* to Britten's *The Turn of the Screw* and Poulenc's *La voix humaine.* The majority of the operas, however, were from the popular composers of the 19th century, including their lesser-known works such as Verdi's *Jerusalem,* Donizetti's *Il Campanello,* Massenet's *Escarmonde,* and Rossini's *Semiramide.*

The Regio was one of the first opera houses to secure the minimum 12% private funding to form a *fondazione* as required by the government by the end of 1999. Its fund-raising goal was $2 million, which it met, giving it a secure financial base. With the arrival of the new millennium, the repertory offered less-often-performed 20th-century and contemporary operas, and it opened the first four seasons in the 21st century with operas such as Stravinsky's *Rake's Progress,* Wolf-Ferrari's *Sly,* Reimann's *Lear,* and Strauss's *Capriccio.* In addition, Penderecki's *Der Teufel von Loudun,* Pizzetti's *Assassinio nella cattedrale,* Gurlitt's *Wozzeck,* Zemlinsky's *Der Zwerg,* Dallapiccola's *Il prigioniero,* Leoncavallo's *Edipo re,* and Previn's *Streetcar Named Desire* were on the boards. The 20th-century repertory does not do as well at the box office as the popular 19th century's does, and with the continual decrease in public funding, more traditional operas have been inaugurating the new seasons, beginning with *Simon Boccanegra,* which opened the 2003/04 season, and then *La bohème,* which opened the 2004/05 season. As the 21st century progresses, the schedule has become more conservative, with the majority of operas from the 19th century and only a couple of 20th-century works, which is unfortunate, since the Regio's forte is in their execution of the contemporary repertory, both Italian and foreign. Their productions of *King Lear* and *Assassinio nella cattedrale* were mesmerizing. A recent season offered *La bohème, Billy Budd, Cenerentola, Don Giovanni, Trovatore, L'amore dei tre re, Anna Bolena,* and *Werther.*

Practical Information

Teatro Regio, piazza Castello 215, Turin 10124; tel. 39 011 88151, fax 39 011 881 5214; www.teatroregio.torino.it.

The season, which runs from October to June, offers eight to nine operas with 5 to 12 performances of each. Stay at the Grand Hotel Sitea, via Carlo Alberto 35; tel. 011 517 0171, fax 011 548 090. It is a 10-minute walk to the opera house. Visit the following: Teatro Carignano, piazza Carignano 6; tel. 517 6246; www.teatrostabiletorino.it (now a home for drama); Teatro Alfieri, Piazza Solferni 4; tel. 562 3800; www.torinospettacoli.it (now the home for comedy and lighter classics); Teatro Nuovo, corso Massino d'Azeglio 17; tel. 650 0211; www.teatronuovo.torino.it (restructured into a modern, multitheater complex with three performing spaces—two "black box" venues, one with yellow seating and the other with blue seating—and a larger, fan-shaped auditorium with red seating for a total of 1,600 seats).

SIXTEEN

∿

Teatro La Fenice and Teatro Malibran, Venice

During the 17th century, Venice was the opera capital of Europe. At the end of the 1600s, 16 theaters in Venice had hosted 388 operas between 1637 and the end of the century. It began in 1581 when the Tron family opened the Teatro Tron as a private playhouse. Although fire claimed it in 1629, the theater was immediately rebuilt, only to burn down again in 1633. Rebuilt for the second time and renamed Teatro San Cassiano, it opened as the world's first public opera house in 1637, with Manelli's *Andromeda*. The 31 boxes on each of its five tiers the Tron family rented to Venetian nobility and foreign princes. The general public was admitted to the hard bench seats in the orchestra section. World premieres of many operas took place here, including Monteverdi's *Il ritorno di Ulisse in patria* and Cavalli's *Egisto* and *L'Ormindo*. This was not, however, the first opera that Venice witnessed. That was back in 1624 when Monteverdi's *Il combattimento di Tancredi e Clorinda* was performed at the Palazzo Mocenigo Dandolo. The success of the Teatro San Cassiano, which survived until the 1800s, led to the opening in rapid succession of several more public opera houses.

On January 20, 1639, the first theater belonging to the Grimani family, Teatro San Giovanni e Paolo opened with Sacrati's *Delia*. It was here that Monteverdi's *L'incoronazione di Poppea* received its prima assoluta. Considered one of Venice's best opera houses when it opened, it was then deemed too far from the center. The theater survived until 1748. Monteverdi's *Arianna* inaugurated the Teatro San Moisè in 1640. For 178 years, the theater hosted glorious opera seasons, including dozens of *prime esecuzioni mondiali* of both major and minor composers: Rossini's *La cambiale di matrimonio, L'in-*

ganno felice, La scala di seta, L'occasione fa il ladro, and *Il Signor Bruschino*; Mosca's *L'apparenza inganna* and *Il finto Stanislao*; Orgitano's *Non crede alle apparenze*; Pucitta's *Werther* and *La burla fortunata*; Paganini's *I matrimonia a forza*; Mellara's *Il capriccio bizzarro*; Calegari's *Il prigioniero*, *Il matrimonio scoperto*, and *Erminia*; Generali's *Misantropia e pentimento*, *Gli effetti della somiglianza, La lagrime di una vedova, La moglie di tre mariti, La moglie giudice del marito, Isabella, Adelina*, and *La sciocca per gli altri e l'accorta per sé*; Orlandi's *Pandolfo e Baloardo*; Coccia's *La verità nella bugia, I solitari, Una fatale supposizione, Arrighetto*, and *Il crescendo*; Mellara's *Il marito imbarazzato*; Celli's *Amore aguzza l'ingegno*; Tadolini's *La fata Alcina*; and eight works by Pavesi, including *L'amante anonimo* and *L'accortezza materna*. The birth of the Teatro Novissimo came on January 14, 1641, with Sacrati's *La finta pazza*, but fire destroyed the structure 6 years later. Opera graced the stage for 38 years at the Teatro SS Apostoli, which opened in 1649 with Cesti's *Orontea*. Cavalli's *Oristeo* inaugurated the Teatro San Apollinare, which was demolished in 1690.

Teatro San Samuele, the second theater owned by the Grimani family, hosted comedy when it opened in 1655 but began staging operas from 1710 until the end of the 1800s, including the world premiere of Donizetti's *Pietro il Grande* in 1819 and Mosca's *La gastalda ed il lacchè*. It attracted an audience with "lower expectations." The families of Capello and Marcello constructed the Teatro Angelo, inaugurated in 1676 with Freschi's *Elena rapita da Paride*. It hosted opera until the end of the 1700s. Pignatta's *Paolo Emilio* inaugurated the Teatro Fantino at the close of the 17th century. It stood until 1720. The Teatro San Salvatore opened in 1661 with Castrovillari's *Pasife*. Built by the Vendramin family, it was considered one of the foremost opera houses in Venice at the time. Rebaptized Teatro San Luca in 1799, it offered among others the prime mondiali of Mosca's *Le gare*, Orlandi's *Il deputato di rocca*, and Donizetti's *Enrico di Borgogna* and *Un follia* in the early 1800s. Renamed Teatro Apollo in 1833, it continued introducing operas with Curci's *Don Desiderio*, Malipiero's *Attila*, Baratta's *Il cuoco di Parigi*, Villanis's *La regina di Leone*, and Petrocini's *La duchess de la Vallière*. It also hosted the opera seasons of Teatro La Fenice after it burned to the ground in 1836 until it was rebuilt. Since 1875 the theater has been called Teatro Goldoni. It presents a range of operas, from *Le nozze di Figaro* to interesting double bills, for example, comparing Pergolesi's *La serva padrona* with Paisiello's, to contemporary fare such as Rota's *Il principe porcaro*. It is, however, primarily a home for drama.

The third theater of the Grimani family, the Teatro Grimani, also known as Teatro di San Giovanni Grisostomo after the nearby church following the Venetian custom, was inaugurated during carnival season of 1678 with Pallavicino's *Vespasiano*. Called the "biggest, most beautiful and richest theater in the city" by the *Mercure Galant* in March 1683, it was built on the very site where the ancient palace of Marco Polo's family, known as Ca'Milion, used to stand. The theater, designed by Tommaso Bezzi (known as Il Stucchino) boasted five tiers of boxes highlighted with caryatids and parapets lavishly decorated with festoons and shields. The coat of arms of the Grimani family was displayed above the proscenium arch, flanked by 10 proscenium boxes. On the ceiling, allegorical images of History of Theater were painted by Giuseppe Cherubini. It hosted numerous operas during the 1700s, including works by Scarlatti and Händel and *Il Mitridate Eupatore*, *Il trionfo della liberty*, and *Agrippina*, which received 27 performances. A genre called "tragic-comedy," which made fun of heroic operas, was performed there for the first time in 1704 with *La fortuna per dote*. The celebrated castrati Farinelli, Caffarelli, and Nicola Grimaldi and the renowned singers Francesca Cuzzoni and Faustina Bordoni sang there. From 1725 on, around half of the opere serie were by Neapolitan composers such as Vinci, Porpora, Leo, and Hasse. In 1730 the theater was described as a "true kingdom of marvels . . . that with the vastness of its magnificent dimensions can be rightly compared to the splendors of ancient Rome and that with the grandeur of its more than regal dramatic performances has now conquered the applause and esteem of the whole world." It premiered Vinci's *Siroe* and Porpora's *Ezio*, and in 1734 Giacomelli's *Merope* was performed. The glory continued until 1751, when a period of rapid decline began, and from then until 1800, opera was rarely performed.

With the fall of the Venetian republic, the theater was entrusted to the provisional municipality in 1797 and from July to October was transformed into the Teatro Civico. With the dawn of the 19th century, it offered the prime mondiali of Calegari's *Irene e Filandro* and Pucitta's *La perfidia scoperta* and *Zelinda e Lindoro*. When Luigi Facchini and Giovanni Gallo bought the building in 1819, it was in a terrible state of disrepair. They restored the theater to its former grandeur, reopening it with Rossini's *La gazza ladra*. But the opera house continued to deteriorate, so Gallo, who had bought out his partner Facchini, did another refurbishment and renamed the theater Emeronittio. *L'elisir d'amore* inaugurated the opera house in December 1834. The next year, Maria Garcia Malibran came to perform in *La sonnambula* on April 8. She refused her fee, telling the impresario to "use it for the theater." The opera house was renamed in her honor. The Teatro Malibran also introduced many operas, including Bornaccini's *Aver moglie*, Gabussi's *Clemenza di Valois*, Mugnone's *Il birichino*, Ricci-Stolz's *Don Chisciotte*, Lorenzi-Fabris's *Maometto II*, and Floridia's *Maruzza*. When Gallo died in 1844, the opera house passed to his son, Antonio, who in 1852 restored the theater's decorations. The Malibran was put up for auction in 1886 and bought by Francesco Baldanello, Emerico Merkel, and Giuseppe Patrizio. It was radically redecorated in an Egyptian style. In 1913 it was closed for restoration, reopening in December 1919 with Verdi's *Otello*. The next year saw Mascagni's *Isabeau*, followed by Giacomo Lauri-Volpi's debut in *I Puritani*. During the 1930s and 1940s the popular Italian repertory prevailed with *Bohème*, *Madama Butterfly*, *Traviata*, *Tosca*, *Pagliacci*, and *Barbiere di Siviglia*. Toti dal Monte sang in *Madama Butterfly*, Carlo Galeffi in *Rigoletto*, Maria del Monaco in *Otello*, to name a few illustrious singers who performed there. In the 1980s, the Malibran hosted some novelties, including the world premiere of Sciarrino's *Cailles en sarcophage*.

The city acquired the theater in 1992 and Antonio Foscari was entrusted with the project to restore it. Enrico Sopelsa supervised the reconstruction. After almost a decade of work, the 900-seat Malibran reopened May 23, 2001. A gala concert with excerpts from operas by Verdi, it being the centennial of his death, Bellini, the centennial of his birth, and Wagner celebrated the inaugural. All three composers had strong ties to Venice. With its reopening and until the Fenice was finished 2 years later, the Malibran reclaimed the role it had played from the last decades of the 1600s until the first Fenice opened at the end of the 1700s, "that of the most important theater in Venice." The opera season began on November 22, 2002, with Massenet's *Thaïs* in a controversial but dazzling production, including a nude female Christ figure. The next season was inaugurated with a novelty, Auber's *Le domino noir*. It hosts part of La Fenice's season.

The Malibran is tucked away on a small piazza, its entrance doors and rows of shuttered rectangular and arch windows blending with the surrounding buildings. The pale-yellow facade is defined by blocks of off-white stone, engaged Corinthian columns with masks of Comedy and Tragedy, arches, and a balustrade. The 900-seat, coral, gray, and beige auditorium holds three box tiers topped by a gallery on the sides and two large balcony tiers supported by Ionic columns in the center. The parapets are adorned with white bas-reliefs of musical and festival symbols, medallions, and faces of Comedy and Tragedy. Mythological subjects were painted on the ceiling.

The story of La Fenice began with the Teatro San Benedetto, constructed in 1755 by the Grimani family, who decided to build a new, elegant theater to regain their leading position in the opera field, rather than fuse new life into the Teatro Grimani. Owned by the Nobile Società, who had purchased their boxes from Grimani, the San Benedetto was inaugurated with Cocchi's Zoë on December 26, 1755. Although fire ravaged the structure the night of February 5, 1774, it was quickly rebuilt, reopening on December 26, 1774, with Anfossi's *Olimpiade*. A short time later, a dispute arose between the Nobile Società and the Venier family, who owned the land, which resulted in a lawsuit. In June 1787, the Società lost both the lawsuit and ownership of the Teatro San Benedetto. Renamed Teatro Venier, it offered numerous *prime esecuzioni mondiali*: Pucitta's *Teresa Wilk, Oh, che cel caso!* and *Lauretta*; Pavesi's *Un avvertimento ai gelosi, Celanira, I pitocchi fortunati,* and *Don Gusmano*; Generali's *Pamela nubile* and *La calzolaia*; Celli's *L'ajo nell'imbarazzo* and *Dritto e rovescio*; Coccia's *La donna selvaggia, Clotilde,* and *Etelinda*; Vaccai's *Malvina* and *Il lupo di Ostenda*; L. Ricci's *I figli esposti*; F. Ricci's *Monsieur de Chalumeaux*; Levi's *Iginia d'Asti*; Nini's *Ida della torre* and *Orgitano*; Buzzolla's *Ferramondo* and *Mastino I° della Scala*; Marliani's *Lazzarello*; Quilici's *Bartolomeo della Cavalla*; Orlandi's *Il fiore*; and Calegari's *Amor soldato*. Gallo bought the opera house and renamed it Teatro Gallo. It presented Mazza's *Leocadia* and Ferrari's *Pipelè*. In 1868 it was baptized Teatro Rossini to honor the two Rossini operas it had introduced: *L'italiana in Algeri* and *Eduardo e Cristina*. It also was the site of the world premiere of Benvenuti's *Il falconiere*; Abba-Cornaglia's *Maria di Warden*; Lorenzi-Fabris's *Gli adoratori del fuoco* and *Refugium peccatorum*; Dallanoce's *Trisi nozze*; Coop Jr.'s *Nemea*; and Baci's *La sirena*. In 1886 it was sold at auction to Baldanello, Merkel, and Patrizio, the same group that had purchased the Teatro Malibran.

Meanwhile, the Nobile Società decided to build a larger and more important opera house. Their petition to the *Consiglio dei Dieci* for permission to build a theater in the Campo di San Fantin area was approved in August 1787. A competition was held and 29 projects were submitted, including ones from Cosimo Morelli, Pietro Bianchi, and Giannantonio Selva. The winner would also receive a valuable gold medal. Selva's plans were judged the best, but the public preferred Bianchi's, resulting in Bianchi receiving the gold medal, and Selva designing La Fenice. Construction began in 1790 and was completed in 2 years, with the inauguration planned for the Festival of the Ascension.

Paisiello, an important composer of the era, was commissioned to write the inaugural opera for the Gran Teatro La Fenice, the theater's original name. On May 16, 1792, *I giochi di Agrigento* opened Venice's most famous opera house, along with the ballet *Amore e Psiche*. It was named La Fenice (the Phoenix), after the mythical bird that rises from its own ashes, to symbolize the resurrection of the Nobile Società after losing ownership of the Teatro San Benedetto. Selva designed the theater in the neoclassical style with a facade of polished ashlar, tympana, and triglyphs and metopes. Francesco Fontanesi executed the interior decorations, which were described in the *Gazzetta Urbana Veneta*: "The picture has all the requirements for effect: clarity of color, harmony, solidarity and lightness, so difficult to combine are admirably united in this work. . . . In the grand opening in the middle [of the ceiling] one sees a sky with different allegorical figures [genii] bearing symbols related to the subject [of opera]. It is so light as to seem truly open. The divisions and ornaments of this picture are of the most pure and finest character, consisting of bas reliefs, rose ornaments, and arabesque of antique style. The parapets of the boxes are not divided as one usually does into so many small squares with the width of every box, but they form a frieze that wraps around each tier. Very pleasing is the quality of the arabesque and the projection that it shows. The quality of the color does not appear entirely satisfying, but as for it all together, it succeeds so if something were executed in a different way, it would not be possible to decide if it would contribute equally to the total beauty that one admires. All 174 boxes of this theater are equally perfect. . . . The grand opening of the stage formed by an architrave and two large pilasters of the finest intaglio, is like the frame of a picture that divides the stage from the theater. All is gilded and solid gold zecchini links everything that is spread in the theater from the ceiling to the parapets to the inside of the boxes."

When La Fenice was constructed, there were 7 working theaters in Venice—San Cassiano (also called San Cassan), San Angelo, San Samuele, San Moisè, San Benedetto (also called San Beneto), San Salvator, and Grimani (also called San Giovanni Grisostomo)—down from 16 in the previous century. Then a decree by Ludovico Breme in 1807 reduced the number to 5: La Fenice, San Moisè, San Benedetto (Venier/Gallo/Rossini), San Salvador (San Luca/Apollo/Goldoni), and Grimani (Emeronittio/Malibran).

After the fall of the Venetian republic and during the period of the provisional municipal government from May to October, the theater held important public exhibitions and patriotic festivals. When the French dominated, it became a state theater. The auditorium was redecorated in sky blue and silver, according to the new Empire style, and a temporary royal box was constructed for Napoleon's visit in December 1807. Algarotti's *Il giudizio di Giove*, a cantata, was presented in the emperor's honor. The next year, Selva was commissioned to "construct a box for the management of La Fenice occupying six [existing] boxes," and Giuseppe Borsato won the competition to renovate the theater in the Napoleonic style. The designs are lost. Only documentation on the ceiling's decoration exists. The subject was the Triumph of Apollo in a Carriage, with Apollo surrounded by a chorus of Muses and laurel-wreath medallions holding portraits of famous people. On the border, pairs of female rulers with lyres alternated with four reliefs alluding to music. It was framed by a frieze with masks and festoons. Mayr's *Il ritorno di Ulisse* celebrated the reopening on December 26, 1808. Over the next several years, the smoke from the oil lamps illuminating the building reduced the decor to an unsuitable state, resulting in the Società hiring Luigi Locatelli in 1825 to study a new means of lighting.

Borsato redecorated La Fenice again in 1828 in late neoclassicism. The parapets of the boxes were adorned with chiaroscuro ornamentation alluding to tragedy and music, which alternated with medallions displaying busts of famous artists on gilded backgrounds. The vaulted ceiling was painted to suggest a cupola with an elaborate rosette in the middle, with lyres and "Dancing Hours." A band of chiaroscuro ornamental motifs on a gold background circled the vault. Chiaroscuro racemes, vases, gryphons, and swans and gilded rosettes also adorned the space. The reopening took place on December 27, 1828, with a performance of Generali's *Francesca da Rimini*.

A devastating fire devoured La Fenice on December 13, 1836, during rehearsals for the Venetian premiere of *Lucia di Lammermoor*, sparing only the exterior walls and the Apollinee room. The *Gazzetta di Venezia* published news of the fire the same day: "The Teatro della Fenice tragically went up in flames last night, though as we write, it is not yet known for certain what ill-fated accident caused it. The fire raged for about three hours, and despite considerable assistance given, the incredible show of bravery and enthusiasm by the city fire-fighters, despite the zeal of all the authorities and all the most important citizens who rushed to the site, the unfortunate blow could not be averted or softened." A recently installed Austrian stove was the cause of the fire. Tommaso and Giambattista Meduna, who would be the architects of the second Fenice, also described the horrible fire. "From the dense smoke that invaded the rooms and was visible through the windows that showed the scene, one could hear and see the fire. Terrified with fear, one very soon sought to escape from the dangers that they were observing." The Fenice, rebuilt by the Meduna brothers, was completed in a year, reopening on December 27, 1837, with Lillo's *Rosmunda in Ravenna*.

The horseshoe-shaped auditorium was decorated in pale yellows, greens, gold, and white. There were five box tiers, and each parapet offered a different decoration on a background of simulated streaked Grecian marble: chiaroscuro ornamentation on the first; bas-reliefs of groupings of shields, helmets, arrows, sacrificial knives, oak branches, masks, nymphs, and elves on the second; putti, lyres, griffins, and cornucopias on the third; fruit, winged female figures, candelabra, handbells, masks, and garlands on the fourth; and plain ornamentation on the fifth. Not everyone was pleased with the new decor, but some, including Locatelli, wrote favorably that the auditorium was very beautiful and bright, with a delicacy of color and splendid harmony.

The Fenice was redecorated for the last time in 1854, a result of the changing tastes. By midcentury, the late neoclassicism looked dated. Eclecticism and ornateness were in fashion. Meduna was entrusted with the project, which called for "ornate splendor and gold," although there were some critics who wrote that the new decor was "corrupting the rococo to the point that it collapses from its own weight" and that everything "repeats ad nauseam." The auditorium, radiating with gold and a dark rose hue, offered three box tiers and two galleries. The parapets were decorated with endless gold filigree, which encircled painted panels of medallions and putti, the work of Leonardo Gavagnin, and flowers executed by Giuseppe Voltan. The royal box, flanked by gilded caryatids, was crowned by the golden Lion of Venice— Pax Tibi Marce Evangelista Meus (Peace to you Marco, my evangelist). This was the appearance of La Fenice when it burned to the ground at the end of the 20th century. After this refurbishment, the theater reopened December 26, 1854, with Petrella's *Marco Visconti*.

World War I closed the building. In 1936 the descendants of the Società relinquished their boxes to the municipality, and the building underwent a major renovation, reopening 2 years later with Verdi's *Don Carlo*. At the same time, it was designated an *ente autonomo*. The opera house remained open during World War II; the only interruption was a joyous one, the announcement of Milan's liberation during a performance of *Madama Butterfly* in April 1945.

During the night of January 29, 1996, La Fenice was once again engulfed in flames. The circumstances right before the fire were suspicious: the fire doors were ajar and flammable materials were scattered around the theater. The building was undergoing renovations when the conflagration occurred. The company contracted to do the work was behind and faced fines of $15,000. Apparently the plan was just to damage the theater, to avoid paying the fine, not destroy it. Ultimately two electricians, Enrico Carella and Massimiliano Marchetti, were sentenced to 8 years in jail for arson, and eight others were found guilty of negligence, including Massimo Carriari, who was the mayor of Venice and president of La Fenice, and the director of La Fenice, Gianfranco Pontel. Opera performances continued in a tentlike structure euphemistically called Palafenice and, beginning in 2001, also in the Teatro Malibran.

The motto for the reconstruction was "Com'era, dov'era" (As it was, where it was). Six companies submitted projects and on June 2, 1997, the Italian firm Impregilo S.p.A. of Sesto San Giovanni was awarded the contract, as their proposal was the most economical. The deadline for completion was September 1999. Only 28 days later, however, on June 30, 1997, the German firm Philipp Holzmann Bauakiengesellschaft Sud of Munich, associated with the Italian group Romagnoli, sued. They had lost the competition, but their project was considered the best technically. Impregilo had omitted the south wing of the theater in their proposal, allowing for a cheaper price. At first Holzmann's appeals were denied, but then the Consiglio di Stato ruled in their favor and after 137 days, or 30,815 hours, of work, Impregilo's contract was revoked. A second competition was held and Holzmann declared the winner, but reconstruction did not begin again until June 1999. Then in February 2001, the mayor of Venice, Paolo Costa, revoked Holzmann's contract, charging the firm with breach of contract because after 597 days of work, or 61% of the 975 days stipulated in the contract, only 5% of the work had been completed. The amount of damages demanded was $250 million. Near the end of 2001, work began again by the SACAIM group, which was awarded the contract to finish the Fenice with a deadline of November 30, 2003. The final cost was $100 million. The architect of the project, Aldo Rossi, was killed in a car crash in 1997.

With 400 security agents patrolling the streets around the building to stop anyone who did not have a ticket, a pass, and identity papers from getting anywhere near the opera house, La Fenice reopened December 14, 2003. "The music tells us that the nightmare is over, the Teatro Fenice has been restored to Italy and the world." With those words, the mayor reopened the city's famous opera house with a gala concert, conducted by Riccardo Muti. The composers on the program all had ties to Venice: Beethoven's *Die Weihe des Hauses*, Stravinsky's *Symphony of the Psalms*, Antonio Caldara's *Te Deum*, and Wagner's *Kaisermarsch* and *Huldigungsmarsch*. But after a week of inaugural concerts and a New Year's Eve gala, the opera house closed for a year to finish the restoration work. On November 12, 2004, *La traviata* inaugurated the first opera season in the new theater.

La Fenice has risen once again from its ashes. The perfectly proportioned white neoclassical facade sparkles with its tetrastyle portico of large Corinthian columns and decorative elements: masks of Comedy and Tragedy by Domenico Fadiga; statues of Terpsichore (Dance) and Melpomene (Tragedy) believed to be the work of Giovanni Ferrari; a lyre with the face of Mercury flanked by trumpets on laurels; a helmet, shield, club, and halberd on oak branches; a thyrsus, vessel, and torch with vine leaves; and in the center, the words Societas MDCCXCII and a phoenix in a wreath of laurels. The 1,099-seat auditorium dazzles in rococo splendor with gold, delicate blue, and rose hues. Horseshoe shape with five tiers, the auditorium is filled with intricately painted festoons of flowers, wreaths of leaves, cherubs, seraphim, nymphs, putti, and medallions. Cherubs support a sky-colored ceiling surrounded by gilded stucco, the work of Osvaldo Mazzoran. Maidens and cherubs swirl around the center chandelier with radiant lights secured to its arms. Torch-like electrified candles ring the tiers. A large gilded phoenix stares out from atop the proscenium. The pre-fire designs and colors were taken from Visconti's *Senso*, a perfectly lit film shot inside La Fenice in 1954. Technically advanced stage machinery replaced the hand-operated pulleys, and extensive fire-safety measures include a sprinkler system. A space suitable for chamber concerts and choral and orchestral rehearsals was added, named the Sala Rossi in memory of the project's architect.

Operatic Events at La Fenice

La Fenice was inaugurated with a world premiere, Paisiello's *I giochi di Agrigento*, and continues to be a stage for them, both important ones and those that have fallen into obscurity. As was the custom, theaters of a certain level commissioned works to open their seasons. Since there were three seasons the inaugural year—Feast of Ascension, autumn, and carnival—there was a need for at least three new operas. Of the four additional operas offered, Bianchi's *Alessandro nell'Indie*, *Tarara*, and *Ines de Castro* and Nasolini's *Tito e Berenice*, three were prime assolute. The first composer of importance after Paisiello was Mayr, whose *Sapho* was offered during the 1793/94 season, followed by Cimarosa's *Gli Orazi ed i Curaz* and *Artemisia*. During the first decade of the 1800s, world premieres such as Pavesi's *La festa della rosa*, *I Gauri*, *Teodoro*, *I Cherusci*, *Amare e non voler essere amante*, and *Sapersi scegliere un vero sposo*; Generali's *Orgoglio ed umiliazione*; and Coccia's *Il sogno verificato* graced the stage.

Rossini arrived at the Fenice with the world premiere of *Tancredi* in February 1813. At the opening night, the Venice paper *Il Giornale* reported that the two prima donnas were indisposed but sang anyway, with the result that

the opera had to be stopped in the middle of the second act. When the singers recovered, the opera was performed in its entirety, and was well received.
The amazing popularity of the aria "di tanti palpiti," however, came with
later performances, when, as the story goes, everyone from gondoliers to the
nobility was singing "Mi rivedrai; ti rivedrò." No one was singing after *Sigismondo*, which inaugurated the carnival season in December 1814. The audience found it boring and, as Alex-Jacob Azevedo reported, "greeted the
production with a unanimous yawn." Rossini, conducting the performance,
was himself seized by this boredom. Never, he said later, had he "suffered so
much at a first performance as at *Sigismondo*."

The prima assoluta of his next work, *Semiramide*, took place in February
1823. The opera was unusually long: the first act lasted for 2½ hours and the
second act for another 1½. Supposedly, it was composed in only 33 days.
Rossini was quoted as saying to Azevedo, "It is the only one of my Italian
operas which I was able to do at my ease; my contract gave me 40 days . . . I
didn't put in 40 days writing it." Regarding the reception of the work, Herbert Weinstock wrote in *Rossini* that "the musical style of the opera per-
plexed most members of the audience, which blew hot and cold during Act
I. Then, perhaps because the first act had acquainted them somewhat with
Rossini's changing, more complex manner, Act II won them over. Enthusiastic applause followed."

Rossini operas were popular and performed often, including *Maometto II*
and *Ricciardo e Zoraide*. Bellini wrote *I Capuleti e i Montecchi* and *Beatrice di
Tenda* for the Fenice, with rival sopranos Giuditta Grisi and Giuditta Pasta
creating the roles. *I Capuleti e i Montecchi*, although written in a hurry, had
a pleasing result. Bellini himself had written to his friend Lamperi, "I find
myself most fatigued. To write an opera in a month . . . is tortuous suffering."
Beatrice di Tenda, however, was a fiasco.

Donizetti was also commissioned to write a couple of operas for Fenice.
His *Belisario* was enthusiastically received in February 1836, Egidio Saracino
wrote in *Invito all'Ascolto di Donizetti*, "for the strong dramatic events, the
precision of the music, for the luxury of the scenes, and for the writing for
the singers that had the novelty to create a grand romantic role for a baritone." On the other hand, *Maria di Rudenz* was a disaster, and after two performances the management pulled it from the schedule, substituting
Parisiana. The operas of Rossini, Bellini, and Donizetti formed the backbone
of the repertory. During this period, Fenice also hosted numerous prime
mondiali by minor composers, including Generali's *Francesca da Rimini* and
Beniowski; Ricci's *Griselda*; Morlacchi's *Ilda d'Avenello* and *I saraceni in Sicilia*;

and Vaccai's *Giovanna d'Arco* and *Sposa di Messina*. It also offered operas by Lavigna, Mellara Carafa, Persiani, Buzzolla, Pacini, Cordella, Ferrari, Nini, Levi, and Malipiero.

Verdi wrote five operas for La Fenice: *Ernani*, *Attila*, *Rigoletto*, *La traviata*, and *Simon Boccanegra*, more than for any opera house except La Scala. *Ernani* was reasonably successful, although Verdi despaired, complaining that if he only had had "singers who could sing [Carlo Guasco was so hoarse that he could barely finish and Sophia Löwe sang flat], *Ernanai* would have been as successful as *Nabucco*." Although the opening scenes of *Attila* were received well enough, as the evening wore on, the applause diminished. It, too, suffered from poor singing. Guasco was still having vocal problems, and Natale Costantini had the flu. A stage mishap did not help. The candles were so smoky that some in the audience had trouble breathing. But with Austria occupying Venice, "Avrai tu l'universo, resti l'Italia a me" (You will have the universe, leave Italy to me) made Verdi a hero and patriotic symbol for Italy's fight for freedom. With *Rigoletto*, Verdi ran into unexpected censorship problems. The Austrian authorities wrote to the management of La Fenice that "it is with profound regret that the poet Piave and the celebrated maestro Verdi could not have chosen a more worthy vehicle to display their talents than the revolting immorality and obscene triviality of the libretto of *La maledizione* (*Rigoletto*) submitted to us for intended performance at the Teatro Fenice. . . . The performance shall be absolutely forbidden." Eventually, a compromise was reached that left the situations mostly unchanged and only the locations and characters' names altered. *Rigoletto* was a major triumph at the premiere and soon played all over Italy. To pass the various local censors at different theaters, it was performed under a variety of names, including *Viscardello*, *Clara di Perth*, and *Lionello*. *La traviata* by many accounts, including Verdi's, was a fiasco. The singers, except for Fanny Salvini-Donatelli "failed to understand the spirit of the opera," and although Salvini-Donatelli possessed a good voice, her hefty physique made it difficult to believe she was dying of consumption. As Verdi wrote to his friend Emanuele Muzio on March 7, 1853, the day after the *prima*, "Is the fault mine or the singers? Time will be the judge." Verdi's last Fenice premiere, *Simon Boccanegra*, as the composer wrote to the Countess Maffei, "was almost a greater fiasco than *Traviata*. I thought I had done something fairly good, but now it seems I was mistaken." Although La Fenice asked Verdi to compose a sixth opera, he refused, replying that they should ask someone "who is better suited to the tastes of the Venetian public."

The novelties continued with Apolloni's *Lida di Granata* and *Pietro d'Abano* and operas from De Ferrari, Tessarin, Villanis, Pisani, Bonamici, Pinsuti, Smareglia, Benvenuti, Coronaro, and Orefice. These, too, fell into oblivion. There were also Italian premieres of *Das Rheingold, Die Walküre, Götterdämmerung, Samson et Dalila*, and Thomas's *Hamlet*. The schedule included operas by Meyerbeer, Flotow, Halévy, Gounod, and Weber. Fenice attracted the best singers: Giambattista Rubini, Grisi, Pasta, Malibran, Enrico Caruso, Toti dal Monte, and Beniamino Gigli.

The middle of the 20th century saw the establishment of the Contemporary Music Festival, which became a venue for the prime assolute of several important contemporary works, including *The Rake's Progress, Turn of the Screw*, and *Intolleranza 1960*. The greatest singers continued to come to the Fenice: Maria Callas, Renata Tebaldi, Marilyn Horne, Mirella Freni, and Luciano Pavarotti. Subsequently, La Fenice was plagued by a small public subsidy and limited theater seating capacity that diminished its role in the international opera scene.

La traviata opened the first opera season after the reconstruction, and it offered a wide-ranging repertory: *Le roi de Lahore, Maometto II, La finta semplice, Parsifal, Pia de Tolomei, Matrimonio segreto*, and at the Malibran, in celebration of the centennial of Goffredo Petrassi's birth, *Morte dell'aria* and *Il cordovano*. As noted in the above repertory, the Fenice showcases lesser-known, infrequently performed works of the giants of 19th-century Italian opera—Donizetti, Bellini, Rossini, and Verdi—and includes works from the 1700s, along with French, German, and other non-Italian operas. Recent operas included *Attila, La scala di seta, Don Chisiotte, Les pêcheurs de perles, Der Freischütz, Tristan und Isolde, Capriccio, Ariadne auf Naxos, Kát'a Kabanová*, Paisiello's *Barbiere di Siviglia*, Guarnieri's *Medea*, along with the more popular fare of *L'elisir d'amore, Otello, Tosca, Don Pasquale*, and *Nabucco*. With its transformation into a *fondazione* and seasons of unusual operas and provocative productions, La Fenice is regaining its past glory.

Practical Information

Teatro La Fenice, campo San Fantin 2519, 30124 Venice; tel. 39 041 786 562, fax 39 041 786 545; www.teatrolafenice.it. The opera season runs from November to October with a break during the summer months. There are eight operas with five to eight performances of each. Teatro Malibran, corte del Teatro Malibran 5886; tel. 39 041 241 8029, fax 39 041 241 8028. The opera season is part of La Fenice's.

The number of operas and performances vary. Stay at the Bauer Venezia, campo San Moisé 1459, San Marco, 30124 Venice; tel. 041 520 7022, fax 041 520 7557. A 5-minute walk from the opera house, the luxurious Bauer hosts the Fenice's pre-opera talks in their Salone delle Feste (Salon of the Festivals). Visit Teatro Goldoni, San Marco 4650/b; tel. 240 2011, fax 520 5241.

SEVENTEEN

Arena di Verona and Teatro Filarmonico, Verona

It is believed that the arena was constructed outside the city walls during the second and third decades of the 1st century AD, at the end of the reign of Augustus, financed by members of local aristocracy. It hosted gladiatorial fights (*munera gladiatorial*) and big-game hunts (*venationes*). These games were an ancient form of funeral celebration, probably of Etruscan origin, so it was common for the aristocracy to promise a gladiatorial spectacle to honor the memory of a loved one. A letter from Pliny the Younger (*Pliny, Epistles, VI, 34*) thanks a prominent Veronese contemporary for providing one: "Gaius Pliny to his Maximus. You did well to promise a gladiatorial spectacle to our Veronese, who have loved, respected, and honored you for some time. Your wife, so dear to you and so rich in virtue was also from Verona. It was opportune to dedicate a public work or spectacle to her memory: nay, really better a spectacle, which is the thing most suited for a funeral. Moreover, it was asked of you so insistently that to deny it would seem not firmness, but excess rigidity. And I once again congratulate you, for in conceding it you were so open and generous: in this way too, one gives proof of magnanimity. I would have wished that the African panthers you had bought in such great numbers had arrived in time: but even if this could not come about because of bad weather, you have merited gratitude all the same, since it was not your fault they could not be exhibited."

When Emperor Gallenus built a new wall in 265, he enclosed the amphitheater inside the city, which ended its most prosperous period. It slowly lost its function as an amphitheater when in 405 the barbaric gladiatorial fights were prohibited by Emperor Honorius and, after another century, the hunts disappeared as well. During the Middle Ages, the paupers and the homeless took up residence and the city inhabitants dumped their garbage there. In 1183 a powerful earthquake struck and collapsed most of the outer wall, according to the *Annales Veronese Antiqui*, edited by Cipolla, which became a source of building materials. Only the *ala* (wing) remained. In fact, there were a series of earthquakes during that period, the last of which hit on Christmas Day 1223 during a spectacle in the arena. In 1278, during a crusade against the Albigensians, 166 heretics were put to death. In 1298 it was decided to use the arches of the arena as a brothel. The arena was a place where duels and bullfights were fought, where riding tournaments and races took place, and where funerals and wedding celebrations were held. And at the marriage of Antonio della Scala to Samaritana di Polenta in 1382, a most spectacular entertainment was performed, called *Il castello dell'Amore* (The Castle of Love).

From the mid-1400s, a series of ordinances were designed to prevent abuse to the amphitheater. In 1568 the city council voted to have the arena renovated, which was paid for by the aristocracy. Jousting tournaments took place during the 17th century. A summer season of commedia dell'arte, tragedies, and farces, with ballet and circus acts performed during the intermission, began in the early 1700s and continued into the early 1800s on a small stage rigged up on a wooden platform. Goldoni in his *Memoires* described it: "The best Italian troupes come here and take turns showing off their talents." Charles de Brosses wrote, "I have never seen so many friars and priests at a procession than I saw . . . going to plays in the Arena (despite the fact that the Bishop of Verona expressly prohibited the clergy from going there)." There were also bull hunts, where butchers trained dogs to slaughter the bulls. As barbaric as it sounds, this was the entertainment mounted to honor Napoleon's visit to the arena in 1805, the same year it was turned into a detention center for Austrian prisoners, who demolished the stage for firewood. The Congress of Vienna took place in Verona during October and November of 1822, and the festivities went on for weeks, including a piece written and conducted at the arena by Rossini called *La Santa Alleanza* (Holy Alliance) that lasted an hour and a half and featured 128 instrumentalists and 121 singers, dancers, and extras. In 1842 his *Stabat Mater* was given just 10 days after it had been performed at the Teatro Filarmonico.

The first experiments for the arena as a venue for opera took place in 1856, organized by the impresario Nunziante, when *Il casino di campagna* and *La fanciulla di Grand* by the Veronese composer Lenotti and Donizetti's *Le convenienze e inconvenience teatrali* and *I pazzi per progetto* were offered. Productions of *Il barbiere di Siviglia* and *L'elisir d'amore* followed. The seeds for the future of opera at the arena had been planted.

The concept of holding regular opera seasons blossomed in the spring of 1913 in a café on the Piazza Bra where Giovanni Zenatello, a Veronese Verdian tenor, and his wife, Maria Gay, a Spanish mezzo, were seated. Zenatello proposed celebrating the centennial of Verdi's birth with a performance of *Aida*. (*Aida* was chosen as it was the most grandiose and least likely of the maestro's operas to be overwhelmed by the sheer size of the venue.) To quote Teodor Mommsen, "One does not go to Rome to accomplish matters of petty routine." After finding the acoustics optimal, chorus director Ferruccio Cusinati, impresario Ottone Rovato, and conductor Tullio Serafin gave their approval of the project, which Zenatello financed at his own expense. A plaque in the arena is dedicated to the inaugural *Aida*: "On the 50th anniversary of performances in this Roman arena, Verona remembers its fellow citizen tenor Giovanni Zenatello, who was its talented promoter, his collaborator Ottone Rovato, and the producers of Verdi's *Aida*: Tullio Serafin, Ferruccio Cusinati, Ettore Fagiuoli, Maria Gay, Ester Mazzoleni, Mansueto Gaudio, Arrigo Passuello, Giuseppe Danise, Ugo Malfatti. 1913–1963." *Aida* became the arena's trademark, with more than 400 performances since 1913. Slowly, the festival grew into the most spectacular open-air operatic extravaganza in the world. Its success is attributed to the arena's phenomenal acoustics: sound reflects off the ancient stones with the same perfection found in the famous Italian opera houses of the 1700s.

The arena was constructed of limestone from the Lessini Mountains, except the vaulting, which was a mixture of pebbles and concrete. The huge, elliptical amphitheater rests on a bed of concrete that covers the entire area. It is situated just outside the most ancient wall of the city. You can get an idea of the original appearance from the northwest side, where a piece of the *ala* still stands. The three orders of arches that formed the original outer wall corresponded to the three orders of seating inside. The simplicity of its modular plan made the measurements of the arena proportional. The two axes of the ellipse that forms the amphitheater measure 250 and 150 Roman feet, establishing a five-to-three relationship. It is the second-largest Roman amphitheater in the world, seating 19,000 for opera performances out of a total capacity of almost 30,000, since part of the seating area is used for the production.

Teatro Filarmonico

L'Accademia Filarmonica was an association of music lovers that was founded in 1543. At the beginning of the 17th century, the idea to construct a theater came about during preparation work for a new site for the academy itself. Designed by Francesco Galli Bibiena, the theater was erected between 1719 and 1729 and finally inaugurated on January 6, 1732, with Vivaldi's *La fida ninfa*. It survived only 17 years. During the night of January 21, 1749, a torch was forgotten in the box of the Marquis Spolverini, and the theater burned to the ground. The academy decided immediately to rebuild, hiring the architect Paglia, who was faithful to the original design by Bibiena. The Filarmonica reopened in 1754 with Perez's *Lucio Vero*, a work soon forgotten.

During the 17th, 18th, and 19th centuries, other theaters were constructed, including the Teatro Ristori, which was erected on the foundation of the Teatro Valle and hosted the world premiere of Sala's *Bice Alighieri* in 1865, and the Teatro Nuovo, which presented during the 1850s the world premieres of Pedrotti's *Fiorina*, *Il parrucchiere della reggenza*, and *Tutti in maschera* and native son Mela's *Il feudatario* and *Cristoforo Colombo*.

During a bombing raid the night of February 23, 1945, the Teatro Filarmonico was destroyed. A decade passed before the Accademia Filarmonica officially announced in October 1955 that the theater would be reconstructed "as it was and as far as possible, how it was." The reconstruction was initiated in 1961 and ended in 1965. The architect, Vittorio Filippini, followed the "line of Bibiena." Although the Filarmonico boasts an impressive main entrance facade lined with six massive Ionic columns forming a colonnade, it is no longer used. The entrance is located on a nondescript side of the building. The gold, red, and ivory, 1,430-seat auditorium offers three box tiers topped by two galleries. There is a large center royal box. The parapets are decorated with gilded ornamentations on an ivory background while pairs of gilded Corinthian columns flank the proscenium boxes and bronze statues of the Muses. The opera house was one of the few early theaters to benefit from improved sight lines. The boxes extend out one in respect to the other and slope toward the stage, which increases stage visibility. There are gilded griffins on either side of a proscenium clock.

Operatic Events at the Arena

On August 10, 1913, *Aida* inaugurated the first summer opera season. Attending the event was a distinguished audience, including several opera composers—Puccini, Mascagni, Zandonai, Montemezzi, Illica, Boïto, and Pizzetti—the publishers Ricordi and Sonzogno, numerous members of the aristocracy, the writers Maxim Gorki and Franz Kafka, and the directors of Teatro alla Scala and Teatro Dal Verme. The gates were opened at 6 p.m. and the ticket holders, who had packed the Piazza Bra in front of the arena all afternoon, entered through the 11 entrances. As the amphitheater filled up, excitement pervaded the air in anticipation of *Aida* performed in an open-air theater. There was also an amusing sign: "Ladies and girls sitting in the VIP section are requested to wear hats of small bulk . . . if you feel that scarves are not enough." A buffet service was available for the VIPs. Promptly at 8:30 p.m., Tullio Serafin raised his baton and the performance began. As a chronicle of the era reported, "there were 120 orchestral players, 12 trumpeters, an on-stage band, a chorus of 180, 50 chorus leaders, 36 ballerinas, 40 boys, 280 extras, and 30 horses and oxen." The sets re-created the grandeur of ancient Egypt and the performance was a triumph. There were eight performances of *Aida* that summer, which was the only opera mounted. *Carmen* followed the next year with 10 performances. This was more an Italian Carmen than a French one, with little in common with the Opéra Comique *prima*. It was turned into a "grand opera" typical of the arena, which included inserting a ballet. The production emphasized the verismo elements of passion, vengeful rage, and sublime tragedy. The more memorable *Carmens* came after World War II, especially those with Franco Corelli and Giulietta Simionato. Bizet's opera is the second-most-staged opera, with more than 150 performances.

World War I closed the arena. The first season after the war opened July 31, 1919, with *Il figliuol prodigy*, a relatively unknown work, which was an attempt to expand the festival's repertory. Over the next 16 seasons, a number of infrequently performed operas were on the schedule: *Il piccolo Marat*, *Le roi de Lahore*, *Mosè*, *Nerone*, *La vestale*, *Isabeau*, *Boris Godunov*, *Les Huguenots*, and *Loreley*. In addition, the season had expanded in 1920 to two operas with further expansion at the end of the decade. In 1922 *Lohengrin* became the first Wagner opera performed. Other Wagner works followed, including *Parsifal*, *Die Meistersinger von Nürnberg*, *Tannhäuser*, and *Die Walküre*. They survived only one season, *Lohengrin* three. The performances continued uninterrupted until the venue closed because of World War II. The last season took place in 1939 with performances of *Rigoletto*, *Tosca*, *Faust*, and Zandonai's *Giulietta e Romeo*.

A variety of organizations and people managed the opera seasons until 1936: Lyrica Italica ARS, 1919/20; Casa Musicale Sonzogno, 1921/22; Ente Autonomo Fiera, 1930/1931; Emilio Ferroni, Ciro Ragazzini, and Gianni Scalabrini, 1932/33; and Ente Comunale degli Spettacoli, 1934/35. In 1936 the Ente Autonomo Spettacoli Lirici was created, with Ente Lirico Arena di Verona assuming the management of the opera seasons. It was suspended between 1940 and 1947 because of the war, with Società Spettacoli arranging the 1946 season. At the end of the 20th century, as required by the Italian government, all the Enti Lirici, of which the arena was one, had to establish *fondazioni* for private support in addition to government subsidies, so it is now Fondazione Arena di Verona.

The seasons began again on August 1, 1946, with *Aida*, featuring Margherita Grandi, Galliano Masini, and Elena Nicolai. *La traviata* followed. For the 1950 season, there were five operas: *Mefistofele, Die Walküre, La bohème, Les pêcheurs de perles* and *La forza del destino*. As the decades progressed, season performances fluctuated between three and six operas, and the repertory became more limited to popular fare, a trend that continues to the present. From 1913 into the 21st century, approximately 60 different operas have been staged, half of which were produced only once. Financial factors influence the choice of operas. When the works are unfamiliar, the seats remain empty. With 19,000 seats to fill almost every night for 2 months, and having to earn around 60% of its budget from ticket sales, the arena is forced to produce only the most popular and best-loved operas in spectacular extravaganzas season after season. Verdi dominates the repertory every season. Fourteen of the maestro's operas have been staged. Of the approximately 275 opera productions given, around 110 have been Verdi operas, with 900 performances out of a total of 1900 performances. In terms of number of performances, after *Aida* and *Carmen* come *Nabucco* and *Turandot*, with around 100 performances each, then *Tosca, Traviata,* and *Rigoletto*, with around 75 performances each.

Filling seats also depends on hiring the appropriate singers: big names with big voices. Some of the most successful artists go back to the early years, Lauri-Volpi in *Turandot*; Beniamino Gigli in *Martha, Les Huguenots, Gioconda, Andrea Chénier*, and *Forza del destino*; Nicola Rossi Lemeni in *Gioconda, Faust*, and *Boris Godunov*; and Maria Callas in *Gioconda, Turandot*, and *Traviata*. Richard Tucker, Renata Tebaldi, Mario del Monaco, Magda Olivero, and Franco Corelli all sang there in the early to mid-20th century. The 1969 season marked the debuts of Plácido Domingo, Birgit Nilsson, and Montserrat Caballé, and the 1970s witnessed the debuts of Luciano Pavarotti in *Ballo in maschera* and Renato Bruson in *Macbeth*. During the 1990s, it hosted the likes of Paolo Gavanelli, Lando Bartolini, Giorgio Zancanaro, José Carreras, Leo Nucci, Dolores Zajick, Deborah Voigt, Roberto Scandiuzzi, Vladimir Chernov, Maria Guleghina, and Juan Pons. In the 21st century, Salvatore Licitra, Ambrogio Maestri, Kristjan Johannsson, Alexandru Agache, and Ramon Vargas have continued the tradition.

To commemorate the centennial of Verdi's death, the arena devoted both its 2000 and 2001 seasons exclusively to the operas of the maestro, transforming the traditional summer festival into Verdi Festivals. This prompted the speculation that the venue would become the Bayreuth of Verdi. Renzo Giacchieri, the *sovrintendente* at the time, denied that, saying, "There was no need for a special festival for the maestro because he is so loved and his operas are an essential part of every house's repertory. His operas have the drama, vigor, power to arouse the feelings, sentiments and emotions of the people. Verdi will continue to play a major role in the repertory at the Arena, but not to the exclusion of the other composers. . . . We began the celebration in 2000 to be the first to commemorate the centennial. If we had waited for 2001, we would have been one of the last." The millennium season offered *Nabucco, Forza del destino, Aida,* and *Traviata,* followed by *Messa da Requiem, Trovatore, Aida, Nabucco, Rigoletto,* and *Traviata* the next summer.

The 21st century ushered in a new production style for the ever-present *Aida.* Conceived by Pier Luigi Pizzi and nicknamed "Blue Aida" (the scenery was all blue), it was a futuristic set with clean, smooth lines, devoid of the usual Egyptian tourist trappings that had been the trademark of arena *Aidas* since its inception. Nonetheless, it stayed true to the composer's intent and contrasted with the ornate excesses of Franco Zeffirelli's new *Trovatore* of gigantic men in armor, enormous turrets, and dozens of horses, the traditional extravaganza one associates with the arena. Giacchieri explained the dichotomy: "The tradition at the Arena must be kept, because there are 19,000 seats to fill every night, but it also is not possible to ignore the new technical and architectural advances which excite the imagination." Recent seasons have offered *Nabucco, Traviata, Rigoletto, Turandot, Gioconda, Bohème,* and *Carmen.*

Operatic Events at the Teatro Filarmonico

After the theater opened in 1732, the opera season became the major artistic and social focus of the city. Some works of note during the 1700s included Traetta's *Olimpiade,* Sarti's *Antigone,* and Cimarosa's *Giumio Bruto.* Near the close of the century, two events stood out. In May 1797, in the spirit of the French revolution of liberty and equality and to glorify the new French regime, the theater was open and free to the public. But just a short time later, on January 21, 1798, there was a celebration to hail the expulsion of the French by the Austrians. During the first decade of the 19th century, the opera house hosted the world premieres of Pavesi's *I castelli in aria* and *La forza dei simpatico;* Mellara's *La prova indiscrete, Berenice in Roma,* and *La Fiera di Livorno*; and Morlacchi's *Il ritratto*. The French returned on November 27, 1807, and the Filarmonico hosted Napoleon at a performance. The mid-1800s saw additional prime mondiali: Pedrotti's *Lina*, *Clara di Mailand*, and *Romea di Montfort* and Sala's *Ginevra di Monreale*.

On January 10, 1844, *Nabucco* became the first Verdi opera performed in Verona. The maestro was in attendance and at the end of the performance was called to the stage to acknowledge the applause. Among the lead singers was his future wife, Giuseppina Strepponi, who had also created the role of Abigaille in the world premiere at La Scala. A critic for the Verona *Foglio* wrote, "The genius that inspired the notes of *Nabucco* is a new star. . . . Verdi's music has its own type of grandeur and originality. The vocal part is simple and expressive. The instrumentation is rich and abundant, but philosophical. It is written with such taste and arranged with such skill that far from detracting from the effect of the singing (which dominates throughout), it sustains that dominion and sharpens its fibre. Indeed, we could even say that through this magical instrumentation Verdi wishes us to penetrate the innermost secret of those affects that the words and notes of the vocal line alone would not be sufficient to disclose." Verdi's operas arrived quickly at the Filarmonico, usually within a year of the prima assoluta. By the end of the 19th century, only eight of Verdi's operas had never been performed in the city. With the dawn of the 21st century, only *Oberto*, *Alzira*, *Il corsaro*, and *Stiffelio* have not been staged. The Filarmonico maintained an ambitious schedule of long seasons with operas by the most famous composers until the theater was destroyed during World War II.

After the theater reopened in 1965, it was placed under the Ente Lirico Arena di Verona (now Fondazione Arena di Verona), which since 1976 has presented an operatic program. The repertory selected, that of neglected, obscure, and contemporary works, was to complement the popular fare at the arena. Included were Chailly's *Una domanda di matrimonio*, Massenet's *Ritratto di Manon*; Busoni's *Turandot*; Zandonai's *Francesca da Rimini* and *Giulietta e Romeo*; Alfano's *Risurrezione*; Auber's *Manon Lescaut* (first performance in Italy); Verdi's *Un giorno di regno* and *Giovanna d'Arco*; Wolf-Ferrari's *I quattro rusteghi*; Tutino's *Cirano*; and the world premiere of Arcà's *Gattabianca*. These were combined with more popular fare, such as *Madama Butterfly*, *Il barbiere di Siviglia*, *Rigoletto*, *Don Pasquale*, and *Traviata*.

In 1994 the Festival di Primavera (Festival of Spring) was begun to showcase the richness of Italy's forgotten music. The festivals had themes: "The Festival Theater and Music of the Republic of Venice" was the theme of the first three. The result was the rediscovery of forgotten works such as Vivaldi's

Il Tamerlano and *La fida ninfa*; Salieri's *Les Danaides*; Farinelli's *Teresa e Claudio*; Rossini's *L'inganno felice*; Boccadoro's *Rimini addio*; Bertoni's *Orfeo*; and the *prima esecuzione assoluta* of Ferrero's *Nascita di Orfeo*. The fourth festival looked toward the Orient in the works of the 1700s with Paisiello's *I'idolo cinese* and Cimarosa's *I turchi amante* receiving their Verona premieres. These unknown operas did not attract many people, resulting in the cancellation of the festival.

With the dawn of the millennium, the Teatro Filarmonico has offered a German opera each season, including *Salome* and *Elektra*, and in 2004 the season opened with *Tristan und Isolde*, the first performance at the theater since 1938. The rest of the program included popular Italian fare, such as *La traviata*, *Un ballo in maschera*, and *L'elisir d'amore*. Recent offerings include *Ernani*, *Falstaff*, *La bohème*, and *Die lustige Witwe*.

Practical Information

Arena di Verona, piazza Bra 28, 37100 Verona; tel. 39 045 800 5151, fax 39 045 801 3287; www.arena.it. The season takes place during June, July, and August. There are five or six operas with between 5 and 18 performances of each. Teatro Filarmonico, via dei Mutilati 4, 37121 Verona; tel. 39 045 8051 891, fax 39 045 8031 443. The season runs from November to March or April, offering four operas with 5 performances of each.

Stay at the Hotel Gabbia d'Oro, corso Porta Borsari 4/a, 37121 Verona; tel. 045 800 3060, fax 045 590 293. A luxurious, historic hotel, it is a 12-minute walk to both the arena and the Teatro Filarmonico. Visit the Teatro Romano and Juliet's balcony.

EIGHTEEN

Teatro Da Ponte, Vittorio Veneto

Until 1866, Vittorio Veneto was divided into two sections known as Cèneda and Serravalle. During the late 1700s in Cèneda, the Nobile Teatro Zuliani hosted performances. Although the theater ceased operations in 1820, the Teatro Nuovo di Società was built to take its place. Subsequently renamed Teatro Verdi, it functioned as an opera house for decades until circumstances forced its conversion into a movie theater, Cinema Teatro Verdi, which is still in operation.

In Serravalle, the first seeds for a new opera house were planted in 1842, when Giuseppe Segusini was chosen as the architect by a society of music lovers who had collected funds to pay for the new theater. Various problems, including finding a suitable location for the building, delayed construction. In 1857 *Il trovatore* was performed in the unfinished building. Finally, in 1879, the Teatro Sociale, as the Teatro Da Ponte was originally called, was inaugurated with *Un ballo in maschera*. The theater was most active during August and September (Fiera di Santa Augusta) and carnival. But the Sociale led a checkered existence until the municipality took it over during the 1920s, at which time it was renamed Teatro Comunale. In 1938 the theater celebrated the 20th anniversary of the Italian victory over the Austrian-Hungarian Empire in November 1918. After World War II, however, decline set in. In 1957 it was transformed into a movie house and renamed Cinema Teatro Rossini. Activity continued until the mid-1980s, but the building steadily deteriorated until it reached such a state of disrepair that it was closed. At the dawn of the millennium, the Rossini was carefully restored under the supervision of Leopoldo Saccon, with Roberto Zecchin in charge of the acoustics and the Fondazione Cassamarca paying the bill. It was renamed Teatro Da Ponte in honor of the poet and librettist Lorenzo da Ponte, who came from the area. The renovated Teatro Da Ponte was inaugurated during the fall of 2002 with *Così fan tutte*, for which Da Ponte wrote the libretto. *Don Giovanni* and *Le nozze di Figaro* followed to complete the cycle of Da Ponte–written libretti for Mozart operas. The Orchestra di Padova e del Veneto played at the opening, marking its first foray into the opera arena.

The neoclassical structure exhibits a symmetrical facade divided into two levels. The lower consists of rusticated stone with masks of Comedy and Tragedy over each of the five entrances. On the upper level, five large rectangular windows are flanked by gilded Corinthian pilasters and crowned with medallions and friezes. The rectangular auditorium holds 400 seats. Because of its small size, it hosts primarily dance and symphonic music concerts and has joined with Comunale in Treviso for opera.

Practical Information

Teatro Da Ponte, via Martiri della Libertà, 31029 Vittorio Veneto; tel. 39 0438 553 836, fax 39 0422 513 311; www.siagrio.it. Teatro Verdi Cinema, via Lioni 9, piazza San Francesco, Vittorio Veneto (Cèneda); tel. 39 0438 551 699.

⌒

NINETEEN

Teatro delle Muse, Ancona

From at least the beginning of the 1600s, private musical activities took place in the palaces of the nobility, in monasteries, and in churches around the city. Because of Ancona's strategic location on the water, a large arsenal existed from which the first public theatrical space was carved, known as the Teatro Arsenale. The Arsenale itself was formed from five corridors and six galleries, three of which were covered by a roof supported by large pilasters and arcades. Two of the galleries served as storage areas. Although open-air performances were not uncommon, it is believed that the performances took place in one of the covered galleries, where a large number of seats were set up, rigorously divided according to class and sex. Three levels of boxes were created between each of the eight large arches. The theater accommodated no fewer than 4,000, of which 500 were usually foreigners. Among the works performed were Bonarelli's *L'Esilio d'Amore* and *Il Medoro*. There was suffi-cient space for a huge, special-effects machine that made clouds fly and rain fall, accompanied by bolts of thunder and flashes of lightning, and created waves in seas sprinkled with rocks and filled with darting fish and various marine monsters that appeared at appropriate places. Carts filled with choruses of gods and semigods descended from the heavens, suspended from enormous belts. In 1632 Bonarelli himself founded the Academy of the "Cal-iginosi" where *La Metamorfosi d'Amore* and *Filli di Sciro*, among others, were performed.

In 1658 a group of aristocracy presented a petition to the civil authorities to erect a theater at their own expense "to perpetuate and in like form of the most famous [theaters] of Italy." The new theater was constructed in the same space of the Teatro Arsenale, reorganizing and enlarging it in such a way to satisfy the needs of the most complex scenic effects and to produce worthy and important spectacles for the passage of princes through the city. Although the theater was completed in 1664, it wasn't inaugurated until the following year with Cavalli's *Il Giasone*. The performance space remained unnamed. It held 54 boxes on three levels, decorated in gold and deep blue. Surviving 35 years, it was thought to be the first permanent theater with boxes in the Marche region. The theater's repertory included Cavalli's *Scipione africano* and *Erismena*, Agostini's *Il ratto delle Sabine*, Bani's *Il figlio delle selve*, and Scarlatti's *Rosaura* and *Tutto il mal non vien per nuocere*. The theater was closed in 1690 and destroyed 9 years later by a fire caused by maintenance workers responsible for dredging the port.

The community quickly decided to rebuild, thanks to the generous offer of four families to contribute 1,000 scudi each toward the total cost of 6,000. The rest of the funds were raised through the sale of boxes. Domenico Egidio Rossi was the architect of the new theater, called Teatro Fenice after the mythical bird that rises from its own ashes. Located in the same place as the two preceding theaters, the structure offered four box tiers, decorated in blue and gold bas-reliefs. The curtain was yellow and deep blue with the coat of arms of the city embroidered in the middle. Two stucco statues of Aurora and Fame flanked the proscenium arch while a phoenix was affixed above the central box, reserved for the authorities. Surrounded by angels, festoons, and the motto Resurgo ab Igne (Resurrected from the Fire), the theater was inaugurated during carnival season of 1712 and remained active until the spring of 1818. Around 250 different works were presented between musical drama and dance. During the first 30 years, serious works were predominant and included Vivaldi's *Siroe, re di Persia*. The schedule then took a decisive turn toward opera buffa and semiseria, with works by Piccinni, Cimarosa, Paisiello, and finally Rossini dominating the boards. The best known singers to perform were the famous castrati Gaetano Majorana (known as Caffarelli), Tommaso Consoli, and Girolamo Crescentini. Despite the prohibition against women appearing on stage, there were some exceptions with some *prime donne* of the times performing, such as Anna Girò, Margherita Gualandi, and Caterina Fumagalli. As the 1700s progressed, other well-known singers of the era appeared. By the 19th century, the Fenice had undergone a series of restorations to extend its useful life to its utmost limit, until finally, in November 1818, the Gonfalonier Giuseppe Ferretti declared that the Teatro Fenice could no longer be used. The building was closed, and it was demolished a few years later.

While discussions began about the construction of a new theater for "the dignity of this respectable city," Ancona enjoyed opera courtesy of a private initiative. A gentleman named Marco Organari obtained permission from the authorities to build a structure in wood outside the port area. The building, known as the Teatro Grande Organari, included three tiers topped by a gallery. For almost a decade, it was the city's most important theater, presenting popular works of the era such as Mosca's *I tre mariti*, Celli's *Il ditto e rovescio*, Fonseca's *Ora non copra amore*, Fioravanti's *La capricciosa pentita*, Mercadante's *Elisa e Claudio*, and Pacini's *Il Barone di Dolsheim*. The final season at the Organari offered Donizetti's *L'Ajo nell'imbarazzo*, reportedly with a mediocre cast, except that of the protagonist, which Girolamo Donati Candetta assayed. Despite the dearth of outstanding singers, the Organari played an important role between the disappearance of La Fenice and the opening of the new theater.

Meanwhile, in February 1819, the municipal council approved the project of Pietro Ghinelli for the new edifice. Gabriele Vignini and Pietro Pasquali were entrusted with executing Ghinelli's plans. They had 40 months to complete the structure. The location chosen was known as Isola delle Carceri (Island of the Prison), where a prison, the customs office, and dilapidated houses were located. The municipality purchased the buildings and the prison itself, which were then razed. All materials recovered from the demolition were used in the new construction, which included not only the opera house but a new customs office, casino, apartments, and houses, the income from which would be used to finance the opera productions. The construction itself, however, was paid for by the sale of boxes. There were 99 *palchettisti* who formed the Società dei Palchettisti. They paid for and owned the new theater. The final cost reached 77,000 scudi. An agreement was drawn up between the municipality and the box holders regarding the management of the theater. The Teatro delle Muse, as the new opera house was named, was inaugurated on April 28, 1827, with Rossini's *L'Aureliano in Palmira*. The cream of Ancona society turned out for the joyous occasion, along with many from other parts of Italy. It was an evening of elegance and lavishness.

The neoclassical facade offered a portico of five massive arches of rusticated stone of Itria. A balustrade separated the lower level from the upper, where six monumental engaged Ionic columns supported a pediment, the tympanum displaying a bas-relief in stucco of Apollo surrounded by nine Muses, the work of Giacomo de Maria. The gold- and wheat-colored auditorium was horseshoe shape, with four box tiers topped by a gallery, for a total of 99 boxes, including 8 proscenium boxes. The parapets of the box tiers exhibited an assortment of gilded, carved wood ornamentation: the first held reliefs of antique masks and gold festoons; the second and fourth were decorated with bacchantes, and the third was painted with designs from antiquity. On the dome, Olympia with the gods among the clouds was painted by Giovanni Bonsignori, who also painted the curtain, which depicted the triumph of Traiano in the port of Ancona with a view of the city.

In 1861 the auditorium was redecorated by Luigi Samoggia. The parapets took on an ivory background with adornments of gilded, carved wood more intricate than the earlier decorations, with festoons of flowers and ornaments. The boxes were enclosed with pilasters, the walls upholstered in red velvet, and gilded corbels were added. The dome, which had been ruined by smoke from oil and candle lighting, was repainted. The reason for the renovation was competition from a new private theater called Teatro Vittorio Emanuele II, erected by Corrado Pergolesi and decorated by Fortunato Morini. In 1864 there was more competition from an amphitheater built by Raffaele Boni, renamed the Carlo Goldoni in 1880 after it received a roof. Both venues survived World War II as movie houses. The Muse did not.

On May 27, 1943, the final performance of the spring season took place, and the last one in the old Teatro delle Muse. On November 1, 1943, the theater was damaged by bombs and a resulting fire. It never reopened for performances. The Allied troops camped out in the theater during their stay in Ancona. A decade after the bombing, contentious discussions began between the box holders, who owned the theater, and the municipality. Three years later, the municipality owned the building. Although the facade had survived undamaged and all the tiers in the auditorium were intact, the roof had collapsed and only one stage wall was standing.

In 1958 Carlo Montecamozzo received the commission to rebuild the opera house. His concept was a completely new structure, but it took a decade before work began, only to be halted by an earthquake in 1972, which damaged the building such that the old plans were set aside. Seven years later, a new contract was given to Danilo Guerri, Paola Salmoni, and Francesco Zaupa for reconstruction, but the plans were not approved until 1988, held up by bureaucratic infighting. Fourteen years passed before the theater was ready. After 59 years of silence, the Teatro delle Muse reopened October 13, 2002, with a gala concert of music by Rossini, Stravinsky, Tchaikovsky, and Verdi. Riccardo Muti conducted. There was much fanfare and some controversy. Apparently the iron balustrades on all three tiers were built so high that Muti joked, "One does not know if we are in jail or you are."

The neoclassical facade of beige brick was preserved. The auditorium, however, is a fusion of the classic with the modern in a harmonious balance.

The piazza outside the opera house was re-created in the auditorium by duplicating the beige bricks and massive arches of the facade for side walls and punctuating them with boxes with wrought-iron balustrades reminiscent of the balconies overlooking the piazza from the surrounding buildings. A 1,057-seat rectangular auditorium replaced the original horseshoe-shaped auditorium, and three steeply graded balconies supplanted the tiers of boxes. A striking steel "fire curtain," designed by Valeriano Trubbiani, displays bronze sculptured images of the sun surrounded by seven telamon angels, a broadside view of an antique ship known as a trireme, 11 hoofed horses, and the Arch of Traiano.

Operatic Events at the Teatro delle Muse

After the inauguration of the Muse in 1827 with Rossini's *L'Aureliano in Palmira*, the Pesaro maestro dominated the repertory for the next few years with *Ricciardo e Zoraide*, *Il barbiere di Siviglia*, *Maometto II*, *L'inganno felice*, *La Cenerentola*, *Semiramide*, and *Mosè in Egitto*. Other popular composers and operas during those first years included Vaccai's *La pastorella feudataria*, *Giulietta e Romeo*, and *Zadig e Astartea*; Coccia's *Clotide* and *Edoardo in Scozia*; Bellini; Pacini; and Ricci. In 1834 *L'esule di Roma* became the first Donizetti work at Le Muse. Within 2 years, his works monopolized the schedule: *Anna Bolena*, *I Capuleti e I Montecchi*, *I Puritani*, *Parisina*, *Olivio e Pasquale*, *Il furioso all'isola di San Domingo*, *Belisario*, *Lucia di Lammermoor*, *Roberto Devereux*, *Gemma di Vergy*, *Torquato Tasso*, *L'ajo nell'imbarazzo*, *Maria Stuarda*, *Marino Faliero*, *Maria di Rudenz*, *Linda di Chamounix*, and *Lucrezia Borgia* (performed as *Eustorgia da Romaneo*). Additional composers included Mercadante and Persiani.

Verdi entered the repertory in 1844 with *Nabucco*, 2 years after its La Scala triumph, and soon eclipsed them all. Until the unity of Italy in 1860, Verdi's operas composed almost 54% of all operas performed at the Muse. As the 1850s drew to a close, the theater introduced three prime assolute by composers from the Marche region: Zabban's *Il conte di Stennedoff*, which enjoyed 7 performances; Boccolini's *La fidanzata di Savoja*, which received only 5 additional hearings; and Grassoni's *Matilde da Valdelmo*, with 14 more recitals. The operas, however, soon fell into oblivion. About the same time, the spring season, in which opera seria and ballet were scheduled and had regularly taken place since the opening of the Muse, became sporadic and disappeared entirely in the 1880s. The winter carnival season, which presented opera buffa and opera semiseria, took place regularly until 1896. Then opera seasons were scheduled almost exclusively for the fall and on special occasions.

During the early years, the opera house attracted a number of important singers of the era, such as Giambattista Rubini, Gilbert-Louis Duprez, Adolphe Nourrit, Carolina Ungher, Giuseppina Strepponi, and Giorgio Ronconi. Around the middle of the century, Carlo Negrini assayed the Duke in *Rigoletto*, with Enrico Crivelli in the title role. Other artists included Pietro Mongini and Giuseppe Fancelli. As the 19th century drew to a close, composers from the verismo school occupied the schedule, including Cilea's *Tilda*; Ponchielli's *La gioconda*; Mascagni's *Cavalleria rusticana* and *L'amico Fritz*; Giordano's *Mala vita*; and the operas of Puccini. French opera was also popular, with works by Massenet, Halévy, Meyerbeer, and Thomas. During the first few decades of the 20th century, before the Muse was closed, Aureliano Pertile, Renato Zanelli, Vittorio Lois, Beniamino Gigli, John O'Sullivan, Toti dal Monte, Giuseppe Taddei, Margaret Sheridan, and Ferruccio Tagliavini sang at the opera house. Despite the outbreak of World War II, the theater kept its doors open, presenting seasons of popular Italian fare: *La bohème*, *Lucia di Lammermoor*, *Il barbiere di Siviglia*, *Tosca*, *La traviata*, *Madama Butterfly*, *Rigoletto*, *Fedora*, and *L'elisir d'amore*. The final season took place in 1943 with *Andrea Chénier*, *Manon Lescaut*, and *Werther* on the boards. When Le Muse shut its doors on May 27, 1943, after the final performance of *Werther*, they would never open again in the old opera house.

After the opera house reopened in October 2002 with an inaugural concert, the opera season followed with three works, *Idomeneo*, *Lucia di Lammermoor*, and *Madama Butterfly*. The second season was also inaugurated with a Mozart opera, *Il re pastore*, followed by a controversial, avant-garde production of *Un ballo in maschera*. *Tosca* completed the schedule. This set a pattern of the season opening with a lesser-known opera, followed by popular Italian fare that was conceived in new, thought-provoking if not always successful or pleasing ways. This allowed the opera house to distinguish itself in a short time as a home for unusual operas and challenging and innovative productions of traditional ones. The artistic bent of the opera house changed directions in 2004 in regard to production style. Instead of another "shocking" production of a popular opera, the *Norma* staged was from the Italian school of Visconti and Strehler where the singing, sets, costumes, and direction were all integrated with the music. Conceived by Hugo De Ana, the production was updated to Bellini's era regarding the sets, costumes, and architecture of the buildings but retained the grandeur of the Italian tradition of singing with studied gestures and grand movements. The season had opened with a double bill of two rarely performed contemporary operas, Stravinsky's *The Flood* and Ravel's *L'Enfant et les Sortilèges*, and closed with *La bohème*. Recent operas included Henze's *Elegy for Young Lovers*, *Die Entführung aus dem Serail*, *Trovatore*, and *Roberto Devereux*.

The Teatro delle Muse, being so new, has not been classified as a *Teatro di tradizione*, which has given the management the freedom to produce what it feels is best. Its activities are supported through a *fondazione* that was established when the theater reopened.

Practical Information

Teatro delle Muse, via della Loggia, 60121 Ancona; tel. 39 071 52525, fax 39 071 52622; www.teatrodellemuse.org.

The season, which runs from November through January, offers three to four operas with three to four performances of each. A convenient, modest hotel is the Roma & Pace, via Leopardi 1; tel. 071 202007, a 5-minute walk from the theater.

TWENTY

Teatro Comunale Ventidio Basso, Ascoli Piceno

The first performances date back to January 1560 in the Palazzo Anzianale. The sala of the Palazzo dell'Arringo also hosted comedies, while entertainment with modest requirements was performed in the piazza in front of the Arringo. Given that no permanent theater existed, the villas of wealthy individuals and convents also served as venues. By the 1700s, the fact that the Arringo held no boxes became a serious problem, and by the 1730s discussions began on constructing a new theater. This resulted in the realization of the Teatro del Legno, the first permanent theater. The Legno opened in December 1746. Biagio Miniera built the theater and executed the decorations, including the stage curtain, which depicted the Ascolanese hero Ventidio Basso on a horse. The auditorium was large, with oil lamps on the proscenium arch and tallow candles in the orchestra area illuminating the space. There were four tiers of boxes, which were the privilege of the nobility, while the orchestra section was for the working class, where rows of high-backed chairs were placed. The working class could purchase boxes only in the late afternoon of the evening performance when all the requests of the nobility had been met. This arrangement left everyone unhappy. So in 1748, the entire second tier and four central boxes of the first were reserved exclusively for the nobility, with the remaining boxes available for anyone who could pay the price.

The Teatro del Legno was constructed of wood—hence its name, Theater of Wood—which carried a great fire risk. This led to discussions in 1792 about the construction of a new theater. To pay for its construction, it was suggested that every noble family purchase a box and, to save on the design, use a project similar to that in Macerata or Jesi, cities where theaters had already been built. But nothing happened. The issue was taken up again in 1827 with a more concrete proposal: the new theater should offer four tiers of 23 boxes each, with the three central boxes of the second tier reserved for the association, the police, and the authorities. The estimated cost was 18,000 scudi. The first plans were submitted in 1829 by Angelo Brizzi, who envisioned a theater located opposite the Palazzo Sgariglia. His plans were rejected because the site was considered too narrow and close to the church Sant'Agostino. Additional plans were submitted, including those by architects Gabriele Gabrielli, Ireneo Aleandri, Giovani Santini, and Luigi Incoronati, locating the theater at different sites around the city. On January 15, 1839, after performances of Il pirata and Il belisario, the Teatro del Legno closed its shutters permanently, after almost a century of hosting opera, ballet, comedy, drama, and balls. There was now a new urgency to erect another theater.

On April 5, 1839, the Società Condominale del Teatro Ventidio Basso was formed by 65 soci whose purpose was to construct, open, and manage the Nuovo Teatro, together with the municipality, using a combination of public and private funds. Aleandri was awarded the commission. The structure, to be located on the via del Trivio, would have 21 boxes a tier, priced at 150 scudi each, except three boxes on the second tier would be the property of the municipality, one for the apostolic delegate, one for the magistrate, and one for the Deputation for Public Entertainment. In November 1839, Aleandri arrived in Ascoli with the architectural drawings and received partial payment of 120 scudi the next month. Insurmountable obstacles surfaced in 1840, causing a delay in the start of the construction and forcing Aleandri to submit a second set of drawings. Finally, the first stone was placed in March 1841, but differences arose when the deputation demanded modifications to the structure that Aleandri felt ruined the internal and external symmetry of the edifice. In January 1845, the deputation signed a contract with Giovanni Battista Carducci to design the decorations of the parapets of the boxes. This was the final straw, as Aleandri believed the decorations destroyed his concept, and he left the project. Luigi Mazzoni was appointed to oversee the construction. All this turmoil resulted in cost overruns with each condominio charged 50 scudi more than the originally stipulated price.

The Nuovo Teatro dei Signori Condomini, also called Teatro Condominale (original name of the Teatro Ventidio Basso) was inaugurated in November 1846 with Ernani for the Grande Fiera di Assegna. The performance was dedicated to the noble and most illustrious gentlemen Gonfaloniere and Anziani and to the town council and theater deputy. The second opera, *I Puritani*, was dedicated to the noble and illustrious ladies Marquess Livia Lomellini and Countess Sgariglia. The diva for the inaugural event, Anna De La Grange, reportedly was paid 10,000 lire in gold. The political situation was delicate that November at the inaugural, and there were shouts of "Abbasso" (Down with) and other offensive yelling outside the opera house, directed at the authorities.

When the theater opened, it contained only the essential structure, so work continued during the season, including reconstructing a block of stone on the side of the building, demolished when a carriage collided with it. In the beginning of the 1850s, the facade was finally completed, and a gas chandelier was added in 1867. Only in 1922 was heating installed. In December 1936, a legal decree of the council of ministers gave the municipality the power to expropriate the privately owned boxes "for reasons of public benefit." The actual handing over by the *condomini* of their share of the building and contents to the municipality took place in October 1941. The Teatro Condominale became the Teatro Comunale. In November 1971, several seismic shocks damaged the theater, forcing its closure for repairs. But when it reopened, the repairs were found inadequate and the theater closed again in 1980, not reopening for 14 years, during which time it underwent a major restoration and renovation. The opera house reopened October 15, 1994, with *Traviata*.

The Ventidio Basso is a somber-looking, neoclassical structure, faced with travertine stone. On the entrance level, the facade offers a colonnade of six Ionic stone columns that extends from the theater. Above the entrance are six engaged Corinthian columns that support an unadorned pediment. Statues of Harmony, Dance, Apollo, Minerva, Comedy, and Tragedy reside in the foyer. The 840-seat, horseshoe-shaped auditorium radiates with red and gold. It holds four tiers of boxes topped by a gallery. Gilded angels, cherubs, putti, and griffins, with lyres, horns, and harps, embellished with wreaths, flowers, and masks of Comedy and Tragedy ornament the parapets, the work of Emidio and Giorgio Paci following Carducci's designs. There are also medallions of Donizetti, Rossini, Verdi, Bellini, Goldoni, and Alfieri. The ceiling shows eight Muses, the work of Ferdinando Cicconi. The stage curtain, by Cesare Recanatini, depicts the Piazza del Popolo, above which is the escutcheon of Ascoli Piceno.

Operatic Events at the Teatro
Comunale Ventidio Basso

After the inauguration of the Ventidio Basso with *Ernani* and *I Puritani*, the operatic schedule continued in the same vein, with works of Bellini and Verdi dominating the stage, especially during the early years: *I due Foscari*, *Nabucco*, *Macbeth*, *I masnadieri*, *Attila*, *Rigoletto*, *Traviata*, and *Luisa Miller*. Donizetti operas held a prominent place in the repertory throughout the 1800s with *Parisina*, *Linda di Chamounix*, *Maria di Rohan*, *Lucia di Lammermoor*, *Lucrezia Borgia*, *La favorita*, and *Don Sebastiano* frequently on the boards. Works by minor composers such as Ricci, Pacini, Mercadante, Petrella, Apolloni, Fioravanti, Ferrari, and Moderati also graced the stage.

For the inauguration of the Ascoli-San Benedetto railroad line in 1886, the Italian Company of Comic Operetta Ciro Scognamiglio presented the program, which is worth mentioning only for the presence of Mascagni, who was on the podium. He returned a decade later to conduct his *L'amico Fritz*. Meanwhile, the theater hosted the *prima esecuzione assoluta* of native son Cellini's *Stefania* in 1892, and Franchetti came to lead his *Germania* 10 years later. Afterward, the mayor invited the maestro and the artists to a reception, but Franchetti did not appear. He was later discovered asleep in his hotel room, still attired in clothes creased and dirty from the evening before! Twenty years later, Zandonai arrived at the Ventidio Basso to conduct his *Francesca da Rimini*.

Although the repertory continued to be dominated by Italian opera, foreign works made some inroads, with French opera the first to find favor— *Faust*, *Carmen*, *Les pêcheurs de perles*, *Werther*, *Manon*, *Mignon*, *La Damnation de Faust*, *Les Huguenots*, and *L'Africaine*. Wagner was performed in 1890, with *Lohengrin* given 12 performances. The first Mozart opera did not appear until 1962, when *Die Entführung aus dem Serail* was staged. Those were the exceptions. The repertory remained exclusively popular Italian fare until the theater was closed 18 years later. The final season offered *Don Pasquale* and *Il trovatore*. The 1980 season was held in the Supercinema with *Lucia di Lammermoor* and *Andrea Chénier*. Then the seasons stopped.

After the Ventidio Basso reopened with *La traviata* in 1994, the programming continued in the same vein with *Barbiere di Siviglia*, *Bohème*, *L'elisir d'amore*, *Rigoletto*, and *Trovatore*.

But with the opera house closed for 14 years, the *appassionati* lost interest and the audience was not well informed, applauding at everything, even in inappropriate places. Nevertheless, there were exceptions in the traditional fare. In commemoration of the 150th anniversary season, Cornacchioli's *Diana Schernita* and Cimarosa's *I Traci amanti*, along with *Cenerentola*, were offered. During the 1998 season, the original *opèra comique* version of *Carmen* was staged but caused confusion because of the spoken French dialogue. As the 20th century came to a close, Cimarosa's *Il maestro di Cappella* was performed, along with *Tosca*, *Lucia di Lammermoor*, and *Madama Butterfly* among others. With the arrival of the 21st century, the popular fare continued. The theater is run by the Assessorato alla Cultura. Recent productions included *La traviata* and *Don Giovanni*.

Practical Information

Teatro Comunale Ventidio Basso, via del Trivio 44, Ascoli Piceno; tel. 39 0736 244 970; www.comune.ascoli-piceno.it.

The season takes place during November and December with two operas and three performances of each, one of which is reserved for students.

∿

TWENTY-ONE

Opera Barga Festival, Barga

Opera Barga Festival came into existence in 1967 in the medieval city of Barga, near Lucca. Founded by Peter and Gillian Hunt, the festival is characterized by the unearthing of operas from the baroque era, along with showcasing modern and contemporary works. With the reopening of the 289-seat Teatro dei Differenti, which dates from the late 1700s and was closed in 1982 for restoration, the festival found a perfect venue for its programming. The small theater size also made it an ideal space for young singers' voices, who fill the roles.

Over the years, the festival has staged more than 40 operas, many given their first hearing in modern times. The schedule sometimes juxtaposes a baroque opera with a contemporary work, for example, Scarlatti's *La caduta dei Decemviri* with Berio's *A-Ronne*. Vivaldi operas play an important role, with *Tito Manlio*, *Orlando*, and *Arsilda, regina di Ponto* having been offered. Other works include Gruber's *Frankenstein*, Händel's *Agrippina*, Melani's *Il potestà di Colognole*, and Kagel's *The Tribune*.

Practical Information

Opera Barga Festival, Teatro dei Differenti, Piazza Angelio 8, 55051 Barga, Lucca; tel. 39 0583 723250, fax 39 0583 723 250; www.barganews.com/operabarga.

The festival takes place in July and offers two to three operas with two to three performances of each.

TWENTY-TWO

~

Teatro Comunale, Bologna

The oldest theater in Bologna, Teatro del Pubblico, also known as Teatro della Sala, opened in 1581 in the Palazzo del Podestà. During the second decade of the 1600s, it offered some of the earliest documented operas in the city, Giacobbi's *L'Andromeda*, Peri's *Euridice*, and Campeggi's *Reno sacrificante*. During the first half of the 1700s, the Pubblico fell into decline and put on only an occasional opera by Scarlatti and Galuppi, among others. It primarily hosted musical shows, intermezzi, and balls but also the type of entertainment that one saw on a public piazza: pallone, acrobats, and tightrope walkers, which prompted one critic to call the theater "nothing more than a vulgar politeama of the third order, unworthy to be located in the historic, austere, and noble Podestà Palace." Adding to the bad reputation was the quality of the public that frequented it. As Corrado Ricci wrote in *Il Teatri di Bologna*, Bologna 1888, "In the auditorium . . . are mainly students desirous to make noise and execute every type of impropriety, and common people eager for vulgarity and buffoonery." The situation had so deteriorated that in 1746, during some musical intermezzi, there was such a crowd and so much obscenity that the theater had to be temporarily shut. Despite the public's increasing desertion of the theater, especially the "quality public" who crowded into the competing theaters, it stayed open until 1765, when it became structurally unstable and was demolished.

The Teatro Formagliari was inaugurated in 1636. Although privately owned, it was open to the public. Located on a small street then called Ponte di Ferro (today's via Farini), the Formagliari hosted operas until 1802, when a fire reduced it to ashes. The prestige of the Formagliari had begun to decline, however, only a couple of decades after it opened, because in 1651 a new theater, the Teatro di Malvezzi, was inaugurated. Located next to the church of San Sigismondo, the new theater became the favorite gathering place for the aristocracy. It was illuminated by candles and decorated with gold and pictures. Although the Malvezzi was enlarged and renovated in 1697, it was always sold out, and those excluded from the theater caused disturbances. Performances were frequently repeated because of the public's enthusiasm. There is a curious anecdote about a nun who so desperately wanted to see a performance of *Pirro* at the Malvezzi in 1719 that she fled her convent in disguise and managed to enter the theater, where no one spotted her all evening. When the performance was over, she knew punishment awaited her if she returned to the convent. She wandered about all night and then headed to Lugo, where she entered another convent, staying there 16 years before deciding to return to her original one in Bologna!

The first Gluck opera in Bologna, *Demofoonte*, was performed in the Teatro Marsigli-Rossi in 1744. Active from at least 1710 with Paisiello composing 24 operas for the theater, including *Il Cairlone*, the Marsigli-Rossi presented other popular composers of the time, such as Galuppi, Piccinni, Jommelli, Scarlatti, Lotti, Hasse, Vivaldi, and Traetta

During the night of February 19, 1745, fire deprived the city of the Malvezzi, which became the major catalyst for construction of a new public theater, the Nuovo Teatro Pubblico (the original name of the Teatro Comunale) that would place Bologna alongside the other major Italian cities that boasted grand opera houses during the 1700s, such as Naples, Rome, and Turin. But unlike those and other major theaters that arose from royal decrees or noble associations, Bologna's new opera house was constructed by a *Comune cittadino* (citizen's municipality) and was the first major opera house owned by the municipality. It should be noted, however, that this citizen's municipality originated from a group of nobility, called *Reggimento di Camera*. The city estimated the construction costs at 20,000 scudi, but the final expense came to 36,000 scudi more, "to satisfy all the contractual debts and existing laws." This led to the selling of 35 of the 99 boxes for private use and permanent ownership, but these box holders differed from those at other theaters. They did not actually own their boxes and were called *prelazionisti*, not *palchettisti*, which meant they had only the right of preemption. It was a type of rent in perpetuity, conceding to the purchaser "the advantage to always have for himself and his family the full, private use of the preselected box . . . but only for heroic works or staged *drammi in musica.*" The *prelazionisti* also had to contribute additional funds for these two types of works, which led to many legal disputes over the years. The vagueness of the contract made it difficult at times to determine how to categorize a particular work. Finally in

1917, with a performance of *Rondine* (because no one could decide if Puccini's opera was a *drammi in musica* or not), the "right of preemption" was limited to only priority in acquiring the box and a certain discount on the price of the rent.

Antonio Galli Bibiena received the commission from the Bologna senate in January 1756 to construct the new theater. The site selected was known as "guasto" (damaged) because it held the ruins of the celebrated Renaissance residence of Bentivoglio, destroyed by a rebellious people in 1507. Located on via San Donato, today via Zamboni, it was purchased in March 1756 from the Marquis Guido Bentivoglio for 17,500 Bolognese lire. The foundation was laid the following month by Bibiena's master builder, Michelangelo Galletti, but controversy arose immediately as to the security of the installation of the perimeter walls and climbed to epic proportions, fueled by the hostility and jealousy of Francesco Algarotti and two prominent local architects, Carlo Francesco Dotti and Alfonso Torreggiani, all of whom lost the competition to design the new opera house. Algarotti dissected Bibiena's designs point by point in his *Saggio sopra l'opera in musica*, from his choice of masonry instead of wood to the errors of the dimensions and proportions of the bell-shaped auditorium. Bibiena defended his use of masonry as the only way to prevent the "deadly danger of fire" and the bell shape because it rendered a "well-suited, expansive sound." Nonetheless, for economic reasons, he was required to reduce and modify his original plans. The facade as originally conceived, however, was not finished until 1935/36, with Umberto Ricci executing the work, which above the portico surrounding the building involved adding tympana above the corner windows and pilasters in the space between the windows. In the auditorium, the decorations on the parapets of the four box tiers were richer and more varied on Bibiena's original drawings, including ashlar on the first level, a more impressive stage curtain, a ceiling decorated as though it were open to the sky, and a proscenium arch with four engaged Corinthian columns ornamented with statues in niches. Only two columns, with a pair of statues representing Music and Dance by Antonio Schiassi, were actually completed.

The Nuovo Teatro Pubblico was inaugurated May 14, 1763, with Gluck's *Il trionfo di Clelia*, a work especially written for the occasion. Bibiena constructed the elaborate sets. A Jesuit priest described the event in his diary: "If one said that for this opera, all of Bologna was enthusiastic and fanatic, it would not say enough. Just imagining the number of foreigners is incredible. . . . At seven in the evening the piazza in front of the theater was already filled to capacity. The door [to the opera house] although rather grand and well fortified, was having difficulty withstanding the onslaught of those who were crowding the entrance to get a good seat. Voices, yelling, blows, turmoil without end." Many technical services were lacking when the Nuovo Teatro Pubblico opened, limiting the production of *dramma per musica*. Primarily drama, games, and mask balls were hosted. Only when the Teatro del Corso opened in 1805, giving the Pubblico competition, did it complete its facilities.

The first major restoration took place between 1818 and 1820 under the direction of the town architect Giuseppe Tubertini and included, among other things, Mauro Berti reconstructing, painting, and decorating the ceiling, which was in a precarious state, and the portrait painter Pietro Fancelli painting the allegories of Music, Poetry, Painting, and History. Carlo Parmeggiani executed further modifications between 1853 and 1854, with gold and red becoming the primary colors in the auditorium. Napoleone Angiolini was commissioned to design the curtain, which depicted the apotheosis of Felsina: Felsina ascends to Apollo's royal palace, introduced to the god by Music, Poetry, and Painting with the Muses and the Seasons in attendance. In November 1931, fire destroyed the stage area and curtain of the theater. After reconstruction work by Armando Villa and the completion of the facade, the theater reopened November 14, 1935, with *Norma*.

The opera house is encircled by an ocher-colored portico on the ground level that contrasts with the off-white upper level, punctuated with arched windows. A white marble bust of native son Ottorino Respighi and bronze reliefs of Verdi and Wagner reside in the vestibule. The 1,034-seat, ivory, gold, and sea-green auditorium, once bell shape but now horseshoe shape, offers four box tiers crowned by a small balcony and a center royal box, in magnificent splendor. The *effigie* (symbol of Bologna) is displayed on the valance above the gold-fringed, green stage curtain. The hallmark balustrade design of Bibiena defines the parapets on all four tiers, with each box appearing to have its own, individual balcony. Gilded medallions, including Metastasio, Maffel, Sophocles, and Goldoni; golden masks of Comedy and Tragedy; and music motifs adorn the proscenium arch. Allegorical figures swirl around the crystal chandelier suspended from the ceiling.

Operatic Events at the Teatro Comunale

Despite the praise critics gave the sets and designs of Gluck's inaugural opera *Il trionfo di Clelia*, they called the discordant music of the opera dull. Nevertheless, the opera enjoyed 28 performances during May and June of 1763 and

Gluck operas remained in the repertory, including *Orfeo ed Euridice* and *Alceste*. During these last decades of the 1700s, several of the operas were *prime esecuzione assolute*, including Sciroli's *Alessandro nell'Indie*, Mysliweczek's *La nitteti*, Manfredini's *Armida*, and Jommelli's *Ezio*. With the dawn of a new century, the operas of Nasolini, Bianchi, Nicolini, and Zingarelli appeared, and as the decade progressed, Paisiello, Paër, Mayr, and Cimarosa were in evidence. What is of note is the absence of works by Cherubini, Spontini, and Mozart during this time.

In 1814 Rossini exploded onto the scene, quickly dominating the stage with 20 works between 1814 and 1833, including *Tancredi, Aureliano in Palmira, La donna del lago, Mosè in Egitto, Sigismondo, Zelmira, Torvaldo e Dorliska, Eduardo e Cristina,* and *Matilde di Chabran*. By the mid-1830s, Donizetti had become a strong presence, usurping Rossini's dominant position with his *Parisina, Belisario, Marino Faliero, Torquato Tasso, Gemma di Vergy, Roberto Devereux, Maria Padilla, Il campanello, Lucrezia Borgia, La favorita, Lucia di Lammermoor,* and *Poliuto*. Seven of Bellini's 10 operas received their Bologna premiere between 1830 and 1837. The minor composers of the era, Farinelli, Coccia, Generali, Pacini, Mercadante, and Pavesi, were heard alongside the greats. And Meyerbeer's Italian operas graced the stage, beginning in 1820 with his French ones, reaching Bologna in the mid-1840s. Other French operas included Auber's *La Muette de Portici*. In 1843 Verdi eclipsed them all with 32 performances of *Nabucco (Nabucodonosor)* followed by 30 of *Ernani*. First performances in Bologna of *I due Foscari, I Lombardi, I masnadieri, Macbeth,* and *Luisa Miller* followed in quick succession, interspersed with Campana's *Mazeppa*, Ricci's *Chi dura vince*, Coppola's *La pazza per amore*, Mazza's *La prova di un'opera seria*, and Cortesi's *Etra L'astrologa*. In 1867 just a few months after its world premiere in Paris, *Don Carlos* was staged to tremendous acclaim.

Angelo Mariani arrived in 1860 to lead the Comunale, and 11 years later he introduced Wagner's operas to Italy. This is how Enrico Panzacchi described the Italian premiere of *Lohengrin* on November 1, 1871: "The Teatro Comunale towards eight in the evening filled up quickly with people serious and solemn. Many had under their arm a large book. Even the ladies entered their boxes and sat down in silence with a certain composed air and solemn expectation. . . . Orchestra seats, benches, boxes, stage boxes all filled; everyone was at his post; almost all the men in white tie and tails, the ladies in elegant evening gowns; the auditorium sounded like the deep buzz of a gigantic beehive. Every once in a while from the top gallery came a very rude grumble, a laugh, a shout, 'viva Verdi, viva Rossini!' but it only lasted a moment." The *Gazzetta dell'Emilia* chronicled the evening with the following: "The performance began at eight o'clock sharp. The prelude was listened to attentively at the beginning and enthusiastically at the end. There was prolonged applause. The first act began. The audience was becoming more captivated with the opera. Enthusiasm reached its peak with the arrival of Lohengrin. The audience requested an encore, but it was not granted. It could not be granted: the dramatic effect would have been lost. . . . The exuberance fell in the second act while the public listened to the duets of Telramund with Ortrud and then with Elsa for more than a half hour, and signs of disapproval were demonstrated in an unbecoming manner. . . . The act concluded well enough when the music became more flowing. The excitement fell a bit during the love duet of the third act because the public expected a 'melody' which never came. . . . But in the finale the patrons warmly received the music and the stage action. When the curtain fell, the public gave their verdict. The majority applauded, but an imperceptible minority disapproved, whistling in a rude manner that was enough to describe the vulgarity of those who did it." The success was even more striking considering that the audience was almost all bourgeoisie from Bologna and intellectuals, musicians, critics, and impresarios from other Italian cities. As Enrico Bottrigari wrote in *Cronaca di Bologna,* "In the choice and preference that one gives to German operas and those which are imitations of it, to be able to say that Bologna, after Paris, had the honor to produce, on its own stage, for the first time in Italy, this novelty, carries much pride." The opera was repeated 18 times and every performance met with success. Verdi attended the November 19 performance but wanted to go unrecognized. Nevertheless, news of his presence spread rapidly and there were numerous shouts of "Long live Verdi." The maestro, however, did not present himself to thank the public but listened to the opera, making numerous annotations on the score that he had brought with him. Bologna established itself as a Wagner stronghold with the Italian premieres of *Tannhäuser, Rienzi* (Wagner watched from a box), and *Der fliegende Holländer* following. There were also productions of the Ring Cycle and *Tristan und Isolde.*

In the fall of 1894, a 27-year-old Arturo Toscanini arrived at the Comunale, leading the Bologna premieres of *Falstaff* and *Cristoforo Colombo* and the *prima esecuzione assoluta* of Canti's *Savitri.* Unlike in other Italian cities, *Falstaff* was not as immediately accepted or acclaimed, but Toscanini's interpretations were clear, impeccable, and flawless. Two years later, Toscanini led two Puccini works, *Bohème* and *Le villi.* He returned to Bologna in 1904 for a couple of seasons, conducting Wagner along with *Dinorah, Butterfly,* and the *prima esecuzione assoluta* of Gnecchi's *Cassandra*. Despite the outbreak of World War I, the 1914/15 opera season took place, with *Barbiere di Siviglia*, *L'Africaine*, *Loreley*, and Fleres's *L'elisir di vita* on the boards. Short opera seasons continued during the war with primarily popular operas of Donizetti, Rossini, and Puccini.

Respighi was born in Bologna, so the Comunale promoted his operas, staging the world premiere of *Semirama* in November 1910 and the Italian premiere of *La campana sommersa*, along with *La fiamma*, *Maria Egiziaca*, *Belfagor*, and *Lucrezia Romana*. Of note was the 1924 season with the return of Toscanini conducting Boïto's *Nerone* with a stellar cast: Aureliano Pertile, Maria Carena, Luisa Bertana, Benvenuto Franci, and Marcello Journet. *La favorita*, Charpentier's *Louise*, *Andrea Chénier*, and *Das Rheingold* were also on the schedule. The repertory between the wars offered mainly the popular operas of Verdi and Puccini, interspersed with lesser-known ones: Certani's *Floriana*, Mascagni's *Isabeau*, Alfano's *Risurrezione*, Mascagni's *Nerone*, Gandino's *Imelda*, Zandonai's *La farsa amorosa*, Mulé's *La monacella della fontana*, and the world premiere of Pratella's *Fabiano* in 1939. World-class artists such as Beniamino Gigli, Giacomo Laura-Volpi, Toti dal Monte, and Ezio Pinza appeared at the Comunale.

At the onset of World War II, the theater maintained a full opera season, including celebrating the 150th anniversary of Rossini's birth with *Il conte Ory*. As the war progressed, the seasons diminished, with only one opera, *Il matrimonio segreto*, in 1944. With the conclusion of hostilities, seven operas were again on the boards by 1947, including both popular fare and unusual ones, *Fidelio*, *Pelléas et Mélisande*, and *Belfagor*. From the 1960s to the early 1990s, noteworthy was the unearthing of forgotten works of Verdi, Bellini, Rossini, and Donizetti—including *I due Foscari*, *Beatrice di Tenda*, *La donna del lago*, *Parisina*, *La favorita*, *Mosè*, *Attila*, *Giovanna d'Arco*, and *I Lombardi*— and performance of 20th-century operas *Doktor Faust*, *Turn of the Screw*, *Histoire du Soldat*, *Pollicino*, *Wozzeck*, *La notte di un nevrastenico*, and *Věc Makropulos* (The Makropoulos Affair) and early works *Armide*, *L'incoronazione di Poppea*, *Serse*, Cimarosa's *Amor rende sagace*, Paisiello's *L'amor contrastato*, and *La serva padrona*. In 1989 the first performance in modern times of Paër's *Achille* took place, and the 1990s witnessed two *prime rappresentazioni assolute*, Testi's *La brocca rotta* and Vacchi's *Il viaggio*.

The Comunale had been one of the more adventurous opera houses in Italy, in terms of repertory and production style, until a severe financial crisis required more traditional fare in its schedule. As the financial situation stabilized, the pioneering spirit returned. Recently, two Respighi operas never staged at the Comunale were brought to light, *Re Enzo* and *La bella dormente nel bosco*. Musicals from the United States are regularly offered, and in 2004 one from South Africa called *African Footprints* was presented. Around half of the schedule is works by Rossini, Donizetti, Bellini, and Verdi. A recent season opened with Beethoven's *Leonora* and included *Elisabetta, regina d'Inghilterra*, *Porgy and Bess*, and *El retablo de Maese Pedro*, along with popular Italian fare such as *Don Pasquale*, *Sonnambula*, *Trovatore*, and *Macbeth*.

Practical Information

Teatro Comunale, largo Respighi 1, 40126 Bologna; tel. 39 051 617 4299, fax 39 051 529 995; www.comunalebologna.it.

The "official" season, which runs from November to June, offers eight operas with six to seven performances of each. There is a preseason of usually two operas with three to six performances of each. Stay at the prestigious Grand Hotel Baglioni, via Indipendenza 8, 40121 Bologna; tel. 051 22 54 45, fax 051 23 48 40; www.baglionihotel.com/hotel_bologna. The luxurious Baglioni is a 10-minute walk from the opera house. Visit the Civico Museo Bibliografico Musicale, piazza Rossini 2, tel. 221117, which contains collections of incunabula, antique musical editions, autographed scores of Monteverdi, Mozart, and Rossini; Teatro Duse, via Cartoleria 42, tel. 231836; and the Aldrovandi Mazzacorati Villa, via Toscana 19, which was built in 1770 by architect Francesco Tadolini and houses a beautiful baroque theater.

TWENTY-THREE

Teatro Verdi, Busseto

A small theater existed in the 2nd-century Rocca (fortress) where music and drama companies of a certain level performed. As a youth, Verdi had conducted *Il barbiere di Siviglia* at the theater. Because this was the town where Verdi was born and grew up, there was a proposal in 1845 to construct a theater in his honor, but the suggestion was not acted upon. Notwithstanding Verdi's initially favorable opinion toward the proposal, his attitude later turned into grand indignation because the town used his name before they even received permission for the construction and also assumed he would compose an opera for the inaugural in which the famous soprano Erminia Frezzolini and tenor Antonio Poggi would sing gratis.

The idea for the theater was relaunched in 1856 when the municipality acquired the Rocca. Verdi continued his strenuous opposition, writing to a dear Busseto friend, "I have always demonstrated to be against the construction of the theater which was too expensive and would be useless in the future." He was especially disconcerted when he learned that the mayor claimed it was to be constructed only for Verdi at the maestro's insistence and promises. Nevertheless, the project was entrusted to Pier Luigi Montecchini, who was requested to make the theater the most splendid and luxurious possible but also to preserve a major part of the walls and preexisting materials of the fortress. His plans were approved in June 1857 and Giovanni Sivelli was contracted for the construction, which lasted from 1856 to 1868. Verdi remained opposed to the theater, not wanting it dedicated to him, but with the intercession of his friend Carrara, in the end he agreed to it. At the inauguration on August 15, 1868, all the ladies dressed in green (*verdi*) and all the men wore green ties to honor the maestro. Verdi was conspicuously absent, but two of his operas graced the stage, *Ballo in maschera* and *Rigoletto*.

The music critic of the *Gazzetta di Parma* described the inauguration very favorably, both regarding the performances and the building itself.

The theater is fully integrated with the antique structure, with a small portico on the ground level. On the steps that lead to the orchestra level, there is a large bust of Verdi by Giovanni Duprè. The 300-seat, red, ivory, and gold, horseshoe-shaped auditorium offers two box tiers topped by a balcony and a royal center box. Giuseppe Baisi and Alessandro Malpeli executed the decorations of gilded stucco with Renaissance themes. There are images of musicians in plaster. Medallions with figures of Comedy, Tragedy, Melodrama, and Romantic Drama embellish the ceiling, the work of Isacco Gioacchino Levi.

Since its opening, the theater has staged almost all of Verdi's operas. Toscanini conducted opera seasons there in 1913 and 1926. Closed for restoration work to conform to building safety codes, the Verdi reopened January 27, 2005, the anniversary of his death, with *Trovatore*. Performances of *Falstaff* followed in October, Verdi's month of birth. Performances of *Traviata* took place outdoors during July in the Campo di San Maria degli Angeli, next to the church where Verdi played the organ as a child.

Practical Information

Teatro Verdi, piazza Verdi 10, 43011 Busseto; tel. 39 0524 931 016; www.bus setolive.com.

The two to three opera productions take place in the Verdi in January and October, with 4 to 5 performances, outdoors in the summer. Visit Casa Barezzi, via Roma 119; tel. 931 117. Antonio Barezzi was Verdi's benefactor, and Verdi married Barezzi's daughter, Margherita. The original furnishings and the piano, acquired around 1835, on which Verdi composed *I due Foscari* are on display. The salon is the home of the Association of Friends of Verdi. The house where Verdi was born (on the second floor) is just outside Busseto in Roncole (tel. 97450). A modest abode, it has been preserved exactly as it was when he lived there. A plaque on the facade recalls that the marquises of Pallavicino, who were the owners of the property, wanted it to remain "as it was." Pietro Cemellati restored it for the centennial of Verdi's death. Visit Villa Sant'Agata, which Verdi had purchased in 1848 and where he lived beginning in 1851. Parts of the villa are open to the public, including Verdi's apartment where one can see the piano Verdi used to compose the operas *Rigoletto* through *Aida* and artifacts and memorabilia of his life and works. Visit Teatro di Villa Pallavicino, an open-air theater where in 2002 *Un ballo in maschera* and *Il trovatore* were performed.

TWENTY-FOUR

Teatro Marrucino, Chieti

At the end of the 18th century, the first theater, Larghetto Teatro Vecchio, was built. Situated on the small square behind where a bank is located today, it offered seats for 200 between three tiers of boxes and a gallery. Only the facade remains. There were a couple of other small theaters in the town, one built by a local businessman and another by a citizen. By the dawn of the 19th century, the city had outgrown these theaters, so there was a great need for a proper theater, which the municipality agreed to build.

The new structure was constructed between 1814 and 1818 on the perimeter walls of a desecrated church. The project was under the direction of Eugenio Michitelli. On January 11, 1818, *La Cenerentola* inaugurated the Real Teatro San Ferdinando, so named in homage to Ferdinand I of Bourbon, king of Naples and of the two Sicilies. Because it was built on church property, the Monsignore Joshua Maria Saggese could demand its destruction, according to the law at the time, which he did in 1851. But influential citizens successfully banded together to prevent the demolition. When Italy was united in 1861, the theater was renamed Teatro Marrucino.

Luigi Daretti oversaw the restoration of 1872, which also witnessed the addition of a top gallery with its own staircase. At the same time, a fourth tier of boxes was added and the auditorium became semicircular, under the careful direction of Giovanni Vecchi and Enrico Santuccione. In 1874 Luigi Samoggia decorated the ceiling, where in the center was a rose carved from wood surrounded by garlands of flowers. Gold medallions with images of Goldoni, Pergolesi, Paisiello, Rossini, Verdi, Shakespeare, Goethe, Alfieri, and allegorical female figures relating to music and theater also embellished the space. The following year saw the addition of a new stage curtain by Giovanni Ponticelli, with a scene of *Caio Asino Pollione and His Triumph*.

The opera house kept up its illustrious tradition until World War II, when it began declining, and was closed in 1950. Fifteen years passed until a project by Renzo Mancini and Nicola Battaglini was finally approved in November 1965. During the restoration, a huge chandelier was hung in the auditorium. The restored theater opened December 11, 1972, to the overture to *La Cenerentola*, the same opera that inaugurated the building in 1818. But only the overture was played, as it was a gala concert and not opera that reopened this opera house.

There are 59 boxes distributed among the four tiers of the auditorium, in addition to 4 proscenium boxes. The orchestra has 166 seats and the gallery 120. On each of the five tiers are clusters of three glass globe lights that illuminate the space, along with a chandelier. Ornamental designs embellish the parapets, contrasting with the plush red of the seating.

Operatic Events at the Teatro Marrucino

The world premieres of five operas by native son Persiani took place at the theater. The first three, *Manfredi di Svevia*, *Malek Adel*, and *Il prigioniero di Palermo*, were between 1855 and 1861 when it was still the San Ferdinanado, and the last two, *Amore e patria* and *L'assedio di Cesarea*, were in 1878 and 1879. (Persiani's final opera, *Bianco di Belmonte*, was never performed.) It also hosted the first performance of D'Annuzio's *La Figlia di Iorio* in June 1904. One of the most famous singers to perform there was the Italian bass Nicola Rossi Lemeni. In 1997 it was named a *Teatro di tradizione*. With a new system of management in place that has allowed cooperation with other Italian opera houses as well as those abroad, the repertory has grown to five operas and four operettas. The schedule concentrates on pieces that work well in a small space. Recent operas include *La traviata*, *Matrimonio segreto*, *Mefistofele*, *Acis e Galatea*, and *Il viaggio a Reims*. Counted among the operettas are *Die lustige Witwe* and *Il paese dei campanelli*.

Practical Information

Teatro Marrucino (Teatro Lirico d'Abruzzo), via C. de Lollis 10, 66100 Chieti; tel. 39 0871 320 007, fax 39 0871 322 379; www.teatromarrucino.it.

The season runs from October to May and offers five operas with two to five performances of each and four operettas with one performance of each. The Harris Hotel, via P.A. Valignani 219, 66100 Chieti; tel. 0871 321 555, fax 0871 321 781, is a 15-minute walk from the theater. The more modest Albergo Abruzzi, via Asinio Herio 20, 66100 Chieti; tel. 0871 41940, fax 0871 4960, is 5 minutes from the theater.

TWENTY-FIVE

~

Teatro dell'Aquila, Fermo

During the 1700s, a wooden theater had been built in the Palazzo dei Priori, but fire claimed it in 1774. It was immediately decided to construct a new theater in a central location, along the steep slope that connects the Piazza del Popolo to the Girfalco. Construction began in 1780 and lasted a decade. On September 26, 1790, the Teatro dell'Aquila was inaugurated with an oratorio, *La morte di Abele*, composed by Giordani (also known as Giordaniello), director of the Cappella Musicale Metropolitana. The architect was Cosimo Morelli, and decorations were executed by Giuseppe Lucatelli. The following year, Giordani's *La distruzione di Gerusalemme* graced the stage. By Carnival 1796, the theater hosted a full roster of activities.

At the dawn of the 1800s, the theater no longer pleased and was too small. Architect Lucatelli was planning to add more boxes when a fire in January 1826 damaged one side of the auditorium. During repairs to the fire-damaged auditorium, 19 boxes were added and the orchestra section was graded to improve sight lines. Since Lucatelli's decorations were lost in the fire, the academies of San Luca suggested that Luigi Cochetti be entrusted with the task. He repainted the ceiling and the curtain. Biagio Berglioni embellished the parapets. For the reopening in 1830, Alessandro Sanquirico painted the impressive backcloth, which showed a Greek-Roman palace surrounded by woods.

For almost two centuries, the Aquila played a central role in the cultural, recreational, and social activities of the city. Then it was closed in 1986 for a restoration that lasted a little more than a decade. Gae Aulenti was responsible for the project. The opera house reopened in 1997 with a concert by the Orchestra Filarmonica of Teatro alla Scala with Wolfgang Sawallisch on the podium.

With the completion of the restoration, opera once again graced the stage. The opera season is short. Usually, two popular Italian operas are on the boards, with an occasional novelty. Among its offerings have been *La Cenerentola*, *La bohème*, and *Rigoletto*. Counted among the novelties has been *L'eroismo ridicolo*. The theater coproduces with Teatro Pergolesi in Jesi. Recent operas include *Andrea Chénier* and *L'elisir d'amore*.

The 650-seat Teatro dell'Aquila offers an elliptical auditorium with four box tiers topped by a gallery. Gilded stucco designs embellish the parapets, and a complex mythological scene that includes Apollo and the Muses decorates the ceiling.

Practical Information

Teatro dell'Aquila, via Mazzini 4, Fermo; tel. 39 0734 284 295, fax 39 0734 28433; www.fermo.net/teatro.

The season takes place during November, offering two operas with two performances of each.

TWENTY-SIX

~

Teatro Comunale, Ferrara

The first permanent court theater was inaugurated in 1531 but survived only a year. Located on the first floor of the Palazzo Ducale, in front of the bishop's palace, it was constructed under the supervision of Ariosto. Next, some local noble families constructed theaters. Enzo Bentivoglio hired Giambattista Aleotti to build the Teatro degli Intrepidi, which was subsequently renamed Teatro degli Obizzi and inaugurated in 1605. Bentivoglio was also instrumental in the erection of the Teatro della Sala Grande in 1610. A huge space holding around 4,000, it was situated on the west side of the Palazzo Ducale, between via Cortevecchia and the former via Rotta. The Teatro Bonacossi opened in 1662 and presented regular programs during both carnival and *fiera* seasons. Located near the church of Santo Stefano in via del turco, the Bonacossi was subsequently renamed Teatro Ristori and served as a movie theater. In 1692 Count Scroffa constructed the Teatro Scroffa, which lasted until the beginning of the 1970s, when it was demolished to widen the via Ponte Reno.

Since all the theaters in the city were privately owned by noble families and had limited seating capacity, in 1773 Cardinal Borghese, the papal envoy to Ferrera, wanted to build a new, elegant public theater with a large number of seats. He requested Cosimo Morelli to make drawings. Morelli proposed a bell-shaped curve, instead of the customary elliptical shape, but the funds necessary for construction did not materialize and the task of building the theater was left to Borghese's successor, Cardinal Carafa. Carafa entrusted the project to Giuseppe Campana, who chose a central location in the city and expropriated the property. Construction began quickly and progressed rapidly. Unfortunately for Carafa, some of the houses

152

belonged to the Camera Apostolica, which was not pleased with this turn of events and forced Carafa to leave Ferrara in great haste. A new legate, Cardinal Spinelli, arrived from Rome in November 1786, and despite only the roof missing from the new theater, stopped the construction. He opened an inquest into Campana's work and found technical irregularities and lack of administrative orders. The building was destroyed. Spinelli then requested advice from two noted architects, Morelli and Giuseppe Piermarini, while entrusting the project to two local architects, Antonio Foschini and Marchelli. In November 1790, approval was received and constructed began, which lasted until 1797. Foschini was subsequently named director of the project, and Morelli proposed numerous modifications. Then a violent, public argument broke out between the two architects over the curve of the auditorium. Both architects wanted elliptical shapes but different types of ellipses! Advice was requested from Piermarini and Simeone Stratico, as well as the academies in Bologna and Parma. The solution combined the best qualities of each in the final shape. Serafino Barozzi was responsible for the interior decorations, and he painted the ceiling with Santi and Zuliani.

Portogallo's *Gli Orazi e i Curiazi* inaugurated the Teatro Comunale on September 2, 1798. But less than three decades later, the building was in need of restoration. Between 1825 and 1826, Giovanni Tosi reconstructed the building while Angelo Monticelli redid the decorations and ceiling. The theater was again redecorated in 1850, and that is the appearance of the opera house today. An orchestra pit was finally created in 1928, and between 1935 and 1937 the secret staircase cardinals took from the passageway of the theater directly to the private rooms of the archbishop was eliminated. During World War II, German troops occupied the theater complex and left it in ruins. The building was only occasionally opened during the early part of the 1950s, mainly for festivals and masked balls, before it was declared unsafe in 1956 and closed. Restoration work took place between 1962 and 1964 under the careful eye of architect Savonuzzi and included the recovery of the decorations of the parapets, which had been painted over, and allowed the theater to be once again opened to the public. The restoration work performed between 1987 and 1989, under the direction of Giulio Zappaterra, was necessitated by new fire and safety codes and the need to restore areas neglected during the restoration of the early 1960s.

The mustard-hued stucco building follows the parallel principle of eurythmic architecture. A seven-arch colonnade of rusticated stone identifies the lower level, above which are rectangular windows crowned with tympanum and smaller square windows. Stores and shops, as was typical of public buildings in the 1800s, are part of the structure. The 890-seat, elliptical, raspberry, gold, and cream auditorium has five tiers. The parapet of each tier displays a different Romantic type of decoration. The first alludes to Music and Dance with flowers, ornamental designs, and the Sphinx; the second suggests Commerce and Agriculture with caducei, ears of corn, fruit, seahorses, and seaweed; the third recalls Poetry with birds, flowers, lyre, and chimera; the fourth is dedicated to Science and the virtues of man, with the insignia of Prudence, Justice, Architecture, and Medicine; the fifth recognizes Drama, Tragedy, and Comedy, with crests of helmets, arms, and shields. The historic curtain by Francesco Migliari depicted an episode from *Orlando furioso*: the delivery of shields to Rinaldo with a view of Ferrera in the background. The ceiling displays four scenes from the life of Julius Caesar.

Operatic Events at the Teatro Comunale

Although Ferrara's theatrical history dates back a few centuries to a performance of *Ercole d'Este*, during the 20th century it opened only intermittently, hosting primarily grand festivals and masked balls. The birth of the Ferrara Musica under Mayor Roberto Soffritti in 1988, which is now united with the Teatro Comunale, has allowed regular opera seasons in collaboration with other theaters in Emilia Romagna. The Ferrara Musica unearthed forgotten and obscure works from the past, such as *Le astuzie femminili*, *Li zite 'n galera*, and *Les indes Galantes*; presented contemporary pieces such as Corghi's *Divara*, Adams's *Death of Klinghoffer*, and Bartók's *A Kékszakállú herceg vára* (Duke Bluebeard's Castle); collaborated with German theaters for *Der fliegende Holländer* and Ligeti's *Le grand macabre*; and offered the usual popular fare of Verdi and Puccini, including *Turandot*, *Un ballo in maschera*, *La bohème*, *Traviata*, *I vespri siciliani*, and *Macbeth*. Recent repertory includes *Andrea Chénier*, *Tancredi*, *Pikovaya Dama* (Queen of Spades), *Pêcheurs de perles*, *Tancredi*, and *Les contes d'Hoffmann*. The theater itself has no internal structure: no permanent orchestra, chorus, singers, sets, or costumes. Orchestras from the collaborating theaters and the Orchestra Città di Ferrera play the operas. The only well-known person with lasting ties to the theater is the conductor, Claudio Abbado, who usually leads an opera each season, which has often been one of Mozart's, including *Le nozze di Figaro*, *Don Giovanni*, and *Così fan tutte*

Practical Information

Teatro Comunale, corso Martiri della Libertà 5, 44100 Ferrara; tel. 39 0532 202 312, fax 39 0532 247 353; www.teatrocomunaleferrara.it.

The season runs from January or February to April or May, offering four productions with two performances of each. Stay at the Astra Hotel, Viale Cavour, 55, 44100 Ferrara; tel. 0532 206 088, fax 0532 247 002. It is a 5-minute walk from the theater.

TWENTY-SEVEN

Teatro Magnani, Fidenza

The first theater in the city was a very small wooden building, located in the vicinity of an old seminary. It hosted local dramatic productions and traveling troupes that offered farces such as *Il bugiardo veritiero* and *Il matrimonio di un morto*. In 1812 an association of wealthy citizens and civil servants joined forces to give the city a theater, located in the area of the ruined church of San Francesco, which today is piazza Verdi. Construction based on the designs of architect Nicola Bettoli began. Soon the building structure was almost completed, but work had to be stopped for lack of funds. Construction did not begin again until 1831, but the association again found the financial burden too much and decided to hand over the building to the municipality. The municipality was happy to receive it, but a decree in October 1838 by Marie Louise, duchess of Parma, who had authority over Fidenza, prohibited the transfer, because "to put in operation the theater and perform all the conditions that entails would impose too much of an expense for the municipality and be much higher than it would be able to sustain in the present economic climate." The result was that the structure was left to deteriorate. The roof collapsed during a violent storm in 1835. Finally, in March 1848, the municipality received authorization to acquire the edifice and land for around 4,000 lire, but not until 1854 did work begin again, mainly to relieve the high unemployment among the working class. Antonio Armarotti was in charge of the project, which took 6 years to complete. He followed Bettoli's original plans. Girolamo Magnani, a native of Fidenza, was responsible for the interior decorations. He also executed the scenery for the inaugural opera.

The Teatro di Fidenza, as it was originally known, was inaugurated October 26, 1861, with *Il trovatore*. The opera was chosen to honor Verdi, who lived nearby. It was hoped that the maestro would accept the invitation of the mayor to attend the opening, but he graciously declined, writing, "One could not show more courtesy than that which you have showed me in these circumstances, but with the utmost sorrow, I am not able to accept the kind invitation. I must leave in the coming month for St. Petersburg where I will present the new opera which I am now writing, and there is a good deal of work to finish what is still missing, which will occupy all my time and forbids me to be distracted for whatever reason. Therefore, please excuse me if I am not able to take advantage of your extreme kindness. Please accept my most heartfelt thanks. With deep esteem, your devoted servant, G. Verdi."

When Magnani died in 1889, the theater was retitled Teatro Magnani, to honor the native son. The Magnani offers a neoclassical-style facade, divided into three sections. The street level is of rusticated stone with three arch openings. The middle level is punctuated by five large windows surmounted by stucco medallions enclosed in lunettes. In the middle is the coat of arms of the city. A pediment, trimmed with dentils under the horizontal cornice, crowns the building with the tympanum displaying a frieze of horns, masks, and a lyre. The 425-seat, horseshoe-shaped auditorium is a precious jewel in red, gold, and ivory, decorated in a neo-Renaissance style with French overtones. It holds three box tiers with 18 boxes per level, topped by a gallery and the former royal center box and proscenium boxes. Stucco and intaglio in gold and white with masks of Comedy and Tragedy ornament the parapets, the work of Giovanni Rusca and Giuseppe Carletti. Gilded columns flank the proscenium boxes. The allegorically painted ceiling dome depicts Melodrama, Comedy, Dance, and Tragedy with dancing putti and small chiaroscuro pictures. There is a clock in the center of the gold and white stuccoed proscenium arch.

Operatic Events at the Teatro Magnani

Despite Verdi's absence, the inaugural was an event of special importance and the orchestra section and the boxes were overflowing with elegantly attired ladies and gentlemen. The gilded decorations sparkled in the brilliance of the oil-lit chandelier. *Il trovatore* was an unqualified success even though the scheduled conductor and native son Giovanni Rossi was replaced by maestro Gaetano Bassoli. Rossi was also a composer, and the opera house hosted the prima assoluta of his fourth opera, *La contessa d'Altenberg*. The Magnani offered several Verdi operas, including *Ernani* conducted by Rossi, and *Rigoletto* in 1888, along with *Lucia di Lammermoor*. To commemorate the centennial of Verdi's birth, *Otello* was presented, with a stellar cast of Claudia Muzio, Fazzini, and Francesco Cigada. During the first few decades of the 1900s, Fidenza enjoyed the voices of Tito Schipa, Mafalda Favero, Lina Pagliughi, Pia Tassinari, and Ferruccio Tagliavini, among others. After the war, the gong of boxing matches and the noise of masked balls replaced the sound of beautiful voices, changing the atmosphere and attracting the lower classes.

During the early 1990s, the Gruppo Marchetti was entrusted with the presentation of a short opera season and offered the popular Italian operas of the 1800s, including *L'elisir d'amore* and *Rigoletto*. At the end of the decade, the theater was closed for restoration work. After the dawn of the millennium, the theater reopened but is hosting only operetta and musicals. Recently, *Die lustige Witwe* was on the boards. The theater is run by the municipality.

Practical Information

Teatro Magnani, piazza Verdi 1, 43036 Fidenza; tel. 39 0524 522 044, fax 39 0524 527 239; www.turismo.parma.it.

~

TWENTY-EIGHT

Teatro del Maggio Musicale Fiorentino and Teatro Comunale, Florence

The main antecedent of opera was the intermezzo, an interlude embellished with music performed between the acts of plays, usually comedies. This was a popular form of entertainment for special occasions at the Medici court in Florence. One such occasion took place in 1598 with the wedding of the Grand Duke Ferdinando de'Medici to Christine of Lorraine, for which Count Giovanni de'Bardi arranged the intermezzo. A group formed around Bardi known as the Camarata dei Bardi, and following their theory and practice, the very first operas were born in Florence at the end of the 1500s. Also part of the genesis of Florentine opera were two pastorals by Emilio de'Cavalieri, *Il Satiro* and *La disperazione di Fileno*, produced for Carnival 1590. Four years later, Corsi and Peri composed music for *Dafne* of which only fragments remain. *Euridice*, the first opera to survive intact, was a wedding gift from Corsi to Maria de'Medici on her marriage to Henri IV of France on October 6, 1600, at the Pitti Palace. The main entertainment at the celebration was *Il rapimento di Cefalo*, with the music by four composers, Caccini, Del Nibbio, Bati, and Strozzi. Opera, however, played a relatively small part in the overall musical entertainment in the city with intermezzi, balls, and masquerades taking the dominant roles. Opera was primarily for state occasions. In 1619 Gagliano's *Il Medoro* was performed to celebrate the election of Cosimo de'Medici's brother-in-law, Emperor Ferdinand II; Caccini's *La liberazione* marked the visit of the prince of Poland, Wladislas Sigismund; and Peri's and Gagliano's *La Flora* celebrated the wedding of Margherita de'Medici to the Duke of Parma.

Florence's first opera house, the Teatro della Pergola, also known as Teatro degl'Immobili, was inaugurated during the 1656 carnival season with Melani's *Il potestà di Colognole*. Cavalli's *L'Hipermestra* was the planned inaugural work for the Pergola, but problems with the stage machinery delayed its production until 1658. The Accademia degli Immobili, founded by Giovanni Carlo de'Medici, built the wooden structure on via della Pergola as a private venue for the Florentine nobility. It was designed by Ferdinando Tacca. In celebration of the wedding of the Grand Duke Cosimo III de'Medici to Marguerite Louise d'Orleans, Melani's *Ercole in Tebe* was performed there in 1661. After Giovanni Carlo's death 2 years later, the theater was closed. In 1688 Ferdinando de'Medici hired Ferdinando Sengher to remodel the building for his marriage to Violante Beatrice of Bavaria, which was celebrated the following year with Pagliardi's *Il greco in Troia*. But after the festivities, Ferdinando deserted the theater and left the bills unpaid. Cosimo III averted foreclosure and reopened the theater with the premiere of Vivaldi's *Scanderbegh* in 1718, followed by Pedieri's *Le fede ne' tradimenti*. More novelties followed, including Pedieri's *La finta pazzia di Diana*, Vivaldi's *L'Atenaide*, and Porta's *Il gran Tamerlano*. For Carnival 1736, Vivaldi's *Ginevra, principessa di Scozia* was on the boards. Usually three to four operas were offered each season, along with an occasional ballet. The Pergola was renovated under the guidance of Antonio Galli Bibiena in the late 1730s, and by 1740, Florence boasted 14 theaters, but La Pergola was the only one devoted exclusively to opera seria.

During the 1800s, in addition to traditional offerings, the Pergola hosted numerous prime assolute, most of which were by minor opera composers whose operas were popular at the time: Celli's *L'amore muto* and *Le due duchesse*; Persiani's *Piglia il mondo come viene*, *L'inimico generoso*, and *Danao re d'Arco*; Luigi Ricci's *Il birraio de Preston*; Federico Ricci's *Luigi Rolla e Michelangelo*; Alary's *Rosmunda*; Apolloni's *Il conte di Konigsmarch*; Badia's *Il conte di Leicester*; Basevi's *Enrico Howard*; Biagi's *La secchia capita*; Campana's *Vannina d'Ornano*, Gialdini's *Rosmund*; Capecelatro's *Gastone di Chanley*; Casella's *Maria Stuarda*; and three operas by local composer Picchi. The final two decades of the century witnessed the introduction of native son Baci's *Rosilde di Saluzzo*, Cottrau's *Imelda*, and Fornari's *Salammbò*. The operas by major composers that received world premieres include Donizetti's *Rosmonda d'Inghilterra* and *Parisina*, and Mascagni's *I Rantzau*. The most famous *prima mondiale* was *Macbeth*. The opera was given so much publicity before its prima assoluta that the Pergola had to open its doors several hours early on the day of the performance to accommodate the crowds. Verdi attended the world premiere of his opera, taking around three dozen curtain calls. Several encores were demanded, including the first part of the duet "Fatale mia donna" and the witches' chorus. It was so successful that a large crowd followed Verdi's carriage back to his hotel. Verdi dedicated *Macbeth* to his father-in-law, Antonio Barezzi, writing on March 25, 1847, "For a long time I have been thinking of dedicating an opera to you, who have been my father, benefactor, and friend. . . . Now here is this *Macbeth*, which I love more than my other operas and thus believe is more worthy of being presented to you." Barezzi replied, "Your gift is extremely precious to me: your recognition of me will always remain engraved in my heart." Operas by Cimarosa, Meyerbeer, Halévy, Auber, and Gomez were also on the boards.

The Pergola, however, was not the only opera house during the 19th century that hosted world premieres in Florence, especially since La Pergola was not considered a major house and presented only opera seria. More than a dozen other theaters in the city offered *prime esecuzioni assolute*, including the Teatro del Cocomero, renamed Teatro Niccolini, with Biagi's *Una congiura* and Cortesi's *L'amico di casa*, among others, and the Teatro Pagliano, which was very active with Bacchini's *La cacciata del duca d'Atene* and *Delmira*; Cianchi's *La gioventù di Salvator Rosa* and *Il saltimbanco*; Cortesi's *La colpa del cuore*; Benvenuti's *La baruffe chiozztotte*; Dechamps's *Il naufragio della fregata La Peyrouse*; Fornari's *Un dramma in vendemmia*; and Sborgi's *Demofoonte* and *Il giorno natalizio*.

La Pergola was remodeled in 1857, which gave the theater its present appearance, although the general structure is original. Currently, it hosts theatrical productions, except during Maggio Musicale, when opera also graces the stage. The Ente Teatrale Italiano owns and operates the theater. The Pergola is considered the "first organic example of an Italian-style theater" with its 1,000-seat, horseshoe-shaped, ivory, gold, and red auditorium of three box tiers topped by a gallery. The parapets are decorated with gilded ornamentation, and the center royal box and proscenium boxes are flanked by ornate pilasters with golden capitals. On the ceiling are angels and other celestial beings.

Two years after the Pergola was remodeled, the idea to build a new open-air amphitheater took hold after fire destroyed the old politeama, located on piazza Indipendenza. In May 1861, the proposal was adopted, and construction finished the next year. Designed by Telemaco Bonaiuti and built at a cost of 410,000 lire, the Politeama Fiorentino Vittorio Emanuele was inaugurated on May 17, 1862, with *Lucia di Lammermoor*. But only a year later, fire erupted during a ball, killing several attendees and destroying the stage.

Rebuilt by Bonaiuti, the amphitheater reopened April 7, 1864. The roots of the Teatro Comunale extend back to the Politeama Fiorentino. Shortly after the amphitheater opened, the *Quotidiano di Firenze* described it as follows: "The facade of the Politeama Vittorio Emanuele, composed of seven arches containing three doors and four windows, already gives the impression of grandeur that one finds upon entering. It is the work of Bonaiuti, who tried to fuse ancient stateliness with contemporary needs. As soon as one enters the theater, there is an elegant colonnade, then a vestibule, and a foyer, supported by four octagonal columns. The cast iron balustrades serve as parapets to the aisles that lead to the steps. For balance, there is an ornamental balustrade on the other side as well. . . . Descending the stairs, one enters the amphitheater, which is in the shape of an ellipse and has the capacity for 6,000 people. Above all, one admires the extremely large stage, which not counting the six proscenium boxes, has a row of 28 boxes on each side that are interrupted in the middle by a peristyle that joins the arena to the entrance hall." The open-air structure acquired a roof in 1882, electricity in 1895, and heating in 1911. The Società Italiana Anonima Teatrale took over its management in 1910, running it for around two decades.

In 1930 the municipality obtained the building, subsequently renaming it the Teatro Comunale. A bombing raid in May 1944 damaged the theater, closing it until 1947. Eleven years later, stability problems caused the building to be shut once again. The reconstruction, which included the addition of a second gallery, lasted 3 years and gave the theater its current appearance. Architect Bartolini and engineer Giuntoli were in charge of the project. The Comunale reopened May 8, 1961, with *Don Carlo*. The theater was subsequently renamed the Teatro del Maggio Musicale Fiorentino after the well-known festival it hosts.

The Maggio Musicale, like other *ente autonomo* and as required by law, has formed a *fondazione*. But with the government's cutting of subsidies and the high number of full-time employees, it has severe financial difficulties that have led to strikes and upheavals. The problems might be solved by either reducing the number of personnel working there, which would probably result in more strikes and upheaval, or reducing the number of operas in the schedule, since the productions are of a high level and the theater does not want to lower the quality. It has put out an appeal for new supporters, especially among private citizens, by offering perks such as being named in the program, better seats, advance purchase of tickets, attendance at rehearsals, and private receptions. There are currently around only 30 major sup-

Semiramide, Rossini Opera Fesival, Pesaro (Amati Bacciardi).

Ser Mercantonio, Teatro Rossini, Lugo (Roberto Cornacchia).

Elektra, Teatro di San Carlo, Naples (Luciano Romano).

Madame Butterfly set design by Paolo Micciché for Arena di Verona (Paolo Micciché).

Faust, Teatro di San Carlo, Naples (Luciano Romano)

*La forza d'amore,* OperaInCanto, Narni (OperaInCanto).

Die Meistersinger von Nürnberg, Teatro del Maggio Musicale fiorentino, Florence (Gianluca Moggi, New Press photo).

Teatro Pergolesi, Jesi, detail of ceiling in auditorium (Karyl Charna Lynn).

Teatro Municipale Valli, Reggio Emilia, detail of box tier parapets (Karyl Charna Lynn).

Teatro Verdi, Trieste, detail of auditorium decoration (Karyl Charna Lynn).

Teatro Comunale, Modena, view towards stage and
historic curtain from royal box (Rolando Paolo Guerzoni).

Teatro di San Carlo, Naples, view from stage towards royal box (Luciano Romano).

Un ballo in maschera, Teatro delle Muse, Ancona (Sandro D'Ascanio).

La donna del lago, Rossini Opera Festival, Pesaro (Amati Bacciardi).

Turandot, Teatro Coccia, Novara (Teatro Coccia).

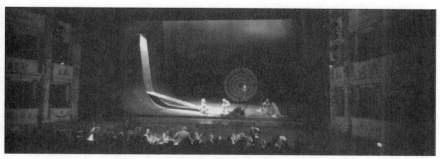

L'Olimpiade, Teatro Comunale, Modena (Rolando Paolo Guerzoni).

Norma, Teatro delle Muse, Ancona (Sandro D'Ascanio).

Teatro Regio, Parma, facade (Karyl Charna Lynn).

Teatro alla scala, Milan, facade with new structure behind (Karyl Charna Lynn).

Teatro Massino, Palermo, facade (Karyl Charna Lynn).

porting members, since Florence is not as large as other cities with *ente autonomo* theaters.

The exterior of the opera house offers a facade of gray rusticated stone, with arched doorways crowned with transoms and golden fleurs-de-lis. Above are seven arch windows flanked by eight Ionic pilasters. The strikingly modern 2,000-seat auditorium retained its original elliptical shape. There are a vast orchestra seating level, a single tier of boxes, and two wide, semicircular galleries, which hint at its origins as an amphitheater. A sea of deep burgundy red seats contrasts with the stark white of the parapets. The dark- and light-gray proscenium arch is crowned by a fleur-de-lis. Starlike lights in a sky-dome ceiling illuminate the space. The Piccolo Teatro is located near the main auditorium. Seating 600, it is a modern space that hosts chamber opera and works better suited to smaller spaces.

There are plans to build a new opera house in a Centro della Musica similar to the Parco della Musica in Rome, which opened in 2003, except Rome's does not offer an opera house. In Florence the new venue would hold 2,200 seats. There would also be a 1,300-seat concert hall, with a covered area between them for refreshments, shops, and other amenities. The estimated cost is between $150 million and $200 million, with completion planned for 2012.

Operatic Events at the Teatro Comunale

After the Politeama Vittorio Emanuele opened in the 1860s, it became the focus of the cultural life of the city, especially after it was enclosed. *Nabucco* celebrated its reopening as an indoor arena in the 1880s. The backbone of the opera repertory was traditional, with operas by Verdi, Meyerbeer, Gomez, Donizetti, Cimarosa, and Halévy and an occasional adventurous work or novelty. In 1896 the number of operatic presentations reached 70 and included such works as *Pagliacci*, *Cavalleria rusticana*, *Zanetto*, *Les pêcheurs de perles*, and *Traviata*. That same year Mascagni made his debut, conducting his own operas. But after that exceptional year, the opera landscape looked bleak, and until 1902, there was little opera. Instead, the circus, baby beauty competitions, and gymnastic demonstrations occupied the stage.

Opera then returned, with some memorable results: Gemma Bellicioni in *Traviata*, Pasquale Amato in *Rigoletto*, Piero Schiavazzi in *Iris*, and Carlo Galeffi in *Guglielmo Ratcliff*. In 1911 some members of the royal family attended Pacini's *Saffo*, and Mascagni conducted his *Isabeau* the next year. One of the first Wagner operas staged, *Die Walküre*, was performed in 1913, followed by *Parsifal*. During World War I, the theater saw an occasional benefit concert and some theatrical works and even served as a costume warehouse. There were regular opera seasons from 1919 until 1928 organized by the Associazione della Stampa Toscana and of the Circolo della Stampa. Operas ranged from baroque to contemporary with artists such as Tito Schipa, Carlo Galeffi, Rosetta Pampanini, Aureliano Pertile, Luigi Rossi-Morelli, Conchita Supervia, Giuseppe Cobelli, and Iva Pacetti. Verdi was the most performed composer between May 1862 and December 1928, with around 200 performances of *Traviata*, followed by *Rigoletto*, *Aida*, and *Trovatore*. Puccini's *Tosca*, Mascagni's *Iris*, and Ponchielli's *Gioconda* were the other most popular works.

The establishment of the Stabile Orchestrale Fiorentina (Permanent Florentine Orchestra), later called Orchestra del Maggio Musicale Fiorentino, in June 1928 paved the way for regular opera seasons and planted the seeds for the Maggio Musicale Fiorentino Festival. The first season yielded fruitful operatic offerings with nine productions: three Puccini, two Verdi, and one each of Alfano, Bellini, Donizetti, and Mascagni, for a total of 38 performances. Seven operas were staged the following year, including *Lohengrin* and *Fidelio*. Although only seven performances of *Norma* were presented in 1930/31, seven different operas were on the boards with 24 performances, including Mascagni's *Pinotta* in 1932/33. The adventurousness infiltrated as well the regular opera season with *Götterdämmerung* and *Francesca da Rimini* and the chamber opera season with *El retablo de Maese Pedro*.

The Politeama Fiorentino Vittorio Emanuele II was designated an *ente autonomo* in 1931. That same year, the Maggio Musicale Fiorentino Festival was established as a triennial event. The goals of the festival were to produce contemporary works, from avant-garde compositions to the most recent creations; to rediscover forgotten works of the great masters and neglected masterpieces and present them in musically authentic versions; and to emphasize the visual aspects in opera through innovative ideas from theater and film producers and famous painters. The first festival opened April 22, 1933, in the Teatro Comunale with *Nabucco*, (at that time early Verdi operas were a rarity), followed by Donizetti's *Lucrezia Borgia* and Spontini's *Vestale*. The success of the first festival led to it becoming a biennial event, with the second one in 1935. On the boards were a *novità assoluta*, Pizzetti's *Orseolo*, Rameau's *Castor et Pollux*, *Mosè*, *Alceste*, *Norma*, and *Un ballo in maschera*. The chamber-music season saw *Le pauvre matelot* and *L'histoire du soldat*. Beginning in 1937 with nine operas, including three world premieres, it became an annual festival, except during World War II.

The Maggio Musicale was the first music festival in Italy and is still the most important. Through the decades it has offered a unique combination of operas, with world and Italian premieres and contemporary works, alongside revivals of forgotten and neglected operas. But despite the large number of *prime esecuzioni assolute* at the festival, including Malipiero's *Venere prigioniera*, *Antonio e Cleopatra*, and *Figliol prodigo*; Frazzi's *Re Lear* and *Don Chisciotte*; Dallapiccola's *Volo di notte*; Pizzetti's *Vanna Lupa*; Bucchi's *Il contrabbasso*; Castelnuovo-Tedesco's *Aucassin ed Nicolette*; Chailly's *Il mantello*; Testi's *Celestina*; Schönberg's *Mano felice*; Sciarrino's *Aspern*; and Vacchi's *Girotondo*, few have survived the test of time. The Italian premieres and contemporary fare offered have faired slightly better, with Stravinsky's *Edipo re*, *Oedipus rex*, *Petrouchka*, and *Persefone*; Spontini's *Olimpia*; Prokofiev's *Voyna i mir* (War and Peace); Dargomisky's *Il convitato di pietra*; and Bartok's *A Kékszakállú herceg vára* (Duke Bluebeard Castle) among them. The unearthed operas such as Purcell's *Didone ed Enea*, Monteverdi's *Vespro della Beata Vergine*, Gluck's *Il cadi' ingannato*, Cavalli's *Didone*, Peri's *Euridice*, and Traetta's *Antigone* were more for curiosity and scholars. There have also been festivals with themes that included Rossini renaissance, early Verdi, historic 20th century, and early Romanticism.

The Maggio Musicale attracted the leading artists of the day. The inaugural season heard Carlo Galeffi, Alessandro Dolci, and Tancredi Pasero in *Nabucco*, Rosa Ponselle in *La vestale*, and Ezio Pinza, Giacomo Lauri-Volpe, and Mercedes Capsir in *I Puritani*. Maria Callas first demonstrated her unique vocal and dramatic style, which revolutionized acting in opera, with *Norma* in 1948, followed by *La traviata*, *I vespri siciliani*, *Orfeo*, *Armida*, and *Médée*. Well-known conductors were on the podium, including Bruno Walter, Claudio Abbado, Wolfgang Sawallisch, Lorin Maazel, Riccardo Muti, and Zubin Mehta.

Florence has a tradition of avant-garde productions. There was a *Tosca* set in Rome during the Nazi occupation, a *Das Rheingold* that opened with the Rhine maidens stark naked, a symbol of their innocence, a *Falstaff* set in a British train station, which prompted shouts of "Povero Verdi" (Poor Verdi), and a minimalist, symbolic *Macbeth*, where not one murder was shown but symbolically demonstrated. The theater has received the award for best production of the year given by the Italian music critics. Operas more suitable for smaller spaces are staged at the Piccolo Teatro. Recently, the Maggio Musicale has offered *Tosca*, *Don Giovanni*, *Turn of the Screw*, and *Boris Godunov*. The regular season fare has included *Khovinchina*, *Così fan tutte*, and both the four- and five-act versions of *Don Carlo* that were set in a historic revival of a Luchino Visconti production. Recent chamber operas included *Where the Wild Things Are*, a double bill of Haydn's *La canterina* and Donizetti's *Pigmalione*, and the world premiere of *Volevo un foglio*. Besides the Teatro Comunale and Teatro Piccolo, performances also take place at the Teatro Pergola and Teatro Goldoni. During the summer, concerts are held in the Piazza della Signoria and Boboli Gardens.

Practical Information

Teatro del Maggio Musicale Fiorentino, Teatro Comunale, corso Italia 16, 50123, Florence; tel. 39 055 427 5367, fax 39 055 239 6954; www.maggio fiorentino.com.

The regular opera season runs from September to December with three main stage operas with five to eight performances of each and three chamber operas with two performances of each. The Maggio Musicale takes place during April, May, and June, offering four operas with five to eight performances of each. Stay at the De Rose Palace, via Solferino 5, 50123 Florence; tel. 055 239 6818, fax 055 268 249; www.hotelderose.it. The small, elegant De Rose is around the corner from the Teatro del Maggio Musicale Fiorentino, a 3-minute walk from the theater. Visit the Teatro della Pergola, via della Pergola 12/32; tel. 226 4335, fax 226 4350; www.pergola.firenze.it. Teatro Goldoni (via Santa Maria 12) is one of the venues for chamber opera; Teatro Verdi (via Ghibellina 99; tel. 239 6242, fax 288 417) was originally the Teatro Pagliano but is now a home for prose; and Teatro Niccolini (via Ricasoli 3; tel. 239 6653) was originally the Teatro del Cocomero but is now a venue for experimental works. Rossini lovers can visit his sepulcher at Santa Croce (piazza San Croce; tel. 244619) and the house where he lived while in Florence, via Cavour, next to the Palazzo Medici Riccardi. A nameplate identifies the house. Biblioteca Marucelliana (via Cavour 43) has conserved 10,000 opera libretti; Palazzo Pitti (piazza Pitti; tel. 238 8611) has a museum of musical instruments, and the Boboli Gardens (piazza Pitti; tel. 218 741) has summer performances.

$\sim$

Teatro Comunale G. B. Pergolesi, Jesi

The first records of opera presentations began in 1715, when the Palazzo dei Priori hosted carnival season with performances of Scarlatti's *L'amore non viene dal caso* and Gasparini's *Flavio Anicio Olibio*. Opera became quite popular with people familiar with the social customs of the art form. A committee known as the Gentlemen Deputies of the Opera was organized, as well as a less formal group called People United for Opera. The Magistrate Room was transformed into a temporary performance space, and in 1727 Orlandini's *Lisetta e Delfo* and *Nino* and Scarlatti's *Tolomeo e Alessandro* were performed. The need and the desire of the city for a permanent performance venue had been made in April 1726, with a formal request to the city council for permission to construct a theater for "public dignity and honest entertainment." The site chosen was called piazza della Morte (today, Piazza della Repubblica). The request was granted, but the location was moved because of complications with the site.

The Jesian painter and architect Domenico Valeri constructed and decorated the wooden theater at his own expense, selling boxes to the nobility, who became the *condomini*, to recoup his construction costs. The theater opened in 1732 with *Nel perdono la vendetta*. History was not kind to the theater, describing it as not very elegant or comfortable and dangerous. It was managed by the *condomini* without any help from the municipality. Beginning in 1773, it was called Teatro del Leone, from the civil coat of arms of Jesi. Twice a year, for carnival and the September fair, musical works were offered, including the prime mondiali of Galeazzi's *Ginevra* and Pergolesi's *Livietta* and *Tracollo*. *Drammi giocosi* from the Neapolitan school were the main fare. The Leone was very active until 1791. It survived another century, however, until fire destroyed it in 1892, with only the walls remaining, which were demolished in 1900. Despite much discussion, the Leone was not rebuilt, although many felt there was a need for a less elitist theater than the Teatro della Concordia.

The birth of the Concordia came about in February 1790 when the nobility of the city and the prelate governor Monsignore Pietro Gravina came to an agreement about the construction of a new theater. Eight noble Jesians were elected deputies and were responsible for the project. They requested authorization to build the opera house on the piazza della Morte (the location originally requested for the Teatro del Leone), an area occupied by slaughterhouses, fisheries, a city garbage dump, execution chambers, and shops that sold flour. The city wanted to renew the area and remove the horrific odor associated with such activities by demolishing the buildings. Construction of a new theater at that location was part of the restoration project, so the request was granted with the condition that the demolished shops be rebuilt and two boxes on the "most noble" tier be donated to the city. Eventually, the city government relented and demanded that two boxes be only sold to the city. Then a property dispute arose with the fraternity that accompanied condemned people to their death that claimed the property was theirs, but the dispute was resolved and the project proceeded. In July the chosen architect, Francesco Maria Ciaraffoni, delivered the plans to the deputies who hired the contractor Pietro Belli for the construction. The first stone was laid in September. The original cost was 16,000 scudi, paid by the sale of boxes: 100 in all divided among the four tiers. Expenses, however, reached 24,000 scudi, and four generous and rich noblemen paid the additional 8,000 scudi. Another architect, Cosimo Morelli, modified the plans to bring optimal acoustics to the auditorium. The Teatro della Concordia was inaugurated during Carnival 1798 with Portogallo's *Lo spazzacamino principe*. In 1835 the fourth tier of boxes was transformed into a gallery by architect Raffaele Grilli, and the center box on the first tier was demolished to enlarge the entrance to the orchestra level. Four years later, a monumental clock was installed on the facade, a gift from Prince Massimiliano of Beauharnais to the citizens of Jesi. In 1880, on the occasion of the 170th anniversary of the birth of the Jesian composer Pergolesi, the Concordia was renamed in his honor, although it actually took 3 years for the new name to become official, since all the *condomini*, administration, and related associations had to sign the documents.

The closing of the opera house for 2 years beginning in 1925 for a much needed roof repair was the catalyst that led to the dissolution of the Società Teatrale, an association of the heirs of the theater's original *condomini*, at the end of the 1928 season. The following editorial had appeared in the local paper around the time of the crisis, "Despite the unfailing good will of each box-holder, it has not been possible to prepare an opera season worthy of our city. The story is by now old and should be resolved with the transfer of the boxes by those box-holders who are not able to or do not wish to pay out for the subvention. The idea of the cession of the theater to the municipality had been launched many times, but it appears that the municipal administration is not entirely interested in this question. The sister cities of the Marchè [region] like Osimo, Fabriano, Senigallia, etc., have resolved the question: is it really impossible to resolve it also in Jesi?" In March 1929, the city acquired the Pergolesi for 247,460 lire.

The Pergolesi was recognized as a *Teatro di tradizione* on May 3, 1968. It is one of the few opera houses in Italy from the late 1700s that has never been destroyed by fire or bombs. The Pergolesi, being a *Teatro di tradizione*, has certain requirements and restrictions regarding its management and opera programming. Its funding still comes entirely from the municipal government, since it has not created a *fondazione* for financing, but the change in the subsidies could affect its future opera seasons.

The Teatro Pergolesi is typical of Marche region architecture—a large-looking building with a small theater: the auditorium runs parallel to the theater's facade. Faced with earth-colored Roman brick, the neoclassical facade displays three levels. On the ground level is a series of arched portals with masks of Comedy and Tragedy in the keystones. The second and third levels are punctuated by Palladium-style windows. A small balcony juts out over the main entrance and a huge clock, flanked by a cornucopia of fruit and mythological birds, crowns the theater. The auditorium is a typical *Teatro italiano*—elliptically shaped with three tiers of boxes topped by a gallery. Intimate in scale and elegantly decorated in predominately green-pastel water colors, reflecting the tastes of the late 1700s when the theater opened, the auditorium boasts gilded ornamentation and bas-reliefs of Pergolesi and Spontini on the proscenium box parapets and plush red seats. The elaborately painted dome ceiling, the work of Felice Giani, depicts mythological scenes from *Apollo's Tale*: Jove and Latona, the Death of Hyacinth, Pastoral Apollo, Apollo and Cassandra, Apollo killing the serpent Python, Apollo and Dafne, Apollo and Marsia, and the Birth of Apollo and Diana. It is surrounded by dancing putti and satyrs, and in the triangular spaces near the proscenium arch, the allegory of Music and allegory of Epics are featured. On the proscenium arch, the allegory of Day and allegory of Night are represented with the allegory of Time in the center, the work of Giuseppe Valesi.

The painted curtain, executed by Luigi Mancini in 1850, and completely restored in 1995, shows the entrance of Emperor Federico II into Jesi in 1216.

Operatic Events at the Teatro Pergolesi

The inaugural 1798 carnival season, besides *Lo spazzacamino principe*, offered Portogallo's *Le confusioni della somiglianza* and Martín y Soler's *La capricciosa correttae*. During the first few decades, operas such as Portogallo's *La donna di genio voluble* and *Le donne cangiate*, Fioravanti's *Il furbo contra il furbo* and *Le cantatrici villane*, Guglielmi's *La serva bizzarra* and *La spelta di uno sposo*, Farinelli's *Teresa e Claudio*, and Mayr's *L'amor coniugale* graced the stage. Sometimes, however, the choice of operas did not please, as during the 1812 carnival season when Mayr's *Elisa* and Trento's *I due vecchi delusi* were mounted. The chief of police wrote to the prefect that there was no applause for either one of the two productions because of the bad selection of subjects and bad singing.

Keeping order in Italian opera houses was no small feat in the 1800s. In 1814 during a performance of *Ser Marcantonio*, the public requested that the second-act duet between the prima donna and the primo buffo be repeated. One of the directors of the theater tried to explain that the prima donna was not in perfect health and that it would not be possible to repeat. This caused such an uproar that the curtain had to be lowered. The following evening, during that same duet, some members of the audience began to whistle, causing the police to enter the box of one of the offenders, arrest him, and escort him home. The result was that bylaws were passed regulating behavior in the theater.

With the arrival of the 1820s, Rossini entered the repertory with *Cenerentola*, *Torvaldo e Dorliska*, and *La gazza ladra*. Bellini followed in 1833 with *Il pirata*, *Straniera*, *Beatrice di Tenda*, and *Norma*. Donizetti was first heard 5 years later with *L'elisir d'amore*, *Lucia di Lammermoor*, and *Roberto Devereux*. There were also operas by Morlacchi, Vaccai, Ricci, Persiani, Pacini, and Mercadante. The first Verdi operas were in 1850, *Nabucco* and *I due Foscari*, followed by *Il Lombardi*, *Luisa Miller*, *Ernani*, and *Traviata*. In 1869 a 20-year-old Jesian singer, Niccolina Favi Gallo, was greatly acclaimed in *Ballo in maschera* and 2 years later in *Trovatore*.

From the opening of the Concordia until 1883, the most popular composers were Verdi and Donizetti, followed by Bellini and Rossini. Of note was the complete absence from the repertory of operas by two Jesian composers, Spontini, who was born near Jesi in Maiolati, and Pergolesi. *La vestale* was staged for the first time for the 100th anniversary of Spontini's birth in 1875 and *Stabat Mater* for the 170th birthday of Pergolesi. The 1885 season featured Lena Bordato in the title role of *Lucia di Lammermoor*, who according to accounts in the local paper, "executed the mad scene with such aplomb that she was obliged to repeat it. After the performance, a torch light procession, complete with citizen's musical band organized by her admirers, accompanied her home." The 1895 season featured *Cavalleria rusticana* only 5 years after its *prima* in Rome. The 1890s, however, witnessed some curious program changes, partially on economic grounds but also reflecting the new tastes of the people. In September 1897, the operetta *I granatieri* replaced the originally scheduled *Norma*, and the next year *Rigoletto* was performed instead of three originally scheduled contemporary operas: *Gioconda*, *Mignon*, and *Bohème*. By 1899 operatic activity ceased altogether when the drama company of Ermete Zacconi took over the theater. The following year saw movies projected in the building. Only in 1903 did opera return to the stage, with *Bohème* and *Il barbiere di Siviglia*, sharing it with movies and plays. In 1908 a noteworthy *Manon Lescaut* was given, which one critic described as "excellent from every point of view. Tina Desana in the title role makes a believable character, with her powerful, clear, and flexible voice, fine artistic talent, exact knowledge of the scene, slim, elegant figure, perfect form, and ability to relate well to the audience." In April 1910, for the bicentennial of Pergolesi's birth, a statue of the composer was erected by Alessandro Lazzerini, and in October performances of *Stabat Mater* and *La serva padrona* took place. The 100th anniversary of Verdi's birth was commemorated in 1913 with a series of performances of *La forza del destino*. Although World War I did not stop productions at the Pergolesi, most were benefit concerts. The traditional opera season returned in 1919, dominated by Puccini works, including the Brescia version of *Madama Butterfly* and *Bohème*.

When the theater reopened with the municipality as the proprietor, the Compagnia dell'Opera Lirica Italiana (Company of Italian Lyric Opera) presented *Cavalleria rusticana*, *Pagliacci*, *Rigoletto*, and *Traviata*. The repertory remained popular Italian fare before, during, and after World War II. Pergolesi operas, however, were included in the schedule, with the 250th anniversary of his birth celebrated in 1960 with *Lo frate 'nnammurato* in a Franco Zeffirelli production from La Scala, conducted by Bruno Bartoletti. The Pergolesi celebrated its recognition in 1968 as a *Teatro di tradizione* by inaugurating the season with Mario del Monaco in *Otello*, directed by Giancarlo del Monaco, and hosting the world premieres of Boccosi's *La lettera scarlatta* in September 1968 and Squadroni's *Calandrino & C* in September 1969.

Between 1970 and 1976, every season offered a contemporary Italian opera, Squadroni's *Un treno*, Mannino's *Vivì*, Strano's *Sulla via maestro*, Fiorda's *Margot*, Rossellini's *Uno squardo dal ponte*, Menotti's *Il ladro e la zitella*, and Napoli's *Il povero diavolo*/Massaron's *La mamma dei gatti*/*Un amore asfissiante*.

Beginning in the mid-1990s, the mission of the Pergolesi has been the rediscovery of the musical patrimony of the Marche by inaugurating each season with an opera rarity by a composer from the region, preferably Jesi. Often the operas were from the 1800s and popular in their day, such as Persiani's *Ines de Castro*, Marchetti's *Ruy Blas*, and Vaccai's *Giulietta e Romeo*, but had fallen into oblivion, overshadowed by the giants of the 19th century, Rossini, Donizetti, Bellini, and Verdi, or they were earlier works such as Spontini's *Teseo Riconosciuto* and Pergolesi's *Il prigionier superbo*. Recently the world premiere of Tutino's *Federico II* was staged, with the remainder of the season filled with popular Italian operas such as *L'elisir d'amore*, *La traviata*, and *Andrea Chénier*.

Practical Information

Teatro Comunale G. B. Pergolesi, piazza della Repubblica 9, 60035 Jesi; tel. 39 0731 538 350, fax 39 0731 538 384; www.teatropergolesi.org.

The opera season, which runs during October and November, offers four operas with two to three performances of each. Stay at the Hotel Federico II, via Ancona 100, 60035 Jesi; tel. 0731 211 079, fax 0731 57221. A resort hotel just outside the old city, the Federico II, is on a direct bus line to the opera house, or it is a 30-minute walk. Visit the statue in the center of town of the famous Jesi composer, Pergolesi, after whom the theater is named.

THIRTY

~

Comitato Estate Livornese and Teatro di Livorno, Livorno

Opera has been present in Livorno since 1658. One of the earliest works heard was *Eurillo* by Margaritoni. In 1843 construction began on the Teatro Leopoldo, named after Leopold II of Lorena, who ruled during that era. Designed by Giuseppe Cappellini, it opened July 24, 1847. The people, however, called the theater Caporali after the two brothers who built it. In 1859 the theater was renamed Teatro Goldoni in honor of the "theater poet" Carlo Goldoni, who in 1742 had staged his comedy *Tonin bella grazia* in Livorno.

Various businessmen, local associations, and organizations established the Comitato Estate Livornese (CEL), Teatro di Livorno in 1930 to organize the opera seasons for the Goldoni. Disbanded during World War II, it was reestablished in 1947 by the city's mayor, Furio Diaz. Recognized in 1967 as a *Teatro di tradizione*, the CEL has three objectives: to celebrate and make better known, especially outside Italy, famous composers, librettists, singers, and conductors who came from Livorno; to explore the lesser-known works of Pietro Mascagni and other composers from the Tuscany region; and to examine and bring to the stage works from the Italian verismo school.

After the war, with the Teatro Goldoni damaged, the company performed in the Teatro La Gran Guardia, which opened in 1955. La Gran Guardia is a nondescript, multipurpose theater, wedged between stores and apartment buildings. The glass-and-pillar facade leads into an art deco–inspired lobby of turquoise and light-colored wood. The 1,600-seat auditorium is divided between an orchestra section and a balcony. After more than 20 years, the Teatro Goldoni reopened in January 2004 and CEL moved their operations back to the opera house. They celebrated the event with a double bill of *Cavalleria rusticana* and *La vida breve*. The Goldoni follows neoclassical principles: the facade is defined by a seven-arch arcade of rusticated stone with Doric pilasters surmounted by seven large arch windows with balustrades running across the lower section. Above, "Teatro Goldoni Anno MDCCC-XLVII" is written with a semicircular window punctuating the crowning tympanum. The delicate green-colored foyer offers painted friezes and plinths bearing porcelain figures. The auditorium is solid and elegant, with the balustrade the exact twin of the stone one that runs the length of the promenade, called the Terrazza Mascagni.

Operatic Events of the CEL

The opera seasons remain dedicated to CEL's goals, and each season there is at least one opera from the verismo school, which includes Mascagni, Cilea, Giordano, Zandonai, and Leoncavallo. The emphasis remains, however, with operas of Mascagni, which led in 1988 to the creation of the Mascagni Project, the unearthing of *Iris* and *Il piccolo Marat*, and launched a Mascagni rebirth. The next several seasons offered the first modern, complete-version performance of *I Rantzau* and *Lodoletta, Amico Fritz, Silvano*, and *Cavalleria rusticana*. *Guglielmo Ratcliff* was revived in 1995 to commemorate both the 50th anniversary of the composer's death and the centennial of its prima assoluta. Another native son, the librettist Ranieri de Calzabigi, was recognized with a concert version of two works for which he wrote the libretto, *Orfeo ed Euridice* and *Don Juan*.

Another project was born during the 1996 season, that of Great Voices to honor singers, especially those from Livorno and Tuscany. Tenor Galliano Masini was honored on the centennial of his birth with the opera in which he made his debut, *Tosca*. The next season it was two Tuscan singers, Titta Ruffo, 120 years from his birth, and Ettore Bastianini, in the third decade since his death, with *Rigoletto*; a new production of *Cavalleria rusticana* for the centennial of Roberto Stagno's death; Maria Callas in the second decade since her passing; and the first performance in Italy of George Gershwin's *Blue Monday* on the 60th anniversary of his death.

The CEL began the Operetta Project in 1996 to recognize and generate more appreciation for Italian operetta. The first production was Mascagni's *Sì*, followed by Pietri's *L'acqua cheta*. It presented its first *novità assoluta*, Tutino's *La lupa*, in 1990. Other operas have included *La Wally, Il tabarro, I pagliacci*, and *La bohème*. As the 20th century drew to a close, *Die Zauberflöte* and

La sonnambula were on the boards, followed by *Carmen, L'amico Fritz, Tosca,* and *La belle Helene* in the new millennium. The company always includes a Mascagni opera in the schedule of popular Italian works with one lesser-known piece, as can be seen by a recent season: *La traviata, Turandot, Cavalleria rusticana,* and *Midsummer Night's Dream.*

The CEL is part of the CittàLirica, a regional project for opera productions that includes the Fondazione Teatro Verdi in Pisa and the Teatro Giglio in Lucca. The three historic theaters in western Tuscany share a single orchestra and productions and coordinate schedules, which are partially based on the training and development of the young artists. The theater also coproduces with other Italian opera houses.

Practical Information

Comitato Estate Livornese, Teatro di Livorno, via Goldoni 83, 57125 Livorno; tel. 39 0586 204 21, fax 39 0586 899 920; www.celteatrolivorno.it.

The season, which runs from October to December or January, offers four productions with two performances each. Stay at the Hotel Città, via di Franco 32, 57100 Livorno; tel. 0586 883 495, fax 0586 890 196. Visit the Fondazione dell'Istituto Musicale P. Mascagni. There are frequent musical events.

THIRTY-ONE

~

Teatro del Giglio, Lucca

During the 1600s, theatrical activities took place in the salons of the grand palaces of the princes and dukes. For public theatrical functions, two halls, one called the Sala del Podestà in the Palazzo Pretorio, and the other in the Palazzo de'Borghi, were adapted and known as the Teatri di Corte. With the increase of theatrical activities, the two halls became insufficient for the needs of the public. So in 1672 the Consiglio della Repubblica decreed the formation of a commission to construct a public theater by restructuring the old convent of the Jesuits at the church of San Girolamo. Designed by Francesco Buonamici and constructed by Giovanni Maria Padreddio, the Teatro Pubblico was inaugurated January 14, 1675, with Ziani's *Attila in Capua* and Sartorio's *La prosperità di Elio Seiano*. The theater held 48 boxes on three tiers, supported by columns of stone that were decorated similarly and modestly. Only the center box was ornamented, for the gentlemen of the governing body. The construction was paid for by the sale of boxes. Orchestra seats were sold separately, either for a single evening or a series of performances.

In February 1688, the carelessness of the verger started a fire that reduced the structure to ashes, leaving only the perimeter walls. In 1692 the theater was reconstructed, opening the following year on December 29, 1693, with Legrenzi's *Giustino* and Gabrielli's *Tiberio a Bisanzio*. Barsotto Barsotti was in charge of the reconstruction. There were now 67 boxes on four tiers. Angelo Livoratti executed the ceiling paintings and Silvano Barbati rebuilt the stage. The artistic activity during the 1700s played an important role in the life of the city, such that in 1754 a special office was created to manage and maintain the theater, called *Cura sopra il teatro* (Care regarding the theater). It functioned until 1799, when Lucca lost its independence and fell under

176

French rule. Renamed the Teatro Nazionale between 1799 and 1805, it entered a period of crisis. Elisa Bonaparte, who ruled Lucca between 1805 and 1814, was not interested in the theater, preferring other activities. Without money, the building was not maintained, finally closing in 1808. Performances were shifted to the smaller, privately run Teatro Castglioncelli.

The Castglioncelli had been erected in 1752 by the Accademia Magis Vigent and substantially modified in 1772 by Ottaviano Diodati. More elegant than the Pubblico, it was restored in 1808 and hosted mainly comic operas, such as Puccini's *Ciarlatano*, which shared the stage with drama and other diversions. It was the only theater in Lucca for a decade until the Teatro Panera reopened in 1817. The Panera had been constructed in 1770 by the Academy of the Collegati. Designed by Michele Lippi, it held four box tiers and a gallery. The sale of its boxes paid for the construction. It was also privately managed and offered comic opera, drama, and even promotional events such as a lottery to encourage attendance. Closed at the beginning of the 1800s, it was reopened in 1817, the same year the Teatro Pubblico was reconstructed. The Panera hosted the prime mondiali of native son Mazza's *La vigilanza delusa*, Speranza's *Egli è di moda?* and *Il postiglione di Longjumeau*, and Valentini's *Il sonnambulo* and *Gli avventurieri*.

Giovanni Lazzarini was entrusted with the rebuilding of the Pubblico, which lasted 2 years. Meanwhile, Marie Louise of Bourbon had become sovereign of Lucca, so she was given the honor of inaugurating the new theater and choosing Teatro San Luigi, Teatro Alfieri, or Teatro Giglio for its name. She chose Teatro Giglio, which was the flower on the coat of arms of the House of Bourbon. The name has remained. Mayr's *La rosa bianca e la rosa rossa* inaugurated the opera house in August 1819. Marquis Antonio Mazzarosa described the auditorium in the *Guida di Lucca* when it opened in 1819: "The auditorium has a pretty shape, carries the voice perfectly, and is large enough for the usual attendance of the public. There are four tiers of boxes, twenty on each tier, and above, a balcony used by the lower classes which one is gratified to see." A chronicler of the time wrote that "the elegant theater with its noble Neoclassic facade is splendid with the innumerable flames, and the ladies in their boxes all bathed with white-camellia face powder." In September the state took ownership of the Giglio and Mazzarosa was charged with its administration. Gas lighting was installed in 1872 and electric lighting followed in 1911. The Giglio was used as a military warehouse during World War I. The building was closed in 1936 for reasons of "security, stability, and decorations," which led to the question of whether the building should be strengthened and stabilized or demolished and reconstructed. The first option was chosen, to be supervised by Righetto Pianucci and with Ezio Ricci responsible for the redecoration. *La traviata* and *Tosca* were on the boards when the theater reopened. Four hundred seats were added in 1957 by replacing the fourth-tier center boxes with gallery seating. On February 20, 1985, the theater was classified as a *Teatro di tradizione*. Restoration work, especially on the facade, was executed at the end of the 1990s.

The large center section of the neoclassical building thrusts out from its side wings, with five arched doorways enclosing a former carriage entrance of ashlar. On the second level, six Ionic pilasters alternate with rectangular windows, each crowned by bas-reliefs of musical subjects. On top, the tympanum, delineated with dentils, displays the red and white coat of arms of Lucca. The 750-seat auditorium offers four box tiers, with open balcony seating in the middle of the fourth and a center royal box topped by a golden crown. On the sides of the fifth tier, directly underneath the roof is a gallery, with columns decorated in gold. Each tier has different decorations: the second displays mythological scenes, putti, and musical instruments; the third shows griffins flanking lyres; and the fourth features urns with leafy branches. On the ceiling surrounding the large center chandelier are mythological figures and griffins.

Operatic Events at the Teatro Giglio

The Teatro Pubblico witnessed intense operatic activity after its opening in 1675, with two opera seasons, one during carnival and the other in the fall, coinciding with the Festival of the Santa Croce. Two different operas were performed, four times a week. Impresarios and companies of actors and singers offered the entertainment. With the dawn of the 1700s, masked balls and intermezzos, which were choreographed dances between the acts to distract the audience from the scene changes, were popular. The 1740s saw three Scarlatti works, *Ezio*, *Olimpiade*, and *Artaserse*, and Pucitta's *L'amor platonico* was introduced at the turn of the century.

The first autumn season at the Giglio in 1819 opened with Rossini's *Aureliano in Palmira*, followed by prime assolute of Pacini's *Temistocle*, Persiani's *Eufemio da Messina*, and Quilici's *Francesca da Rimini*. The Italian premiere of *Guglielmo Tell* took place in 1831, followed by another world premiere, Poniatowski's *Ruy Blas*, during the 1840s. The operas of Rossini, Donizetti, Bellini, and then Verdi, however, dominated the schedule. Renowned singers such as Fanny Tacchinardi, Gilbert-Louis Duprez, Maria Malibran, and Giuseppina Strepponi graced the stage. Beginning in 1840, opera performances were often transformed into patriotic demonstrations, especially those of Verdi's operas, and in 1884 the world premiere of Graffigna's *La pazza per progetto* was staged. As the century was drawing to a close, the operas of Mascagni, Ponchielli, Marchetti, Catalani, and Puccini dominated the schedule. In 1911 Puccini, who had been born in Lucca, returned to direct *La fanciulla del West* and asked the municipality to shorten the stage and create an orchestra pit. The theater reopened its doors after World War I with works by three Lucca composers: Puccini's *Tosca*, Catalani's *Loreley*, and Luporini's *Dispetti amorose*. During the Fascist era, it became a political meeting place, and Mussolini attended a performance of *L'elisir d'amore* in 1930. During the 1950s, *Loreley* and *La Wally* were offered, and *Madama Butterfly* and *Manon Lescaut* celebrated the centennial of Puccini's birth. With the arrival of the 21st century, operas such as *Traviata*, *Turandot*, *Così fan tutte*, *Midsummer Night's Dream*, and *Cavalleria rusticana/La vida breve* were on the schedule. Emphasis remains with popular Italian fare, especially Verdi and Puccini. Recent offerings included *Madama Butterfly*, *La Cenerentola*, *Rigoletto*, and *Acis and Galatea*.

The Teatro Giglio is one of the three theaters involved with the CittàLirica, a regional project for opera productions that includes the Fondazione Teatro Verdi in Pisa and the CEL in Livorno. The theater also collaborates with the Study Center of Giacomo Puccini, founded in 1996 to promote research on Puccini, the music of his time, and opera theater that followed him.

Practical Information

Teatro del Giglio, piazza del Giglio 13/15, 55100 Lucca; tel. 39 0583 46531, fax 39 0583 490 317; www.teatrodelgiglio.it.

The opera season, which runs from September to February, offers four operas with two performances of each. Stay at the Hotel Universo, piazza del Giglio 1, 55100 Lucca; tel. 0583 493 678, fax 0583 954 854; www.universo lucca.com. A favorite with the artists, the Universo is a 2-minute walk from the opera house, which is directly across the piazza. Visit the Fondazione Giacomo Puccini Museum, via di Poggio, corte San Lorenzo 9; tel. 584 028. The house where Giacomo Puccini was born, and where the Puccini family had lived since the beginning of the 17th century, has been turned into a museum about the composer, displaying the piano where the maestro composed *Turandot*, some portraits of his ancestors, letters, and remembrances of his life and work.

THIRTY-TWO

~

Teatro Rossini, Lugo

There were performances of various types in Lugo from at least the 1550s, and the fair seasons had become very well known. A company of comedians performed in Lugo in 1586. Eight years later a presentation of a fable, Pirazzoli's *Filleno*, took place. After the turn of the century, Guarini's *Il pastor fido* was performed at the Teatro Paviglione (Pavilion Theater). By the 1700s, a tremendous number of theatrical events occurred in Lugo, with no fixed venue for performances, so the construction of a permanent theater was deemed necessary. A site was chosen on the periphery of the commercial area, facing the fairgrounds. The new building, designed by Francesco Ambrogio Petrocchi, was supposed to have been modeled after the theater in Medicina, designed by architect Scandellari, but Petrocchi had his own ideas and designed the auditorium in a bell shape. Under the auspices of Cardinal Giovanni Francesco Banchieri, construction began in the summer of 1758, with the citizens of Lugo bearing the cost. For the 1759 fair season, with only the exterior walls and roof finished and 38 temporary small boxes in wood arranged on two levels, the impresario Pasquale Bondini received permission to present Fischietti's *Il mercato di Malmantile*. In 1760 Antonio Galli Bibiena signed a contract to complete the interior, including the stage, boxes, and other permanent seating areas.

The Teatro Sociale, the original name of the Teatro Rossini, was officially inaugurated in 1761 with Vinci's *Catone in Utica*. An inscription in Latin on the facade recalls the construction and opening of the theater. "Theatrum / faustissimis sub auspiciis / Ioannis Francisci Bancherii / Cardinalis amplissimi / Ferrariae ab later legati / acivibus lugiensibus / aere proprio / extrui coeptum atque absolutum / anno ab orbe ristaurato / mdcclxi" (The theater, the construction of which was started at the expense of the Lugo

180

citizens, under the most propitious auspices of the illustrious Cardinal Giovanni Francesco Banchieri, special legate to Ferrara, was finished in the year 1761). There were four tiers with 16 boxes each. Teatro Rossini is regarded as a prototype of the theaters in the theater-rich Emilia Romagna region.

When the municipality took over the theater in 1763, it was renamed the Teatro Comunale. By 1821 substantial restoration work was needed. The town commissioned Leandro Marconi who, with his neoclassical taste, essentially eliminated the work of Bibiena. The bell-shaped curve of the auditorium was transformed into the traditional horseshoe shape and a gallery was added. The proscenium arch and stage were also restructured. Additional changes were made to the decorations in 1855 by Benedetto Crescentini, after which only a few of the masks of Comedy and Tragedy and delicate frescoes remained. It was renamed Teatro Rossini in 1859, to honor its most famous citizen whose father was born in Lugo and who lived there for a couple of years when he was young. A plaque commemorates the event: "I comisi consigliari / nel xxi febbraio mdccclix / vollero per acclamazione / che questo edificio del comune / dal celebratissimo concittadino / averse nome / di / Teatro Rossini" (The commissary council on the 21st February 1859 ordered by acclamation that this building of the municipality have the name of Teatro Rossini after its most celebrated citizen). The theater played an active role in the political and civic life of the city.

The Rossini declined as the 20th century progressed. It was first converted into a movie theater. After World War I and during the dark years of Fascism, it became the focal point for social demonstrations. In September 1956, it hosted its final performances. The theater was abandoned and its doors permanently shut. During the 1960s, there was talk of demolishing it, but because of its civic significance, it was spared the wrecking ball. The project of restoration first surfaced in 1972, but more than a decade passed before it was restored to its original splendor by Pier Luigi Cervellati between 1984 and 1986.

The neoclassical theater displays an austere, earth-colored facade with ornamental pillars and plaster cornices on each level, as was typical of 18th-century buildings. The unusual coral and turquoise blue 446-seat auditorium holds four box tiers topped by a gallery. White stucco relief masks of Comedy and Tragedy and white and gold ornamentation decorate the parapets of three of the box tiers. An 18th-century chandelier from Vienna hangs from the middle of a gilded sunburst of leaves, surrounded by gilded rosettes and ornamentation.

Operatic Events at the Teatro Rossini

Until the first years of the 1800s, the fare was primarily opere buffe, but the theater also hosted drama troupes, masked balls, and festivals. Between 1814 and 1840, works of Rossini dominated the stage, which alternated with operas by Bellini, Donizetti, and Mercadante, among others. The prima assoluta of Sinico's *Alessandro Stradella* took place during the second half of the century, when Verdi works prevailed. At the end of the 1800s, Puccini was first heard, followed in 1900 by Wagner's *Lohengrin*. Two years later, Arturo Toscanini conducted *Aida* there, and in 1905 the premiere of Lugo composer and conductor Pratella's *La Lilia* graced the stage.

When the Rossini reopened in 1986, its intimate size made it the perfect showplace for chamber opera. Located in the Emilia Romagna region, which has an abundant supply of opera houses, it created a unique opera identity by unearthing forgotten, obscure, and never-performed chamber operas from the 1700s opera seria and opera buffa genres. Counted among the resurrected operas were Paër's *Achille*, Galuppi's *Il mondo della luna*, Salieri's *La locandiera*, Stradella's *Il biante ovvero a laurinda*, Jommelli's *Didone abbandonata*, and Lattuada's *Le preziose ridicule*. A decade later, the theater initiated the Rossini opera project to capitalize on Rossini's 2-year stay in Lugo, where he studied singing, composition, and harpsichord. The project concentrated on operas by composers who either influenced Rossini or were influenced by him and theater works by Metastasio. The productions in 2001 included Mosca's *L'italiani in Algeri*, Mercadante's *Elena da Feltre*, Hasse's *Artaserse*, Pavesi's *Ser Marcantonio*, and Gluck's *Il trionfo di Clelia*. This last opera was not successful, so in 2002 both the director and direction of the festival changed. During the next 3 years, the evolution of the farce from Rossini's time to the present, both in Italy and other European countries, was the focus, which led to productions of Milhaud's *Le pauvre matelot*/Chabrier's *Une education manque*, De Falla's *El retablo de Maese Pedro*, and Martinů's *Mirandolina*, among others. Beginning in 2005, the festival returned to its original mission with rarities from the late 1700s, with a double bill of Paisiello's *La serva padrona* and Mozart's *Bastien und Bastienne*. There have also been pairings of 18th-century works with contemporary ones. Recent offerings included Rossini's *La scala di seta* and Respighi's *La bella dormente nel bosco*. Since the repertory is unique, excellent CDs of live performances have been produced by Teatro Rossini and Longiovanni–Bologna.

Practical Information

Teatro Rossini, piazza Cavour 17, 48022 Lugo; tel. 39 0545 38538, fax 39 0545 38482; www.teatrorossini.it.

The opera season is part of the Lugo Opera Festival, which takes place during April and May. There are one or two operas with three performances each. Stay at the Hotel Ala d'Oro, corso Matteotti 56, 48022 Lugo; tel. 0545 22388, fax 0545 30509; www.aladoro.it. A 5-minute walk from the opera house, the Ala d'Oro is in the center of Lugo and has a fine restaurant. Visit the Museum of the House of Rossini, via Giacomo Rocca 14; tel. 38556. The house was originally owned by Rossini's grandfather, and in 1839 it passed to Rossini. Although he never resided there, he took care of it, renting it to relatives. Rossini's father was born in Lugo. When he returned there in 1802 from Pesaro, the young Rossini was taught singing, composition, and harpsichord by Giuseppe and Luigi Malerbi at the Malerbi Canon's School, which was built in the beginning of the 1800s. The Villa Malerbi was the Malerbi's country residence, and the music stand from which Donizetti conducted his *Stabat Mater* in Bologna is preserved there. The collection of Rossini manuscripts that used to be there are now housed in the Trisi Library. The church of Carmine, constructed in the middle of the 1700s in the baroque style by the same architect who built the Teatro Rossini, houses a famous organ built in 1797 by Gaetano Callido on which the young Rossini practiced. Inside the Municipal Residence (the Este Fortress), in the Rossini Salon, hangs a portrait of his mother, Anna Guidarini, the Pesaro singer who married his father, Giuseppe Antonio Rossini, in 1791. A portrait of his father is also there, along with other Rossini memorabilia.

~

THIRTY-THREE

Macerata Opera—Sferisterio and Teatro Lauro Rossi, Macerata

In the 1500s in the Palazzo Comunale, a *sala della commedia* (comedy room) was in operation until 1662, when Monsignore Agostino Franciotti, governor of Macerata, proposed the erection of a permanent theater in the *sala grande* (large room) of the magistrate's palazzo. The project was approved the following year with Giambattista Franceschini entrusted with its execution. On August 31, 1663, for the Feast of San Giuliano, the theater was inaugurated, built at a cost of 450 scudi. Designed by Cornelio Felici and Giulio Lazzarelli, it held 45 boxes divided among the three tiers. Only a year later, it was deemed too small for the needs of the city and demolished. The theater was then rebuilt according to the plans of Giacomo Torelli. In 1684 the performance venue was enlarged by extending it into part of the court room with the addition of a fourth tier and seven new boxes.

In 1765 46 Macerata noblemen formed the *condomini teatrale* under the auspices of Raniero Finocchietti, governor of the Marche region, to build a much larger theater in the same location. The designs submitted by Antonio Galli Bibiena were impossible to realize in the space chosen for the theater, so in 1769 the project was given to Cosimo Morelli, who adapted the plans and constructed the Teatro Condomini, keeping Bibiena's bell-shaped curve, four tiers of boxes, and eight proscenium boxes. The Teatro Condomini was inaugurated January 2, 1774, with Anfossi's *Olimpiade*. It was designed in the late-baroque style, reminiscent of Bibiena's Teatro Comunale in Bologna. During the first few decades of the 1800s, in keeping with the tastes of the times, various renovation and redecorating projects were submitted to impose a neoclassical design, but fortunately none were executed. There was some restructuring, including in 1855 the conversion of the fourth tier of boxes to a gallery, executed by Agostino Benedettelli. The theater was restored in 1870 according to plans of Mario Monti and Luigi Samoggia that included grading the orchestra floor, among other modifications.

The municipality took over ownership of the Teatro Condomini in 1872 when the *condomini* sold their boxes, and a dozen years later the theater was renamed Lauro Rossi to honor the Macerata-born opera composer. In 1919 a citizens' association for public entertainment elected Pieralberto Conti, who personally paid for a production of *La fanciulla del West* at the theater, as its president. Additional work was executed on the building in the mid-1900s. In 1983 the Rossi was declared unsafe and closed. Giancarlo de Mattia was entrusted with the restoration project, which saw a return of the original colors and form to the venue. Gianfranco Pasquali restored the painting and Franco Cudini the wood. Completed in 1989, the renovation cost totaled around $2 million.

The Rossi is a 550-seat, baroque-style gem, decorated in ivory, gold, and bluish gray. There are three tiers topped by a gallery. The delicately carved balustrades that form tiny balconies, a hallmark of Bibiena, are embellished with stucco ornamentation and silvery, light-blue imitation marble. Gray marble columns with gilded Corinthian capitals flank the proscenium boxes. The ceiling is decorated with allegorical motifs, dating from 1870 by Luigi Samoggia. On the stage curtain is displayed the coat of arms of Macerata.

Operatic Events at the Lauro Rossi

A new operatic era began at the Rossi in 1990, thanks to the efforts of Gustav Kuhn. There was an updated production of *Così fan tutte* with the singers clad only in bikinis. During the next few seasons, *Don Pasquale*, *Le nozze di Figaro*, and some minor Rossini works, such as *La cambiale di matrimonio*, *Bruschino*, *L'occasione fa il ladro*, and *La scala di seta*, were on the boards. Then opera left the stage and did not return until 1998, when to celebrate the bicentennial of the birth of Giacomo Leopardi, a commissioned work, *Giacomo mio, salviamoci* by Giorgio Battistelli, received its prima assoluta on July 11, 1998. Verdi's *Oberto*, Maderna's *Satyricon*, *Ozeanflug/Die sieben Todsünden* followed. Most recently, Poulenc's *Les mamelles de Tirésias* was offered. The rarities complement the spectacular, popular productions at the Sferisterio.

The Sferisterio

The Sferisterio, from the Greek *sphaera*, was originally built as a playing field for *pallone a bracciale* (pallone with an armlet), a popular type of ball game dating from the 15th century. The Sferisterio was erected by 100 of Macerata's wealthiest families, who formed the Società Fondatrice di Macerata to pay for the construction. Four architects submitted drawings, and in August 1820, two were selected, those of Salvatore Innocenzi and Signor Spata. But Spata refused to accept the changes requested to his plans and left the project. Innocenzi modified his plans but other problems arose, including the discovery that there were not enough boxes to accommodate all the founding members (originally there were only 40 boxes), which prompted some of the members to threaten to leave. This led to arguments and bad feeling between Innocenzi and some of the members, so a request for new designs went out and in August 1823 Ireneo Aleandri submitted drawings. His plans were accepted, and in December 1823 construction began (ironically, under the direction of Innocenzi). But the project was plagued by problems with the construction companies, contract disputes, cost overruns, and work stoppages that delayed the completion until August 1829. Finally, on September 5, 1829, the Sferisterio was inaugurated with a month-long celebration that included ball games, medieval jousts, horseback tournaments, and fireworks.

Only 2 years after its inauguration, another use for the Sferisterio was found, that of a performance venue. The drama company of Alfonso Frati and Eurenio Lavagnoli staged some plays, followed in 1843 by a comic opera, Fioravanti's *Non tutti i pazzi son all'ospedale*, that only some months earlier had had its prima assoluta at Teatro La Fenice in Naples. In 1850 Shakespeare's *Henry IV* and Pellico's *Francesca da Rimini* were offered, followed by *La pazza di Tolone* with music by Saint Amand-Lacoste. The performances took place in daylight. By 1863 the passion for pallone had waned, and the number of theatrical shows had increased such that a moveable stage was constructed. The Compagnia Favi-Fioravanti presented Von Suppé's *Boccaccio* in 1886 followed by Mosca's *Amori ed armi*. Sport spectacles still took place, and with the arrival of the 20th century, football exhibitions and lawn-tennis were the new passions. The military occupied the Sferisterio during World War I. After the war, in July 1921, the first grand opera, *Aida*, was performed. The final game of pallone took place in 1960, and 6 years later, the arena was restructured into a permanent open-air opera venue. In 1967 *Otello* inaugurated the Macerata Opera and the regular summer opera season.

The Sferisterio is an open-air, hemicycle arena of earth-tone brick that can be viewed as a type of coliseum. On the exterior, a series of archlike impressions on both levels break up the massive brick surface. The coat of arms of Macerata crowns the structure. In 1901 a dedication to the hundred original founders was inscribed on the front: "Ad Ornamento della Città a Diletto Pubblico la Generosità di Cento Consorti Edifice MDCCCXXIX" (To the Decoration of the City to Public Pleasure the Generosity of the Hundred Building Associates 1829). Inside are two tiers of 52 boxes, separated by large Doric columns, in an open-sided gallery setting. A "magistrate" box is located in the center underneath a soaring arch. The stage is set against the straight, massive, former ball-playing wall. The arena accommodates between 3,500 and 4,500 spectators, depending upon the set design. They do not sell obstructed-view seats.

Macerata Opera Events at the Sferisterio

The seeds for a summer opera season at the Sferisterio were planted in 1914 when a group of opera lovers from Macerata visited the arena in Verona. With acoustics of the Sferisterio like those of the arena, mimicking that of a closed theater, a series of performances of *Norma* were planned. The arrival of World War I forced the project to be canceled. After the war, Conti, who was very wealthy and in love with the soprano Francisca Solari, paid for a production of *Aida* at the Sferisterio in 1921. An immense stage was built and electric lighting installed. A huge orchestra, massive chorus, numerous ballet dancers, and a large number of horseback riders were assembled, along with an enormous publicity campaign. People came from all over Italy: 3,000 were seated and another 6,000 standing. It was a tremendous success. The following year *Gioconda* was staged, but it rained and turned into a financial disaster from which Conti never recovered. Nothing happened until 1929 when Beniamino Gigli gave an extraordinary concert, recalling his debut in 1907 at the Lauro Rossi. Opera was not heard again until 1967 when the Macerata Opera, founded by the former baritone Carlo Perucci, was officially inaugurated with *Otello*.

During the early years, it was a small organization with little money. The seasons offered exclusively popular Italian operas of the 19th and early 20th centuries, including some Macerata premieres such as *Turandot*, *Falstaff*, and *Don Carlo*. Then in 1977, *Assassinio nella cattedrale* appeared in the program. The 1980s saw a further broadening of the repertory with foreign works, including *Khovanshchina*, *Elektra*, *West Side Story*, *Zauberflöte*, and *Tannhäuser*. The experiment was not financially successful, and the popular Italian repertory returned. The company spent most of its money on attracting the best singers, including Birgit Nilsson, Franco Corelli, Luciano Pavarotti, Cesare Siepi, Magda Olivero, Leo Nucci, Marilyn Horne, José Carreras, Montserrat

Caballé, Fiorenza Cossotto, Olivia Stapp, Ghena Dimitrova, and Eva Marton.

Meanwhile, the traditional staging and directing gave way to bold, new concepts, some of which bordered on the scandalous. Directors from outside the opera world were hired. Ken Russell reset *Madama Butterfly* in a bordello. Collado advanced the time with each act of *Bohème*: the third act was set during the Nazi era, and Mimi died of a drug overdose in the fourth act. Zefferelli relocated *Carmen* to New York with motorcycle gangs. By the end of the 1980s, the flood of international stars had slowed to a trickle. Around the same time Gustav Kuhn arrived on the scene, bringing more Wagner and Mozart operas to Macerata, which was not popular. As the 20th century came to a close, the seasons had returned to being almost exclusively Italian, with *Attila*, *L'elisir d'amore*, *Nabucco*, *Falstaff*, and *Otello* among others on the boards. The success of the Sferisterio lies in offering popular titles in spectacular productions, which it returned to at the end of the 20th and beginning of the 21st centuries. There was a stunning *Traviata* with a clever play of mirrors conceived by Josef Svoboda; a poignant *Madama Butterfly* set against the backdrop of a symbolic Fujiyama that was in continual transformation by Henning Brockhaus; an awesome *Turandot* with imaginative, multipurpose, monumental spheres; and an award-winning, breathtaking *Aida* by Hugo de Ana. The first few years of the 21st century saw a continuation of popular Italian fare with *Aida*, *Macbeth*, *Norma*, *Tosca*, *Rigoletto*, *Lucia di Lammermoor*, and *Cavalleria rusticana/Pagliacci*. In 2004 with a change in management and the belief that the repertory needed a drastic renewal, operas such as *Les contes d'Hoffmann*, *Francesca da Rimini*, and *Simon Boccanegra* were on the schedule. Recently, the fare is again more popular but still spectacular, with *Don Carlo*, *Andrea Chénier*, and *Tosca*.

Practical Information

Macerata Opera, Sferisterio, piazza Mazzini 10, 62100 Macerata; tel. 39 0733 230 735, fax 0733 261 570; www.macerataopera.org. Teatro Lauro Rossi, Piazza della Libertì 21; tel. 256 306; www.tuttiteatri-mc.net/teatri/laurorossi.

The season, which takes place during July and August, offers three operas with four to seven performances each at the Sferisterio and one opera with two performances at the Teatro Lauro Rossi. Stay at Arena Hotel, Vicolo Sferisterio 16; tel. 230931. A modest hotel, it is a 3-minute walk from the Sferisterio and 8 minutes from the Teatro Rossi.

~

THIRTY-FOUR

Teatro Comunale, Modena

In 1643 the first of several theaters that would be built in Modena opened, the Teatro Valentini. Constructed of wood, it survived 38 years before succumbing to fire on January 20, 1681. The rebuilding of the Valentini began in February 1682, but during construction a boundary dispute between the Valentini family and the Rangoni family erupted, delaying completion until November 1683. Two years later, the Marquis Fontanelli bought the theater, renaming it Teatro Fontanelli. Eleven operas were performed, including a couple of world premieres: Giannettini's *L'ingresso alla gioventù di Claudio Nerone* and Boni's *Il figlio delle selve*. Fontanelli then sold the building to Count Teodoro Rangoni on July 29, 1705, for 65,000 lire. Renamed Teatro Rangoni, the theater began hosting performances that fall, opening with *Il trionfo d'amore nè tradimenti*. During the Rangoni's long life, it introduced Abos's *Tito Manlio*, Scolari's *Il finto cavaliero*, Lampugnani's *La scuola delle cantatrici*, Rutini's *Gli sposi in maschera*, and Paisiello's *Madama l'umorista* and *Il Demetrio*. In fact, several of Paisiello's operas were popular, including *Il re Teodoro*, *Il fanatico in Berlina*, and *Demofonte*. During the last two decades of the 1700s, Pio's *Demofonte*, Sirotti's *La Zenobia*, Giuliani's *Guerra in pace*, Giordani's *La vestale*, and Gazzaniga's *Il divorzio senza matrimonio* were introduced and Sarti, Paisiello, and Cimarosa were the most favored composers.

Next, the Teatro Ducale di Piazza, commissioned by Francesco I, opened in 1656 with Manelli's *Andromeda*. Designed by Gaspare Vigarani, the Ducale contained six boxes on two tiers, elegantly decorated proscenium boxes flanked by Corinthian columns, and benches in the rear. Modena saw its first world premiere in this theater in 1674, Mazzi's *Il principe Corsaro* followed by Acciajuoli's *Il girello*. Also of note were Cesti's *La schiava fortunata* and Cavalli's *Il ciro*. The last operatic performance in the Ducale was Clemente Monari's *Atlanta* performed by a local academy in 1710. The building was razed in 1769.

On March 13, 1686, the Teatro di Corte, commissioned by Francesco II with Tommaso Bezzi responsible for the construction, was inaugurated with Rosselli-Genesini's *L'Eritrea*. It was in a small private room that hosted many productions by the students of the Collegio dei Nobili, including Perti's *L'Apollo geloso* and Pulli's *Il carnevale e la pazzia*. After the Court Theater was enlarged according to the designs of Antonio Cugini in 1749, it was opened to the public, introducing Rutini's *La Nitteti*; Latilla's *Antigona*; Mortellari's *Armida*; Paisiello's *Artaserse* and *Alessandro nelle Indie*; Bortnianski's *Quinto Fabio*; and Bianchi's *Erfile* and *Enea nel Lazio*. With the accession of Napoleon, the theater was rebaptized Teatro Nazionale. Works of Portogallo, Mayr, Vaccai, and Zingarelli graced the stage. It was renamed Teatro Regio in 1804 and finally regained its original name, Teatro di Corte, in 1814. The theater hosted all the *prime esecuzioni mondiali* of operas by the Modenese composer Antonio Gandini—*Erminia*, *Ruggero*, *Antigono*, and *Il disertore*—and almost all by his son Alessandro Gandini—*Demetrio*, *Zaira*, *Isabella di Lara*, and *Maria di Brabante*. The structure was permanently shut in 1859. Three years later, the Teatro Aliprandi opened where the Teatro di Corte had existed. Named after the impresario Achille Aliprandi, the theater hosted three world premieres, Rossi's *Mimì*, Mazzoli's *Adela d'Asturia*, and Buzzino's *L'orfanella di Gand* before burning to the ground in March 1881.

The Teatro Molza, which survived only 36 years, opened December 26, 1713, with Gasparini's *La fede tradita e vendicata*. Built on the initiative of Nicolò Molza and under the direction of Antonio Maria Bononcini, the Molza hosted many operas, including the *prima mondiale* of Schiassi's *La Zanina finta contessa*. The final opera, Scarlatti's *Pompeo in Armenia*, was staged in 1749. The Molza closed in 1764.

Meanwhile, the Teatro Rangoni, after more than a century under the Rangoni family, was transferred in 1807 to a society of *palchettisti* who managed it for almost a decade, before giving it in 1816 to Duke Francesco IV, whose duchy ruled the city at the time. The duke passed it to the municipality, but the boxes were returned to the original owners or their heirs, and the theater was dually owned by a public institution and private citizens. To reflect the new ownership arrangement, the building was renamed Teatro Comunale di via Emilia. In 1813 when *Demetrio e Polibio*, the first of many Rossini operas arrived at the theater, followed by Donizetti and Bellini works, the Italian masters of the 1600s and 1700s disappeared from the repertory.

Other popular composers included Mercadante, Pacini, Petrella, and the brothers Ricci. In 1841 the theater was rebaptized the Comunale Vecchio, because a new municipal theater had opened. It closed its doors in 1859.

The roots for the Teatro dell'Illustrissima Comunità, the original name of the Teatro Comunale, were planted in 1838, when Marquis Ippolito Livizzani, the mayor of Modena, and the Conservatorio dell'Illustrissima Comunità (Conservatory of the Most Illustrious Community) decided to construct a new theater "for the dignity of the city and for the transmission of the scenic arts" to replace the aging Teatro Comunale di via Emilia, which could no longer accommodate the theatrical requirements of the productions or the growing population of the city. Francesco Vandelli, the architect of the project, incorporated in his design for the new edifice ideas from the theaters at Piacenza, Mantua, and Milan. The location chosen for the new structure required the demolition of 12 houses. The new opera house took 3 years to build and cost 722,000 lire, paid for by the sale of boxes in the new theater, the selling of material recovered from the demolition of the houses, and a substantial gift from Friedrich IV. On October 2, 1841, Gandini's *Adelaide di Borgogna al Castello di Canossa*, an opera specially commissioned for the inaugural, opened the Comunale. As a chronicler of the time reported, "Yesterday evening, the solemn opening of this noble and magnificent building under the auspices of the Royal court took place. . . . The magnificence of the decorations renders it most brilliant. . . . The presence of the royal family, ministers, dignitaries, nobility, and the bourgeoisie gave the evening a formal aspect that this tiny duchy had awaited for a long time. The architect, Vandelli received the first applause. The opera was a success and the singers enthusiastically applauded." But *Il ricoglitore fiorentino* had a different opinion, writing that there was "grand confusion in the libretto" and "noise and unevenness" in the music.

The ducal period ended in 1859 when Friedrich V left Modena and the opera house was renamed Teatro Municipale. After the unification of Italy, the coat of arms from the House of Savoy replaced the golden Este eagle above the center royal box. Between 1915 and 1923, the Municipale remained closed. First the military requisitioned the building because of the war, then there was a dispute between the box holders and the municipality, and finally the building was declared unsafe. During this time, the performances took place at the Teatro Storchi.

The Teatro Storchi had opened in the spring of 1889 with Usiglio's *Le donne curiose* with the composer on the podium. Designed by Vincenzo Maestri, it was constructed on land ceded gratuitously by the city. Gaetano Storchi, a wealthy businessman and art lover, paid for the erection of the building, which filled the need in the city for a theater to host popular and escapism entertainment. The theater had two facades, executed in the Greek-Roman style. The horseshoe-shaped auditorium held three tiers that offered mixed boxes and balcony seating, separated by cast-iron columns, and topped by a gallery. The ceiling was painted with an allegorical subject, *The Apotheosis of the Prince of Italian Comedy*. The Storchi hosted five prime assolute, including Gazzotti's *Lo zingaro cisco* and *La procella*. The repertory was predominately popular 19th-century Italian operas. In 1959 after 70 years of opera, the Storchi began hosting only dramatic fare, except when the Comunale was undergoing restoration work. The building was purchased by the municipality and restored during the 1980s.

Meanwhile, the Arena-Teatro Goldoni opened in 1860, surviving three decades and hosting 24 opera seasons between 1867 and 1888, alternating with the Aliprandi and Municipale.

In 1935 an orchestra pit was created in the Municipale, and 21 years later, it regained its original name, Teatro Comunale. As the 20th century drew to a close, the Comunale was closed for a complete restoration, including modernization of technical facilities and restoring the original decor. The red of the orchestra, boxes, and stage curtain in the auditorium gave way to its original rose hue. The restoration cost topped $9 million, paid for by the municipality and region of Emilia Romagna. The Comunale reopened December 20, 1998.

The imposing edifice offers a neoclassical facade. On the ground level is a nine-arch portico, the center of which has four Doric columns supporting a narrow balcony. On the middle level, four Ionic pilasters flank architrave windows topped by bas-reliefs that illustrate the tragedies of Modenese writers, the work of Luigi Righi. Crowning the structure is a statue, *The Genius of Modena*, also executed by Righi. Smaller windows and ornamental wreaths define the attic level. The elliptical, neoclassical, 900-seat auditorium radiates with ivory, gold, and rose. There are 112 boxes distributed in four tiers, topped by a gallery, and the former royal box. The gilded Este eagle with spread wings is again perched atop the center box. Golden figures of mythological subjects embellish the parapets. Fluted, gilded, half-Corinthian columns flank the proscenium boxes, which display frolicking putti on the parapets, and support an architrave adorned with golden lyre and masks. The slightly curved ceiling, embellished with ornamental designs by Camillo Crespolani, displays four figures representing Music, Poetry, Comedy, and Tragedy, the work of Luigi Manzini, that alternate with chiaroscuro medallions of Verdi, Bellini, Donizetti, and Rossini. Toward the center are four medallions of Dante Alighieri, Lucovico Ariosto, Torquato Tasso, and Francesco Petrarca. The historic curtain by Adeodato Malatesta portrays Hercules I d'Este in 1486 visiting the Teatro di Corte under construction in Ferrera.

Operatic Events at the Teatro Comunale

After the inaugural opera by Gandini, the season continued with Merca- dante's *Il bravo*, Bellini's *Beatrice di Tenda*, and Catelani's *Carattaco*. For car- nival season, F. Ricci's *La prigione di Edimburgo*, L. Ricci's *Che dura vince*, and Rossini's *Il barbiere di Siviglia* were on the boards. Donizetti works dominated the 1842 season, being three of the four operas staged. The first of Verdi's operas entered the repertory during Carnival 1843/44 with *Nabucco*, followed by *Ernani*, *I Lombardi*, *I due Foscari*, *I masnadieri*, *Luisa Miller*, *Macbeth*, *Il cor- saro*, *Trovatore*, *Attila*, *La traviata*, *Vespri siciliani*, *Ballo in maschera*, and *Rigo- letto*. The 1859 spring opera season opened with *Aroldo* on May 9 and for three evenings it played to an empty house. The impresario, facing bank- ruptcy, fled and the theater was closed. As the second half of the 1800s pro- gressed, composers such as Apolloni, Gentile, Ricci, and Marchetti were much in evidence alongside Verdi, Donizetti, and Bellini. The mostly Italian repertory was peppered with French grand operas such as *Les Huguenots*, *Faust*, *La Juive*, and *Le prophète*. There were also a few prime mondiali, Gio- vannini's *Irene*, Pedrotti's *Olema*, and Bertini's *Roncisval*.

With the dawn of the 20th century, Giordano, Puccini, Alfano, Mas- cagni, Leoncavallo, Montemezzi, Cilea, Zandonai, and Franchetti were the favored composers. The repertory remained predominately Italian with the works of the verismo school popular, with occasional German and French opera, such as *Siegfried*, *Tristan und Isolde*, *Manon*, *Mignon*, and *Les pêcheurs de perles*. Seasons of popular Italian fare continued during World War II, and between 1937 and 1950 there were three prime assolute, Azzolini's *Wanda* and *Rossana* and Valentini's *Mi-kel*. Beginning in the 1960s, some Modena novelties were staged, including Donizetti's *Rita*, Haydn's *Lo speziale*, Proko- fiev's *L'yubov' k tryom apel'sinam* (The Love for Three Oranges), Rimsky- Korsakov's *Zolotoy petushok* (The Golden Cockerel), and Ghedini's *La pulce d'oro*. In 1964 the Association of the Theaters of Emilia Romagna was founded, which led to coproductions with the operas houses in Reggio Emi- lia, Piacenza, Ferrara, Ravenna, Parma, and Bologna. As the millennium approached, works such as *Otello; Salome; Idomeneo, re di Creta;* and *Tosca* were on the boards.

Designated as a *Teatro di tradizione*, it is in the top 10 in this classification in terms of funding. But with only 20 permanent staff, it has not been afflicted with the financial problems of the *enti autonomi* theaters. With the dawn of the 21st century, the Teatro Comunale formed a *fondazione*. Besides the standard Italian repertory, the offerings have expanded to include more non-Italian, rarely performed, and contemporary works, such as Stockhausen's *Montag aus Licht*, Stravinsky's *Rake's Progress*, and Mascagni's *Le maschere*. The opera house has hosted Italian premiers, such as Adams's *Death of Klinghoffer*, Battistelli's *Prova d'orchestra*, and Betta's *Il fantasia nella cabina*, and commissioned operas for children, including D'Amico's *Lavinia Fuggita* and Scannavini's *Il fantasma di Canterville*. A recent season included *Nabucco, Ariadne auf Naxos, La gioconda, Il trovatore, Three Penny Opera,* and *Peter Grimes*.

Modena is the home town of Luciano Pavarotti and Mirella Freni, so in 2005 the Comunale paid tribute to Freni on the 50th anniversary of her debut, and the opera house was the scene of Pavarotti's second marriage.

Practical Information

Teatro Comunale, via del Teatro 8, 41100 Modena; tel. 39 059 200010, fax 39 059 200025; www.teatrocomunalemodena.it.

The opera season runs from October to April and offers seven operas with two performances of each. The Hotel Centrale, via Rismondo 55, 41100 Modena; tel. 059 218808, fax 39 059 238 202, is a 5-minute walk from the theater.

THIRTY-FIVE

Cantiere Internazionale d'Arte, Montepulciano

The Cantiere was founded by the German composer Hans Werner Henze in 1976 as a showcase for lesser-known operatic works and commissions and as a place for professional musicians and artists to work (without pay) with young talent. After several years, differences surfaced between Henze and the municipality, which played an important role in the project, and Henze left. The Cantiere then declined. With a different director almost every year, it floundered, looking for direction and purpose. As the 20th century drew to a close, stability returned to the festival with a return to Henze's philosophy with operas such as De Falla's *El retablo de maese Pedro* and *Gianni Schicchi* on the boards for the last season of the 20th century. For the first few years of the 21st century, a broad selection of operas was offered. They ranged from the late 1600s to 1700s, *Matrimonio segreto*, *Dido and Aeneas*, and *Maestro di Cappella*, to the 20th century, *The Telephone*, *Voix humane*, and *Il tabarro*; from unusual pieces, Krása's *Brundibar* and Chailly's *Il libro dei reclaim* and *Una domanda di matrimonio*, to perennial favorites, *Madama Butterfly*, *Don Pasquale*, *Nozze di Figaro*, *Falstaff*, and *La sonnambula*.

It should be pointed out that the Cantiere is not a festival but a factory, and the amateurs and professionals that congregate every summer in this small, medieval, hilltop Tuscan village come together to "manufacture" art and culture. Guiding principles include following Henze's original concept, with teaching and experimental works related to the social-cultural environment; keeping close contact with and creating a type of collaboration with local associations and institutions connected to culture in general and music in particular; and encouraging interaction between the national and international professionals and locals.

The festival uses several venues, including the Teatro Comunale Poliziano for operatic works, Cortile della Fortezza for *opere a pezzi* (pieces of operas), and the Teatro dei Concordi in Acquaviva for avant-garde undertakings. The program offers opera, music, theater, and dance ranging from the popular to the experimental.

The Poliziano was originally built in the late 1700s. Damaged by fire, it was reconstructed in 1881 by Agusto Corbi to its present appearance, reopening on April 25, 1882, "with extraordinary pomp." There is a plaque in the entrance hall dedicated "to the glorious memory of maestro Giuseppe Verdi" affixed on July 21, 1901, barely 6 months after the maestro's death. The exterior of the Poliziano fuses red brick, stone, and concrete, with small shuttered windows punctuating the modest facade that was typical of 18th-century Italian theaters. The entrance is through a large arched door. The 300-seat, horseshoe-shaped auditorium of gold, ivory, beige, and red holds four tiers of boxes. Gilded ornamentation embellishes the parapets. Medallions of famous composers and playwrights, including Rossini, Donizetti, Shakespeare, Goldoni, and Poliziano decorate the ceiling. Only the cupola of the auditorium remains from the original structure. The rest of the auditorium was created during the restoration and restructuring of the 1800s.

The Teatro Concordi opened in 1907. It is a small structure with only a single tier in the rectangular auditorium of white and red. Wreath-encircled portraits of composers, including Verdi and Rossini, alternate with lyres on the parapets. Faces of maidens embellish the balcony supports. An allegorically inspired ceiling is painted with seven bell-ringing Muses.

Practical Information

Cantiere Internazionale d'Arte, piazza Grande 7, 53045 Montepulciano; tel. 39 0578 712 228, fax 39 0578 758 307; www.nautilus-mp.com/cantiere. Teatro Comunale Poliziano, via del Teatro 6; tel. 0578 757 281. Teatro dei Concordi, via F.lli Braschi, Acquaviva. The festival takes place from the end of July through the beginning of August, offering two operas with one to three performances of each.

THIRTY-SIX

∼

Associazione in Canto, Narni, Amelia, and Terni

•

In 1782 the Nobile Società Teatrale was formed to finance the construction of a new theater in Amelia, to be built in 2 years and to cost no more than 5,000 scudi. The money was borrowed from the Franchi family, who guaranteed the loan with their property. The members of the Società repaid the loan at the rate of 8 scudi a year. Extensive delays in construction and a devaluation of the currency caused the sum to double before the building was completed. Giuseppe Mattei designed the opera house, selected the site, and purchased the wood. (The all-wood interior was reinforced with concrete in the 1990s.) The Nobile Teatro Sociale, as the Teatro Sociale was originally known, hosted its first performance in 1791, an oratorio in music, before it was finished. Four years later, two farces in music were offered by the Compagnia dell'Impresario Vincenzo Dionisi. During the 1800s, there were several opera productions, including *Don Pasquale*, *Lucia di Lammermoor*, *I due Foscari*, *L'italiana in Algeri*, *Il barbiere di Siviglia*, Pergolesi's *La serva padrona*, Ricci's *Crispino e la comare*, and Donizetti's *Marino Faliero*. In 1881 after a restoration, *La favorita* reopened the Sociale. Some operas were staged in the 1900s, including *Traviata*, *Fedora*, *Cavalleria rusticana*, *Pagliacci*, and Paër's *Il maestro di cappella*. For the 50th anniversary of Verdi's death, *Rigoletto*, *Ballo in maschera*, and *Traviata* were on the boards. The 1960s witnessed *Trovatore* and *Tosca*, among others. Between 1913 and 1977, opera shared the stage with movies. The nondescript exterior, typical of Italian buildings in the 1700s, conceals a jewel of an auditorium. The 300-seat, lyre-shaped space of bluish green, creamy white, dark yellow, and red holds 45 boxes and a gallery. Each tier displays a different ornamentation: the first tier is decorated

197

with rosettes, the second with Greek lyres and vases of red flowers, and the top with vases of multicolored flowers. Chiaroscuro masks of Comedy and Tragedy embellish the proscenium boxes. Putti and Harlequins adorn the dome ceiling.

In Narni, a group of nobility formed the Società Teatrale in the early 1800s to finance the construction of a new theater, replacing an older one located in the Palazzo Comunale that was no longer adequate for the needs of the town. The construction lasted more than a decade because the financial burden became too onerous for the Società and the funding dried up. The municipality took over the project, bringing it to completion. The almost 16,000 scudi cost was double the original budget, to which the Società contributed only 2,500 scudi. Giovanni Santini designed the building, with Enrico Benvenuti and Giovanni Battista Prisco responsible for the paintings and decorations. Giovanni Biagini was the contractor. The new theater, called the Teatro Comunale, was inaugurated in May 1856 with *La traviata*. During the first decades, *Rigoletto*, *Ballo in maschera*, *Faust*, *Forza del destino*, and *Traviata* were the operas most often performed. The first years of the 1900s also witnessed regular opera seasons with similar operas, including *Barbiere di Siviglia*. The horseshoe-shaped, 380-seat auditorium holds three tiers and a gallery. The parapets, with backgrounds of bluish green, maroon, and beige, are embellished with gilded masks of Comedy and Tragedy, faces of women, lions' heads, musical instruments, and wreaths.

In Terni, the Teatro Nuovo was constructed between 1840 and 1848 on the ruins of the 17th-century Palazzo dei Priori, which had been damaged in the 1703 earthquake and subsequently demolished. The new theater replaced the Teatro dei Nobili, which had opened in 1745. Designed by Luigi Poletti, the Nuovo was inaugurated in 1849 with Pacini's *Saffo*. Subsequently renamed the Teatro Verdi in 1908, it reopened with *Otello* after some restoration. Additional work followed in 1930, with *Turandot* reinaugurating the theater. After a bombing raid in 1943/44, only the exterior walls remained. It was reconstructed in the 1950s as an enormous movie theater, following the plans of architect Francesco Leoni. The theater is a somber, concrete structure, with a stately portico of six Ionic columns. Etched in the entablature in bright red letters is "Teatro Comunale Giuseppe Verdi." The red, tan, and white auditorium is contemporary in design and holds three tiers in spacious surroundings.

Operatic Events of Opera in Canto

The seeds for Opera in Canto were planted in 1982 with a performance of Händel's *Il pastor fido* in the Teatro Sociale in Amelia, under the auspices of the Corsi di Musica barocca (Studies of Baroque Music). Three years later, the Estate Musicale Amerina took place again in Amelia with performances of *La serva padrona* and Scarlatti's *La dirindina*. Opera in Canto was officially founded in 1986 for the purpose of diffusing the grand heritage of never-performed Italian music. That same year, the Province of Terni and the Associazione Filarmonica Umbra (Umbrian Philharmonic Association) together offered Pergolesi's *San Guglielmo, duca d'Aquitania* in three cities, Amelia, Narni, and Orvieto. And in 1987 under the sole auspices of the province of Terni, Pasquini's *La forza d'amore* and Rossini's *Il cambiale di matrimonio* were presented in Amelia, Narni, and Terni. The next year, Opera in Canto initiated annual opera seasons with funding from both public and private corporations. The company focused on unearthing forgotten intermezzi of the 1700s (opera buffa), operas from the first decades of the 1800s both popular and unknown, and commissioning and highlighting works of major contemporary Italian composers, including D'Amico, Panni, Betta, Galante, Boccadoro, Donatoni, Pedini, and Pennisi.

The company initially offered popular works alongside the rediscovered operas to build an audience base: Franchi/Anfossi's *Il Baron di Rocca Antica*, Rossini's *Il barbiere di Siviglia*, and Morlacchi's *Il barbiere di Siviglia* and *Cenerentola*. Then only rarities graced the stage. In 1990 it was Donizetti's *Il pigmalione* and *Rita*, Gluck's *L'innocenza*, and Salieri's *Arlecchinata*. The 1991 season saw the unearthing of Morlacchi's *Il poeta disperato* and Hasse's *La contadina*. Beginning in 1992 with Sarro's *Dorina e Nibbio* and Rossini's *L'inganno felice* in the repertory, Opera in Canto came under the management of the Associazione in Canto, which led to contemporary operas making an appearance. In 1995 Betta's *Sabaoth e Sammael* was contrasted to Rossini's *Signor Bruschino*. The next season witnessed the Association's first world premiere, D'Amico's *Farinelli, la voce perduta*. More contemporary works followed, including Boccadoro's *A qualcuno piace tango*, Galante's *Combattimento con l'angolo*, Donatoni's *Alfred, Alfred*, and the world premiere of Pedini's *Così fan (quasi) tutte*. After the dawn of the millennium, money became less plentiful, so the contemporary operas were geared to children, since the company felt that youngsters were more open to new works than adults. This led in 2005 to the world premiere of *Dr. Jekyll and Mr. Hyde*, which the association had commissioned. The company continued to stage forgotten operas, such as Cimarosa's *Il maestro di Cappella*, Salieri's *Prima la musica poi le parole*, Rimsky-Korsakov's *Mozart e Salieri*, Morlacchi's *Saffo*, and Donizetti's *Il campanello*. Some recent rediscoveries include Capua's *La zingara* and Cherubini's *Il giocatore*.

Practical Information

Associazione in Canto, Campocavallo 248, 05024 Giove (Narni, headquarters); tel. 39 0744 992 894; www.operaincanto.com. Teatro Sociale, via del Teatro 22, 05022 Amelia; tel. 0744 978 315. Teatro Comunale, via Garibaldi, 05035 Narni; tel. 0744 726 326. Teatro Verdi, corso Vittorio Emanuele 23, 05100 Terni; tel. 0744 409 100.

Opera in Canto takes place in December, consisting of two operas with three performances of each, in each of the three towns. Terni is the most convenient place to stay, at the Hotel Michelangelo Palace, viale della Stazione, 63, Terni; tel. 0744 202 711, fax 0744 202 7200; www.michelangelo hotelumbria.it. The Michelangelo Palace is a 12-minute walk from the Teatro Verdi in Terni and across the street from the train station with direct links to the other towns.

THIRTY-SEVEN

Teatro Regio, Parma

The first theater of note in Parma was the Teatro Farnese, created from the weapons room on the first floor of the Palazzo della Pilotta between 1617 and 1618. It was the idea of Ranuccio I Farnese, Duke of Parma. During a visit to Florence in 1604, he attended a performance of Peri's *Dafne* that had such impressive stage effects that he decided to build a theater in Parma capable of similar effects to impress important visitors. He hired Giovanni Battista Aleotti, who assembled an expert construction team.

Although the theater was completed in record time, Ranuccio waited in vain for the politically important visit from the Grand Duke Cosimo II de'Medici that was to be celebrated with an elaborate show in his new theater. Although the grand duke had announced a stop in Parma on the occasion of his pilgrimage to the tomb of San Carlo in Milan, he did not make the trip for diplomatic reasons. The theater sat idle for a decade before it hosted its first spectacle, Peri's and Monteverdi's *Mercurio e Marte*, in honor of the marriage between Odoardo Farnese and Margherita de'Medici. The production included a tournament and ended with an incredible shipwreck, for which the orchestra floor was completely flooded with water pumped from tanks beneath the stage. Spectators feared the floor would collapse from the weight of the water. The theater was used only nine times, for visits from royalty and for wedding celebrations. Three of the weddings were for the three marriages of Ranuccio II Farnese: first to Margherita Violante of Savoy, then to Isabella d'Este, and upon Isabella's death, to her sister Maria d'Este. With each opening of the theater, a different production was mounted, either a musical drama, play, or ballet. For Ranuccio II's first marriage, to Violante, Manelli's *La Filo* was staged; Odoardo Farnese's marriage to Dorotea Sofia was commemorated with Sabadini's *Il favore degli Dei*. The last performance was *Venuta di Ascanio in Italia*, presented in honor of Don Carlo, prince of Spain, on his visit to Parma in October 1732.

Afterward, the Farnese slowly deteriorated until a bomb hit it on May 13, 1944, severely damaging the theater. Twelve years passed before the theater was rebuilt, following the original designs. It stands today as an excellent example of a 17th-century aristocratic theater. With its reconstruction, there were a variety of possibilities for its use. The most popular idea was to turn it into a temple for Verdi's music, making Parma to Verdi what Bayreuth is to Wagner and Salzburg is to Mozart, but that did not occur. For the dedication of the theater, the *Requiem Mass* was planned, with Herbert von Karajan conducting and singers Carlo Bergonzi and Fiorenza Cossotto, but problems prevented the planned program from taking place. Finally in 2001, as part of the Verdi Festival, which itself had a few false starts, the Teatro Farnese became one of the performance venues for the festival, which finally took root on the centennial of the composer's death. The Farnese hosted the Project Shakespeare, with performances of *The Tempest* and *As You Like It*.

Located on the first floor of the Pilotta Palace, the Teatro Farnese is constructed of wood, papier-mâché, and painted stucco. It is a structure of enormous dimensions. Decorated by Lionello Spada and embellished with statues by Luca Reti, the Farnese was painted to look like marble and gold, giving the illusion of great wealth and power to its owner. The entrance was via a stately portal, framed by pairs of Corinthian columns surmounted by the Farnese coat of arms. Above the passageway, in the center of the amphitheater, was a box of honor for the ducal family, anticipating the future royal box in opera houses. The stadium-type seating was in a semiellipse and held 14 rows, accommodating 3,000 spectators. Flowing upward from the top seats were two rows of serlian-type upper galleries, which reflected Palladian influence and could be considered a prototype of the vertical box tiers in future Italian opera houses. The stage was the first moveable one in Italy.

Ranuccio I also constructed the Teatro del Collegio dei Nobili in 1685 where acclaimed performances were held. Ranuccio II erected three theaters in Parma. The first, the Teatro della Rocchetta, arose in 1674 with 85 boxes. Given in 1688 to the Count Sanvitalea, it was demolished in 1822. The second, the Teatrino di Corte, built in 1689 and demolished in 1832, was the work of Stefano Lolli. The last and most important, the Teatro Ducale, was designed by Lolli and constructed of wood. Zannettini's *Teseo in Atene* inaugurated the Ducale in 1689. During its heyday, it was renowned in Italy and Europe for its performances, which included *La serva padrona*, *La locanda dei vagabondi*, and Paisiello's *Il barbiere di Siviglia*. Near the end of the 1700s, the

Ducale hosted the *prime esecuzioni mondiali* of Paër's *Griselda* and *Il principe di taranto*, Portogallo's *Un effetto naturale*, Mayr's *L'equivoco*, and Cimador's *Il pagmalione*, among others. With the arrival of the 1800s, the Ducale continued introducing operas: Calegari's *Raoul di Crequi*; Lavigna's *Coriolano*; Guglielmi's *Don Papirio*; Morlacchi's *Corradino* and *Oreste*; Mosca's *Romilda*; Orlandi's *La pupilla scozzese*; Persiani's *Attila in Aquileia*; and Pucitta's *Le nozze senza sposa*. When Rossini's works arrived at the Ducale in 1814, some were well received by the critical Parma audience, such as *Tancredi* and *La Cenerentola*, but others were not, such as *L'italiana in Algeri* and *Il turco in Italia*.

The audience at the Ducale had a penchant for unruly behavior during substandard operas and performances, which began in 1816 with Federici's *Zaira*. The audience whistled and booed the tenor Alberico Curioni, but he would have none of it and shouted obscenities back. Pandemonium followed, such that the chief of police was called, arrested the tenor, and announced a ballet would be substituted. But the evening was not over at the end of the ballet. Curioni returned, apologized, and the opera continued at the exact point where it had been stopped. Curioni got his revenge at the final performance of the opera. In the middle of the opera, he stopped singing and began whistling. There was bedlam. Again the police were summoned. This time he was not only arrested but incarcerated for 8 days and then escorted to the frontier and banished forever from Parma. Two years later, the impresario was imprisoned for the failure of the opening night, charged with "offending the public sensibilities." In 1828 after a performance of *Zelmira*, the theater was closed. It was demolished the next year, when a new ducal theater opened.

The Nuovo Teatro Ducale, called Teatro Regio from 1849, was commissioned by Marie Louise, Napoleon's second ex-wife, Empress of Austria and Duchess of Parma, to replace the small, narrow Teatro Ducale. A site in the area of the former convent of San Alessandro was chosen for the new opera house, and Nicola Bettòli received the commission. Gian Battista Borghesi and Paolo Toschi executed the interior decorations, which had hints of Marie Louise's Austrian and French-empire background. The construction lasted 8 years. Bellini's *Zaira* inaugurated the Nuovo Teatro Ducale on May 16, 1829. Unlike most inaugural gala openings of new opera houses, this one was not a joyous occasion. The audience was not pleased with *Zaira* and gave the work a frosty reception. But there were two reasons for this unhappy event. First, Rossini was invited to compose the inaugural opera, but he said he was too busy to accept the commission. The theater then invited Bellini.

Although he accepted the offer, he refused to use a libretto supplied to him by a member of the board of the opera house. This and the fact that he was a second choice were the primary reasons for the cool reaction of the audience.

The type of neoclassical architecture of the Nuovo Teatro Ducale was called "formal heroism." The facade presented a colonnade of massive Ionic columns bordered by an architrave and thin fascia, imperial-style windows topped by tympana, and a large semicircular window flanked by bas-reliefs of Fame bearing a wreath and horn. A crowning tympanum, distinguished with dentils, held a lyre and masks of Comedy and Tragedy. Tommaso Bandini executed the work. The neoclassical auditorium featured chiaroscuro decorations by Toschi with each parapet of the elliptical hall embellished with different plaster figures: military wreaths, the history of Psyche, medallions with portraits of poets, and garlands of flowers and fruit. The proscenium boxes were ornamented with figures of Fame, bearing wreaths of acanthus, and portraits of illustrious men. The curtain depicted *Triumph of Knowledge*: Minerva sat on her throne with her symbols, a screech owl, an olive branch, and a spear and Justice next to her. Glory and Immortality descend from the heavens to crown the goddess, while on the left the Hours danced.

In 1853 Carlo III of Bourbon decided it was time to update the theater to rank with the most important ones in Europe. He hired Girolamo Magnani to redecorate the ceiling, proscenium arch, and parapets in a more opulent manner. A restoration followed with Luigi Montecchi and Luigi Bettoli entrusted with the work. Electric lights were introduced on the stage in 1907 and later, for the centennial of Verdi's birth, in the rest of the theater. An orchestra pit was also created in 1907 but not transformed into its present form until 1925. The Regio survived both world wars unscathed, but an earthquake in November 1983 closed the theater, which did not reopen until January 8, 1985, with *I due Foscari*.

The neoclassical facade has remained unchanged, but the tasteful, neoclassical style of the auditorium gave way to an elaborate, neobaroque appearance during the 1853 redecoration, which remains today. Radiating gold, ivory, and maroon, the 1,400-seat auditorium holds four tiers of boxes topped by a gallery. Gilded stucco figures and ornaments embellish the parapets. In the center an imposing ducal box is accented with heavy maroon drapery fringed with gold and surmounted by a crown. The ceiling holds images of the ancient father of music Lino, the Greek comic Aristophanes, the tragic Euripides, the Latin comic Plauto, the tragic Seneca, and the poets Metastasio, Alfieri, and Goldoni.

Operatic Events at the Teatro Regio

Despite the poor reception *Zaira* received, it was performed seven more times, with the duke of Modena Francesco IV and his consort, Beatrice Vittoria of Sardegna, attending on May 18, 1829. At a presentation 6 days later, the third act had to be omitted because of the sudden indisposition of the bass, Giovanni Inchindi. Four additional operas occupied the schedule during the inaugural spring season, three of which were by Rossini: *Mosè e Faraone*, *Semiramide*, and *Il barbiere di Siviglia*. For the next several seasons, Rossini's operas dominated the stage with *La gazza ladra*, *Torvaldo e Dorliska*, *L'inganno felice*, *Tancredi*, *Cenerentola*, *turco in Italia*, *Matilde di Shabran*, *Il conte Ory* and *Bianca e Falliero*. Bellini and Donizetti followed, eventually overshadowing the Pesaro maestro with *Il pirata*, *I Puritani*, *La sonnambula*, *I Capuleti e i Montecchi*, *Norma*, *Olivo e Pasquale*, *Parisina*, *Anna Bolena*, *L'elisir d'amore*, *Il furioso*, *Gemma di Vergy*, *Torquato Tasso*, *Lucrezia Borgia*, and *Belisario*. There were also prime mondiali of minor composers: Sarmiento's *Elmina*, Peri's *Ester d'Engaddi*, Savj's *Il Cid*, and Sanelli's *Luisa Strozzi* and *Il fornaretto*. Verdi then arrived and eclipsed them all.

Verdi was born less than 30 miles from Parma, in Roncole, so the city adopted him as its native son, and his operas played and still play a principal role in the Regio's repertory. All of the maestro's works have been staged, beginning in the spring of 1843 with *Nabucco*. The Regio also hosted works by other composers, such as Fioravanti, Mercadante, Rossi, Gnecco, Ricci, Pacini, Cimarosa, Coccia, Vaccai, and Buzzi, and introduced several more world premieres by minor composers: Bandini's *Eufemio di Messina*; Benvenuti's *Guglielmo Shakespeare*; Biletta's *L'abbazia di Kelso*; Guindani's *La regina di Castiglia*; Marchisio's *Piccarda Donati*; Rossi's *Elena di Taranto*; Giovanni Giscala; Rota's *Ginevra di Scozia* and *Beatrice Cenci*; and Sanelli's *Il fornaretto*.

To celebrate the centennial of Verdi's birth in 1913, only works by the maestro were on the program: *Oberto*, *Nabucco*, *Un ballo in maschera*, *Aida*, *Falstaff*, *Don Carlo*, and *Messa da Requiem*. The commemoration of the 50th anniversary of his death in 1951 found *Ernani*, *Don Carlo*, *La battaglia di Legnano*, and *Falstaff* on the boards. From 1829 to 1979, Verdi, Donizetti, and Bellini were the most frequently staged composers as a look at the 10 most performed operas at the Regio shows: 5 were by Verdi: *Aida* (189), *Il trovatore* (177), *Rigoletto* (164), *Ernani* (102), and *La traviata* (92); Donizetti held second place with *Lucia di Lammermoor* (122) and *La favorita* (90), followed closely by Bellini with *Norma* (119) and *La sonnambula* (99).

The 1980s saw a broadening of the repertory to baroque and contemporary operas with several Parma novelties: Rota's *Il cappello di paglia di Firenze*, Gluck's *Orfeo ed Euridice*, Händel's *Rinaldo*, Janácek's *Věc Makropulos* (Makropoulos Affair), Pergolesi's *Lo frate 'nnamorato*, Salieri's *Falstaff*, and Baldassarre Galuppi's *L'arcadia*. During the 1990s, the much postponed Verdi Festival finally took root, offering a couple of the maestro's rarely performed works, *Alzira* and *Le trouvère*, along with the better known Italian version *Il trovatore*. In subsequent festivals, *Nabucco*, *Aida*, and *Ernani* were on the boards. The commemoration of the centennial of Verdi's death in 2001 brought a year-long celebration of the composer's operas, beginning with *Messa da Requiem*, followed by six Verdi operas, *Un ballo in maschera* and *La traviata*, among others. In 2003 Teatro Regio began a 6-year-long celebration known as Buon Compleanno Maestro Verdi (Happy Birthday, Maestro Verdi). Each year on October 10, Verdi's birthday, excerpts from several of his operas are performed in chronological order, which began with *Oberto* in 2003 and ends with *Falstaff* in 2008. This is the schedule: in 2003 *Oberto*, *Un giorno di regno*, *Nabucco*, *I Lombardi*, *Jerusalem*, *Ernani*, *I due Foscari*; in 2004 *Giovanna d'Arco*, *Alzira*, *Attila*, *Macbeth*, *I masnadieri*, *Il corsaro*; in 2005 *La battaglia di Legnano*, *Luisa Miller*, *Rigoletto*, *Il trovatore*; in 2006 *La traviata*, *I vespri siciliani*, *Stiffelio*, *Aroldo*, *Un ballo in maschera*; in 2007 *La forza del destino*, *Don Carlos*, *Aida*; and in 2008 *Simon Boccanegra*, *Otello*, and *Falstaff*.

The history of the Regio is filled with moments of triumph and failure, with glorious evenings, tempestuous evenings, and evenings when audience protest of poor-quality performances stopped them, as documented in *Teatro Regio di Città Parma Cronologia degli Spettacoli Lirici 1829/1979*. The exacting nature of the Regio public first showed itself at the opening night of the second season when the spectators laughed at the *terzetto* of the first act of Vaccai's *Giulietta e Romeo*, disgusted with the singing of Giovanni Cavaceppi (Lorenzo), and the *terzetto* was actually omitted from the next performance. At the world premiere of *Piccarda Donati*, which had only a single performance in 1860, the management had to drop the curtain in the middle of the second act amid a hurricane of yelling and whistling. Carlotta Marchisio, in the title role and sister of the composer, fainted on stage. The following year, Pedrotti's *Fiorina* did not fare any better. The disapproval of the audience manifested itself with yelling and whistling that was so loud that the curtain was lowered in the middle of the second act and the theater's administration was fired. In 1885 Ponchielli attended the Parma premiere of *La Gioconda*, whose final performance had to be suspended because of public protest, which also happened at the Parma *prima* of Pagura's *L'apostata* in 1907, when public protest interrupted the first act and the price of the tickets had to be refunded. But probably the best story took place on the opening night of *La Gioconda* in 1903. Legend has it that when the audience booed Emma Carelli in the title role during the second act, she walked off the stage, and still dressed in her costume and makeup, headed straight to the train station and left Parma.

The vociferous and critical Parma audience still exists today. As reported in the *Parma Gazzetta*, on opening night of Verdi's *Macbeth* during the Verdi Festival 2001, the scheduled Lady Macbeth, Tiziana Fabbricini, canceled, claiming laryngitis. There were rumors, however, that since it was to be her debut at the Regio and she knew the Regio's reputation, there was more behind her cancellation. It seemed that among the *loggionisti*, hostility had been brewing for months against the production and the administration of the festival and was ready to explode on opening night, and she did not want to be the recipient of it. But just in case that did not happen, she sent her troops to ruin it for her substitute and rival, Denia Mazzola. And she did, because as soon as Mazzola entered the stage, one wing of the gallery struck, shouting, whistling, yelling, and booing. Then the rest of the gallery revolted, and nothing could be heard or saved of the evening. In fact, Fabbricini even wrote a letter to the newspaper trying to deny her involvement with the opening night fiasco, claiming, "I am not a mean, evil lady." The *Macbeth* production had been updated to World War I by theater director Dominique Pitoiset, who used the opera to show the horrors of war. At the performance I attended, this annoyed some attendees, who shouted insults during the performance aimed at the director (who had long left Parma). This was also Fabbricini's debut, so she had her troops shouting bravas to drown out the boos at the poor quality of her singing. The situation was explained like this, "Teatro Regio realizes it needs to be the best because the audience are all experts. There is a tremendous pressure to be exceptional, but, of course, we do not always succeed."

Teatro Regio is designated a *Teatro di tradizione* and is first in terms of budget size in that category of theaters. At the turn of the 20th century, the Regio formed a *fondazione*, securing its financial future. The repertory is broad, with non-Italian, early, and 20th-century operas included, such as *Dinorah, Lohengrin, Roméo et Juliette, The Rape of Lucretia, Les contes d'Hoffmann, Camilla,* and *Idomeneo*, along with the usual popular fare, which includes one Verdi opera. Among recent presentations were *Alceste, Il barbiere di Siviglia, Rigoletto,* and *Madama Butterfly*. The Verdi Festival presents two Verdi operas, with recent productions including *Simon Boccanegra, Il Corsaro,* and *Il Lombardi*.

Practical Information

Teatro Regio, via Garibaldi 16/A, 43100 Parma; tel. 39 0521 039 393, fax 39 0521 206 156; www.teatroregioparma.org.

The regular season, which runs from December to March, offers four productions with four performances of each. The Verdi Festival takes place during May and June with two Verdi operas and five or six performances of each, amid a variety of other offerings. Stay at the Park Hotel Stendhal, via Bodoni 3, 43100 Parma; tel. 0521 208 057, fax 0521 285 655. The lavishly refurbished Park Hotel Stendhal is a 5-minute walk from the Regio and offers a superb restaurant. Visit the Teatro Farnese in the Pilotta Palace opposite the Teatro Regio. Also in the Pilotta Palace is the National Gallery (tel. 233 309), where a model of the Teatro Farnese, attributed to Fanti-Rousseau, is displayed. Arturo Toscanini was born in a modest house at via Rodolfo Tanzi 13 (tel. 285 499) in 1867, and for the centennial of his birth the town transformed the house into a museum. There are pictures, letters, numerous recordings, artifacts, and memorabilia from various sources that belonged to the maestro. Arrigo Boïto Conservatory (via del Conservatorio 27) was founded in 1819 by Marie Louise in the ancient convent of the Carmine and is where Toscanini, Verdi, Cleofonte Campanini, and Pizzetti studied. All the principal musical institutions of Parma are located at La Casa della Musica / House of Music (Piazzale San Francesco 1; tel. 031 170, fax 031 106; www.lacasadellamusica.it): Historical Archives of the Teatro Regio (tel. 031 189), which includes original documents, photographs, publications, and posters from 1816 to the present; Multimedia Museum from the Teatro Farnese to the Teatro Regio (tel. 031 170), which contains the history of the opera houses in Parma from the 1600s to today with original documents, publications, photos, and multimedia; Foundation National Institute of Verdi Studies (tel. 031 177), which has archives with original letters and documents of the maestro, as well as a library dedicated to him; International Center of Research on Musical Periodicals (tel. 031 181), which was founded in 1984 and is the only research center in Europe dedicated to the collection and study of musical and theatrical journals from the 1800s to today. You can also visit the neoclassical-style tomb of Niccolò Paganini in the Viletta Cemetery. It is the first aisle to the left. Although he died in Nice, he wished to be buried in Parma, where he had worked for a long time during the Duchy of Marie Louise.

~

THIRTY-EIGHT

Rossini Opera Festival and Teatro Rossini, Pesaro

Pace's *Il mondo lieto* was the planned spectacle for the opening of the Teatro di Corte, erected by Nicolò Sabbatini inside the great hall of the Palazzo Ducale in the early 1600s. The Teatro di Corte was built for Duke Federico Ubaldo, and modeled on the Teatro Farnese in Parma. The theater offered a U-shaped auditorium with tiers of seats bordered by a balustrade that ended in an arched gallery. The stage was joined to the parterre by semicircular steps, permitting the singers to move around during the performance. After the dukedom passed to the Holy See in 1631, the Teatro di Corte was demolished.

The origins of the Teatro Rossini extend back to a group of noblemen, who commissioned Sabbatini to erect a theater to present comedies and other public spectacles inside the old ducal stables at Porta Collina. Less luxurious than the Teatro di Corte, the Teatro del Sole was quickly constructed, opening on February 23, 1637, with Hondedei's *Asmondo*. Although the stage was adequately equipped, the seating area kept the look of the ducal mews. There were a few rows of benches, with seats for noblewomen, government officials, and city employees. The space behind was for the common people to stand. The walls were hurriedly plastered and decorated with the Dance of the Hours of Day and Night. Renovated in 1694, which included adding three tiers of boxes and repainting by Pietro Mauro, it reopened with Tauro's *La falsa astrologa*. In 1723 Anotonio Mauro added a fourth box tier, while in 1788 Andrea Giuliani renovated the decorations and architect Tommaso Bicciaglia extended the atrium. Twenty-eight years later, to construct a new theater, the Teatro del Sole was demolished, except for the monumental entrance door (originally part of the ducal stables) and the atriums. It had been written that "honorable philanthropy brought it to the minds and hearts of the municipality of Pesaro to give work and bread to many people in the calamitous years 1816 and 1817 by almost completely rebuilding the city's public theater from its foundations up." The small Teatro della Pallacorda served as an interim performance venue until the new theater was completed.

The cornerstone for the Teatro Nuovo, as the Rossini was originally called, was laid on April 25, 1816. Construction was completed within 2 years and the theater was inaugurated on June 10, 1818, with *La gazza ladra* and *Il barbiere di Siviglia* conducted by Rossini himself. Pietro Ghinelli designed the opera house in the neoclassical style. There were 99 boxes distributed on four tiers, including the proscenium boxes, topped by a gallery. The horseshoe-shaped auditorium was decorated in the neoclassical style. Giambattista Martinetti was in charge of the decor, and Felice Giani and Gaetano Bertolani were responsible for the decorations of the box tiers' parapets and figures and arabesques in the vault. The painted decorations and carved stucco ornamentation were redone in 1854, and that decor survives today. At the same time, the theater was renamed Teatro Rossini. The building was restored again after the earthquake of October 30, 1930, under the direction of architect Rutilio Ceccolini, reopening with *Guglielmo Tell* on August 30, 1934. Thirty-two years later, the building was declared unsafe and closed. There were cracks in the walls, decayed beams, and water in the subsoil. The restoration took 14 years, under the supervision of Loris Papi, with Carlo Ferretti and Werther Bettini responsible for the decorations. The theater was reopened April 6, 1980, with a concert by Luciano Pavarotti (who has a summer home in Pesaro). That same year, on August 28, the Rossini Opera Festival was launched with a performance of *La gazza ladra*. The last restoration to the building took place in 2002.

The ochre stone facade of the Teatro Rossini follows the principles of the neoclassical school. It is divided into two sections. The lower level is defined by an arch order of ashlar topped by a broken scroll pediment with Ionic volutes that frame a cartouche. On the upper level, two rectangular windows and two unadorned niches flank an arch window bordered by Doric pilasters and topped by a smaller broken scroll pediment with Ionic volutes. A pediment crowns the facade. The 860-seat, horseshoe-shaped auditorium holds four box tiers crowned by a gallery. Cherubs, wreaths, and bouquets of flowers and garlands embellish the ivory and gold parapets. Apollo and the nine Muses are painted in tempera on the ceiling, the work of Luigi Samoggia and

Girolamo Dalpane. The curtain, painted by Angello Monticelli, depicts the Fountain of Hippocrene in a grotto on Mount Helicon where a nymph draws the waters that awaken poetic inspiration. Above, Fame flies toward the city of Athens, depicted in the distance.

The Liceo Musicale Rossini (Rossini Conservatory) located in the Palazzo Olivieri, which was originally built by the Olivieri family as a residence, was officially inaugurated on November 5, 1882, under the direction of maestro Carlo Pedrotti. The building housed a Salone dei Concerti (Auditorium of Concerts), which in 1892 was named in honor of Pedrotti. In the latter part of the 20th century, the Fondazione Rossini purchased the Auditorium Pedrotti for the Rossini Festival to use as a theater, which it restored in 1995. The facade of the Palazzo Olivieri displays classic Italianate features on its peach-colored stone with Palladium-type windows. The Auditorium Pedrotti is a rectangular, 500-seat venue decorated in ivory, red, and beige. Slender fluted Corinthian columns topped by lions' heads support the single tier, with Ionic pilasters embellishing the upper walls.

Operatic Events at the Teatro Rossini and the Rossini Festival

Pesaro commemorated the anniversaries of Rossini's birth and death with performances of his operas, and a statue of the composer was unveiled in the city on August 21, 1864, accompanied by music from his *Gazza ladra*. A week earlier, the Pesaro premiere of *Guglielmo Tell* had inaugurated a Solennità Musicale (Musical Ceremony). When Rossini died in Paris in 1868, Pesaro marked the solemn occasion with Teresa Stolz singing in *Stabat Mater* and performances of *Semiramide* and *Otello*. The first centennial of the birth of the "Swan of Pesaro," as Rossini was known, was celebrated in 1892 with *L'occasione fa il ladro*. The Rossini hosted the *prima esecuzione assoluta* of Mascagni's *Zanetto* 4 years later, under the baton of the composer, with his *Guglielmo Ratcliff* performed during the following carnival season.

With the arrival of the 1900s, Verdi and Puccini operas were much in evidence, along with other popular 19th-century Italian composers and those of the *giovane scuola*. In 1901 *Bohème* was given "splendid" performances as noted in the local journal and enthusiastically received, but the cast of *Rigoletto* was not even fixed 6 days before the first performance. The *La Sveglia Democratica* commented, "The performance of *Rigoletto* that took place during the past week had little success. In the execution of the famous quartet, something did not please, above all the insufficiency of the mezzo soprano, so that one could not enjoy all the exquisiteness of this stupendous passage." The situation got worse, such that some performances of *Rigoletto* were replaced with *Bohème* after the subscribers protested. Only after a better mezzo was found did *Rigoletto* grace the stage again that season. About *La forza del destino* offered a few years later, the chronicle wrote, "It appears that the force of destiny that followed Don Alvaro has taken aim, at least until now, also in the performances of the homonymous opera." The performances of *Adriana Lecouvreur*, which was a novelty for Pesaro, passed "plain and smooth, without shame or praise." Many French and German operas successfully graced the stage, as the local paper recorded, "The evening of *Salome* will remain memorable . . . with an exceptional presentation." *Werther* was "a grandiose success." Other works included *Manon*, *Mignon*, and *Lohengrin*.

Zandonai was an important presence in Pesaro's music scene, conducting many of his owns works there, such as *I cavalieri di Ekebù*, *Giulietta e Romeo*, and *Francesca da Rimini*. Operas by minor composers were also heard, including Soffredini's *Il piccolo Haydn*, Pedrotti's *Tutti in maschera*, and Carloni's *Lezione amorosa*. The 150th anniversary of Rossini's birth in 1942 brought *La gazza ladra*, *Le Comte Ory*, and *Mefistofele*. On a darker side, the 23rd anniversary of the founding of the Fighting Fascists was also celebrated in the theater. More unusual works were on the boards during the 1950s, such as Lualdi's *Le furie di Arlecchino* and Spontini's *Milton*. The 160th anniversary of Rossini's birth brought *Stabat Mater*, *Il barbiere di Siviglia*, and *Guglielmo Tell*. The 1960 season seemed to anticipate the Rossini Festival with a couple of little-known operas of the maestro, *La cambiale di matrimonio* and *Il signor Bruschino*, along with *L'italiana in Algeri* and *Il barbiere di Siviglia* on the boards.

Gianfranco Moretti and Francesco Sorlini were the primary forces behind the creation of the festival, founded to rescue Rossini's obscure and neglected operas, to present his works in their critical edition, and to fill in September the numerous beach hotels that dot Pesaro's Adriatic coast. Unfortunately, the festival now takes place in August, making it impossible to find a hotel room. Moretti explained that no other major composer had so many unknown pieces, and that of the more than three dozen operas that Rossini wrote, only a handful are known. The festival collaborates with Fondazione Rossini, which publishes and produces the critical editions of the maestro's works. The goal of the festival is to present all of Rossini's operas, especially the unknown *opere serie*. Some of the operas it has unearthed include *Bianca e Falliero*, *Ermione*, *Armida*, *Ricciardo e Zoraide*, *Otello*, *Elisabetta, regina d'Ingh-*

ilterra, *Matilde di Shabran*, *Le nozze di Teti e di Peleo*, *Pietra del paragone*, and *L'equivoco stravagante*.

For the inaugural season, the festival opened with *La gazza ladra* in the Teatro Rossini followed by *L'inganno felice* in the Auditorium Pedrotti, the other performance space. However, the limited seating in the festival's two performing venues made it impossible to expand. So in 1988, the 1,500-seat Palasport, the town's sport arena, was transformed into the third venue, Palafestival. Lacking air-conditioning and offering the acoustics of a sport arena, it initially could host only short, one-act operas such as *L'occasione fa il ladro* and *Il signor Bruschino*. But after a generous Rossini lover paid for air-conditioning and acoustic panels (but not comfortable seats), critical editions of Rossini's longer and more demanding works graced the stage, including monumental productions of *Moïse et Pharaon*, *Tancredi*, *Semiramide*, and *Guillaume Tell*.

From the beginning, the festival attracted a range of artists, from big names, often at the beginning or end of their careers, to promising emerging talent. A production of *Ermione* featured Montserrat Caballé, Marilyn Horne, and Chris Merritt, and the bicentennial of Rossini's birth saw Cheryl Studer, Merritt, and Ruggero Raimondi in *Il viaggio a Reims*. Other name artists have included Ruth Ann Swenson, Michele Pertusi, Ferruccio Furlanetto, Mariella Devia, Vesselina Kasarova, and Juan Diego Florez. Many productions, however, offer unknown talent.

The productions range from different and unusual to thoughtful, provoking, and bizarre, sometimes even offensive. *L'Indipendente* complained about the 1992 *Il barbiere di Siviglia*: "How strange a Neogothic *Barbiere* at the Pesaro Festival. [There was] no enthusiasm for the work of director Squarzina." The newspaper *Il sole 24 ore x* on *Barbiere*: "The Rossini Festival opened with an interpretation colored and capricious, but rather modest in the voices and in the orchestra." *Corriere della Sera* on the 1994 *Italiana in Algeri*: "Bottleneck on the stage, soccer players and cyclists, seesaws, trampolines, trapeze, *Italiana* among chaos, but one laughs." *Il Manifesto* on the 1997 *Moïse et Pharaon*: "A seducing Egyptian night, the star of David, the deportations of the Hebrews, the warring Egyptians in a rich and symbolic narration for *Moïse et Pharaon*." But *Il Giornale* commented, "Applause and boos, the spectators are upset with the *Mosè* (*Moïse*) by [director] Howell." Given the rarity of recordings of many of Rossini's lesser-known operas, beginning in 1997 the festival started to produce CDs. The first was *Moïse et Pharaon*, which is a treat to listen to without having to endure the visual excesses and effrontery of the production.

Since the arrival of the 21st century, besides the continuing rediscovery of Rossini's forgotten operas, there have been productions in another venue, the Teatro Sperimentale (Experimental Theater), of operas from the minor composers of the 19th century who were Rossini's contemporaries, Mosca's *I tre mariti*; Generali's *Gli inganni della somiglianza* and *Adelina*; Pavesi's *Il trionfo delle belle*; and most recently, Coccia's *Il mondo delle farse*. Recent Rossini operas include *Bianca e Falliero*, *La gazzetta*, *Il viaggio a Reims*, and *Il barbiere di Siviglia*.

Practical Information

Rossini Opera Festival, Teatro Rossini, via Rossini 37, 61100 Pesaro; tel. 39 0721 33 184, fax 0721 380 0220, 30979; www.rossinioperafestival.it.

The festival takes place during August with five operas and two to five performances of each. During the festival, it is difficult to find a hotel, so contact the Informazioni e Accoglienza Turistica, viale Trieste 164 (tel. 0721 69341, fax 30462) for available rooms. Visit the house where Rossini was born, 34 via Rossini. There is an important collection of publications and pictures from Rossini's time—Liceo Musicale Rossini, via Pedrotti—where it is possible to see the Column Room, the Marble Room, and the Pedrotti Auditorium; Tempietto rossiniano, piazza Olivieri, which contains autographed music scores and memorabilia of the maestro.

~

THIRTY-NINE

Teatro Municipale, Piacenza

The Teatro delle Saline, constructed in 1595, was so named because there were salt deposits beneath the building. In the 1600s, Piacenza saw the birth of two additional theaters, the Teatro Ducale del Palazzo gotico (Ducal Theater of the gothic building), created in a room in the municipal building, and the Teatro Ducale della Cittadella, located west of the Cittadella Viscontea. The Cittadella was considered the most important and aristocratic theater in the city. In the middle of the 1700s, the Teatro Saline was in ruins, disappearing in 1804, and the Cittadella burned to the ground on Christmas Eve 1798.

At the dawn of the 19th century, Piacenza was without a proper theater. The ducal government should have constructed the new building, since it was the owner of the previous theaters, but it was occupied with more urgent matters at the time. In 1802 Pietro La Boubé, a French citizen who had acquired much wealth building on speculation, requested of Duke Ferdinand permission to construct a theater in the Palazzo Nibbiani, which he owned. Modeled on La Scala in nearby Milan, it would be designed by Lotario Tomba. The theater would have been filled with magnificent decorations, offering five box tiers, with 30 boxes to a tier, topped by a gallery, and a grand ducal box. Two foyers were planned, one for the nobility and one for the common people. Ownership and management would have been private, with the sale of boxes paying for the construction. Although there were objections to the proposal, the project was approved, with slight modifications to the ownership and management arrangements: the government would own the theater except for the privately owned boxes and, after a little more than two decades, would also manage the theater. With the death of Ferdinand soon thereafter and the Republic of France assuming the sovereignty, Boubé asked to be released from his project. Then five aristocratic citizens presented the same proposal to the French government, with some minor changes: 12 years after the theater's inauguration, all rights to managing the theater would be ceded to the government, and there would be only 29 boxes per tier. In 1803 permission was received. The site selected for the construction held the palazzo of the late Conte Landi Pietra, whose heirs sold the building to the *soci* (of the society of nobles who paid for the construction.) The interior of the palazzo was demolished, but the exterior walls were preserved. On September 29, 1803, at 4 p.m., the first stone, a marble box with some coins from the era and an inscription of the occasion, was laid during a lavish ceremony, which concluded with "Vive la Republique! Vive Bonaparte! Vive Plaisance!" (Long live the republic! Long live Bonaparte! Long live pleasure!) The construction proceeded rapidly, and within a year the new opera house was finished.

The inauguration of the Teatro Nuovo, the original name of the Teatro Municipale, was originally scheduled for August 19, 1804. After several postponements it finally took place on September 10, 1804, with Mayr's *Zamori*, an opera commissioned especially for the occasion. Despite the absence of the composer, it was a memorable evening: "The abundance of the public was incredible . . . lovers of music came from every part of Italy, . . . many representatives of the French military, including Maresciallo Jourdan, and other foreigners of high rank [were in attendance]." An array of special events included a lavish fireworks display. The opera was a grand success, and afterward, to express their satisfaction, the management presented a superb box of gold to the composer. Tomba designed the opera house in neoclassical style. The auditorium, a three-quarter ellipse, offered four box tiers with a total of 114 boxes, topped by a gallery. In the middle was a royal box, located above the entrance door to the orchestra section and occupying the space of four regular boxes. Bracciolo and Antonini were responsible for the interior design. The total cost was 352,000 lire. Because the work was done so quickly, Galli wrote in 1858 in *Il Teatro comunitativo di Piacenza*, "The ornamentation and embellishments do not correspond to the elegance and perfection of the architecture." After 12 years, as stipulated in the proposal, all rights of the theater went to the government, but Marie Louise, who had recently become the Duchess of Piacenza and Parma, did not want the responsibility of running an opera house, so she passed it along to the municipality with the boxes remaining with their owners. Many boxes are still in private hands today.

Since the Nuovo was constructed in a hurry, it soon needed attention, and in 1826 Alessandro Sanquirico redid the proscenium decorations, painted the stage curtain, and painted a "grand medallion" in the middle of the auditorium ceiling. Local artists executed the work on the fascia between the box tiers and the rest of the ceiling. The neoclassical facade was finally completed in 1830, based on designs left by Tomba and modified by Sanquirico. The interior decor was changed in 1857 to be up-to-date with the tastes of the era. The original blue silk decorating the boxes was replaced with a pink silk and with valences of green. The ivory and gold color scheme in the auditorium was unchanged. Girolamo Magnani redid the ceiling design and the chiaroscuro. Righetti and Soldati were in charge of the plasterwork; Paolo Bozzini and Labò, the gilding; and Cardinali, Rapetti, Borea, and Scaglia, the intaglios. At the same time, gas lighting replaced the oil and candles. In 1895 electricity was installed, and between 1938 and 1939 the third and fourth tiers were converted into galleries. The building was restored at the end of the 1970s and again after the dawn of the millennium, a project that saw the original cobalt blue color restored to the boxes. That work was in preparation for the celebration of the theater's 200th birthday. The president of Italy attended a performance of *Nabucco* in September 2004 to mark the occasion.

The central section of the neoclassical facade extends from the building on the street level to offer a three-arch portico of rusticated stone, originally the carriage entrance. Rows of rectangular and square windows punctuate the upper level, with a balustrade discreetly dividing the two sections. A large terrace with four massive Ionic columns supports the crowning pediment, embellished with the coat of arms of Piacenza. The ivory and gold, 1,055-seat auditorium is decorated in the rococo style, with a touch of neoclassicism. A three-quarter ellipse, it holds two box tiers, two balcony tiers, a gallery, and a large center box. The solid fascias are decorated with intricate gilded ornamentations on the upper four levels, except those of the proscenium boxes, which are gilded balustrades. An ornamental gilded grid divides the ceiling into eight sections. Allegorical images of putti floating on clouds in a vivid blue-sky background adorn the four larger ones, and chiaroscuro putti fill the medallions in the four smaller ones.

Operatic Events at the Municipale

The society of the nobles, who constructed and ran the theater during the first 12 years, were obligated to "furnish to the public suitable and dignified performances in the usual times excluding extraordinary occurrences." The "usual times" referred to carnival and *fiera d'agosta*, when performances were always given. When possible, a spring or fall season was also offered. During the first 5 years, the society mounted three opera seasons a year, with only two on the boards during the remaining 7. The inaugural opera, *Zamori*, was a typical "rescue opera," with a "complex apparatus of plausible surprises." It was performed from September 30 to October 30, for 30 evenings, as was the custom of the time. To defend this practice, a chronicler of the time wrote, "The Italians are not wrong to listen again and again [to the same opera] with delight for an entire month, since it is true that the more one listens to beautiful music, the more one derives pleasure from it without tiring of it." Afterward, Mayr used part of the music for a new opera, *Palmira*, premiered at Teatro alla Pergola in Florence 2 years later, and *Zamori* was forgotten. The season continued with Cimarosa's *Gli Orazi e i Curiazi*. For carnival, Paër's *Griselda*, Orlandi's *Il sarto declamatory*, and Fioravanti's *La cantatrici villane* were given. During the early years, the most favored composers were Cimarosa; Paisiello; Mayr with his *Ginevra di Scozia*, *L'equivoco*, *Lodoïska*, and *Raoul De Crequy*; and native son Nicolini, whose *Il trionfo del bel sesso* and *Traiano in Dacia* were popular. The Municipale also presented the world premiere of his *La feudataria* and *Vitikindo*. Operas from other minor composers, including Gnecco, Zingarelli, Morlacchi, Farinelli, and Pavesi, were on the boards.

Only in 1816 did an opera from one of the great 19th-century composers enter the repertory, Rossini's *L'italiana in Algeri*. During the following 15 years, the Pesaro maestro had hardly any rivals in Piacenza, with works such as *Tancredi*, *Mosè in Egitto*, *La donna del lago*, *La gazza ladra*, *Ciro in Babilonia*, and *Demetrio e Polibio* dominating the schedule. In 1832 Bellini's *I Capuleti e i Montecchi* joined the repertory, and between Carnival 1831/32 and Carnival 1837/38, seven of Bellini's operas were staged; only *Bianca e Fernando*, *Adelson e Salvini*, and *Zaira* were missing from the repertory. In the summer of 1831, the first Donizetti opera, *Olivo e Pasquale*, entered the repertory. During the next 20 years, ending in Carnival 1851/52 with *Don Pasquale*, 22 of the Bergamo maestro's operas were performed, including *L'elisir d'amore*, *Il furioso all'isola*, *Parisina*, *Belisario*, *Gemma di Vergy*, *La favorita*, and *Lucia di Lammermoor*. Donizetti surpassed Rossini in number of performances at the opera house, with more than 100. Works by Mercadante and Ricci were also popular, with *Gabriella di Vergy*, *L'orfanella di Ginevra*, *Gli esposti*, *Chiara di Rosenbergh*, *Emma di Antiochia*, *La vestale*, and *Il giuramento* gracing the stage.

Talking about Verdi with someone from Piacenza was like talking about a family member. Verdi's mother came from the city, and the maestro was born not far away. So they adopted him as one of their own (as Parma had). Of Verdi's 26 operas, 23 have been staged. Only *Alzira*, *Oberto*, and *Un giorno di regno* are missing from the schedule. The spring season of 1843 opened with Mercadante's *La vestale*, followed by the first Verdi opera at the Municipale, *Nabucco* (*Nabucodonosor*). One reviewer wrote, "Perhaps *La Vestale* was more suitable for the singers than *Nabucodonosor*, but no one, except Abbadia [the lead soprano] was deserving of so much music." From 1845 until 1859, a Verdi opera, such as *I due Foscari*, *Giovanna d'Arco*, *I Lombardi*, *Attila*, *I masnadieri*, *Luisa Miller*, *Il corsaro*, *Rigoletto*, *Il trovatore*, *Macbeth*, *La traviata*, and *Aroldo*, opened every carnival season and many of the other seasons as well. Verdi has been the composer most performed and most acclaimed at the Municipale.

The first carnival season not inaugurated with a Verdi opera, 1859/60, was also the first after Italy was united. Apolloni's *L'ebreo* was chosen instead, with three Verdi operas completing the season. Then the French composers found favor. Meyerbeer's *Robert le diable* opened Carnival 1862/63, with *L'Africaine* and *Les Huguenots* following during the last two decades of the 19th century. Halévy's *La Juive* opened Carnival 1879/80, greeted at first with whistles and jeers but finishing with a "splendid outcome" as many journals reported. Thomas's *Mignon*, however, was disappointing. *Libertà* wrote that it was "charming, melodic, and amiable, but inadequate for the stage of our theater, which was accustomed to more grandiose scores." *Faust* was "immensely pleasing," *Carmen* "was initially confusing" but returned some seasons later with happy results. *Manon* had an "unfortunate debut" and received a cold welcome, as did *Le damnation de Faust*. As the century drew to a close, German operas made their appearance, including *Lohengrin*, *Tristan und Isolde*, and Goldmark's *Die Königin von Saba*.

The opera house closely followed the *giovane scuola*, reinforced, perhaps, by the librettist Luigi Illica living in Piacenza. Illica wrote the libretti for *La bohème*, *Tosca*, *Madama Butterfly*, *Iris*, *Andrea Chénier*, *La Wally*, and *Germania*, among others. In fact, 22 titles of Illica were debuted in Piacenza during the last decade of the 19th century and the first couple of decades of the 20th century. Verismo played an important role. *Cavalleria rusticana* opened Carnival 1891/92 as the first opera of this genre to appear. Although it pleased, it was not enthusiastically received, partly because it was so short, and the ballet afterward "was buried by an avalanche of protests." *I pagliacci* inaugurated Carnival 1894/95, and its reception was mixed, receiving applause and boos. The first time these two works were paired took place during Carnival 1897/98 with an unhappy result, attributed to the weakness of the production, caused by monetary constraints imposed by the theater, due to financial problems. The debut of Puccini's *Le villi* was a disaster. The first evening ended under "boos of an implacable public." On the other hand, *Manon Lescaut*, which inaugurated the 1893/94 season, was an extraordinary success as was *La bohème*, which "conquered the public, immediately." His other operas followed and were equally enthusiastically received.

The 1900s also saw the return of world premieres, all promptly forgotten, including Zanella's *La sulamita*, Trecate's *Ciottolino*, Gorgni's *Il sacrifizio*, and Zanaboni's *Casello 83* and *Myrica*. In the 1950s, the season had grown to between six and seven operas, with Italian works dominating the schedule. As the century progressed, the repertory remained predominately Italian with the occasional foreign piece, such as *Věc Makropulos* (The Makropoulos Affair), *Die Walküre*, *Samson et Dalila*, and *Salome*, on the boards. As the 20th century drew to a close, *Stiffelio*, *Tosca*, *Lohengrin*, and *Idomeneo* were in the repertory and most of the productions were either coproductions with other Italian opera houses or productions borrowed from other theaters. This arrangement has seen more foreign works in the repertory and an occasional novelty, such as the first performance in modern times of Possio's *Il fantasia di Canterville*. Counted among recent productions are *Nabucco*, *La traviata*, *Die lustige Witwe*, *Battiglia di Legnano*, and a double bill of *Cavalleria rusticana/ Pagliacci*.

Practical Information

Teatro Municipale, via Verdi 41, 29100 Piacenza; tel. 39 0523 492 254, fax 39 0523 492 253; www.teatricomunali.piacenza.it.

The opera season runs from September to March with six operas and three to four productions. Stay at the Grande Albergo Roma, via Cittadella, 14; tel. 0523 323 201, fax 39 0523 330 548. The artists performing at the Municipale stay at the discreet Grande Albergo Roma, which is a 5-minute walk from the opera house.

FORTY

Teatro Verdi, Pisa

As early as 1613, there was news of a public theater, the Stanzone delle Commedie (Large Room of Comedy), located in the Palazzo Gambacorti and built by the Accademici Lunatici o Stravaganti. Subsequently closed, it deteriorated, such that in 1647 the priors of the city requested Grand Duke Ferdinand II to reconstruct the theater in the same place as the original. Again the city had a public theater, along with the numerous private ones located in the palaces of the nobility, the most famous being the theater in the Palazzo Ceuli, only a few steps from the Stanzone. Over the decades, small changes were made to adapt the theater to the needs of the actors and spectators. In 1684 a major modification became necessary to make the theater more "representative" of the social needs of the era by building three boxes: one for the "Most Serene Princes," the second for the consuls, and the third for the priors. During the following years, these boxes were beautified. The rest of the auditorium held two balconies, one for ladies and the other for "citizens." These were eventually transformed into three box tiers, "to eliminate the confusion and for the best decorum of our city." The reconstruction was executed by Alessandro Saller, the pictorial decorations by Verano Mazzi, and the parapets of the new box tiers the work of Fanucci. Nevertheless, by the middle of the 1700s, Pisa needed a new theater.

In 1765 various projects by Orazio Cecconi, Francesco Bombicci, and Zanobi del Rosso were submitted. Bombicci's was chosen, and Cecconi was responsible for its execution. The work began in 1770. Subsequently, Bombicci managed the project while Cecconi was busy recovering all the material from the old theater to be adapted for the new structure. The noble Prini family owned the building, which they called Teatro Prini. It opened May 18, 1771, with the play *Antigono* by Pietro Metastasio, as a chronicle of the era reported, "Under the protection of S.A.R. it [the theater] had been finished in a year and 27 days by Capo Maestro Cecconi, excellently painted by Mattia Tarocchi, with the curtain the work of the celebrated painter Giovanni Tempesti, all from Pisa." Operas began gracing the stage in 1773, with Piccinni's *Il giocatore fortunato*. Composers whose operas were heard included Piccinni, Paisiello, Andreozzi, Sarti, Cimarosa, Guglielmi, and Anfossi. In 1776 Gazzaniga's *Gli errori di Telemaco* received its world premiere, and 1789 saw native son Nicolai's *La madre colpevole* staged.

The Accademia dei Costanti purchased the theater from the Prini family for 77,000 Florentine lire in 1798, renaming it Teatro dei Costanti. Works by Mayr, Pavesi, Gnecco, Farinelli, Paër, Generali, Fioravanti, Paisiello, and Cimarosa were popular. Rossini operas first entered the repertory in 1814 with *L'italiana in Algeri*. His works were favored along with those of Donizetti, whose first opera was performed at the Costanti in 1818. Paini, Coccia, Morlacchi, and Pavesi were also on the schedule. When the academy was dissolved in 1820, the Università dei Palchisti (University of Box Holders) rescued the theater until an association of 48 noble Pisans formed a new academy 2 years later to purchase the building. With *L'indebolita sua virtù ravviva* (It revives its weakened virtue) as its puzzling motto, the academy rebaptized the theater as Teatro Ravvivati. As the decade progressed, Rossini works slowly dominated the schedule, culminating in 1830 with eight out of nine operas on the season program by the Pesaro maestro. Bellini's operas first arrived in 1832 with *Lo straniera*, but unlike Rossini's successes, the singing of some of the artists was so poor that a riot erupted, and the police had to be called. Ten violent youths were arrested before order was restored. In 1836 the *prima mondiale* of Bini's *Ildegonda* took place. Also on the schedule were Coppola's *La pazza per amore*, Manna's *Jacopo di Valenza*, and Bellini's *Norma* and *Capuleti e i Montecchi*. In fact, Bellini operas dominated the schedule, with Donizetti not far behind, until the arrival of Verdi in 1844 with the Pisa premiere of *Nabucco*. Within a decade, Verdi became the composer most represented. The theater hosted the world premiere of Fiori's *Rizzardo da Milano* in 1850. After 1860 the operatic activity at the Ravvivati began a gradual decline.

The Politeama Pisano opened in 1865 as a theater for the masses with inexpensive ticket prices. Designed by Florido Galli, the Politeama was an immense structure, seating more than 2,000. Hosting opera, operetta, and drama, it witnessed its first opera, Ricci's *Crispino e la comare*, in August 1865. An average of two operas per season graced the stage, usually by the giants of the 19th century, Rossini, Bellini, Donizetti, and Verdi. There were exceptions, including Petrella's *La contessa d'Amalfi*, Fioravanti's *Don Procopio*, De Ferrari's *Pipelet*, and Ricci's *Eran due ed or son tre*. Novelties that had already been offered at the new opera house were sometimes staged in subsequent seasons at the Politeama, such as Nicolai's *I ciarlatani*, Usiglio's *Le donne curiose*, and Marchetti's *Ruy Blas*.

Construction began on a new opera house in March of the same year the Politeama opened. But the need for a new opera house had been felt since the 1830s, when a proposal was received from architect Gherardesca, who foresaw two theaters, one for the day and the other for the evening, using the same stage. It was not acted upon. The location chosen for the new edifice had to be "improved" because, as Giampaolo Testi wrote in *Quattro "Puntate" per una Piccola Storia del Teatro Verdi di Pisa*, "One must not put together in the same boat prostitutes and pimps with the so-called upper classes." As originally promoted, the new theater had a resemblance to the Teatro della Pergola (in Florence) and contained 120 boxes divided among five tiers, one of which was reserved for the king. The initial cost was to be no more than 485,000 lire. Within a week after opening the sale of boxes to the public to finance the construction, 75 had been reserved on the first four tiers, with the owners forming the Società del Teatro. The building was practically paid for. The total cost, however, reached 689,230 lire, which then swelled to 800,000 lire, and was covered by a loan from the Cassa di Risparmio (Savings Bank). The project, initially entrusted to Andrea Scala, was completed by Ranieri Simonelli within 15 months. November 9 was chosen for the inauguration, but unforeseen events delayed the opening for 3 days. On November 12, 1867, Rossini's *Guglielmo Tell* inaugurated the Regio Teatro Nuovo, as the Teatro Verdi was originally called. The nobility and bourgeoisie came from all over Tuscany for the grand opening, and they were not disappointed. There were many suggestions regarding the theater's name: Bellini, Rossini, Galileo.·But Simonelli ironically stated, "We will call it Teatro Nuovo. At least we will be original!" Regio was added, with the gracious concession of King Vittorio Emanuele II.

The Po River overflowed its banks the same year that the Nuovo opened, closing the Teatro Ravvivati. It took 3 years to repair the damage. The building was reopened in November 1870 with *Norma*, which was the only opera offered that season. The next year, three operas graced the stage, Giosa's *Don Checco*, Donizetti's *Gemma di Vergy*, and *L'elisir d'amore*, before the theater was again closed until 1878 for a major restoration under the careful supervision of Gaetano Corzani. The cost of the renovation reached 56,000 lire, 16,000 lire more than the original estimate. The Accademia dei Ravvivati was dissolved in 1878, so when the building reopened September 22, 1878, the box holders were the new owners managing the theater. They formed the Società Anonima, and renamed the building Teatro Rossi to honor the great Livornese actor Ernesto Rossi and also to indicate a new direction for the theater. With the opening of the Regio Teatro Nuovo, the Rossi became a home primarily for drama, although operatic productions continued until 1929.

Meanwhile, Giuseppe Puccinelli acquired the Politeama and restored it. Lehár's *Eva* opened the theater on March 22, 1913, and opera returned to the stage in July with *Il barbiere di Siviglia*, followed by *Traviata*, *Rigoletto*, *Norma*, and *La Sonnambula*. The following season, which ran from January to November, offered 45 performances of nine popular Italian operas. The 1915 season saw seven operas. Then there was silence for a decade while it underwent restoration. The theater reopened April 24, 1927, and *Il trovatore* was performed 3 days later, with six additional operas on the boards during the season. The following year, the Politeama reached the pinnacle of its operatic career, hosting 14 operas between April and August. The theater presented mainly popular composers—Rossini, Bellini, Donizetti, Puccini, and Verdi—and those from the verismo school. The final season took place in 1942, with *Andrea Chénier*, *Cavalleria rusticana/Pagliacci*, and *Il barbiere di Siviglia* on the boards, before bombs struck the edifice, reducing the structure to a heap of ruins.

In 1932 Società Anonima, which owned the Rossi, went bankrupt and the theater was sold at public auction. In 1940 it was granted to the Cassa di Risparmio of Pisa for 40,000 lire, which resold it to the Federazione fascista in 1942. With the fall of Fascism, it was, by law, transferred to the state, which in 1946 conceded the management to the municipality of Pisa. It ended up as a movie house until its doors were shut in 1966. For the next 11 years, it served as a depository for lost objects. But there was a happy ending. As the 20th century drew to a close, it was restored to its former glory. The nondescript exterior belies the ivory and gold jewel of an auditorium inside. There are three box tiers, 20 boxes to a tier, topped by a gallery ringed by a gilded, ornamental metal guardrail and fluted Corinthian columns, which support the ceiling. The parapets are decorated with a variety of colorful painted designs of flowers and masks and gilded stucco.

In 1904 the Regio Teatro Nuovo was renamed Teatro Verdi, to honor the grand maestro, who had died 3 years earlier. By the 1920s, the Società del Teatro, which owned the Verdi, ran into financial difficulties and took out a loan for 175,000 lire from the Cassa di Risparmio to survive. The municipal-

---

ity purchased a box for 4,000 lire to have a say in the assembly of the shareholders of the Società. But with the aging of the theater, cinema gaining in popularity, and competition from the Politeama Pisano, their money problems only grew worse, until the Società dissolved itself in 1935 and the theater passed to the municipality. At the same time, the theater underwent a major restoration in which the fourth and fifth tiers of boxes were transformed into galleries and some of the original decorations were redone. The total cost was more than 1.3 million lire. Over the decades, the building continued to age and the decorations deteriorated, requiring a complete overhaul to rectify the problems, which took place in 1985 under the direction of architect Massino Carmassi. The original lucid colors and ornamentation of the auditorium were restored, the separate side entrance for the galleries was eliminated, the lower gallery was transformed into a type of "open" box seating, and the structure itself was strengthened. During the 4 years of work, operas were performed in the Teatro Tenda (Tent Theater), an enormous canvas tent that normally was the home of rock concerts. The Verdi reopened with the prima assoluta of Simone's *Mistero e processo di Giovanna d'Arco* on October 26, 1989. In 1961 the theater had been recognized as a *Teatro di tradizione*, and at the end of the 20th century, it formed a *fondazione* to guarantee funding in the 21st century.

The Verdi is a parallelepiped, identified by "Teatro Comunale G. Verdi" in large letters stretching across the upper level of the facade, just beneath the pediment. The terra-cotta and gray facade is divided into two levels. The street level is defined by rusticated stone and five arches; the upper level is punctuated by five arch windows and four Corinthian pilasters. The tympanum of the pediment is unadorned. The all-white foyer, with marble floor and Corinthian columns, was characteristic of the era in which the theater was built. The ovoid, 900-seat auditorium radiates in gold, white, and ochre. There are five tiers and a center royal box (now used for stage lighting and equipment). Intricate white stucco decorations of musically inspired allegorical designs, which include masks, horns, and torches, embellished with leaves, flowers, and ribbons, adorn the parapets. Outlined with slender golden lines, the parapet ornamentation harmonizes with the plush beige ochre velvet covering the seats. The historic painted curtain depicts Goldoni reciting his poetry to a group of friends in the Scotto Garden. A swirl of figures, faces, and flowers decorate the dome ceiling. Bernasconi and Quadri were responsible for the auditorium decorations and the stucco, respectively; Andreotti and Mancini executed the pictorial decorations; and Annibale Gatti painted the historic curtain and frescoes.

Operatic Events at the Teatro Verdi

During the first 50 years, the theater dedicated its existence to the performances for which it was built, that of opera. There were four seasons: carnival, Lent, spring, and autumn. During the 1868 season, the first complete season at the new theater, the operas of Verdi were prominent in the repertory, with *Ernani, Rigoletto, Ballo in maschera,* and *Trovatore* on the schedule, along with Mercadante's *Leonora.* Boos and whistles greeted Apolloni's *L'ebreo* when it opened the 1869 season, due to the poor quality of the performance. Petrella's *Le precauzioni,* Ferrari's *Il menestrello,* and *La favorita* followed. The 1870 season was short with two obscure works, Petrella's *Marco Visconti* and Usiglio's *Le Educande di Sorrento.* By the next year, French operas had entered the repertory, with *Faust* and *Robert le diable.* The trend continued with Auber's *La muette de Portici, L'Africaine, Le prophète, La Juive, Les Huguenots,* and *Carmen* on the boards. For *Le prophète,* the public arrived from all of Tuscany and Liguria. There were also works from both major and minor Italian composers, including Marchetti's *Ruy Blas,* Peri's *Vittor Pisani,* Donizetti's *Lucrezia Borgia,* Petrella's *Jone,* Ponchielli's *I promessi sposi,* and Verdi's *Nabucco, Aida, Trovatore, Rigoletto,* and *Forza del destino.* During the last few decades of the 1800s, the Nuovo hosted four world premieres, since forgotten: Buonamici's *Linda Wilson,* Nicolai's *I ciarlatani,* Michieli's *Ericarda di Vargas,* and Ricci's *Ruit Hora.*

The theater played an important role in the life of Puccini. In 1876, when he was 18 years old, he walked from Lucca to Pisa to attend a performance of *Aida.* Apparently he was so inspired by the opera that after the performance he decided to devote his life to writing opera, and 11 years later, on March 15, 1887, the Pisa *prima* of his first opera, *Le villi,* took place. It was a success. At the age of 27, Toscanini, already recognized for his extraordinary talents, arrived in Pisa in 1894 to conduct *Otello* and *Manon Lescaut.* His genius resulted from a perfect fusion of all the elements in the opera, and the success of the performances was stupendous. Ricordi telegraphed Verdi's compliments to the maestro (for *Otello*). Toscanini returned the following season for *Falstaff* and *Cristoforo Colombo* to equal acclaim. Wagner was first heard in 1896 with *Lohengrin,* and as the century drew to a close, popular French and Italian operas, especially verismo, filled the repertory, a trend that continued into the 20th century. The number of operas offered per season varied between two and nine.

The Nuovo hosted some well-known singers of the era, with Marietta Biancolini performing in *Le prophète* in 1877, followed 2 years later with the debut of Maria Leopoldina Paolicchi, who would marry conductor Leopoldo Mugnone. There were also scandals. In 1878 Telemaco Lamponi, the lead bass in *La forza del destino*, was drunk when he performed, resulting in his singing out of tune, which provoked boos, hissing, and whistling from the audience. He responded with obscene arm gestures, and Cesare Di Ciolo was quickly substituted in the part. Lamponi, however, was remembered for a long time in Pisa, as the butt of lewd jokes. After the arrival of the 20th century, native son Titta Ruffo made his debut as Jago in *Otello*. His original name was Ruffo Titta, but an impresario reversed it and it remained so. His talent was discovered when he was 15 years old. Upon returning home after seeing a performance of *Cavalleria rusticana*, he sang the entire opera. Subsequently, he studied at various conservatories and made his debut in his home town before forging an international career.

Mascagni conducted several of his operas at the Verdi, including *Amica*, *Le maschere*, *Iris*, *Guglielmo Ratcliff*, and *L'amico Fritz*. There is a story about Mascagni concerning a rehearsal of *Guglielmo Ratcliff* that had gone on too late. Someone suddenly announced that since it was 6 minutes past midnight, the rehearsal was over. Mascagni then pulled out his watch and said, "It is six minutes to midnight . . . this watch was given to me by Benito Mussolini . . . please," and the rehearsal continued. Zandonai visited Pisa to conduct his *Francesca da Rimini*, *Giulietta e Romeo*, and *La farsa amorosa*. Leoncavallo led his *Goffredo Mameli* and Respighi his *La fiamma*. When Thomas's *Amleto* was staged during the 1925 season, it was a prima assoluta for Tuscany, and 2 years later the *prima mondiale* of Landi's *Laurette* was offered.

Famous singers continued to appear at the Verdi with Tito Schipa as Nemorino; Mario del Monaco as De Grieux and Turiddu; Giuseppe di Stefano as Nadir and Rodolfo; and Beniamino Gigli as Andrea Chénier. Gigli succeeded in creating himself as a "singer of the people" and was also known to be generous. Entering a theater before a performance, he saw a poor lad who had come just to see him waiting outside the stage door, not having the money to buy a ticket to hear him. Gigli realized this and gave the boy the modest sum of 2 lire, enough for two tickets and a bite to eat. An incident of a different sort occurred when Maria Callas came in 1950 to assay Tosca opposite Galliano Masini's Cavaradossi. There was an unusually long intermission between the first and second act. The tenor had not been paid, so he marched into Callas's dressing room and asked, "You receive your fee?" Upon hearing that she had, he exclaimed, "Ah, yes, you know what I say to you? If they do not pay me now, they will not shoot Cavaradossi this evening." Someone pulled out his checkbook, but Masini shook his head; he wanted cash, and until he received it the performance could not continue.

Mozart operas finally reached Pisa at the end of the 1980s when *Le nozze di Figaro* and *Così fan tutte* graced the stage. By the mid-1990s, the repertory included operas from the 17th through the 20th centuries, with works such as *Orfeo ed Euridice*, *Il ritorno di Ulisse in patria*, *La scala di seta*, and *L'assassinio nella cattedrale* and the world premiere of Gurlit's *Wozzeck* on the program. At the dawn of the 21st century, the schedule turned more mainstream with *Simon Boccanegra*, *La sonnambula*, *Werther*, *Die Zauberflöte*, and *Il turco in Italia*. Recent repertory shows a branching out to musicals with *Joseph and the Amazing Technicolor Dreamcoat* and to early operas with Gasparini's *Mirena e Floro* alongside the traditional Italian fare of *Madama Butterfly*, *Cenerentola*, *Gioconda*, and *Matrimonio segreto*. The traditional operas, however, are often presented with a new slant or edition. The policy of the theater is to use young singers, the stars of tomorrow.

The Teatro di Pisa belongs to the CittàLirica along with Teatro Giglio in Lucca and the CEL in Livorno. CittàLirica has joined these three theaters in western Tuscany by sharing one orchestra and productions and coordinating schedules, which are based on the training and development of the young artists. There is a flexibility in the schedules to allow coproductions with other Italian opera houses as well.

Practical Information

Teatro Verdi, via Palestro 40, 56127 Pisa; tel. 39 050 941 111, fax 39 050 941 158; www.teatrodipisa.pi.it.

The opera season, which runs from October to April, offers six operas with two to three productions of each. Visit the Collezione Titta Ruffo in the large corridor of the top gallery of the Teatro Verdi. Inaugurated on April 8, 1961, the collection of the singer's costumes was closed during the opera house renovation but reopened June 9, 1999. It can be visited during the day by appointment or during the intermission of a performance.

FORTY-ONE

~

Teatro Comunale Alighieri and Ravenna Festival, Ravenna

As early as 1556, there was a wooden stage in a room in the Palazzo Comunale (municipal building) for the performance of comedy. Although it was a public theater, between 1683 and 1696 it was used by a private society of influential nobility whose purpose was to make money by offering performances. The demolition of the stage in 1702 became the catalyst for the erection of a new public theater, known as the Teatro Comunitativo, constructed outside the city center according to the plans of Giacomo Anziani. Completed in 1723 and opened the following year, the Comunitativo was shaped like a parallelepiped and displayed a facade of restrained elegance. It was written that "if one did not know the exact location of the theater, and had not paid attention to the inscription, stripped of its few decorative elements, the building could have passed for a warehouse or barracks of the municipal guards." Inside, however, was another matter. The U-shaped, baroque auditorium offered lavish decorations. There were 97 boxes distributed in four tiers, each with individual parapets, richly framed. Of the 97 boxes, 56 were sold to pay for the construction, with the nobility purchasing 30, bourgeoisie 15, the city 5, and the church 6. The theater was enlarged between 1779 and 1782.

The operatic activities at the Comunitativo during the 1700s are not well documented, but starting in 1802 and lasting until 1852, a dozen composers dominated the repertory. Of 170 productions, 24 were by Rossini and 22 by Donizetti. Ten other composers—Bellini, Cimarosa, Mayr, Pacini, Mercadante, Gnecco, Fioravanti, Guglielmi, the brothers Ricci, and Verdi—filled out the repertory with between 5 and 10 titles each. By the 1820s, however,

the Teatro Comunitativo had become inadequate for the growing needs and
dignity of the city. Ignazio Sarti was entrusted with a project to enlarge and
modernize the structure, including fire-safety measures. The project pleased
many because it looked like a new building but was more cost efficient than
actually erecting one. But the project languished because, when compared
with constructing an elegant new building in a centrally located area convenient for everyone that would become the focal point of the city, the idea of
a new theater was preferred. Closed in 1857, the Comunitativo was destined
for other uses.

A commission was formed in 1838 to study the issue. The Meduna brothers were then hired for the project, but controversy began immediately, and
revisions to the plans were necessary. The cornerstone was laid in September
1840, with a buried slab of marble inscribed, "Here one placed the foundation of this theater in 1840 by the Venetian architects Tommaso and Giambattista Meduna." The neighboring houses were knocked down to make
room for the new edifice at the location chosen. Giuseppe Votan and Giuseppe Lorenzo Gatteri were in charge of painting and decorations, with the
gilding done by Carlo Franco. In contrast to the Teatro Comunitativo, the
bourgeoisie had purchased almost two-thirds of the boxes sold. The construction lasted a dozen years when finally, on May 15, 1852, the Teatro Comunale Alighieri was inaugurated with Meyerbeer's *Robert le diable* and Pacini's
Medea. The name of the theater, Alighieri, was proposed by the apostolic
delegate Stefano Rossi to honor the great poet Dante Alighieri, who spent
the last years of his life in Ravenna. The boxes were individually decorated
according to the taste of their owners. Gas replaced the oil lighting in 1863,
and electricity was introduced after the turn of the century. In 1919 Enrico
Piazza redecorated the ceiling, and between 1959 and 1967 the theater was
closed for restoration.

The neoclassical facade of the Alighieri recalls that of La Fenice in Venice, the Meduna brothers' previous commission, with its four-column portico, statues of Muses in niches, and architrave windows. But there are
differences. The Alighieri is a subdued yellow, displays four Muse statues, and
boasts Ionic columns on a pronaos that extends from the building; La Fenice
is white, displays two Muse statues, and boasts Corinthian columns on a portico almost flush with the structure. The neoclassically designed auditorium
of ivory, gold, red, and blue is horseshoe shape and holds 830 seats. There
are 118 boxes on four tiers crowned by a gallery, with the middle section
of the fourth tier also offering balcony seating. Mythological subjects, putti,
cherubs, and gilded music motifs decorate the parapets. The center box of

honor is flanked by Corinthian columns and crowned by allegorical figures. Above the proscenium arch are two angels framing the coat of arms of Ravenna. Flower themes and female figures embellish the ceiling.

Operatic Events at the Teatro Alighieri

With the opening in 1852 of the Alighieri, Verdi, the major opera composer of the time, was prominent in the repertory. Ravenna followed the latest fashion in opera and wanted the composers of the day, which meant that the previous domination of Rossini, Bellini, and Donizetti had all but vanished by the time the opera house opened. In fact, for the first 50 years (1852–1902), of the 120 productions offered, Verdi claimed 33, Donizetti 15, and four other composers, Meyerbeer, the brothers Ricci, Bellini, and Petrella, claimed between 5 and 10. Other composers made brief appearances, including Fioravanti, Apolloni, Cagnoni, De Giosa, Pedrotti, and Marchetti. Of the early ruling three composers, only Donizetti had a strong presence until 1870, and then he disappeared, claiming only three titles for the next 32 years. Bellini totally vanished after 1866, as had Rossini except for a couple of *Barbieres*.

The French grand operas, however, were popular and played a role in the repertory, especially those of Meyerbeer, *Les Huguenots*, *Dinorah*, *L'Africaine*, and *Robert le diable*, which had inaugurated the theater. Other French operas followed, including *Faust*, *Carmen*, *Mignon*, *Le roi de Lahore*, and *Manon*. A few German works appeared, including *Lohengrin* and *Martha*. At the end of the 1800s, works from the *giovane scuola* were popular with *Cavalleria rusticana*, *Pagliacci*, *Andrea Chénier*, *Manon Lescaut*, *Fedora*, and *La bohème* gracing the stage. As the 20th century drew to a close, the repertory included operas ranging from the baroque period through the 1900s, with the trend continuing into the millennium. Some were unknown, others neglected works from popular composers, alongside the perennial favorites: Auletta's *La locandiera*, Pergolesi's *L'olimpiade*, Mascagni's *Le maschere*, Roto's *Cappello di paglia di Firenze*, Rossini's *Il cambiale di matrimonio*, Mozart's *Clemenza di Tito*, Verdi's *Nabucco*, Puccini's *Tosca*, and Donizetti's *Don Pasquale*. Recently, the schedule offered *Battaglia di Legnano*, *Il ritorno di Ulisse in patria*, *Madama Butterfly*, *L'elisir d'amore*, *Werther*, and *Porgy and Bess*.

The Ravenna Festival is a recent arrival in Ravenna, celebrating its 15th anniversary during the 2004 season. Started by Maria Cristina Mazzavillani Muti, wife of conductor Riccardo Muti, the festival hosts primarily international orchestras, ensembles, and soloists, with opera playing only a small part in the more than two dozen scheduled events. The opera programming has been diverse, ranging from obscure works, such as Salieri's *Les Danaïdes*, Cherubini's *Lodoïska*, and Auber's *La muette de Portici*, to less frequently performed operas of celebrated composers, such as Donizetti's *Poliuto*, Bellini's *I Capuleti e i Montecchi*, Verdi's *Attila*, to more popular works, such as *Così fan tutte*, *Don Giovanni*, *Macbeth*, *Cavalleria rusticana*, and most recently, *Faust*. There have been productions from the Vienna State Opera and visiting Russian companies: Marinsky Theater, Helikon Theater, and Festival of White Nights performing *Boris Godunov*, *Lady Macbeth of the Mtsensk District*, and Stravinsky's *Mavra*.

Practical Information

Teatro Comunale Alighieri, via Mariani 2, 48100 Ravenna; tel. 39 0544 32 577, fax 39 0544 215 840; www.teatroalighieri.org. The season, which runs from November to March or April, offers six operas with two to three performances of each. Ravenna Festival, via Dante Alighieri 1; tel. 0544 249211, fax 0544 36303; www.ravennafestival.org. The festival takes place during June and July. The number of operas and performances varies.

Stay at the Bisanzio, via Salara 30, 48100 Ravenna; tel. 0544 217111, fax 0544 32539. The centrally located Bisanzio is a 5-minute walk from the theater. Visit the Dante Museum and Tomb, Teatro Rasi, and Museum of Mechanical Musical Instruments.

FORTY-TWO

~

Teatro Municipale Valli, Reggio Emilia

At the end of the 1500s, there were two theatrical venues. One was located in the Palazzo del Monte di Pietà and was known as the Sala delle Commedie (also referred to as the Sala del Ballone). It catered to the nobility who invited their own guests to amateur entertainment, at least initially. Le Commedie was on the east side of the building, rectangular, its height reaching to between the second and third floors, and the stage located on the north side of the room. The layout of the venue suggested that of an amphitheater, with wooden stadium-type seating on three sides and a box in the center that was a little higher, furnished with a carpet and armchairs for the duke and the court. The other venue, known as Teatro dell'Arte, was located in a district populated by inns, taverns, and bordellos and was open to the paying public for professional companies of *comici dell'arte*, evidence of which was a request made on April 14, 1589: "The comedians . . . desire to have license . . . to perform comedy for thirty or forty days." In 1624 the Sala delle Commedie became the venue for both functions. It was outfitted with a permanent stage and renamed Teatro di Reggio. Between 1635 and 1637 it was reconstructed into the emerging "Italian theater" style, a U shape that widened at the ends with four levels of boxes for which the nobility drew lots. Comedies, tragedies, tragic-comedies, ballets, and tournaments were offered as entertainment. The ballet and tournaments were performed in the orchestra section, which had no fixed seating. Gradually, *dramma musicale* and *dramma per musica* were organized on an irregular basis by private impresarios or traveling troupes, supplanting the other types of entertainment. Correspondingly, the venue was adapted to the new performance require-

233

ments. The stage became the only performance space, containing structured sets and moveable scenery, with an area at the foot of the stage set aside for the orchestra. The orchestra section, no longer used for presentations, was reconfigured between 1645 and 1675 into a keyhole shape, and 12 rows of permanent bench seating were installed, with 2 additional rows of seating added on the sides.

The theater, which had been entirely occupied by the oligarchical citizens, was progressively turned into a municipal theater. It was renamed Teatro dell'Illustrissima Comunità di Reggio and opened to the public, with the seats in the orchestra section offered for sale and the boxes owned by the local nobility. Works such as Cavalli's *Il Giasone* and *Antioco*; Cesti's *La Dori*, *Argia*, and *L'Orontea*; and Ziani's *Le fortune di Rodope e Damira* were on the boards. In 1675 the side seating in the orchestra was eliminated and the royal box substantially enlarged and embellished. The reason was that the Duke Francesco II d'Este had taken an interest in the theater, attaching it to the dukedom and increasing the number of commissioned operas. The theater was reconfigured between 1686 and 1700 into a U shape, the orchestra section widened, and permanent, individual seats replaced the benches. During the last decade of the 1600s, all the *drammi per musica* were world premieres, including Ballarotti's *Ottaviano in Sicilia* and *La caduta de'decemviri* and Pollarolo's *Almansorre in Alimena*, *L'Oreste in Sparta*, *L'enigma disciolto*, and *L'Ulisse sconosciuto in Itaca*. The scenery of many of the operas was executed by Ferdinando Galli Bibiena and Francesco Galli Bibiena. In 1700 all the seats in the orchestra section were removed. By the 1730s, the opera house had lost its luster and a new theater was erected.

The Teatro dell'Illustrissimo Pubblico, also known as the Teatro Cittadella because it was constructed on the west side of the wall of the old Cittadella, took only a year to build. Based on the designs of Antonio Cugini, a student of Ferdinando Galli Bibiena, it was inaugurated in April 1741 for *fiera* with the prima assoluta of Pulli's *Vologeso re de'Parti*. De Lalande in his *Voyage en Italie* wrote in 1765, "The auditorium is grand, and the boxes are slightly curved, like bathtubs that had been arranged one next to the other; what is a bit disturbing is that the boxes protrude progressively outward, each one a few inches from the next as they get farther from the stage. The architect wished to procure the best sight lines for the performance, but one wished that he had done so without the drawback of this bothersome decoration of the boxes being uneven. . . . The stage protrudes quite a bit into the orchestra area so one hears the actors very well." The auditorium was in a U shape with delightful pictures decorating the parapets and the inside of the boxes, but the box holders were prevented by agreement from displaying their family coats of arms. Only the ducal box had that privilege. The proscenium boxes were at the disposal of Her Royal Highness.

The theater usually hosted two opera seasons, fair and carnival. During the first two decades, operas such as Gluck's *Demofoonte*, Auletta's *Orazio*, Lampugnani's *Il gran Tamerlano*, Perez's *Didone abbandonata*, and Pescetti's *Adriano in Siria* and novelties such as D'Avossa's *Lo scolaro alla moda*, Galuppi's *Lucio Papirio*, and Scarlatti's *Alessandro nell'Indie* were offered. Until 1761 there were several commissioned works, assayed by singers on the duke's payroll, but from 1761 until the end of the century, the number decreased substantially to only a half dozen. As the 18th century ended and a new one dawned, Cimarosa, Paisello, and Zingarelli became the favored composers, with *Gli Orazi e i Curiazi*, *Il matrimonio segreto*, *Il barbiere di Siviglia*, and *Giulietta e Romeo*, among others, performed. There were also operas by Nasolini, Nicolini, Pavesi, Cimadoro and Mayr. Rossini's works first appeared during the summer of 1814 with *L'inganno felice*; *Aureliano in Palmira* and *L'italiana in Algeri* followed. The rest of the Pesaro maestro's operas soon dominated the schedule. The beginning of the 1830s witnessed the operas of Bellini and Donizetti eclipsing those of Rossini, and monopolizing the repertory until the mid-1840s, when Verdi entered the scene with *I due Foscari*, *Macbeth*, *Nabucco*, *Ernani*, and *I masnadieri*. Luigi Ricci was another popular composer, with performances of *Il nuovo Figaro*, *Chiara di Rosenbergh*, and *Eran due ora sono tre*. At the beginning of the 1840s, two operas by native son Peri, *Il solitaria* and *Circe*, had their world premiere.

The population of the city, being attuned to the comportment of the modern European bourgeoisie, hired architect Pietro Marchelli in 1838 to make important modifications to the structure, including a new facade that offered a portico with three arches as a carriage entrance. The old portico was left for those arriving by foot, but lost its importance when the crowning tympanum surmounting the entrance door was demolished. In the early morning hours of April 21, 1851, after a rehearsal of Peri's *La Tancreda*, scheduled for performance April 29, a fire destroyed the old auditorium and stage of the Cittadella. The idea to reconstruct the ruined sections was immediately dismissed and a proposal to erect a new opera house took hold, with the project assigned to Cesare Costa.

Since the construction would take a long time, the orchestra company, fearing unemployment, assumed the task of constructing a small, temporary theater "in the halls of that which burned." The Teatro Filarmonico, named after the Orchestra Filarmonica (and also known as Teatro dei Filodrammatici) and based on the plans of engineer Tegani, was inaugurated in January 1852 with a *melodramma semiserio*, Villanis's *La regina di Lione*, although *Rigoletto* was the preferred inaugural opera. But because of its subject matter, it was deemed immoral and forbidden to be staged. The horseshoe-shaped auditorium held 41 boxes and a reduced orchestra section. During its brief existence of 7 years, it introduced several operas to the city: *Luisa Miller*, *Poliuto*, *Il trovatore*, *Rigoletto* (as *Viscardello*), *Giovanna d'Arco*, Petrella's *Marco Visconti*, Apolloni's *L'ebreo* (as *Lida di Granata*, 1856) and the prima assoluta of Peri's *Orfano e diavolo*.

Work began during the summer of 1852 on the Teatro Comunitativo di Reggio, the original name of the Teatro Municipale Valli, and in April 1853 Peri was invited to compose the inaugural opera. The sale of boxes helped pay for the construction, which lasted 5 years. On April 21, 1857, the world premiere of *Vittor Pisani* inaugurated the opera house. *Vittore Pisani* was not well received. One reviewer wrote that, "although the performance was optimal, it did not meet, in its complexity, the favor of the public. The music of Peri was worthy, but too languid and hardly suitable for an evening of grand entertainment." Another critic wrote, "It did not please, in fact it almost bored so that it only received cold applause the first evening." However, its success increased with the remaining performances of *Vittor Pisani*, prompting the librettist of the opera, Francesco Maria Piave, to write to Ricordi on May 4, 1857, "The opera of Peri continues to please and will be the work with which Mongini prefers to debut with in Padua." The opera house was almost universally praised: "The people who were crowding the theater this first evening will never finish clapping their hands and cheering Costa in admiration for the shape given to the theater and for the well-suited position of the boxes . . . with the ability to see the entire stage from every angle." One critic, however, complained that the portico had too many columns and statues, that the windows were too many and too small, and that the entrance to the orchestra section was too narrow. On January 16, 1887, the opera house was illuminated for the first time with electricity.

Twenty years after the Teatro Filarmonico closed, substantial thought was given to reusing the area of the old Teatro Cittadella. In 1877 a society was founded for the purpose of constructing a politeama on the site that should be "adaptable to every type of show, lyrical, dramatic, dance, or equestrian." Although it was a private society, it was formed to a great extent by private citizens, not nobility, who received the land free from the municipality. The construction of the new building was entrusted to Achille Grimaldi. The Politeama Ariosto was inaugurated on May 11, 1878, with Lecocq's *Giroflé-*

Giroflà, presented by the Compagnia Italiana di Operette Comiche led by Filippo Bergonzoni. The theater was built with cast iron. The semicircular auditorium held three tiers; the first and third were galleries and the second held boxes. In 1927 an orchestra pit was added and the equipment for putting on horse shows was removed. Anselmo Govi redecorated the space with frescos from the late-Liberty period. The cupola was particularly interesting, depicting episodes from *Orlando Furioso* surrounded by a fillet filled with verses from the poem.

> *Le donne, i cavalier, l'arme, gli amori,*
> *le cortesie, l'audaci impress io canto*
> *che furo al tempo che passaro i Mori*
> *d'Africa il mare*

(I sing of the women, knights, fights, loves, chivalry, and bold adventures that took place when the Moors crossed the African sea [to Europe to try to conquer it].)

On the curtain, Govi created an imaginary scene of the Villa Mauriziano, residence of the queen of poetry. The Politeama was dedicated at that time to Ludovico Ariosto. After World War II, it was used to show films and host variety shows. The passing of the Teatro Ariosto to public administration in 1981 led to a total renovation of the structure to meet fire and safety codes and a return to its original function as a theater.

The Teatro Comunitativo di Reggio was declared unsafe after Carnival 1924/25 and closed. Reconstruction went on for 13 years. The opera house reopened in October 1938 with *Tosca*. In 1957 the centennial of the theater's birth was marked by the transfer of the management from private to public administration, although half of the boxes remained with the heirs of the original *condomini*. At the same time, the theater was rebaptized Teatro Municipale. In 1980 Valli was added to the theater's name to honor a popular actor from Reggia Emilia, Romolo Valli, after his death. The auditorium was restored between June and October 1999 under the direction of Mauro Severi at a cost of 2 billion lire.

The Teatro Municipale Valli is a monumental structure with striking features, covering an area of more than 10,000 square feet. The main facade is divided into two sections. The lower one displays a long colonnade of 12 Doric columns that stretches the length of the building, supporting a large terrace above. On the upper section, 14 Ionic pilasters alternate with 13 windows, each crowned with a fronton and a bas-relief with a musical or dramatic motif. In the middle, the coat of arms of the city of Reggio Emilia is displayed. Crowning the main facade are 14 statues representing Tragedy, Vice, Glory, Drama, Virtue, Truth, Instruction, Pleasure, Fable, Jest, Dance, Caprice, Comedy, and Sound. More statues crown the side facades: Silence, Curiosity, and Remorse on the left, and Painting, Modesty, and Moderation on the right. There are additional statues on the terrace level: on the left, Medea, Oedipus, Achilles, and Actilius Regulus, and on the right, Haranguer, Prometheus, and Daedalus. Bernardino Catelani selected the allegorical themes for the decoration, while the statues themselves were executed by several artists: Attilio Rabagli, Prudenzio Piccioli, Antonio Ilarioli, Giovanni Chierici, and Ilario Bedotti. The 1,100-seat, ivory, gold, and red auditorium is horseshoe shape with four tiers of boxes topped by a gallery. There are a total of 106 boxes and the former ducal box. Gilded, carved wood decorations embellish the ivory-colored parapets, with different ornamentations on each level that decrease in lavishness as the tiers go higher. The royal box is framed by columns with thin, gilded caryatids. The ceiling, executed by Domenico Pellizi, is divided into four large sections representing Melodrama (Metastasio with Pergolesi and Bellini), Tragedy (Alfieri with Monti and Maffei), Choreography (Viganò with Gioia), and Comedy (Goldoni with Nota and Cecchi). The smaller sections are decorated with allegorical figures symbolizing the various theatrical arts. The stage curtain, the work of Alfonso Chierici, shows the Italian Genius inviting the Fine Arts to take their inspiration from the glorious history of Italy.

Operatic Events at the Teatro Municipale Valli

After the Municipale was inaugurated with *Vittore Pisani*, the season continued with *Anna Bolena*, *Norma*, and *Simon Boccanegra*. Verdi arrived in Reggio Emilia on May 10, 1857, to supervise the production of *Simon Boccanegra*, recently introduced at La Fenice. He immediately began working, but the rehearsals were proceeding slower than planned, so the theater offered *Norma*. It was a disaster. Verdi wrote to Ricordi on May 29, "The other evening they made a fiasco with *Norma* such that I had never seen before. The opera was not finished: shouting, booing, threatening the director and management, not only in the theater and atrium, but under their windows. A horror!"

The cast of *Simon Boccanegra* was the same as the one that had been praised in *Vittore Pisani*, but Verdi was not satisfied with the orchestra or the conductor. Piave, the librettist, had written to Ricordi, "The chorus, specially the men, are good, but the conductor . . . and the orchestra . . . leave much to be desired." The opera opened June 10 to a sold-out theater. Although the prologue was well received, the first part of act one was met with silence, followed by technical difficulties that kept the curtain from rising on the second part. Verdi went running to the stage, yelling, "Pull!" to the incompetent stagehand, who replied, "What is this pull?" Verdi retorted in Parmesan slang best left untranslated. Verdi, nonetheless, wrote to Ricordi on June 14: "*Simon* went well the first evening; it was coolly received the second, and last evening went excellently." Verdi operas dominated the repertory, for both fair and carnival seasons, with *I Lombardi, Ernani, I due Foscari, Rigoletto, Trovatore, Traviata,* and *Un ballo in maschera* repeated many times. *Attila, Masnadieri, Macbeth,* and *Luisa Miller* were offered in only one season. Donizetti works were also very popular, from the inaugural season's *Anna Bolena* to *Poliuto, Lucrezia Borgia, Lucia di Lammermoor, La favorita, L'elisir d'amore,* and *Maria di Rohan. Don Sebastiano, Gemma di Vergy, Marino Faliero,* and *Belisario* appeared in only one season. *Don Pasquale* was not performed at the Municipale until 1967; it had been relegated to the less illustrious theaters that catered to opera buffa. Bellini operas also made a strong appearance with *Norma, Sonnambula,* and *I Puritani* repeated often, along with infrequent performances of *Beatrice di Tenda* and *I Capuleti e i Montecchi.* Operas from minor composers Pacini, Pedrotti, Petrella, Cagnoni, and Fioravanti were also much in evidence. Foreign operas that had been missing from the seasons began making an appearance again. French grand opera was particularly well liked, with *Faust, L'Africaine, Les Huguenots, Robert le diable,* and *La Juive* in the schedule. Wagner, however, ignored during the entire 1800s, finally appeared with *Lohengrin* in January 1900 followed by *Tannhäuser, Die Walküre,* and *Tristan und Isolde.*

Novelties were often not well received. De Giosa's *Don Checco* had a "most unhappy outcome" and was pulled from the schedule after one performance, and Cagnoni's *Michele Perrin* met an identical fate. But the outcome was different for the prima assoluta of Franchetti's *Asrael* on February 11, 1888. Puccini had attended the dress rehearsal that had taken place 4 days earlier, and critics from all the major Italian newspapers descended upon Reggio Emilia for the premiere. They were unanimous in their praise. As one critic wrote, "It was an unconditional success. If there are only two performances of the opera, it is sufficient to launch the name of Franchetti."

The Municipale hosted opera seasons during World War I but closed September 27, 1942, after the three-opera fall season of *Carmen, Mefistofele,* and *La Wally,* because of World War II, reopening a few weeks after liberation, on June 9, 1945, with *Andrea Chénier*. Well-known artists such as Magda Olivero, Giulietta Simionato, Tito Schipa, and Giuseppe di Stefano graced the stage. In 1957 there was a special centennial celebration season with *La bohème*, *Falstaff*, *Die Walküre*, *Nabucco*, and *Khovanshchina* on the boards. During the late 1960s and early 1970s, the repertory became more adventurous, with the presentation of both new and long-forgotten Italian operas such as *Il figiuol prodigo*, *Venere prigioniera*, *La serva padrona*, *Assassinio nella cattedrale*, and *Job*, and broad, with foreign works such as *Salome*, *Kát'a Kabanová*, *Prodaná nevěsta* (The Bartered Bride), and *A Kékszakállú herceg vára* (Duke Bluebeard's Castle), among others. That trend has continued into the 21st century with seasons offering early 1700s operas, such as *L'incoronazione di Poppea*, *Olimpiade*, and *Orlando*, lesser-known operas of famous composers, such as *Maria Stuarda*, *Tancredi*, *Le Comte Ory*, and *Pêcheurs de perles*, and 20th-century works, such as *Rape of Lucretia* and *Aufstieg und Fall der Stadt Mahagonny*. In 2002 the world premiere of Alberto Colla's *Il processo* was staged. Recently, *Ritorno di Ulisse* and *Peter Grimes*, among others, were in the repertory.

Practical Information

Teatro Municipale Valli, piazza Martiri 7 Luglio, 42100 Reggio Emilia; tel. 39 0552 458 811, fax 39 0552 458 822; www.iteatri.re.it.

The season, which runs from January to May, offers four productions with two to three performances of each. Stay at the Mercure Astoria Reggio Emilia, viale L. Nobili, 2, 42100, Reggio Emilia; tel. 0522 435 345, fax 0522 453 565. A favorite with the opera singers, the Mercure Astoria is a 3-minute walk from the opera house, which is just around the corner.

~

FORTY-THREE

Teatro dell'Opera, Rome

Cavalli's *Scipione Africano* inaugurated Rome's first public opera house, the Teatro Tordinona, in the mid-1600s. Although Pope Clement IX had given Count Giacomo d'Alibert permission to construct the theater, the next pope, Innocenzo XI, was extremely hostile to opera and had the theater closed, and from 1674 to 1690, the Tordinona remained silent. It was reopened January 5, 1690, and 3 years later Carlo Fontana set forth a grandiose reconstruction project to enlarge the building, which was approved by Pope Innocenzo XII. Six tiers were erected, with 35 boxes to a tier, in addition to those on the ground level, with the original location reversed. The design of the auditorium was one of the first examples of a truncated ellipse. The Tordinona reopened January 25, 1696. Then the next year, Pope Innocenzo XII, the same pope who gave approval only a couple of years earlier for the reconstruction and enlargement that cost thousands of scudi, ordered the theater demolished. In August 1697, the demolition occurred. With Rome bereft of a proper performing venue, in 1717 Count d'Alibert's son constructed the Teatro delle Dame, also known as Teatro Alibert, for opera seria. Possibly designed by Matteo Sassi, it was enlarged in 1720 by Francesco Galli Bibiena, who shaped the auditorium with a "phonetic curve," which was a compromise between a rectangle and a horseshoe. It presented the first performance ever in 1788 of Anfossi's *Artaserse*, which was poorly received. The reviewers wrote that "Anfossi has aged and is no longer a good maestro." In 1799 the prima assoluta of Mosca's *Amore e dovere* took place.

Meanwhile, the Tordinona was rebuilt in 1733 with the consent of Clemente XII. Designed by Domenico Gregorini and Pietro Passalacqua, the four-tier auditorium was a truncated oval resembling a horseshoe and had 26 boxes to a tier. A fifth tier was added in 1734. Fire reduced it to ashes in

1781. Reconstructed and renamed Teatro Apollo, it became Rome's greatest theater of the 19th century, hosting the *novità assolute* of both minor and major composers: Mosca's *Silvia e Nardone* and *La vedova scaltra*; Pacini's *Il corsaro*, *Furio Camillo*, and *Il mulattiere di Toledo*; Pucitta's *La festa del villaggio*; Ricci's *Fernando Cortez*; Terziani's *L'assedio di Firenze*; Vaccai's *Virginia*; Donizetti's *Adelia* and *Duca d'Alba*; Rossini's *Mathilde de Shabran*; and Verdi's *Il trovatore* and *Un ballo in maschera*. The last two operas garnered the most attention. The *Gazzeta Musicale* reviewed the opening of *Trovatore* on January 19, 1853: "The composer merited this resounding success, for he has written in a new style, filled with Castilian characteristics. The audience listened to each number in total silence, applauding at every pause. The end of the third act and the entire fourth act caused such fervor that they had to be repeated." The premiere of *Ballo* in Rome was the result of Verdi's problems with the Neapolitan censors. The papal censors, however, required that the action be relocated to Boston and the king become a governor. The critics wrote that the "orchestration was intelligent and dazzling in uniting dramatic truth with melodic beauty." "Viva Verdi" became the battle cry against Austrian oppression, using the dual meaning of the composer himself and the acronym VERDI, or Vittorio Emanuele, re d'Italia. The Apollo was razed near the end of the 1800s.

In 1727 the Teatro Valle was built by Domenico Valle. It, too, hosted world premieres by both minor and major composers: Morlacchi's *Il Simoncino* and *La principessa per ripiego*; Pavesi's *Il giuocatore* and *Le donne fugitive*; Ricci's *Amina*, *Il sonnambulo*, and *Chi dura vince*; Rossi's *Il disertore svizzero* and *Le fucine di Bergen*; Tritto's *Lo specchio dei gelosi*; Coccia's *Il matrimonio per cambiale* and *Rinaldo d'Asti*; Conti's *L'audacia fortunata*, *Bartolomeo della Cavalla*, and *I finti sposi*; Cordella's *La rappresaglia* and *Il contraccambio*; Cortesi's *Almina*; Mellara's *La voce misteriosa*; Orlandi's *La sponsa contrastata*; Pacini's *La gioventù di Enrico V*; Tadolini's *Il credulo deluso*; Donizetti's *L'ajo nell'imbarazzo*, *Olivo e Pasquale*, *Il furioso all'isola di San Domingo*, and *Torquato Tasso*; and Rossini's *Demetrio e Polibio*, *Cenerentola*, and *Torvaldo e Dorliska*. The latter was a fiasco. As noted in the *Notizie del giorno* on January 18, 1816, "The reception of the *opera semiseria* called *Torvaldo e Dorliska*, new music by *signor maestro* Rossini, has not lived up to the hopes that were reasonably conceived for it. It should be said that the subject of the very dismal and uninteresting libretto has not awakened Homer from his sleep, for which reason it was only in the introduction and the beginning of a trio that the famous composer of *Tancredi*, *La pietra del paragone* etc. was recognizable." The Valle was subsequently converted into a playhouse.

The largest opera house in Rome during the 1700s was the Teatro di Torre Argentina, designed by Girolamo Theodoli. Built by Duke Sforza-Cesarini, the Argentina was inaugurated January 13, 1732, with Sarro's *Berenice*. The building was rectangular, with a horseshoe-shaped auditorium holding six tiers of 31 boxes each. Duke Francesco Sforza-Cesarini commissioned Rossini to write *Il barbiere di Siviglia*, which he called *Almaviva* in a futile attempt to avoid competition with Paisiello's opera of the same name. Paisiello had a loyal following called *paisiellisti*, and his *Il barbiere di Siviglia* was very popular. They resented this young composer (Rossini was only 24 at the time) writing on the same subject. Opening night, which occurred less than 2 months after the fiasco of *Torvaldo e Dorliska* at the Valle, was also a disaster. The *paisiellisti* jeered, shouted, and whistled during the entire performance. Of course, Paisiello's *Il barbiere di Siviglia* has fallen into oblivion and Rossini's is one of the 10 most popular operas. Times change. The Argentina also introduced the Pesaro maestro's *Zoraide in Granata*, *La Cenerentola*, and *Adelaide di Borgogna*.

Two of Verdi's lesser-known operas debuted at the Argentina: *I due Foscari* and *La battaglia di Legnano*. The reviews for *I due Foscari* were favorable, with the *Rivista di Roma* writing, "It appears that Verdi has rid himself of his previous style, to return to the source of emotion and passion . . . where each character expresses his own passions in an inherently dramatic way." When *La battaglia di Legnano* was premiered, Rome was in political turmoil, its citizens ripe for a patriotic opera. The opening chorus of "Viva Italia! Sacro un patto, tutti stringe i figli suoi" (Long live Italy! A sacred pact binds all her sons) was met with shouts of "Viva Italia, Viva Verdi," and the fourth act was repeated in its entirety. The *Pallade* wrote, "Verdi has broken away from the old conventions, his spirit needing freedom as Italy needs independence." There were also numerous prime mondiali of minor composers, including Neri's *Talestri, regina d'Egitto*; Pacini's *Cesare in Egitto*, *Il saltimbanco*, and *Gianni di Nisida*; Poniatowski's *Bonifazio de'Geremei*; Sampieri's *Il trionfo di Emilia*; Sangiorgi's *Edmondo Kean*, *La mendicante*, *La demente*, *Iginia d'Asti*, and *Diana di Chaverny*; Terziani's *Alfredo*; Valentini's *Gli Aragonesi in Napoli*; Van Westerhout's *Cimbelino's*; Cordella's *Lo sposo di provincial*; Dall'Olio's *Don Riego*; Morlacchi's *Le Danaidi*; and the Roman composer Vera's *Adriana Lecouvreur*.

As the 19th century progressed, the aristocratic Teatro di Torre Argentina's limited space had become too confining and the upper council of public works had deliberated about demolishing the glorious Teatro Apollo, so there was a critical need for a new royal theater, which prompted the engineer Adolfo Lepri to submit a project for a theater that would have been elegant enough to replace the Teatro Apollo and appeal to the noble audience of the Argentina. Lepri proposed to locate his Teatro Regio in the Villa Colonna, on the grounds of the ex-convent of the San Silvestro at Quirinale. But the cost of his project was prohibitive, around 10 million lire, so it was never considered.

In 1877 Domenico Costanzi presented his concept for a new opera house as a 3,000-seat politeama, designed by Achille Sfondrini. The aristocracy and upper bourgeoisie objected to the "popular" aspect of the building as well as its decentralized location. This resulted in a compromise. The opera house would be a building of mixed character, with three tiers of luxurious boxes suitable for the most aristocratic society topped by large, primitive balconies for the lower classes. The cost reached 2 million lire, which was much higher than Costanzi's original budget, forcing him to sell much of his property. The foundation was laid in 1879 and the theater completed on schedule. It was named Teatro Costanzi after its owner. The inauguration took place on November 27, 1880, with *Semiramide* and was an event of great importance for the city. "The performance was set for eight o'clock in the evening, but already by seven, a large crowd had gathered around the entrances and a long line of splendid carriages were passing on the narrow street. The royal family arrived at the theater between two squads of cuirassiers in full dress uniform and at their entrance, the orchestra and the band played the Royal March. King Umberto, Queen Margherita, and the best of Roman aristocracy were in the opera house. The queen was dressed in a white, rose, and blue gown with a diamond tiara resting on her blond hair. The king was in tails. A spreading murmur of admiration rose from every section of seats when the auditorium was illuminated and a deserving, seemingly endless applause welcomed the two principal men responsible for the project, Costanzi and Sfondrini," according to Sandro Rinaldi's description of the inaugural evening of the Costanzi in *Il Teatro Costanzi* (1880–1926).

The opera house itself was described on the *«Album Ricordo» del Teatro Costanzi della stagione 1908–1909* as being "in the Renaissance style with a slight tendency towards Baroque, uniting in itself the multiple qualities of splendor, grandeur, and elegance. . . . The spacious dome was wonderfully painted by Brugnoli with allegorical figures from the Beaux Arts, the races and the tournaments of antiquity, and gave the structure a quality of slenderness. The principal facade displayed 16th century characteristics, windows with arch orders, pilasters, and balustrades." The critics did criticize the orchestra pit, accusing the architect of "excessive Wagnerian characteristics." (The orchestra pit was first introduced in Germany, by Wagner, who

wanted the orchestra hidden under the stage.) The critics were not enthusiastic about the performance itself, which was criticized. As one reviewer
wrote, "The public admired the theater, but the performance remained
scarcely satisfying."

Costanzi's dream was to make his theater another Teatro Massimo, but
the goal eluded him. Except for the disastrous inaugural season, the performances were almost always sold out, but that did not translate into sufficient
funds to resolve the financial crises that Costanzi continually experienced.
The culmination came when the second performance of the final opera of
the 1881 season, La forza del destino, had to be canceled because the artists
refused to begin the performance, knowing that they would not be paid. Costanzi, realizing the difficulties in managing his theater, proposed to the
municipality to buy his theater on very favorable terms, but the mayor was
occupied with reconstructing the Teatro Argentina and was not interested.
The last years of his life were filled with problems and concerns about the
management of this beloved theater, into which he poured all his wealth.
When Costanzi died in October 1898, his son Enrico took over the administration together with Vicenzo Morichini. For the next decade, they continued the work of Enrico's father. Enrico died in 1907, and his heirs kept the
management of the theater with Morichini. Morichini made an agreement
with the municipality for the 1908 season, under whose auspices it unfolded.
At the end of the season, in July 1908, the theater was sold for 865,000 lire
to the Società Teatrale Internazionale (STIN).

STIN hired various impresarios to arrange the seasons, but by 1926 the
financial situation of STIN was untenable and the building was sold to the
government of Rome. The theater was closed for restructuring and restoration and renamed the Teatro Reale dell'Opera. The project, entrusted to
Marcello Piacentini, included moving the main entrance from the narrow
side street of via Firenze to the main thoroughfare of via Viminale, renovating the orchestra pit, improving the technical capabilities of the backstage
area, adding an immense chandelier, and transforming the lower gallery into
a fourth tier of boxes. This was the same recommendation that the critic
D'Arcais made in the Roman newspaper L'Opinione in his review of the Costanzi inaugural in 1880. "I believe that to move the winter performances and
the public from the Apollo to the Costanzi, a modification is necessary.
Three tiers of boxes are not enough for a city like Rome and two galleries
seem to me excessive. Can't the engineer Sfondrini substitute another box
tier for the first gallery?"

On February 27, 1928, the opera house reopened its doors with Boïto's

Nerone. When Italy became a republic, the *Reale* (Royal) was dropped from the name. In 1957 major financial difficulties began to manifest themselves at Dell'Opera, bringing uncertainty as to the future and the need to reduce the activities if the federal government did not intervene. This was a problem that affected all the *enti lirici*, of which Teatro dell'Opera was one. It took 10 years before the laws that governed the *enti lirici* were changed, giving them advantages and benefits. At the end of the 1990s, the opera house underwent additional work to meet fire and safety codes, renovate the auditorium, and modernize the backstage technical equipment. It reopened in 2000, prepared for the 21st century.

The building offers an austere facade with symmetrical lines of travertine stone punctuated by nine long rectangular windows. A bronze bas-relief of the Muses crowns the structure. Busts of Volpi and Beniamino Gigli reside in the entrance foyer, where a plaque commemorates Domenico Costanzi. A bust of Verdi is located by the grand staircase. The 1,600-seat, gold and red auditorium holds four box tiers topped by a gallery. Lavish gilded stucco of sphinxes, Muses, acanthus leaves, musical instruments, scrolls, and cornucopia adorn the hall. Allegorical figures surround the massive, circular chandelier hanging in the center of the cupola. Arabesque arches buttress the gallery ceiling. The paintings were the work of Brugnoli, the sculptures by Boggia, and the gilding by Pavone. On the proscenium arch "Vittorio Emanuele III Rege, Benito Mussolini Duce, Lodovicus Spada Potenziani, Romae Gubernator Restituit MCMXXVI–VIII" (Victorio Emanuele III, King, Benito Mussolini, Leader, Lodovicus Spada Potenziani, Roman Governor, Restructured 1926–28) is inscribed.

Operatic Events at the Teatro dell'Opera

Vincenzo Jacovacci, who had directed the Teatro Apollo, was chosen by Costanzi to organize the seasons at his theater. Unfortunately, the performance standards were so poor that after the inaugural gala only 500 people showed up for the second performance of *Semiramide*. *Norma* and Rossini's *Otello* did not fare much better. Only *Trovatore*, with tenor Antonio Rossetti, was met with approval. Jacovacci died in March 1881, so Costanzi entrusted the second season to Boccacci, who was much more successful. Almost all the performances sold out. Two world premieres were also presented, Orsini's *I Burgravi* and Pellegrino's *Fayel*. Glory reigned at the Teatro Costanzi beginning in 1885, when Guglielmo Canori became the impresario, as he was able to obtain the services of the outstanding artists and conductors of the time.

It was a hard blow for Costanzi when Canori left for the rebuilt Teatro Argentina. With Canori gone and the country experiencing economic crises, Costanzi agreed to grant a 3-year contract to the publisher Edoardo Sonzogno to manage the opera house. His competition for one-act operas led to the debut of Mascagni's *Cavalleria rusticana* in May 1890 and the introduction of the verismo style. This was the opera house's first important world premiere. With Leopoldo Mugnone on the podium and Gemma Bellincioni and Roberto Stagno in the leading roles, it was a triumph without precedent. Although Mugnone conducted the same pair of singers in the second- and third-place winners, Spinelli's *Labilia* and Ferroni's *Rudello*, those works fell into oblivion. There were high expectations for Mascagni's next opera, *L'amico Fritz*, which was introduced the following year, and although the work was successful, it was not on the same level as *Cavalleria rusticana*. Mascagni kept close ties with the Costanzi, and was on the podium for four more world premieres of his works, *Iris*, *Le maschere*, *Lodoletta*, and *Il piccolo Marat*. He also conducted the *prima mondiale* of Leoncavallo's *Majà*. During the final two decades of the 1800s, operas by minor composers were also introduced, Gnaga's *Gualtiero Swarten*, which was notable only for Francesco Tamagno in the title role and the conducting of Toscanini, Vallini's *Il voto*, Setaccioli's *La sorella di Mark*, and Floridia's *La colonia libera*.

In April 1893, Verdi went to Rome for the first staging there of his *Falstaff*. When the curtain fell on act 2, King Umberto I and Queen Margherita invited the composer to the royal box, accompanying him to the front. Then they slowly stepped back, allowing Verdi to savor the applause alone. The next important *novità assoluta*, *Tosca*, took place on January 14, 1900, with Mugnone on the podium and the composers Mascagni, Marchetti, and Cilea in the audience. Queen Margherita arrived during the first intermission, dressed in a pretty white gown with lace. It was a tumultuous event, as Alfredo Mandelli described it in *Il Teatro dell'Opera Roma*: "Leopoldo Mugnone, right before he was to conduct, found a delegate from the police headquarters in his dressing room to warn him: «Maestro, do not be frightened, whatever happens, immediately play the Royal March.» . . . «It appears that there is a plot, one talks of a bomb.» Mugnone, by chance, had already been faced with a bomb in a theater, at the Gran Teatre del Liceu in Barcelona. Certainly, he was not pleased. An ill-defined tension ran through the theater. It has been speculated that Mugnone, himself, inadvertently instigated the unrest by trying to emulate Toscanini by insisting on starting the performance on time, but the usual latecomers, who expected to enter the auditorium after the opera began, started a protest which was mistaken for a riot, so soon after the beginning [of the performance], someone who knew, yelled, «lower the curtain!» Nothing. Then the Royal March. After a few more interruptions, came the calm and the performance was a success. Five curtain calls after the first act, only two after the second, and seven at the end." The reviews were split, some were favorable and others unfavorable.

World premieres were offered almost every season for the first quarter of the 20th century. Although most were successful when introduced, except for *Tosca* and a rare staging of Zandonai's *Giulietta e Romeo*, Mascagni's *Le maschere*, or *Il piccolo Marat*, both the operas and the composers are now only footnotes in history: Mascheroni's *Lorenza*, Bustini's *Maria Dulcis*, Robbiani's *Esvelia*, Tommasini's *Uguale Fortuna*, Gasco's *La leggenda delle sette torri*, Monleone's *Arabesca*, Malipiero's *Canossa*, Mariotti's *Un tragedian florentina* conducted by the composer, Romani's *Fedra*, Nepomuceno's *Abul*, Mansilla's *Ivan*, Poggi's *Bufera d'amore*, Vittadini's *Anima Allegra*, Giovannetti's *Petronio*, Michetti's *La gratia*, Bianchi's *La Ghibellina*, Riccitelli's *I compagnacci*, Barilli's *Emiral*, Robbiani's *Anna Karenina*, and the final opera introduced at the Costanzi, Laccetti's *Carnasciali* in February 1925. At that point, the opera house had presented around four dozen *prime esecuzioni assolute* during its 45 years of existence.

There were also numerous foreign opera novelties for Rome, many of which the Romans did not welcome or understand. For the performance of *Salome* it was written, "At the end of the single, long act, the public, which had remained attentive, astonished, and subdued, almost in a unexplained stupor, erupted in applause. But the applause was not unanimous. If there was from one side enthusiasm, from the other indignation, surprise, confusion, and perplexity." The performance of *Pelléas et Mélisande*, however, was not even allowed to finish. "The public which listened at La Scala to *Pelléas et Mélisande* remained a little disoriented faced with the novelty of the work, but on the whole, gave it a respectable welcome, and listened with profound attention. . . . However, a little later, the Roman public . . . not wanting to listen to reason, did not let the performance reach its conclusion." *Don Carlo* opened the final season at the Teatro Costanzi on January 2, 1926, which concluded with Cimarosa's *Il matrimonio segreto*. Of particular note were the Roman premieres of *Turandot* and *Khovanschina*. Some of the outstanding artists of the era who performed at the Costanzi included Titta Ruffo, Emma Carelli, and Beniamino Gigli, after whom the piazza in front of the opera house is named.

When the theater reopened as Teatro dell'Opera in February 1928, the Rome premiere of *Nerone* graced the stage. The inaugural season also featured Stravinsky's *Rossignol* (*The Nightingale*). The next season offered the Rome debut of Claudia Muzio as Violetta with the acclaimed Russian bass Fyodor Chaliapin as Boris Godunov. Mussolini supported the theater, guaranteeing its success during the Fascist era. Every season included at least one *prima assoluta*. Between 1928 and 1960, there were almost four dozen additional world premieres, most forgotten: Mulè's *Dafni*; Casavola's *Il Gobbo del Califfo*; Peragallo's *Ginevra deli Almieri*; Ghislanzoni's *Re Lear*; Guerrini's *La vigna*; Guarino's *Balilla*; Persico's *La Locandiera*; Casavola's *Salammbò*; Veretti's *Burlesca*; Pizzetti's *Lo Straniero*; Ferreri's *La vedova scaltra*; Alfano's *Cyrano di Bergerac* and *Il dottor Antonio*; Napoli's *Il tesoro*; Malipiero's *Ecuba* and *I capriccio di Callot*; and Rossellini's *Racconto d'inverno*. Some composers traveled to Dell'Opera to conduct their world premieres, including Casella for *La donna serpente*, Zandonai for *La farsa amorosa*, Savagnone for *Il drago rosso*, and Respighi for *La fiamma*.

During World War II, many of Italy's artists returned to their homeland, bringing prestige to Dell'Opera. Since Mussolini was allied with Hitler, German operas, especially those of Wagner, held a prominent place in the repertory, and several complete cycles of *Der Ring des Nibelungen* were mounted. On November 3, 1942, Tullio Serafin, who was the director of the opera house at the time, staged the Italian premiere of a German opera banned by the Nazis, Berg's *Wozzeck*. The Nazis declared the work "depraved" and its composer a "degenerate." Serafin left the Dell'Opera shortly thereafter. After the war, a curious incident regarding the liberty of music critics occurred. Two critics reviewing for *Tempo* and *Avanti*, respectively, wrote scathing critiques of Allegra's *Romulus*, also implying political favoritism in getting the opera produced. The next day, Allegra brought a lawsuit against the critics for "defamation of his integrity as an artist." Three composers testified at one of the hearings. Petrassi and Pizzetti were against Allegra. Alfano defended him. The judgment was against the two critics, but to avoid a widening of the scandal, the president of the Società for writers and publishers obtained a withdrawal of the suit, resolving it with no winners or losers.

Important artists performed, both during and after the war, including Franco Corelli, Tito Gobbi, Giuseppe di Stefano, Nicolai Gedda, Ferruccio Tagliavini, Lauri-Volpi, Mario del Monaco, Leonie Rysanek, and the legendary Maria Callas, who was at her peak in the early and mid-1950s. She overwhelmed the audience in 1954 with her *Trovatore*, followed by a stupendous *Medea*. But in 1958, only a few years later, in the season opener of *Norma*, the protests and scandalous behavior of the audience were so hostile that she withdrew from the production after the first act. Her rendering of the famous

Casta diva was routine, not what one would have expected from an artist the caliber of Callas, so amid some applause was prolonged hissing and booing and a certain coldness on the part of the public. The reaction did not please Callas, who barricaded herself in her room and decided not to continue. After a wait of 40 minutes the audience was informed, and the opera house erupted into a cacophony of clamor that continued to the Hotel Quirinale, where she was staying.

Since 1960 around 20 additional world premieres have graced the stage, most since forgotten: Zafred's *Ameleto* and *Wallenstein*; Mortari's *Il contratto*; Mannino's *Il quadro delle meraviglie* and *La stirpe di Davide*, both conducted by the composer; Chailly's *L'idiota*; Ferrero's *Charlotte Corday*, *Salvatore Giuliano*, and *Marilyn*; Fiume's *Il tamburo di anno*; Allegro's *L'isola degli incanti*; Bussotti's *Fedra*; Banchieri's *La pazzia senile*; and Rossellini's *Uno sguardo dal ponte*.

The theater has experienced good times and bad, strikes and uncertainty, and political turmoil and huge deficits but has always managed to survive. There have been worthy performances and questionable ones. There have been tempestuous times and dramatic moments, usually tied to money problems and union agitation. One such period was in 1976, when the entire staff was fired and a new team put in place. Another was May 1999, which was especially turbulent: the theater had to form a *fondazione*, as required by law. A new team took over management, Sinopoli and Ernani, whose stated objective was to produce at least 100 performances each year and occupy a position to rival Teatro alla Scala, Milan's famous opera house. But in January 2000, after only a brief time at the opera house, both Ernani and Sinopoli resigned (although their resignations were refused by the mayor) and the season opened without having been introduced.

The season-inaugural opera, *Tosca*, marked a historic occasion: 100 years ago, the prima assoluta of Puccini's masterpiece was given on the same stage. Since the opera house was still undergoing renovation, it opened only to celebrate the 100th birthday of *Tosca*, which was presented in semistaged form with Luciano Pavarotti, Juan Pons, and Ines Salazar and Plácido Domingo conducting. After the performance, the theater was closed and the season known as the Stagione del Grande Giubileo del 2000 (Season of the Grand Jubilee of 2000) continued with *La bohème* at the Teatro Brancaccio. The Teatro dell'Opera reopened in March 2000 with a concert version of *Siegfried*. The first fully staged work, *Le jongleur de Notre Dame*, arrived in April and showed the modernized stage to its fullest, to a surprisingly empty house. During the first few seasons of the 21st century, contemporary operas played a large role, with the staging of Respighi's *Marie Victoire*, Stravinsky's *Histoire du soldat*, Pizzetti's *Assassinio nella cattedrale*, Wolf-Ferrari's *Sly*, Henze's *Pollicino*, Petrassi's *Il cordovano*, Bacalou's *Estaba La Madre* (commissioned by the Teatro dell'Opera), and Betta's *Il fantasia nella cabina* along with the popular 19th-century repertory and the occasional early period work, such as Monteverdi's *Il combattimento di Tancredi e Clorinda*. The Terme di Caracalla was reopened again in 2001 after a very long hiatus to host a summer festival. Although the first two seasons saw only ballet, opera returned to the stage in 2003 with *Carmen* followed by *Nabucco* and *Trovatore* in 2004.

Most seasons offer at least one novelty; the company's forte is the execution of unusual works. The repertory covers a broad spectrum of operas as shown by a recent season that included *Semiramide*, *Attila*, *Thaïs*, *Das Rheingold*, *La Sonnambula*, *Der Aufstieg und Fall der Stadt Mahagonny*, and *Edipo Re*, among others.

Practical Information

Teatro dell'Opera, piazza Beniamino Gigli 8, 00184 Roma; tel. 39 06 481 601, fax 39 06 481 8847; www.opera.roma.it.

The season, which runs from September to June, offers 11 operas with five to eight performances of each. During July and August, opera takes place at the Terme di Caracalla with 2 operas and six performances of each. Stay at the Hotel Universo, via Principe Amedeo 5/b; tel. 06 476 811, fax 06 474 5125; www.rosciolihotels.com. The stylishly renovated Universo is a 4-minute walk from the opera house. Visit the locations where Puccini set each act of *Tosca*: the 15th-century church of Sant'Andrea della Valle, the Palazzo Farnese (now the French Embassy), and the Castel Sant'Angelo. Visit a couple of the smaller Roman opera companies: Teatro San Pietro, via Santa Maria Mediatrice 24/26 (tel. and fax 6601 7910, cell 347 879 2958; www .teatrosanpietro.org), and Musica & Musica, Chiesa di San Paolo, via Nazionale (tel. 482 6296; www.musicaemusicarsrl.com). See the Museum of Musical Instruments / Museo degli Strumenti Musicali, piazza Santa Croce, where there is a collection of more than 3,000 pieces.

FORTY-FOUR

~

Festival Internazionale,
San Gimignano

The Festival Internazionale began as a summer opera festival in 1929, with performances of *Il trovatore* taking place in the Piazza Duomo. The festival subsequently expanded to include concerts of classical, jazz, and popular music; plays; and cinema, but opera has remained its heart. For the festival, the main piazza is converted into a 250-seat, outdoor opera house by erecting a temporary stage and rows of seats. The orchestra sits in front of the stage at audience level. The buildings surrounding the square become the "theater walls" and an archway, which leads into the square, acts as a formal entrance. Yellow and blue lights illuminate the surrounding towers for a stunning effect.

The inaugural season offered another Verdi work, *Rigoletto*. The second season also had two operas on the schedule, *Lucia di Lammermoor* and *Andrea Chénier*. Then the number of operas per festival began to vary from one to six, but the repertory continued in the same vein with popular Italian fare. There was a predominance of Verdi and Puccini operas with some offerings from the verismo period, including *Cavalleria rusticana* and *I pagliacci*, although during certain times the offerings were more adventurous, with *L'incoronazione di Poppea*, *L'histoire du Soldat*, *The Telephone*, *Il segreto di Susanna*, *Gianni Schicchi*, *Gloria*, and *Tamerlano* on the boards. Many operas are staged, others are presented in concert form, and operetta is occasionally part of the program. Different companies from around Italy are invited to perform. The festival has returned to a more conservative vein with *Rigoletto* and *Bohème* as recent productions.

Practical Information

International Festival, Sala Consiliare, Commune of San Gimignano; tel. 39 0577 941 269.

The opera part of the festival takes place during August, offering two operas with two performances of each. Stay at the Hotel L'Antico Pozzo, via San Matteo 87, San Gimignano; tel. 0577 942014, fax 0577 942 117. In the heart of the old town, the Antico Pozzo is a 5-minute walk from the festival. Visit the Palazzo Vecchio del Podestà, Piazza Duomo, dating from the 12th century, where a theater operated in 1537.

FORTY-FIVE

~

Teatro Verdi Musica Festival, San Severo

Performances were first held in a room of the centrally located municipal building. The first real and proper theater in the city was inaugurated on November 21, 1819. Named the Teatro Reale Borbone (Royal Bourbon Theater), since the area was under the rule of the House of Bourbon, it was constructed of wood. There were three box tiers topped by a gallery, modest decorations, and seats for 300. It served San Severo (Foggia) well for more than a century, but by the beginning of the 1920s the building was in such a terrible state of disrepair that it was more economical to build a new theater instead of restoring the old one. The result was the construction of the Teatro del Littorio, which opened December 19, 1937, with *Andrea Chénier*. It was so named in honor of the Fascist regime that was in power when it opened. In 1983 the theater was renamed Teatro Giuseppe Verdi. The operas take place as part of the music festival. Recent works include *Bohème* and *Rigoletto*.

Practical Information

Teatro Verdi Musica Festival, corso Garibaldi, piazza Municipio, 71016 San Severo (Foggia); tel. 39 0882 241 323, fax 39 0882 359 316. The season takes place in December, offering two operas with two performances of each.

⌐◞

Festival dei Due Mondi, Spoleto

Documentation exists showing musical activities dating back to 1636 with a performance of Campello's *Gerusalemme captive*. Castelli's *Il favorito del principe* followed 3 years later. As in other Italian cities, opera was the "pleasure of princes." But as early as 1667, on the initiative of the Accademia degli Ottusi, a public theater was in operation, the evidence for which was that the city council offered boxes for sale in the Teatro di Piazza del Duomo, also called Teatro della Rosa. Constructed of wood, the building held 60 boxes distributed on four tiers. It is believed that the structure was located on the footings of an ancient duke's palace. Modernized in 1749, the Rosa reopened 2 years later as the Nuovo Teatro di Spoleto with Jommelli's *Ipermestra*. Illuminated by oil lamps, whose smoke caused substantial damage, the building was restored in 1817. Among the illustrious guests was Rossini, who visited twice. The first time he attended an opera, he sat in the box of a Mr. Gonfaloniere, commenting, "Signor Gonfaloniere, I give my congratulations to the orchestra [composed of all local musicians] and my condolences to the singers." On the second visit, he slipped in unnoticed during a rehearsal of *L'italiana in Algeri* and replaced the contrabass player, playing the instrument at the end of the opera to the delight of the public.

By the mid-1800s, the Nuovo Teatro di Spoleto had outlived its usefulness and the town needed a new theater. The location chosen was in the area of the ancient church of the monastery of Sant'Andrea. The owner of the land, Filippo Marignoli, ceded it to 91 local citizens who formed an association for the purpose of erecting the new building. Constructed over the course of a decade, between 1854 and 1864, at a cost of 360,000 lire, it was designed by Ireneo Aleandri. The Teatro Nuovo was inaugurated on August 3, 1864, with Sangiorgi's *Guisemberga da Spoleto*. There were four box tiers topped by a gallery. Of note was the chandelier in the auditorium, decorated with gold zecchini and holding crystal tulip fixtures of oil lamps, later replaced by electric bulbs. The curtain was decorated with a painting showing the defeat of Annibale under Spoleto. During carnival the theater hosted overcrowded masked balls, causing rapid deterioration. The building was restored in 1933.

The facade of the Nuovo displays two distinct sections. The triple-arch lower part is of ashlar and decorated with medallions of Rossini, Alfieri, Goldoni, and Metastasio. Statues occupy the lower four front rectangular niches. The upper part is a mustard color, highlighted with three arches that mirror those below, and framed by Ionic pilasters. Bas-reliefs of musical motifs decorate the facade. The 800-seat, five-tiered, ivory, gold, and maroon auditorium curves in the traditional horseshoe shape. The parapets are meticulously decorated with putti with bows and arrows, figures engaged in diverse activities, and faces and masks of Comedy and Tragedy. Clusters of Muses with horns evoking Apollo and chiaroscuro putti at play embellish the proscenium area. On the ceiling are allegorical figures, nymphs, maidens, and flying horses.

With the completion of the Teatro Nuovo, the old theater was no longer needed. However, the residents of Spoleto were interested in preserving the venue, but with a new layout and design and constructed in masonry. Under the guidance of Giovanni Montiroli, the opera house, renamed Teatro Caio Melisso after one of the Spoletian writers from the time of Augusto, was completed in 1880. It was also known as the Nobile Teatro di Spoleto. The front of the theater is of polished beige stone, with steps and flooring in red brick. The facade has no architectural design or features, as was the custom during the era in which the theater was originally constructed. The 350-seat, red, ivory, and gold auditorium holds three tiers of boxes topped by a gallery. Parapets are decorated with chiaroscuro angels, lyres, and masks of Comedy and Tragedy, while the ceiling features Apollo and the nine Muses—Clio, Euterpe, Thalia, Melpomene, Terpsichore, Erato, Calliope, Urania, and Polymnia—and between the Muses, putti clutching lyres. The curtain shows the apotheosis of Caio Melisso with a background of fortress towers.

It was the presence of these two gems of opera theaters that attracted Gian Carlo Menotti, founder of the Festival dei Due Mondi, to Spoleto. With the town forgotten and on the verge of bankruptcy, it was an ideal match. Festivals attract people and money. When the festival began in 1958, it was considered innovative, the first of its kind in uniting so many varied and diverse art forms in one place at one time. The Festival dei Due Mondi officially opened June 5, 1958, with Verdi's *Macbeth*, directed by a young Luchino Visconti with a young Thomas Schippers on the podium. The primary purpose was to showcase the arts and discover new, young talent. By employing unknown artists, the festival was both affordable and able to do the unusual, the experimental, and the avant-garde. Due Mondi hosts opera, chamber concerts, ballet, experimental theater, art exhibitions, and film. Francis Menotti, Gian Carlo Menotti's adopted son, explains their philosophy: "Art is not entertainment, but an offspring of society. Artists are important in the community and essential in its development." The festival attempts to eliminate the inherent barriers between the various art forms and between the arts and the general population by being accessible to everyone.

Operatic Events of the festival at Teatro Nuovo and Teatro Caio Melisso

The operas of the inaugural season indicated the eclectic orientation the festival's operatic repertory would adopt. Besides the 19th-century opening opera, two were from the 1700s, Cimarosa's *Il maestro di cappella* and Pergolesi's *Lo frate 'nnammorato*, and two were contemporary works, Bucchi's *Il giuoco del barone* and Hoiby's *The Scarf*. Forgotten and unusual works and premieres played an important role, many of which only rarely appeared in regular opera house repertories: *Ognennïy angel* (The Fiery Angel), *Lyubov'k tryom apel'sinam* (The Love for Three Oranges), *Der Prinz von Homburg*, *Il conte Ory*, *L'histoire du Soldat*, *Il furioso all'isola di San Domingo*, *Markheim*, *The Mother*, *Il giuramento*, *Ledi Makbet Mtsenskovo uyezda* (*Lady Macbeth of the Mtsensk District*), *Antony and Cleopatra*, *Paolino*, *Hydrogen Jukebox*, *Apollo et Hyacinthus*, and *Die tote Stadt*. The directors often had a theater or film background and offered experimental, avant-garde productions before crossover directors became commonplace in the opera world. Louis Malle directed *Der Rosenkavalier*; Roman Polanski *Lulu*; Ken Russell *Madama Butterfly*; Günther Kramer *Elektra*, *Wozzeck*, and *Jenůfa*; Patrice Chéreau *L'italiana in Algeri*; and Visconti *Macbeth*, *Duca d'Alba*, *Salome*, *La traviata*, and *Manon Lescaut*. Productions are rarely repeated, although the operas are.

After the festival was on firm footing, Menotti added his own operas to the schedule: *Vanessa*; *The Saint of Bleeker Street*; *The Medium*; *Tamu-Tamu*; *The Consul*; *The Old Lady and the Thief*; *The Telephone*; *The Lie of Martin*; *The Egg*; *The Last Savage*; *Juana, la loca*; *Maria Golovin*; *Goya*; and *Amahl and the Night Visitors*. More recently, despite the small venue, some monumental operas have been offered (with reduced orchestras), including *Voyna i mir* (War and Peace) and *Lohengrin*. With the advent of the 21st century, the repertory has remained unusual with *Eine florentinische Tragödie*, *Carmina Burana*, and the 1847 original version of *Macbeth*. Recently, Ullmann's *Der Kaiser von Atlantis* and Händel's *Oreste* were on the schedule.

Practical Information

Festival dei Due Mondi, piazza del Duomo 8, 06049 Spoleto; tel. 39 0743 220 320, fax 39 0743 220321; www.spoletofestival.it.

The festival takes place during June and July, comprising one to three operas with between one and six performances of each. Visit Teatro Romano, piazza della Libertà, and the ruins of a Roman amphitheater, via Anfiteatro.

FORTY-SEVEN

Puccini Festival, Torre del Lago

In 1924 Puccini, before he left for a clinic in Brussels, said to his friend Gio-
vacchino Forzano, referring to his house on the lake in Torre del Lago, "I
always go behind here and then with the boat I go to hunt snipe . . . but one
time I would like to go behind here to listen to my operas in the outdoors."
Six years later, Forzano established a festival to honor Puccini's memory and
fulfill the maestro's wish. On August 24, 1930, the first Puccini Festival was
inaugurated with *La bohème* in a temporary theater, Carro di Tespi Lirico, in
the Piazzale Puccini, the square in front of the composer's house on the
shores of Lake Massaciuccoli. The stage was supported by piles fixed in the
water. On the podium was the composer Mascagni, with Forzano directing.
Soon after its inauguration, the festival sailed into rough waters with the
Fascist rise to power, managing only a single season in 1937, that of a concert
with Licia Albanese as one of the soloists. It came back to life in 1949 with
the staging of *La fanciulla del West* to commemorate the 25th anniversary of
the composer's death. The 1950s brought some of Puccini's best loved works:
Madama Butterfly, *Tosca*, and *La bohème*. When in 1966 the Teatro dei Quattromila (Theater of the 4,000, so named for its seating capacity, although it
actually holds fewer spectators) was erected on reclaimed land to the north
of Puccini's house, the festival gradually became an annual summer event.

Between the festival's founding in 1930 and 2005, only 51 seasons had
taken place. Although political factors and World War II played a role, the
main barrier was lack of funds. For that reason, on September 15, 1990, the
Fondazione Festival Pucciniano (Puccini Festival Foundation) was established to bring financial stability and ensure its future. Until the end of the
20th century, the festival was sometimes called "a little local event," mainly
because of its inadequate and uncomfortable facilities, although some pro-

ductions also suffered from lack of inspiration. Already in the mid-1990s, the foundation began planning the erection of a new open-air theater with facilities and acoustics to place it on a level with other major Italian summer festivals. Finally, with the dawn of the 21st century, the town of Viareggio purchased the land around the Teatro dei Quattromila to establish a 270,000-square-foot Parco della Musica (Music Park), which would include a 3,100-seat Teatro al Aperto (Outdoor Theater), a 600-seat covered studio theater (if it rains, the opera still goes on, albeit with a reduced audience), and a museum, rehearsal space, and workshops carved out of abandoned buildings on the site. Italo Insolera is coordinating the $60 million project.

Located near a very small marina and overlooking the beautiful natural setting of Lake Massaciuccoli, the Teatro dei Quattromila is entered via a Japanese-style bridge of wooden planks, raised when the performance begins. The natural beauty is somewhat spoiled by the theater itself, a 4,000-seat, massive conglomeration of steel and fiberglass that resembles a sport stadium, and omnipresent mosquitoes.

Operatic Events at the Teatro dei Quattromila

The Puccini Festival was founded to present, examine, and perpetuate Puccini's operas in a theater near the house where the maestro composed several of his works. Puccini wrote only 12 operas—*Le villi, Edgar, Manon Lescaut, La bohème, Tosca, Madama Butterfly, La fanciulla del West, La Rondine, Il trittico (Il tabarro, Gianni Schicchi, Suor Angelica),* and *Turandot.* With *Le villi* and *Edgar* justifiably forgotten, *Il trittico* so short they are all performed in one evening, and *Rondine* not often staged, there are only six viable operas to fill the repertory every season. With these same works on the schedule, season after season, occasionally works of Puccini's contemporaries were performed, like *Andrea Chénier,* and the pairing of *Gianni Schicchi* with *L'heure espagnole,* and *Cavalleria rusticana* with *La vida breve.* Most seasons, however, offer an all-Puccini repertory with three or four out of these six operas: *Madama Butterfly, Tosca, La bohème, Manon Lescaut, Turandot,* and *Fanciulla del West.* To add some variety to the same operas, a project called "scolpire l'opera" (to sculpture the opera) was introduced during the first seasons of the 21st century with productions designed by well-known painters and sculptures. The centenary of *Madama Butterfly* was also the 50th Puccini Festival, so an extraordinary program was offered. There was a special preseason performance of *Madama Butterfly* in May and the first-ever staging at the festival of *Edgar* in August, with artists such as Andrea Bocelli, Sylvie Valayre, Juan

Pons, and Marcello Giordano performing. Over the decades, other well-known artists had been welcomed at the festival: Beniamino Gigli, Ferruccio Tagliavini, Giuseppe di Stefano, Franco Corelli, Luciano Pavarotti, and Mario del Monaco among the male artists and Magda Olivero, Katia Ricciarelli, Fiorenza Cossotto, Eva Marton, and Ghena Dimitrova among the female artists.

Operas at Torre del Lago are large-scale presentations of Puccini's works. The drawback to such productions is the risk inherent in experimentation. Often, when a production deviated from the tried and true, it was a financial or other type of disaster. Although the *scolpire l'opera* had successes, it also suffered failures. Nevertheless, the concept of spectacular Hollywood-like productions of opera outdoors works in this setting, if the singers have strong voices to carry a great distance, since the acoustics are notoriously poor.

Practical Information

Puccini Festival, piazzale Belvedere 4, 55048 Torre del Lago; tel. 39 0584 359 322, fax 39 0584 350 277; www.puccinifestival.it.

The season runs during July and August with three to four operas and three to five performances of each. There are very few hotels in Torre del Lago. Plan on staying in nearby Viareggio. Visit Villa Puccini in Torre del Lago (tel. 341 445). Puccini purchased the villa after the success of *Tosca*, and he composed *Manon Lescaut*, *Madama Butterfly*, and parts of *La fanciulla del West*, *La rondine*, and the *Trittico* there. The maestro restructured the house to its current form, which has remained unchanged from the maestro's time, except for the square in front of the house added after Puccini's death. In 1919 a noisy, smelly peat factory opened next to his villa, forcing him to move to Viareggio, where he built a house on previously purchased land he had at the corner of via Buonarroti and via Marco Polo. There he composed *Turandot* before leaving for Brussels in November 1924, where he died. The house is now privately owned. At the Puccini Festival Foundation, piazzale Belvedere 4; tel. 350567, fax 350277, the artistic patrimony of Puccini is promoted and preserved, and you can learn about the plans for the Parco della Musica.

~

FORTY-EIGHT

Teatro Petruzzelli and Teatro Piccinni, Bari

Small theaters existed in Bari during the 1700s. One was in the realm of the royal convent in Puglia, which during carnival hosted "pleasing comic shows." A larger theater, the Teatro del Sedile located in the Palazzo del Sedile on the Piazza Mercantile, was in operation by 1804 and hosted dramatic works. It held two or three tiers of boxes for families and some seats for single people. The cost of the theater was paid for by the sale of boxes and individual seats. It survived until July 13, 1835, when during a dramatic performance, someone shouted, "Save us, the theater is falling." There was a structural crack in the wall, and the theater collapsed.

That calamity resulted in the construction of a new theater, the Teatro Piccinni. Antonio Niccolini, who had rebuilt the Teatro di San Carlo in Naples, received the commission to design the structure in 1836, but work did not begin until 1840. The theater was finally opened 14 years later, on May 30, 1854. The proposed name of the opera house was Regio Teatro Maria Teresa, in honor of the consort of Ferdinando II, but Maria Teresa did not give her consent, so when it was inaugurated, it had no name.

There are conflicting sources concerning the inaugural work. According to Dinko Fabris and Marco Renzi, editors of *La Musica a Bari dalle cantorie medievali al Conservatorio Piccinni*, the reporter Stanislao d'Aloe claimed it was *Il trovatore*, but the "better informed" Giulio Petroni wrote that it was a "mixed performance with the first act from Pergolesi's *Elena di Troia* and the second and third act from *Poliuto*. The Web site of the Teatro Petruzzelli (www.Teatro-petruzzelli.puglia.it) states it was *Poliuto* that inaugurated the theater. The issue of the name for the theater was taken up on January 8,

1855, when it was decided to call it Teatro del Municipio, but a few weeks later, on January 23, it was decided instead to name it after the Barese musician Piccinni. The cost of construction was 90,000 ducats. As in other Italian theaters, works of Rossini, Bellini, Donizetti, and Verdi dominated the boards, but the Piccinni also hosted Mercadante, Petrella, Sarro, Pedrotti, and what was considered a most modern work at the time, an opera called *Dolores* by Auteri-Manzocchi. The Piccinni also presented the *prima mondiale* of Caracciolo's *Maso il montanaro*. Despite the small stage, operas such as *Les Huguenots*, *Il Guarany*, *Ruy Blas*, *Mefistofele*, *Faust*, *Fra diavolo*, *Dinorah*, *Carmen*, and *Lohengrin* were in the repertory. The most popular operas were *Il barbiere di Siviglia*, *Nabucco*, and *Madama Butterfly*.

The Piccinni is a long building, extending an entire city block. The facade is divided into three distinct sections. The most prominent is the center, which is faced with white stone and offers a colonnade of substantial Doric columns surmounted by Ionic pilasters. The coat of arms of Bari embellishes the crowning pediment. The flanking wings are rose-colored rusticated stone topped by two levels of windows, crowned by a typanum. The ornate, 850-seat, ivory, red, and gold auditorium holds four tiers of boxes topped by a gallery. In the center is an imposing royal box, draped with maroon and gold and topped by an enormous crown. The dome is decorated with allegorical images, the work of Luigi de Luise and Leopoldo Galluzzo.

In the last quarter century of the 1800s, the Piccinni was deemed inadequate for the diverse cultural needs of the city, so in 1877 the city council offered free public land for the realization of a politeama that would be able to satisfy the needs of the Bari population and guarantee accessibility also to the lower classes. The first project, submitted by Gaetano Canedi, was praised by the public and approved by the city council but refused by the prefect on procedural grounds. The municipality then reopened the competition and the businessmen brothers Onofrio and Antonio Petruzzelli offered to finance the project if it was based on plans from their brother-in-law, Angelo Messeni. A contract was drawn up between the city and the Petruzzelli brothers, and Messeni submitted his first plans in 1896. They were approved at the end of the year. He envisioned a theater of enormous dimensions, which were drastically reduced for economic reasons but still much larger than either the Piccinni or the project proposed by Canedi. The first stone was laid in June 1898, with construction lasting almost 5 years. The Politeama Petruzzelli was inaugurated on February 14, 1903, with *Les Huguenots*. The Petruzzelli brothers had received permission from the town to name the theater after themselves, since they had invested much of their wealth in its construction.

In November 1956, the Petruzzelli obtained the classification of *Teatro di tradizione*, which entitled it to receive support from the region and the municipality. With a change in laws, in October 2003, the opera house formed a *fondazione*, allowing it to raise funds privately and enjoy other benefits. A suspicious fire destroyed the theater in October 1991. Only the exterior walls survived. The theater's ex-manager, Ferdinando Pinto, was found guilty of arson and sentenced to 8 years in prison. There is a difference of opinion, depending on with whom one speaks, about who set the fire. Some believe the former manager was guilty, but others feel it was an accident, caused by some kids who made a small fire that got out of control. The opera seasons were transferred to the Piccinni, but it had been closed for several years on the grounds that it was unsafe, since it did not meet the building codes. This required special permission every time the theater opened for performances, with the mayor assuming the responsibility and overruling the veto of the supervising commission, which was evidently scared by the Petruzzelli case, according to the *Giornale della Musica*, no. 150, June 1999.

The government offered around $10 million toward the rebuilding effort. Although reconstruction began in 1993 and was to be completed in 1,000 days, it was halted after only a few months by the Messeni-Nemagna family, heirs of the original owners, when they suspected irregularities in the financial calculations. Only the cupola had been restored. The problems of reconstruction were complicated by the fact that the town owns the land and the Messeni-Nemagna family the building. After a long hiatus, reconstruction began again under the Consorzio recupero patrimonio artistic (Consortium to Recover Artistic Patrimony). The *fondazione* raised around $30 million through a lottery to complete the reconstruction.

The Teatro Petruzzelli represented an important example of the so-called 19th-century politeama. The theaters were enormous and could accommodate a couple of thousand spectators. The Petruzzelli itself occupied 4,843 square meters and was characterized by an enormous cupola of iron and glass. The building was the color of red brick, except for the triple-arched entrance, which was faced with white ashlar adorned with musical and dramatic motifs. Decorative pilasters, arched windows, and balustrades defined the facade, which displayed busts of Verdi, Rossini, and Bellini in niches above the center windows. A relief of Apollo crowning the Muses adorned the pediment. The red, ivory, and gold auditorium was designed by Raffaele Armenise, who drew inspiration from Teatro alla Scala in Milan, Teatro di

San Carlo in Naples, and the Palais Garnier in Paris. The large auditorium of 2,200 seats held five tiers: two box tiers, two tiers with balcony seats in the center and boxes on the sides, topped by a gallery. The ornately decorated ceiling displayed various scenes, including one of a bullfight.

Operatic Events at the Politeama Petruzzelli

When the Petruzzelli opened, with its abundant balcony and gallery seating, it was praised as a politeama. Operas by composers from Puglia found a home here. The inaugural season presented the prima assoluta of native son La Rotella's *Dea*, alongside *Andrea Chénier*, *Il trovatore*, and *Aida*. Subsequent seasons offered native son Paisiello's *Pirro*, *Elfrida*, and *La serva padrona* with the Italian and French grand opera repertory. The Petruzzelli also welcomed operas by Wagner and those from the Russian repertory, including *Boris Godunov*. These works then disappeared from the schedule and *Boris Godunov* was not staged again for more than 70 years. As journalist Franco Chieco commented about the Petruzzelli repertory, "Debussy, German Romantic, National Slavic School and representatives of the Vienna school are unknown [in Bari]. Of Bellini we know only *Norma* and *Sonnambula*, but scarcely *I Puritani*. With Donizetti we stop at the three most popular operas, *Lucia*, *L'Elisir*, and *Don Pasquale*, and darkness on the Neapolitan School, except for the unofficial season when Piccinni's *Cecchina*, and Paisiello's *Barbiere* were performed." Mascagni was one of the most popular composers at the Petruzzelli, with 116 performances of his works between 1903 and 1982, and for 15 seasons *Cavalleria rusticana* was in repertory.

Artists such as Lina Pagliughi, Beniamino Gigli, Toti dal Monte, Aureliano Pertile, Gino Bechi, Gina Cigna, Gianni Pederzini, Rosetta Pampanini, Tito Schipa, Mario del Monaco, and Lauri-Volpi graced the stage during the first part of the 20th century and Alfredo Kraus, Katia Ricciarelli, Luciano Pavarotti, Leo Nucci, Maria Chiara, Cornell McNeil, Piero Cappuccilli, and Renato Bruson during the latter half.

The 1950s and 1960s saw contemporary works such as Rota's *Il cappello di paglia di Firenze*, and the first Mozart works, while the next decade offered mainly "popular" titles, such as *Cenerentola*, and many titles of Verdi, including *Macbeth*, *Otello*, *Simon Boccanegra*, and *Don Carlo*. The 1980s were distinguished by the presentation of the Neapolitan school, with Piccinni's *Iphigénia en Tauride* given its first execution in modern times, and 20th-century works such as *Rake's Progress*.

With the destruction of the Petruzzelli in 1991, it became difficult to produce an opera season. For a few years in the mid-1990s, performances were mounted in the Arena di Vittorio, but the venue was not well suited for opera, so the opera seasons were moved to Teatro Piccinni. The 1996 opera season, known as Barilirica 96, was the first organized by the Ente Lirico Concertistico Pugliese and under the guidance of Fabris, whose goals were the rediscovery of forgotten works of the 1700s from the Neapolitan school and the reestablishment of Piccinni as an important musician. The program included the *prima esecuzione moderna* of Provenzale's *Stellidaura vendicante*, along with the popular *La traviata*, *Il barbiere di Siviglia*, and *Matrimonio segreto*. Subsequent seasons witnessed the first performance in modern times of *La finta camerara* by Bari native son Latilla, who was also the uncle of Piccinni, and Vinci's *I Fidanzati in Galea* (*Li Zite 'n Galera* in Neapolitan dialect). The latter was given at the Castle Svevo. The ambition proved short-lived. The cultural council of Bari, which organizes the schedule, now offers predominately popular Italian fare. Recent repertory includes *Don Giovanni*, *La Cenerentola*, *Ariadne auf Naxos*, *Così fan tutte*, *Otello*, *La bohème*, and *Lucia di Lammermoor*.

Practical Information

Teatro Petruzzelli, via Cavour, 70121 Bari; tel. 39 080 524 1741, fax 39 080 521 0527; www.teatro-petruzzelli.puglia.it. Teatro Comunale Piccinni, Corso Vittorio Emanuele, 70122 Bari.

The opera season, still at the Teatro Piccinni while reconstruction continues, takes place from October to April and offers seven operas with two to five performances of each. Stay at the Palace Hotel, via Lombardi 13, 70122 Bari; tel. 080 521 6551, fax 080 521 1499; www.palacehotelbari.it. The perfect hotel for opera lovers, the Palace offers a special guest room called *camera della musica* (music room), where there is high-quality stereo equipment, a CD player, and a large selection of CDs, books, and newspapers on opera. It is a 5-minute walk to the Teatro Piccinni and 10 minutes to the Petruzzelli. Visit the Casa Piccinni, Vico Fiscardi 2, Piazza Mercantile, 70122 Bari; tel. 574 0022, fax 579 4461. The birthplace of Piccinni has been restored and turned into a museum of the composer.

~

Teatro Alfonso Rendano, Cosenza

From the end of the 1700s to the beginnings of the 1800s, there was a dignified and active operatic and theatrical life in Cosenza. It unfolded in two
private theaters, owned by the noble families Miletto and Contestabile, as
well as in the palaces of the patrician citizens. There had also been a luxurious public theater, Teatro Real Ferdinando, which had been built in a school
owned by the Jesuits. But after persistent demands of the Jesuits to have it
razed, King Ferdinand II ordered in 1853 that the theater be demolished.
Opera performances also took place in the Teatro Garibaldi, and the 300-
seat Teatro Baraccato, known as the Baraccone Ligneo and erected by private citizens who were lovers of the arts. Then in 1876 the municipality
decided to demolish the Baraccone in a much contested decision. This was
the catalyst for the construction of a new theater to replace the demolished
Teatro Real Ferdinando, as the Garibaldi was deemed inadequate for the city.

In 1877 *Il Giornale di Calabria* reported, "The municipality will loan a
million lire for the construction of public buildings, among which is a theater." From all the plans submitted, the one of Nicola Zumpano was selected
with the construction assigned to Paolo Greco. More than three decades
passed, however, before the Teatro Comunale, the original name of the Teatro Rendano, opened. First, there were money problems, and the construction was suspended. The minister of Public Works authorized additional
funding, and a new contract was signed in June 1899. The structure was
finally completed, and all appeared ready for the gala inaugural with an opera
by native son Alfonso Rendano planned. Then in October 1902, a piece of
ceiling three feet by four feet fell, putting the building's safety in question
and forcing a postponement of the inaugural. Next, an earthquake struck in
1905, forcing another delay, and then a problem with the lighting surfaced.

This provoked the following comment on September 16, 1906, in the local paper: "One was hoping that for September 20 it would be possible to finally open the theater, if only for a half hour, to admire it; on the contrary . . . but for now one is not able to talk about the inauguration because . . . there is no light." It was not until November 20, 1909, that the Teatro Comunale was inaugurated, with *Aida*, not with Rendano's opera as originally planned. This prompted the local newspaper, *Il Giornale di Calabria*, to denounce the "crazy hurry" with which the inauguration was arranged once the theater was finally completed, but it was not stingy in its praise for the decorations of the auditorium, that "dazzled by the vision of the arts which it created."

Meanwhile, the inhabitants were growing impatient with the delays plaguing the Comunale and other performing venues sprang up. Some were ephemeral, functioning just for a season, and others more permanent, such as the Teatro Grisolia. The Grisolia was one of the longest functioning theaters in the city. It was owned by Baron Grisolia, who hired the theater agent Enrico Mirabelli to organize opera seasons, and beginning in 1904 companies from Milan and Naples were brought to his theater.

During the Fascist era, the Comunale was used for propaganda and demonstrations, and in 1935 the opera house was rebaptized in honor of Rendano. Severely damaged in August 1943 during an aerial bombardment, it was not restored until the 1960s, reopening in 1967. But it was rough going and opera was suspended in 1972 and did not take the stage again until 1977, when the theater received the classification of *Teatro di tradizione*. The Rendano was closed once again in 1990 for 4 years, to bring the building up to fire and safety standards, reopening in 1994 with a full opera season. It is managed by the municipality.

The Rendano is a neoclassical building, with the facade divided into two levels. The lower level of ashlar extends from the building, offering a covered archway that was originally a carriage entrance. The upper level is divided into three sections by pairs of white Ionic pilasters framing three arched windows on a stucco facade. Musical symbols, instruments, and masks embellish the front. The coat of arms of Cosenza crowns the building. The sparkling ivory, gold, and red, 800-seat auditorium is in the traditional horseshoe shape, with three tiers topped by a gallery. Musical instruments and flowers of gilded stucco decorate the hall and Muses and masks of Comedy and Tragedy ornament the proscenium arch. The original ceiling, executed by Enrico Salfi, reproduced the allegory of the Performing Arts with Music, Dance, Comedy, Tragedy, Opera Buffa, and Opera Seria. It was not restored but replaced in 1966 with acoustic panels of aluminum decorated with a cloud-filled sky. The original curtain, designed by Domenico Morelli and realized by Paolo Veltri, was also not restored. A magnificent chromatic chandelier hangs in the center of the hall.

Operatic Events at the Teatro Rendano

Rendano's *Consuelo* was originally planned to inaugurate the new opera house, but those plans had been made several years earlier. With a new management in place when the Rendano was inaugurated, *Aida* was the chosen opera instead, which stirred up much controversy. *La Scintilla* published this question in its paper on November 25, 1909, "Why prearrange the inauguration of the theater when there was no special occasion that would require it just now . . . being that the *Consuelo* was exiled from the program assumed by the management, when the cost of the artistic company should have been absolutely enormous." *Il Giornale di Calabria* also complained. Nevertheless, *Aida* inaugurated the new opera house with Emilia Corsi in the title role. She was described as having "delicate inflections in her voice and sometimes the sustaining force of well-delivered high notes." The success of *Aida* did little to quell the diatribe surrounding the staging of the next opera, *Mefistofele*, but the public loved it, applauding warmly at each performance. *Rigoletto* concluded the inaugural season.

Carlo Gargiulo, the impresario who had been excluded from arranging the opening season, also hurled harsh criticism, charging that no opera on the schedule was by a Calabrese composer, neither Cilea nor Rendano. Gargiulo had offered *Adriana Lecouvreur*, but it was declined. But the work was staged during the second season, along with *Cavalleria rusticana*, *I pagliacci*, and *Carmen*. About the season it was written, "Rosina Cesaretti had interpreted her part of Carmen very well, she had a good voice and received much applause. Carlotta Marini interpreted Micaela in a way that left the public content, but was not well suited for Lola and Nedda. . . . Aldo Stanzani was a good Don Josè: his voice was effective and his experience on the stage pleased, . . . and in the part of *Escamillo* Luigi Silvetti's voice had been admired and the applause was merited. . . . Admired as always [was] the orchestra and the talented maestro Biondi, . . . only the disharmony of the chorus and the absolute deficiency in the appearance and the ugly execution of the dance [distracted]." The 1911 season featured *Il trovatore*, *La traviata*, and *Tosca*. By 1913 the number of opera offerings had jumped to eight. Besides the popular Italian works of *Il barbiere di Siviglia*, *Lucia di Lammermoor*, *La forza del destino*, and *Norma*, it included *Fior d'Alpe*, an opera by native son Giacomantonio.

The season was presented by the Compagnia Lirica Internazionale Borboni, with "splendid receipts at the box office and thunderous applause inside the theater by an overflowing public" as noted in *Storia del "Rendano"* by Amedeo Furfaro.

World War I closed the theater in 1915. Opera did not return to the stage for 5 years, not until *Rigoletto* was performed in 1920. Despite the absence of some members of the orchestra, who were left in Paola because of a train strike, it was deemed a success. The programming continued with works of the popular Italian composers such as Bellini, Cilea, Donizetti, Giordano, Leoncavallo, Ponchielli, Puccini, Rossini, and Verdi. Verdi was the most popular, followed by Puccini. Bizet and Thomas were the only non-Italian composers whose operas were on the schedule. A novelty, *Julia* by native son Quintieri who also conducted, was offered during the 1922/23 season. The story of Julia made such a positive impression on the public that the final applause lasted a half hour, as described by Furfaro in *Storia del "Rendano."* It was a notable success that the Cosenza composer would experience elsewhere in the next stages of his artistic career. When the Rendano did not offer an opera season in 1921, the Teatro Politeama, originally called Politeama Alhambra, did, with *La bohème*, *Tosca*, *Lucia di Lammermoor*, and *Wally*. But there was never any competition between the two theaters. The Politeama was severely damaged in 1943 during World War II, along with the Rendano.

Opera returned to Cosenza in 1957, but at the Teatro Citrigno with *Il trovatore*, *Lucia di Lammermoor*, *La bohème*, and *Rigoletto* gracing the stage. The Rendano reopened a decade later with *La traviata*, and a couple of novelties, Quintieri's *Liliadeh* and the first Mozart opera, *Don Giovanni*, at the theater. The first Wagner work, *Lohengrin*, arrived the following season. Although opera floundered during the 1970s with no seasons at all between 1972 and 1976, it returned to the stage in 1977 with *Un ballo in maschera* and *Madama Butterfly*. The next year, two of Giacomantonio's operas, *La leggenda del ponte* and *Quelle signore*, were offered along with popular Italian fare. The 1980 season brought Capizzano's *Amalia* with *Werther*, *Così fan tutte*, and Paisiello's *Il barbiere di Siviglia* along with the traditional Italian fare as the decade progressed. Verdi and Puccini remained the most popular composers.

When the theater reopened in 1994 after the restoration, the artistic direction aimed toward adventurous seasons. There was a reexamination of repertory lost or buried in the past and a look at modern and contemporary opera. The traditional operas were approached in a new way. There was experimentation using directors from the film world and cross-referencing with ballet and drama. One unusual opera was scheduled each season. The first year of this new approach saw only 250 people in the audience for the double bill of Rota's *La notte di un nevrastenico* and Poulenc's *La voix humaine*. But they persisted with lesser-known contemporary and foreign operas: Battiatoi's *Il cavaliere dell'intelletto*, Rimsky-Korsakov's *Motsart i Sal'yeri* (Mozart and Salieri), and the resurrection of Schubert's *Die Zwillingsbrüder* and *Der vierjährige posten*. The audience slowly returned. As the 20th century drew to a close, the repertory covered the spectrum, from Vivaldi's *L'Olimpiade* and Paisiello's *Le due Contesse* to the world premiere of Michele dall'Ongaro's *Il filo*. There was a cultural exchange with Finland with the dawn of the 21st century that saw the first performance in Italy of Rautavaara's *Aleksis Kivi* and the unearthing of Cilea's *Gina*. In 2002 Rendano's *Consuelo*, the opera that was supposed to inaugurate the opera house, was finally staged. (It had had its world premiere instead in Turin in 1902). There are coproductions with opera houses around Italy and in France. The Rendano continues with adventurous repertory as a recent season shows with Cilea's *L'arlesiana*, *Albert Herring*, and *Traviata*.

Practical Information

Teatro Alfonso Rendano, piazza XV Marzo, 87100 Cosenza; tel. 39 0984 813229, fax 39 0984 74165; www.comune.cosenza.it/rendano.

The season runs from October to December, offering three operas with two to three productions of each. Stay at the Royal Hotel, Via Molinella 24, Cosenza, Calabria; tel. 0984 412461, fax 0984 412 165. In the new section of town, the Royal is a 20-minute walk from the opera house. Visit the Associazione Alfonso Rendano in nearby Carolei, birthplace of the composer Rendano.

FIFTY

Teatro Politeama Greco, Lecce

In 1882 Enrico De Cataldis and Donato Greco requested permission from the municipality of Lecce to construct a large theater in the square of San Martino, near the Castle Carlo V. Construction began in 1883 and was completed at the end of 1884. The Politeama Principe di Napoli, as the Politeama Greco was originally called, was inaugurated with *Aida* on November 15, 1884. With the facade of an amphitheater, it held a 600-seat orchestra section, 80 boxes, and two galleries. It was furnished with 90 tanks of water that would be activated in case of fire, because it was constructed of wood and illuminated by gas. The stage was mobile with special technical devices to allow the theater to also host equestrian shows. The ceiling exhibited a fresco of a mythological scene, created by Carmine Palmieri. In 1913 the Politeama was restructured, taking a form more suitable for an opera house and removing the dangerous fire hazard. Stone replaced the wood, and heating and electricity were installed, replacing the gas. The auditorium was decorated with gilded stucco, velvet, and mirrors. Allegorical figures and portraits of great Italian composers, executed by Palmieri, decorated the ceiling and proscenium arch. The number of seats was increased to 1,500. It reopened in the spring of 1913 under its new name, Politeama Donato Greco, after its architect. The main force behind the operatic aspects was Tito Schipa, who was the artistic director at the beginning of the 1920s. It is currently used as a movie theater but also hosts the opera season, along with other shows of various types.

Operatic Events at the Politeama Greco

Lecce cannot claim, as can most other Italian cities, much of an operatic heritage. Operas by the popular Italian composers, such as Verdi, Donizetti,

Bellini, Rossini, Giordano, Puccini, Mascagni, Leoncavallo, Cilea, and Boïto, and French composers Meyerbeer and Bizet dominated the repertory. In 1969 the Politeama Greco was recognized as a *Teatro di tradizione*, which initiated the current opera structure. As the 20th century drew to a close and the 21st century appeared, the repertory, which had been mainstream with operas such as *Adriana Lecouvreur, I Capuleti e i Montecchi, Macbeth*, and *La traviata*, began offering unusual repertory, combining early 1700s (*Ariodante, Rinaldo, Agrippina*) forgotten or rarely performed works of famous composers (*Il viaggio a Reims, La figlia del reggimento, Le convenienza ed inconvenienza, Tancredi, I due Foscari, Attila*) and 20th-century pieces (*Cappello di paglia di Firenze, Il segreto di Susanna*), alongside popular fare (*Il trovatore, Tosca, Il trittico, Aida*). In 2004 both Massenet's *Manon* and Puccini's *Manon Lescaut* were on the boards, allowing a comparison of the two works. There have also been single performances in concert form of obscure operas. Recently, with a change in direction at the opera house, the repertory has become less adventurous, with *Les pêcheurs de perles, Cenerentola*, and *Carmen* on the boards.

Practical Information

Teatro Politeama Greco, via XXV Luglio 29, 73100 Lecce; tel. and fax 39 0832 241 468; www.provincia.le.it.

The season, which runs from January or February to April or May, offers three opera productions with two to five performances of each.

FIFTY-ONE

Festival della Valle d'Itria, Martina Franca

The seeds for the Festival della Valle d'Itria were planted on the evening of January 2, 1958, at the Teatro dell'Opera (Rome) during a performance of *Norma* with Maria Callas in the title role. Callas, feeling slighted by her cool reception and indignant that someone had shouted "Torna a Milano" (Return to Milan), refused to return for the second act. Alessandro Caroli, who eventually became the vice-manager at RAI, was in the audience that evening and recalled that the original version of *Norma* was for two sopranos, Norma and Adalgisa. The commonly performed version is for one soprano, Norma, and one mezzo, Adalgisa. So he asked himself (as quoted in *Miracolo a Martina* by Antonio Rossano), "Why not restore the roles exactly as Bellini wanted them?" Many years passed before the festival became reality, with help from Paolo Grassi, then *sovrintendente* of La Scala, who gave his support to the idea and mobilized the talent. Gluck's *Orfeo ed Euridice* (French edition) inaugurated the first Festival della Valle d'Itria on August 25, 1975, on an open-air stage in the courtyard of the Palazzo Ducale. There were also concerts, recitals, lieder, and other types of programming. It has been referred to as the Spoleto of the south.

The festival rediscovers obscure, neglected, and rarely performed works by Pugliese composers from the Neapolitan school, the lesser-known bel canto repertory, French operas with an Italian influence, and European composers who resided in Italy and France. The philosophy is to perform uncut versions with the certified original text in stylistically correct, interpretative vocal techniques of the era. From a scholarly point of view, this can be interesting, but for everyone else, it has the potential to bore, as often there are good reasons a work has been cut, has fallen into obscurity, or has only certain versions staged. So it is not unexpected that during the early years there were many detractors. (The thinking in southern Italy was more provincial than that up north.) "This Festival is useless. It is an exhibition of the unpopular, the arrogant, and the elite who want to humiliate the simple people. Enough with this garbage" was written in *Contrappunti*, July 1999, "Miracle or Fable" by Franco Chieco. There were also chronic money problems and at times it looked as if the festival was doomed. Two weeks before opening night in 1979, the festival was 50 million lire short. Caroli called a press conference, saying, "I have invited you to show you the festival program, however, I have the thankless task to announce that the festival will not take place." Franco Punzi, the mayor of Martina Franca, resolved that situation, and against all odds the festival has survived, even thrived, celebrating its 30th anniversary during the 2004 season.

The Cortile del Palazzo Ducale is transformed into an outdoor opera house during the festival. Overlooked by the windows of offices from which birth, marriage, and death certificates are issued, the courtyard acquires an elevated temporary stage, an "orchestra pit" that is situated at audience level, weather-resistant scenery, rows of black fiberglass seats and hard wooden benches. One hopes it does not rain.

Operatic Events of the Festival in the Cortile del Palazzo Ducale

Since the festival began in 1975, it has brought to light the first complete performances in modern times of many operas, including Auber's *Fra diavolo*, Mercadante's *Il giuramento*, Cimarosa's *Le astuzie femminili*, Traetta's *Iphigénia en Tauride*, and Bellini's *La straniera* and *Il pirata*. There was a comparison of Paisiello's and Rossini's *Il barbiere di Siviglia*, the two-soprano version of *Norma* that inspired the festival in 1977, and during the 25th season, the Italian premiere of Massenet's *Roma*. Other curiosities included the original 1857 *Simon Boccanegra*, the French edition of *Lucie de Lammermoor* and *Le trouvère*, and the uncut version of Traetta's *Ippolito ed Aricia*, which did not end until 2 a.m., when most of the audience were already at home, asleep.

With the arrival of the 21st century, more obscure, but interesting operas have been unearthed that fit the festival's goals: Gounod's *Le reine de Saba*; Donizetti's *La zingara*; Rossini's *Ivanhoe*; Paisiello's *Il due contesse* and *Proserpine*; Meyerbeer's *Gli amori di Teodolinda*; Giordano's *Siberia*; and Mercadante's *Le sette ultime parole di nostro signore sulla croce*. Recently, Gomes's *Salvator Rosa*, Donizetti's *Pietro il Grande*, and Gounod's *Polyeucte* have graced the stage. There appears to be no limit to the number of lost or forgotten operas.

Practical Information

Festival della Valle d'Itria, Martina Franca, Centro Artistico Musicale "Paolo Grassi," Palazzo Ducale 1, 74015 Martina Franca; tel. 39 080 480 5100 (during festival) and 39 080 430 2751, fax 39 080 480 5120; www.festivaldella valleditria.it.

The season, which takes place during July and August, offers three operas with two performances of each. Stay at the Park Hotel San Michele, viale Carella 9, Martina Franca; tel. 080 480 7053, fax 080 480 8895. A supporter of the festival, the San Michele is a 5-minute walk from the courtyard of the ducal palace where the performances take place and hosts the artists', journalists', and festival parties.

FIFTY-TWO

~

Teatro di San Carlo, Naples

In 1618 Vincenzo Capece constructed a theater for comedy, called Teatro dei Fiorentini, where according to Benedetto Croce in *I teatri di Napoli*, "only rare and poor rudimentary musical dramas [were] performed until 1651." The first opera heard in Naples, possibly Monteverdi's *Il Nerone*, was at the royal palace the same year the Fiorentini was erected. In 1619 Cavalli's *Veremonda* was offered. The first opera house in Naples, Teatro San Bartolomeo, was constructed around 1620 and owned by the Santa Casa degli Incurabili (Holy House of the Incurables). Originally deemed unacceptable for opera, because of its unbecoming state, it was so neglected and damaged during the fighting and turmoil of 1647 and 1648 that upon restoration it was a splendid theater, worthy of hosting operas. Operatic performances were then held at the San Bartolomeo, with Cirillo's *Giasone*, *L'Orontea*, and *Il ratto d'Elena*, and Alfiero's *La fedeltà trionfante* gracing the stage.

It was Scarlatti's move to Naples in 1682, however, that transformed the city into an important operatic center. His works were regarded as the beginning of the 18th-century Neapolitan school, which put Naples in as dominant a position in the opera world in the 1700s as the Venetian school had been in the 1600s. An essential ingredient of Neapolitan opera was the variety and degree of stylization of the different types of arias, giving opera a less rigid structure. *Pompeo* was Scarlatti's first work performed in Naples at the royal palace and again in 1684 at the Teatro San Bartolomeo. Other Scarlatti works included *Flavio*, *Rosaura*, *Odoacre*, and *Caduta dei Decemviri*. The early 1700s saw a brief flowering of Pergolesi's operas: *Sallustia*, *Il prigioniero fortunato*, and *La serva padrona*. But the glory of the Teatro San Bartolomeo was short-lived. During the night of February 6, 1681, fire destroyed the theater. It was rebuilt and reopened 2 years later. Although it was described in its day

277

as "pleasing," there were only two box tiers, which forced some nobility to find places in the orchestra level until 1698, when the addition of three more box tiers allowed the nobility to be accommodated in the style to which they were accustomed. At the same time, the theater was beautified to match the opera houses in other Italian cities.

"Although King Charles of Bourbon assuredly did not love music, as any glance into the royal box would reveal, he gossiped during the first half of the opera and slept during the second half," as De Brosses noted in *Le Présidente de Brosses en Italie, Lettres familières éreites d'Italia en 1739 et 1740*, "he held in highest regard royal decorum and wanted everything in his court to be splendid." When the captain of his guard, Lelio Carafa, Marquis d'Arienzo, counseled the king to change the management of the San Bartolomeo and restore his subsidy, he obliged. New singers were hired, including Gaetano Majorana, called Caffarelli, but in October 1734, when a performance of Pergolesi's *Adriano in Siria* was not popular, the impresario was changed again, with Angelo Carasale as the new head. He offered *Nemica amante*, *Merope*, and *Cesare in Egitto* in 1735/36. For the 1736/37 season, Sarro's *Alessandro nelle Indie* and Leo's *Farnace* were on the boards. There were also spectacular ballets the likes of which Naples had not previously seen.

By the mid-1730s, the Bartolomeo had become too small to accommodate the requirements of the new luxurious court, and its location was not convenient for the king, who visited the theater often. Discussions began in mid-1736 to construct a new opera house, better situated and more luxurious. Giovanni Antonio Medrano was hired to design the new theater, and he studied the plans of the major Italian theaters of the time, especially the Teatro Argentina in Rome and Teatro Filarmonico in Verona. Medrano's drawings were approved in March 1737, and a contract was signed, with the construction job awarded to Angelo Carasale. The Santa Casa degli Incurabili agreed to transfer the Bartolomeo to the king in April 1737 for payment of 2,500 ducats annually as compensation for lost theater profits. The cost of the new opera house was calculated at 75,000 ducats, including the cost of purchasing the San Bartolomeo. Completion was scheduled for October 1737 with the theater finished in every part except the stage, which would be the job of the future impresario. The San Bartolomeo was torn down in July and the wood was reused to build a chapel on the site called la Graziella.

The new opera house was named San Carlo in honor of the king's patron saint. It was completed on schedule at a final cost of 100,000 ducats, including in that the value of the San Bartolomeo. King Charles had contributed 32,000 ducats toward the cost. The *palchettisti* of the Bartolomeo quickly purchased boxes in the new theater, as close to the royal box as possible. There were six box tiers, of which the first four were for the nobility. The price of the boxes was 770 ducats on the first and second tiers and 580 ducats on the third and fourth. In addition, the *condomini* paid an annual fee, 230 ducats for the first two tiers, 200 ducats for the third, and 180 ducats for the fourth, to cover the costs of the productions and the management of the theater. Rules were established to maintain order: it was prohibited to go on stage, to clap during the performance, to request an encore (the king was exempt), and that servants in livery enter the orchestra level.

On October 23, 1737, the imposing facade of the theater was revealed with the following inscription: "Carolus Vtriusque Siciliae, Rex. Pulsis. Hostibus. Constitutis. Legibus. Magistratibus. Ornatis. Litteris. Artibus. Excitatis. Orbe. Pacato. Theatrum. Quo. Se Populus—Oblectaret. Endendum—Censuit. Anno. Regni. IV. Ch. R. MDCCXXXVII" (Charles, King of the Two Sicilies, defeated the enemy; instituted laws and the magistracy, favored the humanities, gave impulse to the arts, with the world at peace agreed to the construction of this theater for the enjoyment of the people, in the 4th year of his reign, 1737). The inscription was removed during the reconstruction following the 1816 fire. Domenico Sarro's *Achille in Sciro* inaugurated the opera house on November 4, 1737, the feast day of the king's patron saint. The local newspaper, *Gazzetta di Napoli*, described the gala event as being attended by "an incredible number of distinguished people, with all the boxes overflowing with ladies wearing the richest gowns and most precious gems, attended by gentlemen in tails for this most magnificent gala, the purpose of which was to make public their jubilation at the inauguration of the opera house." The five boxes to the right and left of the royal box were filled with members of the court. Francesco Milizia in his book *Del Teatro, in 1794* described the theater: "The San Carlo is horseshoe-shaped, that is to say it is a semi-circle in which the extremes are prolonged in an almost straight line as they approach the stage. . . . There are six levels of boxes with a superb royal box in the middle of the second level. . . . The stairs are magnificent, the access, vestibules, and corridors are spacious; the entrance, divided into three parts, has some decoration that could have been more majestic and significant." De Brosses wrote that it was "a room that overwhelms by its grandeur and magnificence." Royal blue and gold decorated the auditorium, which held 184 boxes in its six tiers, in addition to the royal box. The coat of arms of the Kingdom of the Two Sicilies and three gilded fleurs-de-lis of the House of Bourbon were displayed around the ornately decorated proscenium arch. Twenty-one heraldic symbols of the ruling dynasties surrounded these royal coats of arms. The king entered the theater by means of a private, covered corridor directly from his royal palace. Oil lamps and more than a thousand candles illuminated the hall. The number of candles at each box indicated the social rank of its occupants.

Carasale remained the impresario for the first 4 years. Very much in the king's favor, he was promoted and regarded as the king's right-hand man, but then misfortune befell him. The royal auditors were dissatisfied with his accounting of the money and denounced him. He was victimized by the very people in whom he had placed his trust, such that in 1739 he requested to be released from the contracts he had assumed. In May 1741, he left the San Carlo, transferring to the Teatro Nuovo. But 2 months later he was arrested and sent to the prison of the Vicar. In October 1741, he was transferred to the Fortress Saint Elmo, where in March the following year he died of a stroke. The successor of Carasale, Domenico Luigi Barone, played a pivotal role in having Carasale removed from the San Carlo. Barone, having established himself as author and conductor of popular comedies, asked in 1741 to be employed in the royal service as "director of royal entertainments." This was only possible with Carasale "out of the way." Called the inspector of the Reale Teatro San Carlo, Barone remained at the head of San Carlo until 1747, entering into unscrupulous contracts with singers and ballerinas based on their beauty, not their ability. Diego Tufarelli took the helm from Barone in 1747, remaining until 1753. He received a subsidy of 3,000 ducats to run the theater and offer 70 performances a year.

Since the San Carlo was constructed only for opera seria, the Teatro Fiorentini was the home for opera buffa until 1820, during which time it played a role in introducing numerous works, including six by Cimarosa, *L'Armida immaginaria*, *La ballerina amante*, *Il marito disperato*, *La ballerina amante*, *Le astuzie femminili*, and *Il falegame*; five by Giuseppe Mosca; six by his brother Luigi Mosca; Paisiello's *Pirro* and *L'amor contrastato*; Fioravanti's *Liretta e Giannino*; Carafa's *La gelosia corretta*; Cordella's *Una folla* and *L'azzardo fortunato*; Capotorti's *L'impegno superato*, *Le nozze per impegno*, *Bref il sorgo*, and *Ernesto e Carina*; and Rossini's *La gazzetta*. This was the Pesaro maestro's second opera for Naples. It took place in September 1816 and was a failure, holding the stage only a few evenings. It was never restaged in Naples or anywhere else during Rossini's lifetime.

In 1799 Alfieri's *Virginia* was staged at the Fiorentini the same evening as one of his tragedies at the Teatro Fondo, with *Virginia* receiving much more applause. A critic then wrote, "Comedies are the only subjects and feelings in which the audience delights." Actually, since the early 1700s, opera buffa was so much in vogue that the Fiorentini was not large enough to present all the comic operas desired by the public, so two new theaters were built. Construction on the first one began in 1718. Called the Teatro Pace because of its proximity to the Ospedale della Pace (Hospital of Peace), the theater opened in 1724 with Vinci's *La mogliere fedele*. The theater did not have a happy existence. Small and not well located, it hosted inferior companies that resulted in scandalous occurrences with inferences of "friendship with the women." Often no one rented it. The Pace was closed in 1749 by order of the king because "obscenities" were committed there and its proximity to a monastery was causing "problems."

The second theater, originally called the Teatro Nuovo di Montecalvario but known today as Teatro Nuovo, was constructed by Carasale and Giacinto de Laurentiis who employed the architect Domenico Antonio Vaccaro to design it. Inaugurated in 1724 with *Sagliemmanco falluto*, by an unknown composer, and Saddumene's *Lo simmele*, the Nuovo offered five tiers with thirteen boxes a tier and an orchestra section with 200 seats. The auditorium was so symmetrical and well arranged that one could see as well from the side boxes as from the center ones. The architect for the Spanish king, Canevari, judged that Vaccaro had created "the possible from the impossible."

The theater presented the *prime rappresentazioni assolute* of at least a hundred comic operas by both major and minor composers, of which almost none have survived: Guglielmi's *L'inganno amoroso* and *Chi la dura la vince*; Cimarosa's *Le trauma deluse* and *L'impresario in angustie*; Combi's *La sponsa e l'eredità*; Bona's *Il tutore e il diavolo*; Grazioli's *I furbi burlati*; Altavilla'a *Le nozze di un principe*; Casella's *L'innocenza conosciuta*; Capotorti's *Gli sposi in rissa*; Battista's *Esmeralda* and *Il corsaro della Guadalupa*; Valentini's *Amina, Ferdinando*, and *Lo spettro parlance*; Traversari's *Il fuorbandito di Montalbore* and *La lettera di raccomandazione*; Carini's *La gioventù di Enrico V* and *I sposi fuggitivi*; Buonomo's *Cicco e Cola*, *Una giornata a Napoli*, *Enrico III*, and *L'ultima domenica di carnevale*, to list but a few. Composers De Joannon, Balducci, and Agnelli each introduced 3 of their operas, Rossi and Conti 4, Cordella 5, Ricci 6, and Aspa 14. A chronicler of the era noted that Rossini preferred Cimarosa's *L'impresario in angustie*, now completely forgotten, to the composer's famous *Matrimonio segreto*. Tastes change. During the time Donizetti was music director at the San Carlo, he introduced 7 of his 70 operas: *La zingara, Il fortunato inganno, Emilia, Otto mesi in due ore, Le convenience e le inconvenience teatrali, Il campanello*, and *Betly*. They ranged from *dramma semiserio* (semiserious drama) to *dramma giocoso* (humorous drama), from *melodramma romantico* (romantic melodrama) to *farsa* (farce). The theater today hosts experimental shows.

In 1776 construction began on the Teatro del Fondo. Completed in 3 years, the theater was designed by Francesco Securo and paid for by the Casa militare del fondo della separazione dei lucre. Operas by Paisiello, Cimarosa, and Tritto were on the boards during the final two decades of the 18th century, including *prime assolute* such as Cimarosa's *Gli amanti alla prova, Il fanatico burlato*, and *La pastorella riconosciuta*. During the days of anarchy in January 1799, the Fondo was renamed Teatro Patriottico and presented Monti's *Aristodemo*. Unfortunately, the work was deemed unpatriotic and the theater was closed, not reopening until March with *Catone in Utica*. The Fondo, like the Nuovo, hosted dozens of *prime mondiali*. Cordella introduced four of his operas and Aspa six, others included Tritto's *Zelinda e Rodrigo*; Vicenconte's *Evelina*; Butera's *Angelica Veniero*; Casella's *L'equivoco*; Chiaromonte's *Fenicia* and *Caterina di Cleves*; Coppola's *Achille in Sciro*; Altavilla's *Il debito* and *I pirati di Baratteria*; Balducci's *Il sospetto funesto* and *L'amante virtuoso*; and Rossini's *Otello* in 1817. About *Otello* Stendhal wrote, "I came to Naples transported with hope. . . . I began with *Otello*. Nothing colder. It must have taken a lot of *savoir-faire* on the part of the writer of the libretto to render insipid to this degree the most impassioned of all dramas. Rossini has seconded him well." During Donizetti's tenure at San Carlo, he offered six of his works to the Fondo: *La lettura anonima, Il borgomastro di Sardaam, Gianni di Calais, Il giovedí grasso, I pazzi per progetto*, and *La romanziera e l'uomo nero*. During the latter part of the 1800s, the Fondo was renamed Mercadante. It continued to host long forgotten world premieres, including Bonamici's *Un matrimonio nella luna*; Cellini's *Vendetta sarda*; Coop Jr.'s *Teresa Raquin*; and Musone's *Cameons, Wallenstein*, and *Carlo di Borgogna*. The extant Mercadante occasionally hosts musical programs.

Only 30 years after the opening of the San Carlo, its interior was "beautified" for a new queen, Maria Carolina, archduchess of Austria. The court architect, Ferdinando Fuga, was entrusted with the work. More restoration was carried out in 1797 for the visit of Maria Clementina of Austria. On February 12, 1816, rehearsals were just finishing when sparks from an oil lamp ignited a fire that reduced the San Carlo to ashes. Within 6 days, however, King Ferdinand ordered the theater rebuilt, under the direction of Antonio Niccolini. It was reconstructed in record time following Medrano's original plans. The only changes made were to enlarge the stage and improve the acoustics. The San Carlo reopened January 12, 1817, the king's birthday, with Mayr's *Il sogno di Partenope*, a work specially commissioned for the reopening. At the inaugural, the boxes closest to the royal box were filled with members of the court; other boxes held various dukes and princes. Stendhal wrote about the 1817 opening night, "There is nothing in all of Europe that I would say comes close to this theater; they all pale in comparison. The eyes are dazzled, the spirit enraptured." An orchestra pit was created in 1872 at the suggestion of Verdi and electricity installed in 1890. The structure was slightly damaged during World War II but quickly repaired, hosting performances for the benefit of the Allied troops and civilians, who sat in the upper two tiers. Closed at the end of 1980s for restoration work, the opera house reopened in the early 1990s.

The neoclassical facade extends from the building with a covered ashlar archway, adorned with friezes. The dominating central one depicts Apollo holding a lyre surrounded by the nine Muses with their symbols. A balustrade wraps around the structure, separating the lower section from the upper, where the names of Italian composers and writers—Pergolesi, Iommelli, Piccinni, Alfieri, Metastasio, and Goldoni—and there is a row of 14 imposing Ionic columns. Large statues of Paisiello and Cimarosa reside in the entrance foyer. The 1,444-seat, horseshoe-shaped auditorium offers six tiers. The red, ivory, and gold colors introduced after the unification of Italy supplanted the original royal blue hues. The parapets are adorned with gilded putti with musical instruments and other elaborate gold ornamentation. An enormous crown graces the top of the royal box and angels hold open elaborately draped blue curtains embroidered with gold. The royal coat of arms, gilded Muses with their instruments, and a crown surmount the proscenium arch. Camillo Guerra and Gennaro Maldarelli were responsible for the decorations. The ceiling painting, by Giuseppe Cammarano, depicts Apollo introducing the world's greatest poets to Minerva. The curtain, the work of Giuseppe Mancinelli and dating from 1854, represents Parnassus, the sacred mountain of Apollo and the Muses.

Operatic Events at the Teatro di San Carlo

The repertory was composed exclusively of *drammi per musica* or opera seria. These works about the feats and exploits of the gods and heroes, kings and emperors, condottieri and priestesses filled what was known as the "tragic theater" of the time. The repertory "seria" was privileged and often the exclusive domain of the principal theater of a city, and foremost of a royal theater. The tragedies, as opposed to the comedies or opera buffa, conferred an elite social status and aristocratic position. It was the most sumptuous and expensive repertory, in an exclusive position to confer dignity and prestige to the theater that hosted it. The tragedies expressed the ideology of the ruling classes; the heroes and condottieri were symbols of the sovereigns and the government. The backbone of the repertory of the 1700s, with at least one to five operas each season, was based on libretti by Metastasio. For the inaugural season, there were three operas in the schedule: the inaugural work, *Achille in Sciro*, with 14 performances, Leo's *L'Olimpiade* with 10, and Vinci's *Artaserse* with 16. The early years saw works by Auletta, Hasse, Porpora, Perez, Latilla, Manna, Ristori, Sarro, Duni, and Cocchi. By the mid-1750s one found Jommelli, Galuppi, Conti, Traetti, Piccinni, and Paisiello alongside the earlier composers. As the Neapolitan school enjoyed growing success with both opera seria and opera buffa, Naples became the capital of European music, attracting foreign composers such as Gluck, Haydn, Johann Christian Bach, and Hasse. It drew celebrated singers, from "La Bastardella" (Lucrezia Anguiari) to "La Cochetta" (Caterina Gabrielli), and the castrati Farinelli (Carlo Broschi) and Caffarelli (Gaetano Majorana).

In January 1799 during the days of anarchy, the theater stayed open, hosting Tritto's *Nicaboro in Jucatan*. After 3 days of difficult combat, the French entered the city. They removed "Reale Teatro" from the manifestos and rebaptized the San Carlo "Teatro Nazionale." Performances of *Nicaboro in Jucatan* continued, with an anthem added before the performance, arousing the public seated in the orchestra and balconies to scream "Viva la libertà! Morte al tiranno!" (Long live liberty! Death to the tyrant!).

San Carlo's golden age began with the impresario Domenico Barbaia. Although the Neapolitan school was keeping up with the latest trends with composers Pacini, Zingarelli, and Mercadante, Barbaia looked to the future, beyond the limitations imposed upon the opera house because of tradition. He signed Rossini to a contract as music director of the San Carlo and the Fondo and also required him to compose two operas a year for Naples, for an annual salary of 8,000 francs. Rossini arrived in the spring of 1815 and was ready with his first offering, *Elisabetta, regina d'Inghilterra*, in October 1815. It was a spectacular occasion. Not only did the opera open the San Carlo's fall season, but it also honored the name day of Francesco, hereditary prince of the Two Sicilies, which meant that Ferdinand I, Maria Carolina, the hereditary prince, and the court were all in attendance. Although parts of the opera were borrowed from other Rossini works—the overture and act 1 cavatina of *Elisabetta* came from *Aureliano in Palmira*, the act 2 orchestral prelude was originally written for *Ciro in Babilonia*—the opera was the first without recitative secco. He composed the title role for Isabella Colbran, who would become his wife. *Ricciardo e Zoraide* fared better after the failure of *Otello* at the Fondo, but *La donna del lago* was met with indifference at its opening, although at the second performance it was better received. *Armida*, with its palace and enchanted garden, appearances and disappearance of demons and furies, chariots pulled by dragons, and dances of nymphs, recalled the "machinery operas" of the 17th and 18th centuries, but at the same time there were hints of French grand opera yet to come. Despite the lavish production, neither the opening-night audience nor the critics liked it. *Mosè in Egitto*, however, was a resounding success. Other premieres included *Ermione*, *Maometto II*, and *Zelmira*. *Zelmira* was Rossini's last work for San Carlo, so he lavished particular attention upon it, despite a dreadful libretto. It was well received by both the audience and the press. Introduced on February 16, 1822, *Zelmira* played until March 6, on which evening King Ferdinand attended the performance, to show his gratitude to the departing maestro and singers.

Artists of the era who sang at the San Carlo included Giuditta Pasta, Maria Malibran, Giovan Battista Rubini, Adolphe Nourrit, and Gilbert-Louis Duprez. In fact, the great rivalry between the two French tenors (Nourrit and Duprez) ended with Nourrit committing suicide in Naples on March 7, 1839, after a benefit performance at San Carlo.

After the departure of Rossini, Barbaia contracted Donizetti to be music director at the San Carlo. He stayed until 1838, when difficulties with the management over censorship of his *Poliuto* prompted him to leave for Paris, where a contract with the Opéra was waiting and *Poliuto* was transformed into *Les martyrs*. Not until 1848—8 months after Donizetti's death—was *Poliuto* performed at the San Carlo. The Bergamo maestro composed 29 operas for Naples, including 15 for San Carlo. The first was *Alfredo il Grande*, which was poorly received; *Elvida* was a one-act opera, with the sovereigns of Naples attending the opening. Donizetti told Mayr "*Elvida* is not a grand thing . . . but if I catch the cavatina of [singer] Rubini, it will be enough for me." *Gabriella di Vergy* was written for his own amusement and was first presented only in 1869, after Donizetti's death. *L'esule di Roma* was an enormous success because of the vocal interpretation of Luigi Lablache. Despite the success of *Il pario*, Donizetti wrote to his father, "I made mistakes in some parts and I will try to repair them." *Il castello di Kenilworth* was a disaster, booed off the stage, as was *Il diluvio universale*. *Imelda de'Lambertazzi* received little praise, gained much infamy, and had only one performance. *Francesca di Foix* received a "cordial" welcome and *Fausta* a warm one, as did *Sancia di Castiglia*. *L'assedio di Calais* was moderately successful. *Roberto Devereux* was characterized as a "nuova opera" at the time and was more successful at its La Scala premiere. *Maria Stuarda*, however, was banned by decree from the chief of police and was rewritten and performed as *Buondelmonte*; not until 1865 could *Maria Stuarda* be staged at San Carlo. *Lucia di Lammermoor* was the most successful of Donizetti's operas. In fact, as Mario Baccaro wrote in *Centi anni di vita del Teatro di San Carlo, 1848–1948*, an unhappy and ill-advised friend said to Donizetti, "It is a pity that Bellini was dead! *Lucia* would have been a perfect subject for his temperament, all passion and melancholy." To which Donizetti, a little annoyed, replied, "I will put my little bit of talent to work to succeed." After the triumph of the first performance of *Lucia*, Donizetti saw this friend again. He stopped him and said, "I hope that you were content with my *Lucia*. Did I do wrong to the friend Bellini? I thought to invoke his beautiful spirit and that had inspired me!" In *Lucia* Donizetti created one of the "highest levels of expression in 19th-century Italian melodrama; the melodies possessed extraordinary freshness and pure vocal accents," Giampiero Tintori wrote in *Il Teatro di San Carlo*, volume 1. Donizetti's final opera, *Caterina Cornaro*, failed at the San Carlo, with loud whistling and booing. Around four dozen of Donizetti's 70 works have been staged at the opera house. Barbaia also spotted another musician early in his career, Bellini. The opera house introduced *Bianca e Fernando* in 1826 but as *Bianca e Gernando* so as to not offend the Bourbons with a name of the family. Eight of Bellini's 10 works have graced the San Carlo stage.

Unlike his famous predecessors, Verdi had a troubled relationship with the San Carlo. His music was greeted with hostility from those who felt Mercadante was the beacon of the Neapolitan tradition; he had trouble with the authorities and problems with the censors. Although he was commissioned to write three operas, only two reached the stage. The first was *Alzira*. Verdi had written to Cammarano, the librettist for *Alzira*, "I received the line of action of *Alzira*. I am very happy with every relation. I read the tragedy of Voltaire which in your hand became an excellent melodrama. I am accused of loving to make a fuss and to treat the singers badly: do not pay heed to that, put the passion and you will see that I will write tolerably." Verdi was not satisfied with the reception the Neapolitans gave *Alzira* at its *prima mondiale* on August 12, 1845. His second opera for San Carlo, *Luisa Miller*, was planned to premiere in the beginning of October, but Verdi was quarantined in Rome for 2 weeks because of a cholera epidemic, delaying his arrival in Naples. When he finally arrived, the management did not pay him his fee. Verdi wrote demanding they pay him 3,000 ducats immediately or he would break the contract, adding, "Today I will go again to the rehearsal, but I will not tomorrow." The management did not appreciate his threats and placed him under house arrest. The problems were soon resolved and the rehearsals continued. The opening, which took place on December 8, 1849, was a success. The theater commissioned Verdi to write a third work, and for the commission Verdi chose as his subject the actual assassination of Gustavus III of Sweden at a masked ball in 1792. The opera was originally called *Gustavo III*, but Verdi sensed there might be problems showing the killing of a king on stage, so he moved the action to 17th-century Stettin, in Pomerania, and changed the title to *Una vendetta in domino*. The censors still forbade the opera to proceed. Verdi was then given a new libretto, prepared by the management of the theater, with the title *Adelia degli Adimari*, set in 14th-century Florence. Verdi refused to write the opera as the censors demanded, so Teatro Apollo in Rome became the recipient of Verdi's opera known today as *Un ballo in maschera*. Nevertheless, Verdi works dominated the stage during the second half of the 19th century, with only two of his operas, *Un giorno di regno* and *Jerusalem*, not in the repertory. He was also persuaded in 1872 to become the artistic director for the one season during which *Don Carlo* was staged in a revised edition and *Aida* enjoyed its Neapolitan premiere.

The great Romantic period in opera gave way to Puccini and *giovane scuola* (Mascagni, Leoncavallo, Giordano, Cilea). Although Leoncavallo was a Neapolitan, he experienced his greatest success, *I pagliacci*, in Milan. *Pagliacci* was in the San Carlo repertory, however, along with *La bohème*, *Edipo re*, *Zazà*, and *Zingari*, among others. Almost a dozen of Mascagni's works were offered, ranging from *Cavalleria rusticana* to *Nerone*. And between 1915 and 1922, he was the house conductor. Both Giordano's *Andrea Chénier* and Cilea's *Adriana Lecouvreur* were in the repertory for several seasons. Even some of their forgotten works received a hearing. All of Puccini's works have graced the stage except *Edgar*. The first Wagner opera, *Lohengrin*, was heard in 1880, and Richard Strauss came to Naples in 1908 to personally conduct the Italian premiere of *Salome*.

There was no shortage of well-known singers, including Tito Schipa, Beniamino Gigli, Toti del Monte, Fyodor Chaliapin, and Aureliano Pertile, although one of the most famous Neapolitan tenors, Enrico Caruso, performed only during one season, 1901/02. Apparently a reviewer referred to him as a baritone in a production of *L'elisir d'amore* and he was so offended that he never again sang in the city of his birth. Outstanding conductors also stood on the podium, such as Arturo Toscanini, Leopoldo Mugnone, Eduardo Vitale, Ettore Panizza, Vittorio Gui, and Gino Marinuzzi. Meanwhile, works of Alfano, Zandonai, and Pizzetti were introduced. In 1927 the San

Carlo was organized as an *ente autonomo*. After World War II, Renata Tebaldi made her Naples debut as Violetta, and Maria Callas sang during the 1948 through 1951 seasons, and again in the 1955/56 seasons. The schedules were long and varied, with as many as 20 operas on the boards, including lesser-known and contemporary works such as Alfano's *Il Dottor Antonio*, Petretta's *I promessi sposi*, Cilea's *Gloria*, Napoli's *I pescatori*, Spontini's *Fernando Cortez*, Gargiulo's *Maria Antonietta*, and the Italian premieres of Berg's *Wozzeck*, Schönberg's *Von Heute auf Morgan*, and Orff's *Der Mond*. The number of productions and performances were gradually reduced from 20 between 1946 and 1967 to 11 by the 1975/76 season and down to 8 by the end of the century. The trend to offer unusual and rarely staged works continued into the early 1980s, then the repertory became more mainstream.

Beginning in 1979 and continuing to the present, one of San Carlo's goals is the rediscovery of the 18th-century opera buffa of the Neapolitan school. Among those unearthed have been Cimarosa's *Li sposi per accidenti* and *Il marito disperato*; Pergolesi's *Il faminio*; Jommelli's *La schiava liberate*; Scarlatti's *La Dirindina*; and Paisello's *Il divertimento de' numi*, *L'idolo cinese*, *L'osteria di marechiaro*, and *Il socrate immaginario*. Another mission has been to stage forgotten operas of famous composers that have included Verdi's *I due Foscari* and *Gustavo III*, Rossini's *Tancredi*, and Bellini's *Beatrice di Tenda*.

Until 1998, the government had been paying almost all of the San Carlo's bills. Since then, the opera house has been transformed into a *fondazione* and has private sponsorship for productions, along with public money. Founding members paid around $275,000 and subscribing members a minimum of $5,500. Nevertheless, after the turn of the millennium there was a financial crisis, and San Carlo employees protested in the streets because they had not been paid. The 2002/03 season had only six operas, including *Powder Her Face*, *La battiglia di Legnano*, and *Orfeo ed Euridice*, alongside the Italian favorites. The season was increased to seven offerings for 2003/04, including *Elektra*, *Faust*, *I Domenico*, *Il turco in Italia*, and *Gustavo III*. As the first decade of the 21st century progressed, the number of operas continued to increase, productions became more adventurous, and the repertory broadened to include foreign and contemporary works, such as *Ledi Makbet Mtsenskovo uyezda* (*Lady Macbeth of the Mtsensk District*), *La creazione*, *La Statira*, along with popular titles such as *La bohème*, *Il turco in Italia*, and *Trovatore*. A recent season offered a wide range of operas. *Tristan und Isolde* inaugurated the season, with *Die Walküre*. *Pikovaya dama* (Queen of Spades), *Roméo et Juliette*, *Rigoletto*, *Tosca*, *L'elisir d'amore*, and Paisiello's *Il socrate immaginario*, continuing the revival of forgotten Neapolitan-school works.

In 1937 the Arena Flegrea, planned by Giulio De Luca, opened. During the 1950s and 1970s, it hosted regular summer seasons of opera. Then the arena was abandoned and it slowly deteriorated. Finally restored, it began hosting summer opera again in 2004, with *La bohème*. *Il trovatore* followed the next season. The repertory is of popular Italian operas.

Practical Information

Teatro di San Carlo, via San Carlo 98F, 80133 Naples; tel. 39 081 797 2111, fax 39 081 797 2306; www.teatrosancarlo.it.

The season runs from December through November and offers between 9 and 10 operas with five to seven performances of each. Stay at the Hotel Majestic, Largo Vasto a Chiaia 68; tel. 081 416 500, fax 081 410 145; www.-majestic.it. Around a 20-minute walk from the San Carlo, the Majestic is in the heart of Naples. Visit the Palazzo Reale, piazza Plebiscito, tel. 580 8111. Designed by Domenico Fontana for Viceré Ferrante di Castro in 1600, it was the official residence of King Charles of Bourbon, who constructed the Teatro di San Carlo. See also Castle Sant' Elmo, piazzale S. Martino, tel. 578 4030 (the builder of San Carlo, Carasale, was imprisoned and died here in 1742); Teatro Mecandante, piazza del Municipio 1, Royal, tel. 551 3396, www.comune.napoli.it (originally the Teatro Fondo, it hosts mainly drama); Teatro Nuovo, via Montecalvario 16, tel. 425 958; and Teatro Bellini, via Conte di Ruvo 14–19, Toledo, tel. 549 9688 (a jewel of a theater where musicals in English are performed). During the summer, outside of Naples, make sure to catch the Festival musicale di Villa Rufolo, Società dei concerti di Ravello, via Trinità 3, Ravello; tel. 858 149; www.ravelloarts.org. Built in the 12th century, the villa in Ravello is where Wagner composed parts of *Parsifal*. During the summer, there are outdoor concerts and a mini-Wagner festival with orchestra and singers on a specially constructed platform perched above the sea on the Almalfi coast.

FIFTY-THREE

Teatro Municipale G. Verdi, Salerno

At the beginning of the 1850s, there was a strong need to give the city a new theater and heated debate about where the building should be located. This, combined with the problems of financing the construction, delayed any decision. Finally on December 15, 1863, the city council accepted the proposal of the mayor, Matteo Luciani, and approved construction in the piazza of San Teresa. The project and the direction of the work were awarded to Antonio D'Amora and Giuseppe Menichini, who based their measurements and proportions on the Teatro di San Carlo in Naples.

The basic structure was finished on October 1, 1869, and decoration of the interior began under the supervision of Gaetano D'Agostino. The Teatro Municipale was inaugurated on April 15, 1872, with *Rigoletto*. In March 1901, a couple of months after Verdi's death, his name was added to the theater's title. A major earthquake in 1980 made the building structurally unstable and the theater was closed for 14 years. Finally rebuilt, the Verdi was inaugurated on July 6, 1994, during the celebration of the 50th anniversary of the Salerno capitol.

A portico extends from the facade, which is punctuated by three elongated arch windows crowned by a tympanum. The theater is decorated in an iconographic manner, beginning with the entrance foyer. The images show that the building is a temple of music, and especially of bel canto. The peristyle is supported by faux marble columns with neo-Pompeian motifs. In the middle of the peristyle is a sculpture by Giovanni Battista Amendola representing a dying Pergolesi, which symbolically transports the audience into the temple of music. The red, ivory, and gold auditorium offers four tiers topped by a gallery. Medallions with effigies of Italian composers, poets, and painters ornament the parapets of the boxes. The ceiling, painted like a sky by Di Criscito, represents the consecration of the hall to the grand season of Italian opera, and the curtain celebrates the history of the city with an event from the summer of 1871, *The Ejection of the Saracens from Salerno*, the work of Domenico Morelli.

Since the theater reopened, after the devastating earthquake, the repertory has steadily grown and expanded from initially popular Italian fare to include some lesser-known works. A recent schedule offered *Il capello di paglia di Firenze*, *Die lustige Witwe*, and *Tosca*.

Practical Information

Teatro Municipale G. Verdi, via Roma, Salerno; tel. 39 089 662 141; www .salernocity.com/tempo/teatro.

The season runs between October and May, offering three operas with three performances of each.

FIFTY-FOUR

~

Teatro Lirico, Cagliari, Sardinia

The Politeama Regina Margherita, constructed in the second half of the 1800s, hosted opera until 1942, when fire destroyed it. The building was not reconstructed. The other opera venue, the Teatro Civico, was demolished by bombs in 1943. After the war, with no proper theater, opera found a home in the auditorium of the Conservatorio di Musica and in a 2,000-seat movie house known as the Massimo, built in 1947. Structural problems, however, forced the abandonment of the Massimo. With the city bereft of a proper opera venue, work began in 1977 on an auditorium for the conservatory Pier Luigi da Palestrina. Upon its completion, opera seasons continued in this 1,000-seat opera house known as the Teatro Lirico Palestrina. They were short, with works such as Verdi's *Otello* gracing the stage. The theater was situated on viale Regina Margherita.

In 1964 an architectural competition was held to construct a proper theater for the city. Thirty-four design plans were submitted. Eight were accepted, and the drawings from Luciano Galmozzi, Teresa Arslan, and Francesco Ginoulhiac were selected as the winners. A site was selected on the periphery of the city, in an unappealing commercial zone at the foot of an old castle. Several events delayed the construction, including strikes and the discovery of water underneath the building site. Work finally began in 1971, but 22 years passed before the opera house was completed. The Teatro Comunale was inaugurated on September 2, 1993.

The Comunale is a huge building, rising like an enormous concrete and glass sculpture defined by geometric forms and angles of various sizes and shapes fused together. The roof, which measures 54,000 square feet, is covered by a gigantic sheet of patina copper. The contemporary-design, 1,650-seat auditorium of white and red holds a large orchestra section with two large balconies rising above. The stark, angular parapets of the two balconies sweep around the fan-shaped space, thrusting forward at each end to hint at the traditional horseshoe shape. The proscenium arch is paneled with gypsum and wood.

The Teatro Comunale is one of two structures where the Teatro Lirico di Cagliari (Lyrical Theater of Cagliari) performs. The other, an *anfiteatro Romano* (Roman amphitheater), dates from the 2nd century BC. Since the outer walls, spiral staircases, and performance area had survived through the centuries, the amphitheater was restored in 2000 to host performances. The 6,000-seat arena is located within a fortress that dominates Cagliari. It is the third-most-important structure of its kind, after the Roman Colosseum and the arena in Verona.

Operatic Events at the Teatro Comunale

Since the opening of the Teatro Comunale, the opera seasons have progressively become more adventurous. Beginning in 1998, each opera season has opened with the first performance in Italy of an unusual work: Wagner's *Die Feen*, Smetana's *Dalibor*, Tchaikovsky's *Cherevichki* (Little Boots), Strauss's *Die Ägyptische Helena*, Weber's *Euryanthe*, Tchaikovsky's *Oprichnik*, Schubert's *Alfonso ed Estrella*, and Enescu's *Oedipe*. The remainder of the season usually offers popular operas, mainly in the Italian vein, although *A Village*, *Romeo and Juliet*, and *Dialogues des Carmélites* have been staged along with a good dose of Verdi (*Rigoletto*, *La traviata*, *Macbeth*, *Simon Boccanegra*), Puccini (*Madama Butterfly* and *Turandot*), and Mozart (*Le nozze di Figaro*, *Don Giovanni*). Opera is also part of the summer festival, which takes place in the *anfiteatro Romano*, and *Carmen* was recently offered.

Practical Information

Teatro Lirico, Cagliari, via Sant'Alenixedda 111/E, 09128 Cagliari; tel. 39 070 40821, fax 39 070 408 2251; www.teatrolirico.tiscali.it.

The season runs from January to July, offering four to five operas with seven performances of each. The summer production takes place in the amphitheater.

FIFTY-FIVE

Teatro Massimo Bellini, Catania, Sicily

In 1693 an earthquake struck Catania, destroying the city. As part of the reconstruction plans, a public theater was included. The city entrusted Salvatore Zahra Buda with the project to erect the structure on the Piazza Nuovaluce, the area of the present Teatro Massimo Bellini. The plan of the Teatro Nuovaluce was grandiose in all respects. The first stone, however, was not laid until 1812. Then after various events, the work was suspended, and the money allotted for the theater was used instead to build an offshore jetty to defend against the Algerian pirates that plagued the area during that time. Some years later, the senate voted to give the city a smaller, alternative performing venue, which was constructed in a former warehouse. Called the Teatro Comunale Provvisorio (Provisional Municipal Theater), it opened June 9, 1822. The most important event that the Comunale (then called Teatro Coppola) hosted was the Catania premiere of *Norma* in November 1835, only 2 months after native son Bellini's death in Paris. This is how *Il Telegrafo Siciliano* described it: "The evening of November 10 was for Catania a time of sadness and joy. *Norma* was being performed for the first time, but it was being performed after the irreparable loss of its composer. The theater was all in mourning. The Cantanese were weeping for Bellini but applauding *Norma*. They applauded the artists who performed in the opera and while raising their hand in a sign of general acclamation, tears were running down their faces, a sign of a deep sadness." At the premiere, the third tier of boxes was closed because of structural problems with the building, which emphasized the need to build a new opera house. (The theater was destroyed during an aerial bombing raid in 1943 and not rebuilt.)

In 1870 the architect Andrea Scala was charged with finding a suitable location for the new theater, choosing the Piazza Cutelli. Financial problems thwarted the project, so it was decided to restructure the Arena Pacini, converting it into a politeama. The *condomini* of the Società Anonima del Politeama financed the construction of Scala's project, assisted by Carlo Sada. But the Società went bankrupt, and the municipality took over. The city preferred Sada and wanted the structure converted into a theater instead of a politeama. Sada submitted his first designs in 1874. Finally in July 1880, after Sada had submitted his 14th set of plans, the municipality awarded him the commission, and 6 months later, construction began. The city had authorized 605,000 lire, but the final cost reached 975,620 lire, still considered a modest sum for the era. Although construction was completed in 7 years, a cholera epidemic delayed the inauguration for another 3. There was great excitement in the city in the days leading up to the inauguration of the new opera house. The main streets were lined with large posters with the bust of Bellini and "Feste Belliniane" on them. In honor of the inauguration, King Umberto I gave the city an elephant that had been a gift from the emperor of Ethiopia. But either from seasickness, a disease already contracted in Africa, or being enclosed in a cage in the Bellini Gardens, a few days after it arrived in Catania, the elephant died.

On May 31, 1890, *Norma* inaugurated the Teatro Massimo Bellini. This is how Antonino Cristadoro chronicled the inaugural evening: "The crowd hastened to the piazza Nuovaluce, anxiously awaiting the opening of the 22 doors to the theater. . . . Finally at eight-thirty in the evening, the entrance doors were unlocked and the ticket-holders entered according to where their seat was located; the spacious theater filled with light, rich with gold, artistically conceived and constructed by the expert engineer Carlo Sada gave a charming and imposing impression. The ladies and gentlemen gradually began to enter . . . it would be a long story if one described all the very low-cut evening gowns and cleavage . . . the men in the boxes wore white tie and tails, while those in the gallery and the orchestra level wore black suits; the theater was overflowing; a majestic appearance. . . . At nine in the evening, maestro Rossi gave the first sign of the baton to the 66 orchestral players; a deep, attentive silence followed; as soon as the first notes of the *Homage to Bellini* by Mercadante were sounded, the audience called for the royal anthem, which was immediately played among applause, and immediately afterwards the *Homage to Bellini*, which received frenzied applause. When the applause finished, the audience shouted for Sada, who came in front of the curtain, twice, to thank the public . . . moved, touched, confused and timid because he was a modest man. At nine-thirty, with complete silence in the auditorium, the orchestra began the overture to *Norma*; the grand historic curtain of Catania was raised and the opera began, by the composer who had no rival."

Mariella Costa Chines described the facade of the new opera house as "very attentive to the play of chiaroscuro on the surface, harmonizing the deep opening of the portico with the grand arcade of the level above, where single columns and pilasters are paired with columns supported by large bases . . . and the deep cornices extend around the two levels of the building. . . . The theater was illuminated with little gas flames that came out of 406 spouts and looked like orange butterflies." Ironically, the city administration forgot to send Sada an invitation and he had to buy a ticket for the opening of his theater, according to Giuliano Consoli in his article "Il Teatro dei catanesi costò meno di un milione" (The theater of the Cantanese cost less than a million). Then he had to wait several months before being paid by the municipality for his work.

On July 7, 1900, the Teatro Sangiorgi opened with *La bohème*. Designed in a late-Liberty style, it hosted opera, operetta, and drama. Eventually abandoned, the Teatro Bellini purchased the building in the last decades of the 20th century after a decade of negotiations. Under the careful eyes of Salvatore Boscarino, Giovanni Pennisi, Paolo Paolini, and Matteo Arena, the theater was restructured and restored in 3½ years. The cost reached almost $7 million. It reopened November 16, 2002. With only 477 seats, it offers contemporary and chamber opera, operetta, prose, and experimental theater, works suited for smaller spaces.

On May 31, 1990, the Massimo Bellini celebrated its centennial with another lavish production of *Norma*. Bathed in bright lights for the celebration, with the dates "1890–1990" fashioned in red and pink flowers in the garden on the renamed piazza Bellini, Catania's opera house began its second century in grand style. Initially, the theater was run by impresarios, and then the Società Anonima Imprese Teatrali took over, followed by the Sindacato nazionale orchestrale fascista (Fascist National Orchestral Trade Union). After World War II, the Ente Musicale Catanese (Catania Musical Body) managed the Massimo Bellini until the municipality assumed responsibility in 1966. Two decades later, the opera house became an *ente autonomo regionale* and was classified as a *Teatro di tradizione*. In March 2002, with the change of the laws governing opera houses in Italy, it formed a *fondazione* to help support its activities in the 21st century.

A creation of eclectic styles, the theater fuses the neoclassical, Renaissance, and neobaroque. Niches contain busts of composers surrounded by putti and musical motifs; above, lyres and masks decorate the frieze. The windows, delineated by Corinthian columns, are etched with lyre; allegorical statues, mythological animals, and putti playing lyres are on a crowning balustrade, and at the summit is a lyre with a star shooting out, all of which gives the facade a unique appearance. The 1,250-seat, gold, ivory, and red, horseshoe-shaped auditorium radiates in splendor. There are four box tiers topped by a gallery. In the middle, the red-and-gold-draped royal box is surmounted by two putti flanking a crown. Intricately formed stucco ornamentations adorn the parapets, the work of Andrea Stella. The ceiling frescoes picture the apotheosis of Bellini, surrounded by allegorical illustrations from *Norma*, *Il pirata*, *La sonnambula*, and *I Capuleti e i Montecchi*, executed by Andrea Bellandi. Around the perimeter are small medallions of Pacini, Donizetti, Verdi, Cimarosa, Rossini, and other Italian composers. The subject of the stage curtain is imaginary. Painted by Giuseppe Sciuti, it shows the victory of the Cantanese over the Libyans.

Operatic Events at the Teatro Massimo Bellini

"The beginning of the inaugural evening at the Massimo was filled with enthusiasm which diminished as the evening progressed. The *Norma* was disappointing," reported the *Corriere di Catania* on June 1, 1890. "La Damerini (Norma) without being a celebrity, was an optimal artist and a good singer . . . but Giannini (Pollione) left much to be desired. . . . La Boronat (Adalgesia) will be a good singer when she improves her middle and lower range. The orchestra could have been much, much better." The rest of the inaugural season's Bellini Festival offered *Aida*, *Gioconda*, and *Faust*. In fact, the first decade was unremarkable. But things improved with the arrival of the 20th century, and operas such as *Tosca*, *Fedora*, *Andrea Chénier*, *Lohengrin*, *Loreley*, *The Damnation of Faust*, *Thaïs*, and *Isabeau* were on the boards.

The Massimo Bellini has always made Bellini the focal point of its activities, and hosted celebrations that revolved around the anniversaries of Bellini's birth, death, and the world premiere of *Norma*. The 100th anniversary of the composer's birth, which took place in November 1901, was marked by a production of *Norma*. There was a centennial celebration of the world premiere of *Norma* on December 26, 1931, with another production of the opera, under the baton of Antonio Guarnieri. The centennial commemoration of Bellini's death in 1935 featured a season of only Bellini operas: *Beatrice di Tenda*, *Norma*, *Capuleti e i Montecchi*, and *Puritani*. The 150th anniversary of the maestro's birth was celebrated in 1951 with another season of Bellini operas: *Norma*, *Il Pirata*, *I Puritani*, and *Sonnambula*. *Norma* opened the bicentennial celebration 2000/01 season, which included three of the Cantanese maestro's operas and continued into the 2001/02 season with *La straniera*. Besides staging all of Bellini's works, the Massimo has offered works as diverse as *Il prigioniero*, *Job*, *Jeanne d'Arc au bûcher*, the Italian premieres of Nabokov's *La morte di Rasputin* and Strauss's *Guntram*, and the *novità assolute* of Zafred's *Kean*, Mannino's *Il ritratto di Dorian Gray*, and Bussotti's *Bozzetto siciliano*. Verdi operas are also a favorite. Recent repertory, besides Bellini operas, included *Jenůfa*, *Un ballo in maschera*, *Don Pasquale*, *Madama Butterfly*, and *Götterdämmerung*.

Practical Information

Teatro Massimo Bellini, via Perrotta 12, Catania 95131; tel. 39 095 715 0921, fax 39 095 31 18 75; www.teatromassimobellini.it.

The season runs from November or December to May or June with five operas and between 7 and 10 performances of each. Visit the Museo Civico Belliniano, piazza San Francesco d'Assisi 3 (tel. 34 15 23), which is located in the house where Bellini was born. There is a large collection of pictures, musical scores, documents, and personal objects of the composer in the museum. Bellini's tomb is located in the nearby cathedral.

FIFTY-SIX

Teatro Vittorio Emanuele, Messina, Sicily

As early as the 16th century, performances took place in the villas of noble families, open-air theaters and, for solemn religious occasions, at religious institutions. The first public theater with paying spectators opened in 1579 with productions financed by the senate of Messina and included *Judith* by Stefano Toccio. In 1629 the senate allocated money for a municipal theater, to be located in a disused armory of the city where arms and munitions were stored. Known as della Munizione, the space was restructured into a proper theater in 1724 and named Teatro della Munizione (Theater of the Fortification). Opera performances continued despite the plague of 1743 and the earthquake of 1783, after which the theater received a new facade. In the early 1800s, consideration was given to razing the structure and building a new one on the same location, to better accommodate the needs of the growing city. But that plan was ultimately abandoned, because the limited space would have required demolition of several private residences for a large enough structure. In 1827 the prima assoluta of Valenti's *Il capriccio drammatico* took place, and between 1831 and 1849 the theater hosted the world premieres of six of native son Laudamo's operas, *Gli amori di tre selvaggi*, *Adda*, *regina di Caria*, *Ettore Fieramosca*, *Un fiasco alla moda*, *Clarice Visconti*, and *Ernani in contumacia*. The Munizione was leveled in the earthquake of 1908.

The decurion of the city began asking Ferdinand II of Bourbon, king of the Two Sicilies, for a new theater starting in 1827, deploring the fact that the city did not have a suitable performing venue. There was much polemic about this deficiency, with the newspaper *Il Faro* publishing in 1836 a tongue-in-cheek commentary that the Messinians savor entertainment of every type and pleasure of every sort, except a theater. Many reasons delayed the erection of a new building, not the least of which was financial. Finally, on October 2, 1838, the king announced the building of the long-awaited new theater. A competition was held and all the architects in the Kingdom of the Two Sicilies were invited to submit drawings. The Neapolitan architect Pietro Valente was chosen for the project, and that so angered local architects that they delayed the start of the construction for some years with their protests. The first stone was finally laid on April 23, 1842, with Antonio Manganaro in charge of the construction.

The site of the new theater was in the Pozzoleone district, on the via Ferdinando (today's Garibaldi), the city's most elegant street. But an old Bourbon prison stood there, which compromised the prestige of the area. So the prison inmates were transferred to the Rocca Guelfonia (Guelfonia Fortress) and the structure razed. The reasoning behind the construction by the crown was to give the aristocracy and well-to-do a place for amusement to distract them from the revolutionary winds blowing through intellectual circles. The date of the inauguration was set for the 42nd birthday of King Ferdinand II.

The Reale Teatro Santa Elisabetta (original name of the Teatro Vittorio Emanuele), named in honor of the mother of King Ferdinand II, opened January 12, 1852, with the world premiere of Laudamo's *Il trionfo della pace*. All the aristocracy were present at the inaugural, along with the most noted artistic and literary personalities of the time. A chronicler wrote about the abundance of stunning women, the beauty of the new luxuriously illuminated auditorium, the magnificence of the performance, and the high quality of the artistry, especially soprano Giula Sanchioli. Laudamo also conducted.

When the Real Teatro Santa Elisabetta opened, the times were still politically troubled, with the Revolutionary Committee of Messina secretly fighting the throne. For the inauguration of the new opera house, the *Comitato Rivoluzionario* asked the citizens to boycott the opening, but the plea fell on deaf ears as the local inhabitants did not want to miss such a grand event. The theater became the main gathering place in the city for the upper classes and aristocracy. A cafe, restaurant, billiard room, small reading room, and the *Circolo della Borsa* were added to the building. After the liberation of Sicily and the annexation of the Kingdom of the Two Sicilies to the Kingdom of Italy in September 1860, the city council changed the name of the theater to Teatro Vittorio Emanuele II. An overflowing crowd gathered at the theater, decorated with the tricolored flag of a united Italy, to celebrate the annexation. Two years later, King Vittorio Emanuele II attended a production given in his honor at the theater named in his honor. Other honored guests included King Umberto I and Queen Margherita, Vittorio Emanuele III, and Constantine, czar of Russia.

The opera house followed neoclassical principles with a facade of three orders. Extending out from the frontal was a three-arch portico supporting a terrace above. The sculptor Saro Zagari created bas-reliefs of Epicarno, Filemone, Cecilio, Plauto, Metastasio, Goldoni, Alfieri, Niccolini, Ennio, Pacuvio, Rossini, Bellini, Mida d'Agrigento, Aristosseno, Paisiello, and Cimarosa. Crowning the building were the sculptures "Ercole at the Cross-roads between Vice and Virtue," "La Coronation of Ercole," and a marble group representing "Time that discovers Truth and Messina, enchanted by her light, stretches to embrace her." The horseshoe-shaped auditorium offered four tiers of boxes topped by a gallery. It was finished with red velvet, and decorations of pure gold embellished the walls. The legend of Colapesce was painted on the ceiling dome, realized by Renato Guttuso.

On December 28, 1908, 4 hours after a performance of *Aida*, a devastating earthquake hit. Although the theater remained standing, it was rendered unsafe, and it was closed. The Teatro Mastrioieni, located on via San Cecilia and Viale San Martino, was the first theater to host opera after the quake. Built in 1910 and named after the theater impresario who had died in the earthquake, the 1,200-seat Mastrioieni was the work of engineer Vinci. It was demolished in 1930.

More than seven decades passed before the doors of the Teatro Vittorio Emanuele II officially reopened January 7, 1986, with the same opera that was on the boards before the earthquake struck 78 years earlier, *Aida*. A concert had been given by the London Philharmonic Orchestra on April 24, 1985, but the structure was closed immediately afterward to complete the restoration work. Tito Varisco was the architect in charge of the reconstruction. Although the original facade remained, the luxurious auditorium was not rebuilt. A 1,000-seat modern hall with two box tiers and two galleries replaced it. But it is an unusual configuration: the orchestra level is so steeply graded that the seats at the rear almost reach the first tier of boxes, which only partially circle the auditorium. Then instead of the second box tier, there is a balcony, with the second box tier above it. A gallery crowns the hall. Wood covers the walls, contrasting with blue gray velvet seats and a plain black proscenium arch. The ceiling shows a view of the sea with mermaids, alluding to the city's water location.

Operatic Events at the
Teatro Vittorio Emanuele

The inaugural season ran from January 12 to March 23, 1852, with 23 performances of *Marino Faliero*, as *Il Pascià di Scutari* (changed by the royal censors to avoid anti-Bourbon references), 12 performances of *Orazii e Curiazi*, and 8 of *Don Pasquale*. Nobile-Valore-Romano managed the schedule. The next season was produced by Gustavo Galeotti and Rossi and ran from December 1, 1852, to May 8, 1853, with four Verdi operas, *Ernani, Nabucco, I Lombardi*, and *Macbeth*; Pacini's *Maria Tudor d'Inghilterra*; Donizetti's *Poliuto*; Rossini's *Barbiere di Siviglia*; and Battista's *Ermelinda*. For the third season, Pasciuto was the impresario, and he presented *Rigoletto* (as *Viscardello*), *Trovatore*, Ricci's *Crispino e la comare*, Pacini's *Saffo*, and Bellini's *Il pirata* between November 12, 1853, and April 8, 1854. These were typical seasons during the first decade. There was a different impresario every season, with a mixture of operas by major and minor composers, as well as Laudame's final *prima mondiale*, *Caterina Howard* in 1859.

On December 15, 1860, the theater reopened as the Vittorio Emanuele with Verdi's *La battaglia di Legnano* followed by Mercadante's *Eleonora*. Operas of Verdi, Rossini, Bellini, and Donizetti were prominent in the schedule, sharing the stage with an assortment of entertainment, ranging from concerts and ballet to magicians with trained dogs. Although the opera seasons offered predominately Italian fare by the popular composers of the day, a season of French operetta, including works by Offenbach and Lecocq, took place in 1876 and several French grand operas were staged, *Les Huguenots, Faust, Robert le diable, La Juive, L'Africaine*, and *Le prophète*. Around the turn of the century, there were a few prime mondiali, Trimarchi's *Rita Ferrant* and Casalaina's *Aretusa* and *Attollite Portas*. Until the earthquake damaged the theater in 1908, Verdi works dominated the repertory, with *La traviata* offered in more than a third of the seasons and *Il trovatore* in more than a quarter. Marchetti's *Ruy Blas* and *Lucia di Lammermoor* were also very popular. When the 20th century arrived, composers from the verismo school replaced the 19th-century composers in popularity.

Since the reopening of the opera house in 1986, the repertory has been predominately mainstream Italian operas of the 18th and 19th centuries with an occasional operetta. With the dawn of the new millennium, *Macbeth, Così fan tutte, Turandot, Die lustige Witwe*, and *La sonnambula* were on the boards. A smaller performance venue called the Sala Laudamo, named after the Messina composer who introduced all his operas at the theater, is located in a wing of the Teatro Vittorio Emanuele. It hosts operas from the 17th and 20th centuries more suitable for smaller spaces. Works such as Tutino's *l tradimenti*, Busoni's *Arlecchino*, and Pergolesi's *Livietta* and *Tracollo* have been presented. Recent productions in the Sala Laudamo include Tutino's *Il gatto con gli stivali* and Betta's *Il fantasma della cabina*. Recent operas at the Vittorio Emanuele are *La traviata* and *Manon Lescaut*.

Practical Information

Teatro Vittorio Emanuele, via Pozzoleone, 98122 Messina; tel. 39 090 572 2111, fax 39 090 343 629; www.teatrodimessina.it.

The opera season runs from November or December to April or May, offering four operas with three to four performances of each. Stay at the Jolly Hotel Messina, via Garibaldi 126, 98100 Messina; tel. 090 363 860, fax 090 590 2526; www.jollyhotels.it. It is a 2-minute walk from the opera house, directly across a main road.

~

FIFTY-SEVEN

Teatro Massimo, Palermo, Sicily

The oldest extant theater in Palermo was established in 1676 by Marquis Valguarnera of Santa Lucia, who rented the "storehouse" in his palazzo "per farsi la comedij" (for the performance of comedies). It became known as the Teatro di Travagalini but was also called Teatro di Santa Caterina, after the church next to it. During the 1650s, the Teatro Misericordia hosted the union of musicians who presented opera, including Cavalli's *Giasone*, to a more refined public. In 1693 a new theater, Teatro di Santa Cecilia, was inaugurated with native son Pollice's *L'innocenza pentita*, and the musicians left the Misericordia for the Santa Cecilia. That same year, the Travagalini, renamed the Teatro di Santa Lucia, was enlarged and beautified, to stay competitive with the new theater. Opera buffa was the dominant fare before a devastating earthquake closed it in 1726. Sixteen years passed before the Santa Lucia reopened, transformed into a richly decorated little "*Teatro all'i-taliana*" with four tiers of boxes, 15 to a tier, and room for 500 spectators, ready to compete with its rival, the Santa Cecilia.

After the court of Napoleon transferred to Palermo during the 1799 revolution, Queen Maria Carolina frequented the Teatro di Santa Lucia, so it was again renamed Reale Teatro Carolina in her honor. The theater was enlarged to 700 seats and restructured under the direction of Nicolò Puglia. Rossini, Donizetti, Mozart, and Bellini operas dominated the repertory, and on January 7, 1826, it hosted the *novità assoluta* of Donizetti's *Alahor in Granata* with virtuoso singers, including Antonio Tamburini in the title role. The journal *La Cerere* wrote, "This self-disciplined composer had the prudence to adhere to the middle point between the beauty of the old music and the impetus of the new." The operas of several minor composers of the 19th century were also introduced: Mosca's *Federico II*, *La gioventù di Enrico V*, and *Attila in*

Aquileia; Agnelli's *La notte di Carnevale, I due gemelli,* and *Giovanni Vallese;* Pacini's *Maria Tudor d'Inghilterra* and *Medea;* Raimondi's *Andromaca* and *Il no;* and Valentini's *Ildegonda.* In fact, until 1844, the repertory was limited because of the small space in the theater, and Cimarosa, Mayr, Rossini, and Bellini dominated the stage. During the 1850s, more prime assolute of forgotten composers graced the stage: Butera's *Atala* and *Eena Castriotta;* Coppola's *L'orfana guelfa* and *Fingal;* Moscuzza's *Stradella;* and Platania's *Matilde Bentivoglio* and *Piccarda Donati.* The structure and decorations of the theater continued to be improved with the addition of eight proscenium boxes to bring the total to 92. The Marquis Valguarnera sold the building in 1837 to Angrea Bignone. The Teatro Carolina was renamed Teatro Bellini in 1860 to honor the Sicilian composer, and gas lighting was installed. Opera seasons continued, and in 1865 Platania's *La vendetta slava* was introduced. Singers such as Tamagno, Grassi, Hausmann, and La Blanché graced the stage.

Serious discussions began in 1851 about the need for a new opera house because of the limited stage area and seating capacity of the Teatro Carolina. The first proposal had been made by Domenico Caracciolo around the turn of the century, with the building to be located where the Massimo is today. There was also talk of erecting a "palace theater" similar to that of the Teatro di San Carlo in Naples. Another proposal came in 1845 from royal architect Michele Patricolo, with his theater situated on the Piazza Marina. In 1851 Giuseppe Di Martino was entrusted with the project for the new theater, but it never came to fruition. Between 1859 and 1860, the Bourbon government authorized a competition for a new opera house, but that came to naught as the government fell when Giuseppe Garibaldi entered Palermo. Finally, in 1864, the mayor of Palermo, the Marquis of Rudinì, organized an international competition for a new theater, "desiring to make up worthily for the lack of a theater related to the increased population and the needs of the people." Thirty-five projects were submitted and the first prize awarded to Giovan Battista Filippo Basile in 1868. Part of the requirement of the competition was a cost estimate within certain limits, which Basile failed to include, so the results were annulled. (There are other versions too involved to discuss here as to why the competition was annulled.) Much polemic ensued over the next 5 years. Basile then submitted a less expensive project and was awarded the commission in 1874, as well as its direction. The site selected required the demolition of two monasteries, much to the dismay of the clergy. The first stone was laid on January 12, 1875, with the Mayor Emanuele Notarbartolo attending the ceremony. Basile wrote of his design, "A theater which rises in isolation and is the grandest for a large city, must

have on all its facades . . . elements of the monumental and grandiose order
. . . of classicism." It was described as a "colossal and magnificent building."
Construction was stopped in 1881, however, thanks to a zealous municipal
engineer, who found cost overruns. The municipality revoked Basile's contract, accusing him of financial incompetence. Basile withstood the slander
and gossip with dignity, but it took a toll.

The long delay in the building of the Massimo resulted in the construction of a politeama, designed by Giuseppe Damiani Almeyda. Named the
Teatro Politeama Garibaldi, after the Italian patriot who liberated Palermo,
it was inaugurated on June 7, 1874, with Bellini's *I Capuleti e i Montecchi*.
Opera activities were then transferred to the Politeama. Subsequently, prose
held the stage. The facade of the Politeama reveals hints of Spanish influence. The building is semicircular, with porticos on two levels, the lower one
of fluted Doric columns and the upper of fluted Ionic columns. A triumphal
arch defines the principal entrance crowned by a horse-drawn chariot. A
relief of putti with musical instruments extends across the arch, flanked by
musical motifs. The unusual 1,860-seat auditorium is shaped like a U, with
the ends on the two lower box levels curving toward each other. Beige floral
designs and sky-blue geometric patterns adorn the box tier parapets, contrasting with the strong red of the seats. Open wooden-bench seating prevails
on the upper levels, the area illuminated by wrought-iron candelabra. A huge
bust of Garibaldi is located above the proscenium arch. White marble Muses
flank a recessed arcade above the stage, and gilded relief ornamentation rings
the sky-blue dome ceiling.

In 1890 construction on the opera house began again *status quo ante*. For
a while, the municipality considered turning the project over to Alessandro
Antonelli, but in the end, Basile was summoned to finish it because the city
wanted the theater completed for the exposition, which was impossible. But
only a few months after work began, a tired and embittered Basile died at
the age of 66, on January 16, 1891. Only 4 days later his son, Ernesto, was
entrusted with the completion of the theater, which took another 6 years
and cost 7 million lire. The work was executed by the firm of Casano and
Corrao. Ernesto Basile wrote that, "among the buildings of our times, theaters present the most distinctive character of monumentality and also the
most decided artistic character. From the theater every idea of usefulness is
excluded, every thought of utility is practically banished: they are erected for
the sole purpose of public recreation. . . . The theater is exclusively a work
of luxury, in which the art must, without a doubt, be displayed and sparkle."

The most awaited opening of the theater had been threatened the day before by the prefectural commission refusing to grant the certification for the stability of the theater, which aroused the most intense joy among the clergy as they still had not resigned themselves to the demolition of two monastaries to make room for the opera house. The clergy claimed that in the early years of the Massimo a ghost of a monk, who had been buried in the church of one of the destroyed monasteries and whose bones were dug up by the demolition, wandered around the theater. The Catholic paper of Sicily, La Sicilia cattolica, proclaimed, "The Teatro Massimo is the work of iniquity. . . . It rises on the ruins of the Church of the Stimmate of San Giuliano, and the monumental San Agata of Scorrugi."

The Teatro Massimo, although not finished, was inaugurated on May 16, 1897, with Verdi's Falstaff. The local newspaper wrote about the opening, "Not much attention was paid to the opera, which was given a worthy execution, because everyone was admiring the magnificent building, so much so that no one listened to the bells that announced the beginning of the acts. . . . At 9 p.m., maestro Leopoldo Mugnone climbed onto the podium and the orchestra struck up the royal march with resounding applause of all present." The auditorium was described as having "elegance, aristocracy, and splendor in perfect uniformity and correctness of the lines, with enviable decorations and beautiful pictures." The public was very enthusiastic about their new theater and at the inauguration shouted for Basile to come out on stage and cheered, "Long live Basile." Another journal, Omnibus, published the impressions of a polemical reporter, "Whoever wanted to reach the stairs of the theater on the evening of the opening had to navigate through a mound of obstacles: tables, buckets, small and large carts, bricks, concrete blocks, and other horrors. It was dangerous, without exaggerating, not only for getting your clothes dirty . . . but for falling into some ditch full of mortar." The theater held 2,200 spectators, with 500 each in the orchestra section and gallery and 1,200 in the five rows of boxes. The best artists of the era decorated the stage.

The Massimo was constructed to satisfy three needs: a place to hold the opera season, a place for masked balls during carnival, and a place for a club for the nobility. There had been an elitist and rigid order in the allotment of boxes: the first tier for the military and government officials, the second for aristocrats, the third for the rich bourgeoisie. The orchestra level and gallery were for the other classes, which included a diverse public whose interest was either the opera itself—a new opera or a long awaited revival—or a particular singer. The theater was managed by private impresarios until 1936, when the figure of the sovrintendente (general director) was born with the transformation of the Massimo into an *ente autonomo*, its financing secured by public funds.

Meanwhile, the Teatro Bellini had progressively declined, until it was turned into a movie theater in 1907. It was then sold at public auction to LoBianco. They restored the building, giving it a new outlook and purpose, that of hosting operetta and variety shows. After the war, the Bellini became a cinema again. During the 1950s, Nico Pepe and Aldo Giuffrè experimented with returning the antique decor to the theater, and in 1963, for a year and a half, life returned to the opera house with concerts and movies. Then on March 14, 1964, a devastating fire closed the building. A pizzeria was set up in front of the destroyed Bellini, whose neoclassical facade served as backdrop. In 2000 the management of another theater, Teatro Biondo, patched it up. Reopening in December that same year, it had only the basic structure of the auditorium and boxes. Luca Ronconi read two poems from *Divine Comedy*. Then in May 2001, after 40 years, the first show was put on. It has subsequently, during the Massimo's season, become a venue for experimental and chamber operas and works more suitable for smaller spaces. It seats 274.

The Massimo, from its opening in 1897 through January 1974, had hosted 4,450 performances of 308 different titles when, after a concert performance of *Nabucco*, it was declared unsafe and closed. The opera seasons were transferred to the Politeama Garibaldi. On May 12, 1997, after 23 years and $50 million in renovation costs, the city finally reopened their opera house, just for the evening, with Claudio Abbado conducting a concert that began with the famous chorus of the enslaved Hebrews, "Va'pensiero," from *Nabucco*. Only the orchestra level and two box tiers were completed, and the tickets to the "opening" were exorbitant. This led to speculation that this preopening was purely political. A group of students protested the "show." The reopening was also a happy occasion. As *Il Mediterraneo* wrote, "The hope is that the completion [of the Massimo] corresponds to the disinfection from the mafia." The city had to wait until April 1998 before renovations were completed and opera seasons could begin once again. As required by law, the Massimo formed a *fondazione* at the end of the 20th century. But during the first few years of the 21st century problems emerged. The directors of the opera house were fired almost annually, with charges ranging from megalomania, tokenism, and poor programming to corruption and excessive debt. Well-known stage directors and singers refused to work there. But the seasons continued. A new administration had found the right formula for the opera seasons, which have continued uninterrupted both at the Massimo and the Bellini, where early 1700s intermezzi and experimental opera grace the stage.

The Massimo is an enormous building of local tufaceous stone that joins distinctive forms and styles. Neoclassical lines with a touch of art nouveau fuse into various geometric shapes and compositions. The rectangular pronaos of the Grecian-style portico is united with the curvature of the Roman rotunda by monumental fluted Corinthian columns. These columns continue on the building itself as engaged columns alternating with two levels of arched windows. The frieze holds an enigmatic inscription by an unknown author, "L'arte rinnova il popolo e ne rivela la vita vano delle scene il diletto ove non miri a preparer l'avvenire" (Art renews the people and reveals life. The enjoyment of the shows is empty where its purpose is not to prepare for the future). Two bronze lions, evoking Drama and Opera, by Civiletti and Rutelli, guard the steps that lead into the opera house. The horseshoe-shaped, 1,350-seat, golden-glittering auditorium holds five tiers topped by a gallery. Musical motifs, theatrical masks, putti, medallions, and festoons of flowers and fruit, foliage and baskets adorn the parapets. Rich "wooden" drapery, topped by a vase of flowers forming a semicircle and flanked by eagles and caryatids, frame the center royal box. Salvatore Valenti was responsible for the decorations, which included covering all the wooden and stucco ornamentation with sequin gold to contrast with the dark red velvet of the seats and valences of the boxes. The dome ceiling, painted by Rocco Lentini, was conceived as a type of immense wheel whose gilded spokes contrast with the azure-sky background. Female figures and angels surrounded by putti with musical instruments are painted on separate panels of canvas (referred to as petals). The center circle depicts "The Triumph of Music." The stage curtain, realized by Giuseppe Sciuti in tempera on reinforced canvas, represents *The Coronation of Ruggero II, King of Sicily, in Palermo.*

Operatic Events at the Massimo and Politeama Garibaldi

Although the Politeama Garibaldi had originally been constructed to host variety shows, opera also graced the stage until the Massimo opened. One coup of the Garibaldi was the arrival of Arturo Toscanini for the 1892/93 season, where he conducted several works, including *Rigoletto, Loreley, Die fliegende Holländer,* and *Norma.* The Politeama also attracted some of the best singers of the era, including Francesco Tamagno and Nellie Melba. With the opening of the Massimo in 1897, the Politeama's operatic activities came to a halt. When the Massimo was closed in 1974, the operatic life of the Politeama was revived until 1998, when the Massimo was reopened. In the meantime, it hosted an assortment of entertainment.

It was written that the inaugural *Falstaff* at the Massimo featured an "excellent protagonist" in Arturo Pessina. The first season offered two other works, *Gioconda* with a little-known, 24-year-old tenor, Enrico Caruso, as Enzio, under the baton of Leopoldo Mugnone, and *Bohème*. *Bohème* had previously triumphed at the Garibaldi in 1896 and was again a success on the stage of the Massimo. The following season saw 17 performances of Massenet's *Le roi de Lahore*, and then money problems closed the theater in 1899 and 1900. It reopened in 1901 with verismo operas playing a prominent role. When Ignazio Florio took the helm in 1906, guiding the Massimo for the next two decades, he offered the Palermo premiere of several operas, especially French and German, including *Tristan und Isolde*, *Le damnation de Faust*, *Salome*, and *Thaïs*. Some of the notable singers included Toti dal Monte, Beniamino Gigli, Tito Schipa, and Ezio Pinza. Composers came to conduct their operas: Puccini, *Rondine* and *Il trittico*; Zandonai, *Francesca da Rimini* and *Giulietta e Romeo*; and Marinuzzi, *Palla de'Mozzi*. Alfano took the helm in 1940 for a season, offering Sicilian composer Mulè's *La Zolfara*.

The 50th anniversary of the theater was celebrated with a repeat of the inaugural season, *Falstaff*, *Gioconda*, and *Bohème*, among other works. The 1949 season witnessed the Italian premiere of Szymanowski's *Król Roger* (King Roger) and Maria Callas as Brunhilde. Callas returned for *Norma*, and Renata Tebaldi arrived in 1953 for *Mefistofele*. That same year, forgotten operas of famous composers, including *Beatrice di Tenda*, *Il pirata*, *I Capuleti e i Montecchi*, and *Giovanna d'Arco*, and lesser-known contemporary works such as Alfano's *Cyrano de Bergerac* and Tommasini's *Il tenore sconfitto* were revived. By the end of the 1960s many foreign works, for example, Bartók's *A Kékszakállú herceg vára* (Duke Bluebeard's Castle), Smetana's *Prodaná nevěsta* (The Bartered Bride), and Massenet's *Don Quichotte*; neglected Italian operas, including *La favola d'Orfeo*; and contemporary ones, such as Pizzetti's *Iphigenia*, Malipiero's *Sette canzoni*, and Dallapiccola's *Il volo di notte*, had been offered at the Massimo. Legendary voices of the era also graced the stage, often at the start of their careers, including Franco Corelli, Magda Olivero, Victoria de Los Angeles, Mario del Monaco, Giuseppe di Stefano, Luciano Pavarotti, Cesare Siepi, and Giuseppe Taddei.

With the closure of the Massimo in 1974, opera returned to the Garibaldi, staging an unusual repertory, *Il guarany*, *La cecchina*, *Il prigioniero*, and *Iphigénie en Tauride*. Between 1978 and 1988, the emphasis continued on operas fallen into oblivion, contemporary works, and Palermo *prime*, including *Turn of the Screw, Il ritratto di Dorian Gray, Jenůfa, Ognenniÿ angel* (Fiery Angel), and *Voyna i mir* (War and Peace). By the last seasons at the Politeama, the repertory had become more mainstream with *Così fan tutte, La fille du regiment, Le nozze di Figaro,* and in commemoration of the Massimo's centennial, *Falstaff.* The only unusual fare was *Agrippina.* Finally, in April 1998, *Aida* inaugurated the first opera season at the Massimo since 1974. As the 1900s drew to a close, *Werther, Bohème, Der Rosenkavalier, Tannhäuser,* and *L'italiana in Algeri* were on the boards. On October 5, 2002, a world premiere took place, Sollima's *Ellis Island,* about Italians emigrating to America. During the first couple of years of the 21st century, there was a mixture of the old, *Mitridate Eupatore,* the 20th-century, *Mose und Aron,* and more popular fare, *Madama Butterfly, Don Giovanni, Trovatore, I Capuleti e i Montecchi,* and *Contes d'Hoffmann.* Recently, the repertory mix has continued with *La serva padrona,* the world premiere of D'Amico's *Dannata Epicurea* (both at the Teatro Bellini), *Pelléas et Mélisande, Bohème, Andrea Chénier,* and *Ariadne auf Naxos.*

Practical Information

Teatro Massimo, piazza Verdi, 90138 Palermo; tel. 39 091 581 512, fax 39 091 605 3324; www.teatromassimo.it. Teatro Bellini, piazza Bellini 7, 90133 Palermo; tel. 39 091 743 4312; www.teatrobiondi.it.

The season runs from November to June and offers 10 operas with 6 to 12 performances of each. The Politeama Garibaldi, piazza Ruggero Settimo, Palermo (tel. 39 091 605 3315) is undergoing renovation.

FIFTY-EIGHT

~

Taormina Arte Festival, Taormina, Sicily

The Taormina Arte Festival began in 1954 as the Rassegna del Cinema, sponsored by the local tourist office. The Estate Musicale joined the Rassegna del Cinema in 1962 but had financial difficulties. Then, in 1976, the local tourist office sponsored the Festival Internazionale Teatro Taormina, which was also a financial disaster. The current Taormina Arte Festival was founded in 1983 with the subtitle Rassegna Internazionale di Cinema-Teatro-Musica (International Review of Cinema, Theater, and Music). The focal point of the festival is the performances that take place in the Teatro Antico, also known as the Teatro Greco, although there is a dispute among experts as to whether its origin is Greek or Roman.

Evidence points toward a Greek beginning for the amphitheater, since Taormina was originally a Greek polis and every Greek village had a theater. The belief is that the Romans just enlarged the theater to fit their needs. Also, the presence of a certain type of stone around the stage, which was used in ancient Greece, adds to the evidence of its Greek origin. However, others believe that it had been constructed by Roman engineers to serve exclusively the Greek citizens, which explains all the Greek inscriptions found in the theater. There is also debate about the date of construction. If the Greeks built it, it would date to the mid-third century (CE), when Hiéron II was the tyrant of Syracuse.

The Teatro Antico is an amphitheater perched high in the hills of Taormina, with Mount Etna and the Bay of Naxos in the background. It is difficult to image a more magnificent setting for Sicily's second-largest (the one at Syracuse is larger) amphitheater, which required 100,000 cubic meters of stone. The semicircular amphitheater is 150 feet wide, 360 feet long, and 60 feet high. It was divided into five sections known as *diazomata* by the Greeks and *praencinctiones* by the Romans. Corinthian columns in various stages of ruin are strewn around the stage, with bases and pieces of other columns nearby. Encircling the amphitheater were two rows of arches, of which only a small section remains. The inside row contained red brick with low arches, and the outside held high arches. There was seating for 5,400 on stone steps. Today the spectators are accommodated on wooden benches and fiberglass seats.

Operatic Events in the Teatro Antico

Opera made its first appearance at Taormina in 1990, when a double bill of *Cavalleria rusticana* and *Pagliacci* was offered as part of the Festival dell'Opera Siciliana at the Teatro Antico. The following season, Giuseppe Sinopoli conducted *Lohengrin* as part of the Taormina Arte Festival itself, with Siegfried Jerusalem in the title role and Wolfgang Wagner directing. In 1992 *Elektra* graced the stage. The festival's brief foray into opera was not successful. Most of the failure was attributed to Sinopoli's choice of heavy German operas for an Italian summer festival in Sicily.

The lesson was well learned when, after more than a decade of silence, opera again joined the summer festival in 2003. The operas chosen, *Turandot* and *Traviata*, were by Italy's most popular composers, Puccini and Verdi. They were performed in repertory with Marco Balderi conducting both and an Italian cast of singers. In 2004 the most popular French opera, *Carmen*, joined a popular operetta, *Die lustige witwe* on the program.

Practical Information

Taormina Arte Festival, via Pirandello 31, 98039 Taormina; tel. 39 0942 21142, fax 39 0942 23348; www.taormina-arte.com. Teatro Antico, via Teatro Greco 40, Taormina; tel. 39 0942 23220.

The season takes place during July and August as part of the Taormina Arte Festival and offers two operas with two performances of each. Stay at the San Domenico Palace, piazza San Domenico, Taormina, Sicily; tel. 0942 23 701, fax 0942 62 55 06; www.thi.it/italiano/hotel/san_domenico. Originally a Dominican monastery, with breathtaking views of the sea and Mount Etna, the luxurious San Domenico Palace is a 10-minute walk from the Teatro Antico, in the old city.

Glossary

Album "ricordo"   "I remember" album, usually a pictoral commemorative publication
Assessorato alla Cultura   department of culture in the city government
Carnivale (stagione)   Carnival season (opera season held during carnival)
Carroccio   war chariot of the Italian communes
Commedia dell'arte   an Italian improvised drama based on plot outlines
Commedia per musica   comedy for music; comic opera
Condominio (condomini, pl.)   co-owner of the theater; shareholder of an association; box holder in a theater
Dramma giocoso (drammi giocosi, pl.)   humorous drama
Dramma per musica   drama for music, serious opera
Duce   leader; title used for Mussolini
Ente autonomo (enti autonomi, pl.)   public corporation; self-governing body (opera house classification)
Ente autonomo regionale   self-governing regional body (opera house classification)
Ente lirico autonomo (enti lirici autonomi, pl.)   self-governing opera corporation
Farse per musica, farse giocosa   farce for music, type of comic opera
Fiera (stagione)   fair season (opera season held during fair)
Filarmonico   philharmonic
Fondazione lirica (fondazioni liriche, pl.)   opera foundation
Fondazione di diritto privato   private foundation
Liberty style   Italian version of art nouveau
Loggionisti   opera aficionados who sit in the top gallery, or loggione
Loggione   large gallery; also referred to as piccionaia
Melodramma (medodrammi, pl.)   sensational or romantic play interspersed with songs and musical accompaniment; serious opera; also called dramma per musica
Melodramma giocosa   sensational or romantic play interspersed with songs and musical accompaniment that is humorous; comic opera
Nobile Società   noble association, usually formed to pay for opera house construction

Novità assoluta   world premiere; literally, absolute novelty
Opera buffa (opere buffe, pl.)   light or comic opera
Opera seria (opere serie, pl.)   serious or tragic opera
Palazzo Comunale   city hall or municipal building
Palchettista (palchettisti, pl.), palchista (palchisti, pl.)   box holder in a theater; co-owner of the theater; shareholder of an association
Palco (palchi, pl.)   box in an opera house
Platea   orchestra level
Piccionaia   top gallery in an opera house; literally, pigeon loft
Politeama   very large theater for the people that hosts a variety of shows; nonelitist theater
Prima (prime, pl.)   premiere
Prima esecuzione (prime esecuzioni, pl.), prima rappresentazione (prime rappresentazioni, pl.)   first performance
Prima esecuzione moderna   first performance in modern times
Prima assoluta (prime assolute, pl.), prima mondiale (prime mondiali, pl.)   world premiere
Rocca   fortress
Sala   room, theater, or (opera) house
Sala del Consiglio   council chambers; council room
Sala delle Commedie   house of comedies; theater of comedies
Socio (soci, pl.)   member of an association or society
Società   association; society
Società Amici della Musica   association of the friends of music
Società dei Palchettisti   association of box holders
Sovrintendente   general director (of the opera house, company, or festival)
Stagione (stagioni, pl.)   (opera) season
Teatro (teatri, pl.)   theater
Teatro Antico   Ancient Theater
Teatro Comunale   Municipal Theater
Teatro di Corte (Teatri di Corte, pl.)   Court Theater
Teatro Grande   Great Theater
Teatro del Legno   Wood Theater
Teatro di tradizione   Theater of Tradition (opera house classification)
Teatro Nazionale   National Theater
Teatro Novissimo   Newest Theater
Teatro Nuovo   New Theater
Teatro Piccolo   Little Theater
Teatro Pubblico   Public Theater
Teatro Regio, Teatro Reale   Royal Theater
Teatro Vecchio   Old Theater

Selected Bibliography

Aiolfi, Renzo. *Il Teatro a Savona 1583/1984*. Savona: Coop Tipograf, 1984.

————. *La facciata del Teatro Chiabrera e L'opera del Brilla*. Savona: Priamar, 1992.

Amadori, Gianluca. *Fenice cronaca di un rogo annunciato*. Venice: Filippi Editore, 1999.

Ambiveri, Corrado. *Operisti Minori dell'ottocento italiano*. Rome: Gremese, 1998.

Andò, Caterina, ed. *31 Maggio 1890–1990: Per il centenario dell'inaugurazione*. Catania, 1990.

Antonini, Alberto, and Bruno Macaro., eds. *Un Teatro, Una Città, Il Coccia di Novara*. Novara: Interlinea Edizioni, 1993.

Arata, Stefano. *La storia del Teatro Municipale di Piacenza*. Piacenza, 1994.

Arruga, Lorenzo. *Vent'anni di storia del Rossini Opera Festival*. Milan: Rizzoli, 2001.

Atti e Rassegna Tecnica della Società degli Ingegneri e degli Architetti in Turin, N. 9–10, 1973.

Baroni, Daniele, ed. *Teatro Lauro Rossi*. Macerata, 1989.

Bassini, Arnaldo. *Il sipario di Antonio Rizzi*. Cremona: Editoriale Pizzorni, 1995.

————, ed. *Il Teatro Ponchielli di Cremona*. Cremona, 1995.

Basso, Alberto., ed. *Storia del Teatro Regio di Torino*, 5 vols. Turin: Cassa di Risparmio di Torino, 1978–1988.

Bedini, Gilberto, ed. *Il Teatro del Giglio a Lucca*. Lucca: Teatro del Giglio, 1991.

Bellei, Enrico, ed. *Il Teatro Comunale di Modena*. Modena: Comune di Modena, 2000.

Bellotto, Francesco. *L'opera teatrale di Gaetano Donizetti*. Bergamo, 1992.

Bertinelli, Carlo. *Il Teatro Comunale "Giuseppe Verdi" di Padova*. Padua, 1998.

Bimestrale di informazione musicale e culturale del Teatro alla Scala. Milan, 1995–1996.

Bondoni, Simonetta. *Teatri Storici in Emilia Romegna*. Bologna, 1982.

Borelli, Lia, and Rosanna Monti. *Guida al Teatro del Giglio*. Lucca, 1988.

Brancati, Antonio. *Vicende architettoniche e struttutali del Teatro Rossini*. Pesaro, 1985.

Brusatin, Manlio, and Giuseppe Pavanello. *Il Teatro La Fenice: I Progetti, L'Architettura, Le Decorazioni*. Venice: Albrizzi Editore, 1987.

Bussetti, Francesco. *Armonico e bello in tutte le sue parti*. Terni: Editoriale Umbria, 1995.

Calcagnini, Gilberto. *Il Teatro Rossini di Pesaro fra spettacolo e cronaca 1898–1966*. Fano: Editrice Fortuna, 1997.

Capelli, Gianni. *Il Teatro Farnese di Parma, Architettura, Scena, Spettacolo*. Parma: PPS, 2000.

Carmassi, Massimo. *Il restauro del Teatro Verdi di Pisa*. Pisa: Pacini Editore, 1994.

Castoldi, Maria Teresa, and Valeria Piasentà. *Dal Mito alla Scena*. Novara: Istituto Geografico de Agostini, 1989.

Catalogo delle manifestazioni 1928–1997. Florence: Le Lettere, 1998.

Ceccarelli, Rosita Bassini. *Il Teatro Sociale di Amelia 1782–1991*. Assisi: Edizioni Thyrus, 1996.

Cervellati, Pier Luigi. *Il Teatro Rossini di Lugo*. Bologna: Nuova Alfa Editoriale, 1986.

Cervetti, Valerio, Claudio Del Monte, and Vincenzo Segreto. *Teatro Regio di Città Parma Cronologia degli Spettacoli Lirici 1829–1979*, 5 vols. Parma: Grafiche Step Cooperativa Editrice, 1979–1989.

Coarelli, Filippo, and Lanfranco Franzoni. *The Verona Arena: Twenty Centuries of History*. Verona: Ente Autonomo Arena di Verona, 1972.

Comuzio, Ermanno. *Il Teatro Donizetti*. Bergamo: Stamperia Stefanoni, 1995.

———, ed. *Gianandrea Gavazzeni Testimone del Tempo*. Bergamo: Poligrafiche Bolis, 1994.

Comuzio, Ermanno, and Andreina Moretti. *Bergamo durante gli anni di Giovanni Simone Mayr*. Bergamo, 1995.

Conati, Marcello, ed., and Richard Stokes, trans. *Encounters with Verdi*. Ithaca, NY: Cornell University Press, 1984.

Conti, Mauro. *53rd Il Maggio Musicale Fiorentino*. Florence, 1990.

Contrappunti, April–July 1999.

Corriere della Sera, July 1996 to December 2004.

Croce, Benedetto. *I Teatri di Napoli*. Milan: Adelphi Edizioni, 1992.

Danzuso, Domenico, and Giovanni Idonea. *Cento anni di un teatro*. Catania, 1990.

———. *Musica, Musicisti e Teatri a Catania: dal mito alla cronaca*. Palermo, n.d.

Davoli, Susi, and Paolo Ricci. *Immagini di pietra*. Reggio Emilia: Edizioni Tecnograf, 1999.

De Carlo, Donato, and Filomena Scalzo. *Il Teatro Sociale di Como*. Bergamo: Società dei Palchettisti, 1988.

De Filippis, Felice, ed. *Centi anni di vita del Teatro di San Carlo, 1848–1948*. Naples: Editori Riccardo Ricciardi e Gaetano Macchiaroli, 1948.

Degani, Giannino, and Mara Grotti, eds. *Opere in musica: 1857–1976*, 4 vols. Reggio Emilia: Edizione del Teatro Municipale di Reggio Emilio, 1976.

Degrada, Francesco. *Giuseppe Verdi, l'uomo, l'opera, il mito*. Milan: Skira, 2000.

Dell'Ira, Gino. *I teatri di Pisa (1773–1986)*. Pisa: Giardini Editori, 1987.

Deputazione del Teatro Grande, ed. *Teatro Grande Brescia dal 1800 al 1972*. Brescia, 1972.

Esposito, Valter, Stefano Filippi, and Luigi Marangon, eds. *Il Teatro La Fenice 14–21 Dicembre 2003*. Padua: Il Prato Casa Editrice, 2003.

Fabbri, Paolo, and Nullo Pirazzoli. *Il Teatro Alighieri*. Ravenna: Edizioni Essegi, 1988.

Fabbri, Paolo, and Roberto Verti. *Due secoli di teatro per musica a Reggio Emilia*. Reggio Emilia: Edizione del Teatro Municipale di Reggio Emilio, 1987.

Fabris, Dinko, and Marco Renzi, eds. *La Musica a Bari*. Bari: Levante Editore, 1993.
Faitelli, Federica. *Luoghi d'Italia: Lugo*. Florence: Octavo, 1998.
Ferrari, Luigi. *La Scala: Breve storia attraverso due secoli*. Milan: Teatro alla Scala, 1981.
Forlani, Maria Giovanna. *Il Teatro Municipale di Piacenza 1804–1984*. Piacenza, 1985.
Frassoni, Edilio. *Due secoli di lirica a Genoa 1772–1960*, 2 vols. Genoa: Siag, 1980.
Furfaro, Amedeo. *Storia del Rendano*. Cosenza: Edizioni Periferia, 1989.
Gazzetta di Parma, 1998–2004.
Gazzetta del Sud, May 12, 1997.
Gherpelli, Giuseppe. *L'Opera nei teatri di Modena*. Modena: Artioli Editore, 1988.
Giornale di Sicilia, May 9–13, 1997.
Gori, Gianni. *Il Teatro Verdi di Trieste 1801–2001*. Venice: Marsilio, 2001.
Harris, Cyril. *Illustrated Dictionary of Historic Architecture*. New York: Dover, 1983.
Il Giornale, November–December 2004.
Il Mediterraneo, May 11, 1997.
Il Teatro Comunale nelle origini e nella storia. Treviso: Biblioteca Comunale di Treviso, 1980.
Il volto della città. Lugo: Edizioni Eggegi, 1997.
Iovino, Roberto. *Il Carlo Felice due volti di un teatro*. Genoa: Sagep Editrice, 1991.
La Repubblica. Rome, 1998–2004.
La rivista illustrata del Museo Teatrale alla Scala, Milan, Summer 1992 to December 1995.
La Stampa, November–December 2004.
Leone, Giovanni. *L'opera a Palermo dal 1653 al 1987*, 2 vols. Palermo: Publisichula, 1988.
Liburdi, Daniela. *Titta Ruffo I Costumi Teatrali*. Pisa: Pacini Editore, 1993.
Luna, Luca. *Teatro Ventiodio Basso*. Ascoli Piceno: D'Auria Editrice, 1996.
Maggio Musicale Fiorentino. *Per una storia del primo festival musicale italiano*. Florence: 1986.
Mancini, Franco, and Maria Muraro. *I teatri del Veneto*. Venice: Corbo e Fiore, n.d.
Manifesti in vicende musicali pesaresi dal 1864 al 1932. Pesaro, 1999.
Martellucci, Gloria. *Teatro Massimo, Palermo*. Palermo, n.d.
Matteucci, A. M., and Lenzi, D. *Cosimo Morelli e l'architettura delle legazioni pontificie*. Bologna: University Press, 1977.
Mocenigo, Mario. *Il Teatro La Fenice: Notizie storiche e artistiche*. Venice, 1926.
Molonia, Giuseppe. *L'archivio storico del Teatro Vittoria Emanuele*, 2 vols. Messina, 1990.
Motta, Fermo Giovanni, ed. *Teatri delle terre di Pesaro e Urbino*. Venice: Electa, 1997.
Musica&Arte. Quaderni del Museo Teatrale alla Scala. Milan, June–October 1996.
Musica e Musicisti, May 1903.
Musini, Nullo. *Il Teatro Girolamo Magnani di Fidenza 1861–1961*. Fidenza, 1961.
Natale, Mario, ed. *Spoleto trent'anni di festival: 1958–1987*. Spoleto, 1988.
———. *Spoleto trentasei anni di festival: Aggiornamento 1998–1993*. Rome, 1994.
Opera Now, 1996–2005.
Paci, Libero. *Lo Sferisterio: una attrezzatura cultural*. Macerata: Comune di Macerata, n.d.
Parlapiano, Rosalia, and Loretta Mozzoni, eds. *Le stagioni del Teatro Pergolesi 1798/1998*, 2 vols. Milan, 1998.

Pasini, Roberto, and Remo Schiavo. *The Verona Arena*. Verona: Arsenale Editrice, 1995.

Raimondi, Silvia. *Oltre Il Velario*. Milan: Silvana Editoriale, 1993.

Romagnoli, Sergio, and Elvira Garbero, eds. *Teatro a Reggio Emilia*, 2 vols. Florence: Sansoni Editore 1980.

Roscioni, Carlo Marinelli, ed. *Il Teatro di San Carlo*, 2 vols. Naples: Guida Editori, 1988.

Rossano, Antonio. *Miracolo a Martina*. Bari: Uniongrafica Corcelli Editrice, 1999.

Sainati, Fabrizio. *Teatro Rossi: Lo splendore e l'abbandono*. Pisa: Pacini Editore, 1997.

Salvarani, Marco, ed. *Le Muse—Storia del Teatro di Ancona*. Ancona: Il lavoro editoriale, 2002.

Santarelli, Cristina, and Franco Pulcini. *Lo Spettacolo: La Musica, Il Teatro, Il Cinema*. Busto Arsizio: Bramante Editrice, 1987.

Saracino, Edigio. *Invito all'ascolto di Donizetti*. Milan: Mursia, 1984.

————, ed. *Tutti I Libretti di Donizetti*. Milan: Garzanti, 1993.

Scaglione, Nicola. *La vita del Teatro Vittorio Emanuele*. Messina, 1933.

Segalini, Sergio. *La Scala*. Paris: Sand, 1989.

Sforza, Francesco. *Grandi Teatri Italiani*, Rome: Editalia, 1993.

Sicilia Magazine: Speciale Teatro Massimo Bellini Supplemento al N.6 di SM, Catania, 1989.

Siegfried, Albrecht. *Eine Reise zu den oberitalienischen Theatern des 16–19 Jahrhunderts*. Marburg: Jonas Verlag, 1991.

Tamburini, Luciano. *I teatri di Torino*. Turin: Edizioni dell'Albero, 1966.

Teatro alla Scala: un palco all'opera. Milan: Skira editore, 2004.

Testi, Giampaolo. *Quattro "puntate" per una piccola storia del Teatro Verdi in Pisa*. Pisa: Nistri Lischi Editori, 1990.

Tintori, Giampiero. *L'origine del Teatro Fraschini di Pavia*. Pavia, 1983.

Tommasi, Rodolfo. *Il Teatro Comunale di Firenze: presenza e linguaggio*. Florence, 1987.

Travaglini, Vincenzo, ed. *Il Teatro dell'Opera di Rome*. Rome: Ufficio Stampa, 1989.

Trezzini, Lamberto, ed. *Due secoli di vita musicale: Storia del Teatro Comunale di Bologna*, 3 vols. Bologna: Nuovo Alfa Editoriale, 1987.

Trubbiani, Valeriano. *Il Sipario Tagliafuoco*. Ancona, 2002.

Ucello, Giovanni. *Lo spettecolo nei secoli a Messina*. Palermo, 1986.

Ufficio Stampa e P.R. dei Teatri. *Teatro Ariosto*. Reggio Emilia, 1984.

Vespa, Bruno, ed. *Verdi e L'Arena*. Rome: Edizioni Fotogramma, 2001.

Vogue Italia, Teatro alla Scala 1946–1996. Milan, 1996.

XIX *Maggio Musicale Fiorentino*. "Il Teatro Comunale di Firenze." Florence, 1956.

Zietz, Karyl Lynn. *Opera! The Guide to Western Europe's Great Houses*. Santa Fe: JMP, 1990.

————. *Opera Companies and Houses of Western Europe, Canada, Australia, New Zealand*. Wilmington NC: McFarland & Co., 1996.

————. *Breve storia dei teatri d'opera italiani*. Rome: Gremese, 2001.

Index of Artists, Architects, Conductors, Directors, and Rulers

Index of Theaters

About the Author

Karyl Charna Lynn, an author, critic, and lecturer, is a noted international expert in the opera world. She has written six books on opera houses, companies, and architecture, including *The National Trust Guide to Great Opera Houses in America* and *Opera Companies and Houses of Western Europe, Canada, Australia, and New Zealand*. She is an opera critic, interviewer, and feature writer for *Opera Now* in London, *Oper Orpheus International* in Berlin, and *Opera-Opera* in Sydney, Australia. Her writings have taken her to more than 250 opera houses around the world. She speaks four languages and is listed in *Who's Who in America*, *Who's Who in the World*, *Who's Who in American Women*, and *Who's Who in the East*. She studied at Phillips Academy, Andover, the University of Pennsylvania, and American University and has lectured widely on Italian opera houses, their architecture, politics, and performances.